Informality and Monetary Policy in Japan

The political economy of bank performance

T0300470

The success – and recent misfortunes – of the post-war Japanese economy have been among the most debated points in modern economics. Many explanations focus on cultural and institutional factors, and in particular on the role of 'informality' (networks organising business activity and government policy).

This book provides the first quantitative and qualitative assessment of informality in the implementation of Japanese monetary policy. Having been based in Japan for three years, two years of which were spent at the Institute for Monetary and Economic Studies at the Bank of Japan and the Japanese Ministry of Finance, Adrian van Rixtel brings a unique 'insider–outsider' perspective to the subject.

ADRIAN VAN RIXTEL is a senior economist at the European Central Bank. His work has appeared in leading academic journals and in publications including *The Economist* and *The Wall Street Journal*.

Informality and Monetary Policy in Japan

The political economy of bank performance

Adrian van Rixtel

CAMBRIDGE
UNIVERSITY PRESS

CAMBRIDGE UNIVERSITY PRESS
Cambridge, New York, Melbourne, Madrid, Cape Town, Singapore, São Paulo

Cambridge University Press
The Edinburgh Building, Cambridge CB2 8RU, UK

Published in the United States of America by Cambridge University Press, New York

www.cambridge.org
Information on this title: www.cambridge.org/9780521781794

First published 2002
This digitally printed version 2007

A catalogue record for this publication is available from the British Library

ISBN 978-0-521-78179-4 hardback
ISBN 978-0-521-03944-4 paperback

In memory of my father

Human life lasts but an instant. One should spend it doing what one pleases. In this world fleeting as a dream, to live in misery doing only what one dislikes is foolishness.   J. Yamamoto (Sparling 1992, p.33)

Contents

Figures

Tables

Acknowledgements

This book is a revised and updated version of my doctoral research at the Faculty of Economics and Econometrics of the Free University of Amsterdam. During my time there I was also affiliated with the Tinbergen Institute. I am grateful to both institutions for giving me the opportunity to conduct this research, which was finalised while I was on the staff of De Nederlandsche Bank, before my subsequent move to the European Central Bank. Needless to say, my views in no way represent those of either De Nederlandsche Bank or the European Central Bank.

I acknowledge, with gratitude, the support and assistance of many individuals in conducting my research over the years. First and foremost, I am most grateful to Hans Visser for his patience and confidence. It takes a lot of courage for a supervisor to approve a research proposal that aims at investigating empirically a topic of such a delicate nature as informality in monetary policy. I am also deeply indebted to Juro Teranishi for accepting an unknown, 'aggressive' Dutchman as his research student. His advice and teaching substantially enhanced my knowledge of Japan and the Japanese economy, and the wonderful parties that he and his wife gave increased my appreciation of the delights of *sake*. Otto Swank's creative thinking in times of academic trouble and his useful criticism helped in many ways to improve my research. I am also grateful to Age Bakker, Sylvester Eijffinger, Hans Eijgenhuijsen and Joop Stam for reading the original final draft.

During my three years in Japan, several institutions were of great importance to my research. The teachers of the Japanese Language Course at Tsukuba University helped me to acquire a basic knowledge of Japanese. The seminars at the Institute of Economic Research of Hitotsubashi University were excellent opportunities to test my ideas. I would like to thank the participants for their comments, in particular Hidekazu Eguchi, Kyoji Fukao, Shin-Ichi Fukuda and Juro Teranishi. For almost two years the Institute for Monetary and Economic Studies of the Bank of Japan provided an excellent research environment. I cherish the memories of long discussions with staff members, visiting scholars and other research students in the evenings, private skiing lessons in Niigata, the wonderful restaurant in Roppongi and the convenience of the in-house dry-cleaning services. The dedication and professionalism of the Bank of Japan's staff made a lasting impression on me, and certainly contributed to my decision to become a central banker myself. Two months at the Institute of Fiscal and Monetary Policy of the Ministry of Finance gave me the opportunity to complete my picture of the Japanese monetary authorities. I am grateful to the many staff members who patiently answered my sometimes delicate questions.

I wish to thank several other people who helped me in numerous ways during my stay in Japan. Karel van Wolferen gave me the idea of investigating informality in Japan. Tatsuhiko Kawashima of Gakushuin University and Naoyuki Yoshino of Keio University provided important suggestions and ideas. I am also deeply indebted to the present and former staff members of the Ministry of Finance and Bank of Japan, private bankers, academics, journalists and others who agreed to be interviewed. For reasons that will be apparent, many of them cannot be named. Seiichi Tsurumi of the Federation of Bankers' Associations of Japan not only provided the financial data on Japanese banks, but has also been a true friend for many years. Aaron Cohen of Daiwa Securities shared his views on the Japanese financial system and provided critical comments. René and Yukiko Belderbos, Avital Goren-Bandel, Ashima Jain, Yabukin Masae, Michio, Nobue Nochi, Zsolt and Zsuzsa Radak, Bogdan Szydlo, Guillermo Sotomayor Valle, Yupana Wiwattanakantang and Kyung-wha Yoon all showed what friends are for. Onno Steenbeek has been a loyal and pleasant companion inside the Japanese monetary bureaucracy. Bob Dekle and Frank Packer were the best *senpai* a new student of Japan could hope for. At Hitotsubashi, Hiroki Nogami was an excellent tutor, and Mrs Okado frequently helped to retrieve information from the Nikkei Database System. My research in Japan was supported by financial assistance from the Japanese Ministry of Education, Nissan, NWO, Shell Nederland BV, Pacific Investments and the Tinbergen Institute.

I would like to address a special word of thanks to Wolter Hassink. He is the co-author of chapter 8, which is to be published in the *Journal of the Japanese and International Economies*. I have very much enjoyed our collaboration over the years and would like to thank him for his continuing friendship and support. Special thanks also to Ashwin Rattan of Cambridge University Press, who steered the book through reviews and production and who turned out to be not only an exceptionally patient person but also a very understanding one.

Several friends, family members and colleagues provided indispensable editorial assistance. I would like to name in particular Ioana Alexopoulou,

Isabella Asaro, David Marques, Els van Rixtel, Melanie Shah and Zoë Sobke. I am indebted to my father for putting large sets of data into spreadsheets. I must apologise to my family and friends for the times when I cut myself off a little while I was writing some of the chapters of this book. Their support has been more important than they may have expected. Indeed the endless encouragement and wise advice of my parents has proved invaluable throughout my career. I thank Cristina de la Infiesta for her ongoing support. This book is dedicated to my father, who did not live to see it published.

ADRIAN VAN RIXTEL

1   Introduction

'...why do covert instruments such as moral suasion often receive a substantial emphasis in the actual operation of monetary policy whereas they are discussed as an afterthought in most textbook accounts of monetary policy?'

J.F. Chant and K. Acheson (1986)

1.1   Aims

During the 1980s and first half of the 1990s, the economic success of a significant number of Asian countries attracted a great deal of scientific attention. Many studies were conducted that tried to explain this success, often resulting in claims that these economic 'miracles' happened mainly because of some peculiar characteristics of these countries' economic systems and the role of government – i.e. economic policy (see, for example, Wade 1990; Chowdhury and Islam 1993; World Bank 1993; Abegglen 1995; Johnson 1995c; Weiss and Hobson 1995; Aoki et al. 1996; Fruin 1998; Weiss 1998). Against the background of these claims it is not surprising that some studies came up with concepts such as 'Asian Capitalism' or 'Asian Network Capitalism' as possible alternatives to Western capitalist systems (Johnson 1993, p.65; Fruin 1998; Research Project Team for Japanese Systems 1992). Informality was often mentioned as characteristic of these Asian economies: informal forms of industrial organisation, informal networks to organise business and informal factors in the formulation and implementation of government economic policy. Examples of such informality are the informally organised business groups that dominate the Japanese and Korean economies (the *keiretsu* and *chaebol*, respectively), the informal business networks of the overseas Chinese and informal networks for policy co-ordination between public and private spheres (Song 1990; Gerlach 1992; World Bank 1993; Abegglen 1995; Fruin 1998).

In more recent years, however, after the major crisis that hit most countries in Asia in the late nineties, a reverse pattern can be identified, in its extreme form reflected in a 180-degree shift from 'Asian Miracle' and 'Asian Capitalism' to 'Asian Crisis' and 'Crony Capitalism' (see for example, Centre for Economic Policy Research 1998; World Bank 1998; Claessens et al. 1999; Flynn 1999).[1] Now, analyses focus on the perceived weaknesses of the 'Asian Model', consisting of a lack of disclosure and transparency, inadequate corporate governance, 'cronyism' and corruption, a general lack of clear rules and 'rule of law', and the limitations of informal guidance and informal network relations. To some extent this new attitude reflects the 'business cycle' of economic ideas and fashion. Such an attitude risks moving from one extreme to the other, ignoring the remarkable economic achievements of many Asian countries in the past decades (see, for example, Wade 1998). However, it is clear that certain characteristics of the economic development process in East Asia in particular have reached their limits, and that a general reorientation of economic structures, policies and ideas is needed, in particular as regards the functions of government.

It is also clear that such reassessment is needed for Japan, given the severe economic and banking problems of the nineties, and in the field of Japanese economic studies the role of government in the successful development of the post-war Japanese economy has increasingly become the subject of academic debate. On the one side is the so-called market school, which denies substantial contributions of government intervention to this economic development and stresses the importance of the market mechanism. On the other side is the interventionist or government-control school, which sees Japan's economic success mainly as the result of government economic policy. This school even claims that mainstream economic theory such as is used by the market school cannot explain the economic development of Japan, mainly because it would neglect important institutional factors. In line with the studies on Asian economic development mentioned, the interventionists put forward informality as one of the most important of these factors. They concentrate in particular on the use of informal co-ordination mechanisms as important policymaking tools between the public and private sectors, and of informal instruments in the implementation of economic policy. The importance of informality in Japanese economic policy has also been put forward more recently by other schools, which are collectively typified in this study as network schools. These schools adopt hybrid interpretations, their orientation being located between the interventionist and market schools. They see the Japanese government not as strongly interventionist, but stress the use of market-conforming methods of economic policy,

---

[1] An early and famous critical assessment of 'Asia's Miracle' has been Krugman (1994).

in particular the use of informal networks. They share the criticism of the interventionist school that economics ignores important institutional factors, in particular informality.

This study takes up the gauntlet thrown by the interventionist and network schools and includes explicitly informal factors in the analysis of Japanese monetary policy, one of the major pillars of Japanese economic policy. It concentrates in particular on the implementation of micro monetary policy, which consists mainly of prudential policy (Goodhart 1995). It departs from the exclusive qualitative and non-empirical character of most studies that proclaim the importance of informality in Japanese economic policy, and tries to fill the gap left by the absence of quantitative empirical studies on this topic. Both qualitative and quantitative empirical studies on the relevance and importance of informality in the implementation of Japanese prudential policy in particular will be conducted.

1.2   Method

In the development of this study, three major difficulties were experienced. First, as is reflected by the citation on page 1, very little attention is paid in economic theory to the possible importance of informality in the implementation of monetary policy. This negligence has resulted in the lack of a clear theoretical framework on this topic, which could be used as the starting point for an empirical investigation. Second, from the beginning of this study I was uncertain whether objective data sources on informal aspects of Japanese monetary policy could be found. In this sense, the study started as a leap in the dark. Furthermore, the delicate nature of the topic made it often impossible to obtain the data through official channels, which forced me to use often lengthy and time-consuming alternative routes. Finally, there was the obvious language barrier: the few objective data sources on informal aspects that I found were without exception in Japanese.

To cope with these difficulties, I chose the following approach, which is essentially a research strategy consisting of three stages. In the first stage, I developed the theoretical framework of the study. This framework is based on existing studies on the Japanese political economy. The political economy can be defined as the set of relationships between the political system, the government bureaucracy and the economic system. I concentrated in particular on the characteristics of the relationship between the Japanese government bureaucracy and the economic system, the relationship that constitutes economic policy. The investigation of the relevance and importance of informality as an institutional characteristic of Japanese economic policy is one of the central elements in the field of

Japanese political economy studies. Consequently the analysis of these studies resulted in an overview of the informal instruments that are said to be important in the implementation of Japanese economic policy and thus, being a part of this policy, hypothetically in the implementation of Japanese monetary policy. The research of the existing literature was augmented by interviews with various Japanese legal scholars. I then linked these informal instruments with the implementation of Japanese monetary policy in general and prudential policy in particular. In the second stage, I conducted a large number of interviews to find out, firstly, which of the informal aspects mentioned in the literature would offer possibilities for successful empirical investigations and, secondly, to understand the operation of the monetary bureaucracy and thus to set out its institutional framework. In total, more than 250 interviews were conducted during the period 1990–1998 with current and former staff members of the Japanese Ministry of Finance (MoF) and the Bank of Japan (BoJ), private bankers, economic and legal scholars and journalists. The results from the first and second stage were combined in the third stage, in which I investigated qualitatively and quantitatively the use of certain informal instruments by the monetary authorities. This empirical research was largely based on original Japanese-language sources. I have not tried to build an all-encompassing model of the use of informal instruments in the implementation of Japanese monetary policy, concentrating instead on those informal aspects for which objective data were available and which consequently could be investigated empirically.

1.3   Outline

The study is organised in three parts, which correspond roughly with the three stages of the research strategy. Part I (chapters 2–4) sets out the theoretical framework. Chapter 2 describes the existing theories on the Japanese political economy and economic system. It focuses on the controversies between the various schools regarding the nature and effectiveness of the Japanese government's intervention in the economy, or Japanese economic policy. The chapter pays attention to studies that criticise economics as being unrealistic in the sense of neglecting informality as an important institutional characteristic of this policy. Following the overview of chapter 2, chapter 3 presents an analysis of informal factors which are said to be important in Japanese economic policy. It is shown that informality applied to studies of the Japanese economic system involves commonly and predominantly two issues: administrative guidance and informal networks. Administrative guidance, a form of moral suasion, consists of published and unpublished administrative guidance, the former being circulars or *tsūtatsu* published by the MoF. Informal networks are based on personal relationships resulting from common institutional relationships (*amakudari* or 'old boy' networks) and shared university backgrounds (*gakubatsu*), and are used in either the formulation or implementation of economic policy. Finally, chapter 4 presents an operational framework for subsequent analysis of informal aspects in Japanese monetary policy. Following Goodhart (1995), I distinguish between macro and micro monetary policies. Macro monetary policy is aimed at the realisation of macro-economic policy goals such as price stability or full employment. By micro monetary policy is meant the monetary authorities' concerns with the structure and stability of the banking system. In the rest of the study I concentrate predominantly on this latter part of monetary policy. Integrating corporate governance and prudential policy, one of the main elements of micro monetary policy, the chapter proposes a model of 'hierarchical delegated monitoring' for the governance of Japanese banks.

Part II (chapters 5 and 6) treats the institutional framework of the study, which consists of the financial system and monetary authorities. Chapter 5 describes the Japanese financial system and the pre-1998 reform regime. In the institutional analysis, the year 1998 is of considerable importance, given the major institutional reforms that occurred then. The chapter starts with an historical analysis of the development of the post-World War II financial system, and describes the financial institutions. It presents an institutional empirical analysis of the MoF and BoJ, and investigates the relevance and importance of the informal aspects of Japanese economic policy such as described in chapter 3 for the implementation of Japanese monetary policy. The chapter analyses the circulars or *tsūtatsu* published by the MoF – i.e. the published administrative guidance – and finds little evidence of the use of these circulars in the MoF's macro monetary policy in particular. The chapter provides, where possible, evidence of the use of unpublished administrative guidance by the MoF and BoJ. Furthermore, it presents information on the university background (*gakubatsu*) and the mechanism of *shukkō* or temporary external assignment of their staff members. The chapter also contains a translation of the Ministry of Finance Establishment Law, one of the very few Japanese financial laws that have not been translated officially. In chapter 6 the institutional reforms of 1998 and the banking crisis of the nineties are investigated. The chapter pays attention to the process of financial reform and the rise and collapse of the so-called 'bubble' economy. The description of the specific institutional reforms in 1998 are embedded in an analysis of the policy reaction to the banking crisis, in which the relevance and importance of informal aspects are discussed in particular. In the policy reaction, I distinguish seven phases: the initial policy response (1990 to June 1996), administrative and financial reform (June 1996 to January 1997), the end of 'too big to fail' (January 1997 to January 1998), scandals, public funds and financial reform (January 1998 to June 1998), administrative reform and intensifying crisis (June 1998 to October 1998), financial revitalisation (October 1998 to July 2000) and the consolidation of prudential policy (July 2000 to January 2001). It is shown that the policy response to the banking crisis was based on regulatory forbearance and financial reform. I assert that the former was to a significant degree related to the existence of strong and intimate informal network relations between the monetary authorities and private banks.

Finally, part III (chapters 7 and 8) contains two empirical chapters. Chapter 7 investigates qualitatively the informal network of *amakudari*, i.e. retired staff members from the MoF and BoJ on the boards of private banks. Based on an analysis of around 45,000 personal profiles of board members of private banks, I present a data analysis of the positions of former MoF and BoJ staff members on the boards of directors of the major Japanese private banks during the period 1975–1993. The results show that the movement of former MoF and BoJ staff members into these positions can be explained only at the firm level, and involves elements of patterned equalisation, bureaucratic intervention and career management. Comparison of the 1993 figures on *amakudari* with those for 1999 lead to the tentative conclusion that the presence of MoF and BoJ retirees on the boards of private banks has decreased in recent years. However, it is also explained that further research in this respect is needed, given the use of different data sources and the possibility of substitution effects towards other private and public landing-spots for former MoF and BoJ staff members. Chapter 8 explores quantitatively the impact of *amakudari* on bank performance. I formulate three hypotheses that are linked to the three aspects of the explanation of the presence of MoF and BoJ *amakudari kanryō* on the boards of private banks for the period 1975-1993 such as described in chapter 7: 'buying influence' (reformulation of patterned equalisation), ex-post monitoring in the context of prudential policy (bureaucratic intervention) and career management. The results show that the movement of MoF and BoJ retirees into the boards of private banks is negatively related to profitability and positively related to certain governance variables. Furthermore, I find that MoF/BoJ *amakudari* appointments have a positive impact on the development of profitability and lending to risky industries. In particular this latter finding casts doubts on the credibility of the hypothesis that *amakudari* is successfully used as an instrument of prudential policy. Thus, it is concluded that the movement of ex-MoF and ex-BoJ staff members into private banks can be most aptly explained by 'buying influence' behaviour. I present further evidence of the detrimental effects of the re-employment of MoF and BoJ retirees on the boards of private banks. All in all, I conclude that the practice of *amakudari* seriously impaired the performance of Japanese banks during the period 1975–1993.

Finally, chapter 9 draws some lessons from the Japanese experience with informal instruments and presents some forward-looking conclusions.

Part I

Theory

2   The political economy and economic system of Japan: a survey of literature, conflict and confusion

> Whatever may be said about Japan, the opposite may also be true.
>
> L. Hollerman (1988)

2.1   Introduction

As President Kennedy already knew, success has many fathers and failure few. By almost any economic standard, the post-war economic development of Japan can be characterised as a success. Very few industrialised countries boast a similar persistent combination of low unemployment, low inflation and high economic growth. Not surprisingly, this success has become the main topic of many studies in economics, and in other disciplines such as political science and sociology as well. Various theoretical schools try to claim success by declaring it in accordance with their own analytical frameworks and resulting conclusions. Consequently, as will be argued in this chapter, the field of Japanese economic studies has become a battleground of academic conflicts, characterised by significant polarisation and politicisation. These conflicts result mainly from prevailing differences of opinion regarding two fundamental issues.

First, Japanese economic studies have, like other fields in economics, been hit by the controversy between activist and non-activist policies, the contrast between belief in government intervention and faith in the free market (Schmiegelow 1986b, p.ix; Morris-Suzuki 1989, p.195; Itoh 1990, p.159). This debate will be clearly reflected in section 2.3 in the opposing views of the interventionist and market schools, with the interventionists drawing the conclusion that the alleged successful Japanese experience with industrial policy offers important lessons not only for developing countries, but for the industrialised world as well.[1] Furthermore, the debate between government intervention and free-market dominance as the main characteristic of the Japanese economic system can be found

---

[1] See for example Johnson (1982, 1988, and 1993), *Tokyo Business Today* (1991) and Tyson (1993).

in the analyses of economists whose main work has no linkage with this specific economic system whatsoever, but whose general conclusions are applied to it eagerly. For example, Milton Friedman stated: 'The image of the Japanese having had an industrial policy that explains their success is a myth. The fact of the matter is that the most successful components of Japanese development proceeded against the advice of the government' (Johnson 1988, p.1).

Second and most importantly, conflicts have surfaced regarding the explanations and usefulness of mainstream economic theory with respect to the Japanese economic system. The critics, predominantly originating from political and social sciences, but also including some prominent Japanese academic economists, blame traditional (mainstream) economics for being unrealistic and narrow, putting too much emphasis on markets and neglecting the importance of comparative institutional differences, history, culture and social factors. For example, K.G. van Wolferen launched a sharp attack on mainstream or neo-classical economics in an essay called 'Is Economic Science Worth Anything? The Conceptual Mismatch Between Economic Theory and Japanese Reality' (van Wolferen 1997). Not surprisingly, this criticism of mainstream economic interpretations of the Japanese economy has been counter-attacked in return, for example in Evans (1990), where it is asserted that 'standard economic analysis has a good record of understanding the major elements of the Japanese economy'.

Without doubt, Chalmers Johnson, the leading proponent of the interventionist school and a political scientist, is the most critical analyst of contemporary Japanese economic studies. In his sharp attack on the state of affairs in the contribution of economics to a better understanding of the Japanese economic system, he asserts that 'what has to be stressed is that the Western world is without any widely agreed-upon theoretical explanation for Japan's post-war economic performance and that professional economics in the United States has virtually abandoned the effort' (Johnson 1988, pp.1–2). According to Johnson, Japan's post-war economic development poses a significant number of anomalies for 'Western' economic theory, a development in which specific institutional characteristics were of great importance (Johnson 1988, 1993). To be able to explain the Japanese economic system, Johnson (1988) emphasises that economics needs to incorporate explicitly the study of institutions and institutional differences, and therefore should move towards the study of political economy.

The criticism of Johnson has been shared in recent years by a growing number of authors who have also stressed the importance of the explicit inclusion of institutional characteristics in studies of the Japanese economic system, the lack of attention to these aspects in traditional economic analyses of Japan and the consequent need to move from economics to political economy, which as a result has received more attention in Japanese economic studies. Kumon and Rosovsky (1992, pp.1–2) describe this development as follows:

> The movement from economics to political economy is significant; it certainly means more than simply the desire to include political factors in understanding Japan's current position and future prospects. The recent revival of political economy was a direct result of increasing dissatisfaction with the perceived narrowness and lack of realism that characterised much of traditional economics, with its almost exclusive emphasis on markets and simultaneous de-emphasising of history and institutions. The revived political economy approach intends to reintroduce the missing ingredients: primarily government, but other social forces as well . . . It was fairly clear that modern Japanese economic history could not adequately be analysed without reference to public policy and institutions.

The movement towards political economy is also recognised by Morris-Suzuki. In her view, the common feature linking contemporary Japanese economists is 'their rejection of the conventional, relatively narrow interpretation of "economic" phenomena. Each in his own way has tried to overstep the boundaries that have confined most modern economic thought, in Japan and elsewhere, and to reintegrate the economic with aspects of the political, the social, and the cultural . . . there appears to be an attempt to rediscover lost elements of that earlier concept of "political economy"' (Morris-Suzuki 1989, p.195). As will become clear in the following sections, numerous other studies, such as Murakami (1982), Okimoto (1989), Kumon (1992) and Murakami and Rohlen (1992), are punctuated with this criticism of the traditional theories and explanations of the Japanese economic system. The criticism of mainstream economics is translated by some Japanese economists into uniquely Japanese cultural explanations of post-war Japanese economic development. For example, Morishima (1982) explains Japan's economic success in terms of Confucianism and Shintoism; in the work of Y. Murakami, Japanese collectivism is set against Western individualism, the former making the difference in Japan's successful economic development.[2]

As will become clear in the following analysis, these two major controversies in the field of Japanese economic studies, i.e. the contrast between belief in government intervention and faith in the free market

---

[2] See Morishima (1982) and Morris-Suzuki (1989), pp.176–177. For Murakami's interpretation see Morris-Suzuki (1989), pp.185–187. The importance of cultural values is also stressed in Okimoto (1989) and Kumon and Rosovsky (1992). A vast amount of literature exists that emphasises the cultural uniqueness of Japan (*Nihonjinron*); see Mouer and Sugimoto (1986) and Buruma (1989).

and the criticism of mainstream economics in neglecting comparative institutional differences, are embedded in different interpretations of the Japanese political economy. From a general perspective, the political economy can be defined as the set of relationships between the political system, the government bureaucracy and the economic system. This chapter will focus explicitly on the characteristics of the relationship between the Japanese government bureaucracy and the economic system. In this regard, the Japanese political economy is important for two reasons.

First, knowledge of the various interpretations of the Japanese political economy is indispensable in order to understand the relationship between the government bureaucracy and the economic system, especially regarding the nature and level of government intervention in the economy. Section 2.3 will be devoted to various interpretations of this specific relationship.

Second, analysis of the Japanese political economy is necessary in order to understand the different interpretations of the alleged relevance of informal aspects as institutional characteristics of the public–private sector relationship within the Japanese economic system. This debate will be presented in chapter 3.

It must be stressed that the focus on interpretations of the Japanese political economy in this chapter is inspired by the alleged negligence of fundamental institutional characteristics of the Japanese economic system in traditional economic analyses. This study is not interested in the specifics of the Japanese political system and the relationship between the political and economic systems.[3] However, because discussions of the fundamental institutional characteristics of the Japanese economic system, such as its nature and in particular the importance of informal factors and the relationship between the Japanese bureaucracy and economy, are predominantly concentrated in the rapidly growing literature on the Japanese political economy, such literature is relevant to this study. In order to put the different theories with respect to the Japanese economic system and the alleged relevance of informal aspects in the right perspective, we must now analyse some varying interpretations of the Japanese political economy.

2.2   The Japanese political economy

The Japanese political economy has formed the basis of many studies, for example Johnson 1982; Horne 1985; Eads and Yamamura 1987; Hamada

---

[3] For these aspects see, for example, Johnson (1995b), Richardson (1997), Pempel (1998), Curtis (1999) and Stockwin (1999).

and Horiuchi 1987; Kosai 1987; Yamamura and Yasuba 1987; Hollerman 1988; Inoguchi and Okimoto 1988; McCall Rosenbluth 1989; Okuno-Fujiwara 1991; Calder 1993; Ramseyer and McCall Rosenbluth 1993; Weiss and Hobson 1995; Johnson 1995c; Vogel 1996; Banno 1997, 1998; Cargill et al. 1997; Amyx 1998; Carlile and Tilton 1998a; Fruin 1998a; Gibney 1998a; Ramseyer and Rosenbluth 1998; Schwartz 1998; Beason and James 1999; Katayama 2000. These authors focus primarily on the influence of various interest groups, especially big business and political parties, on the formulation and consequent implementation of Japanese economic policy, the role of the government bureaucracy in the economic system and the relationships between various ministries. In these studies, generally five models of the Japanese political economy can be distinguished: the 'Japan, Inc.', bureaucracy-led, pluralistic, consensual policy and pluralistic network models. The broad structure of this classification is based on Kosai (1987), Okimoto (1988, 1989), Noble (1989) and Murakami and Rohlen (1992).[4]

The 'Japan, Inc.' model

The first school to be discussed is the 'Japan, Inc.' model, or the 'ruling-triad' model, which dominated in particular early thinking about the Japanese political economy. This model departs from the notion that power in Japan is concentrated in the hands of the collective leadership of three groups: big business (*Zaikai*), the government bureaucracy and the Liberal Democratic Party (LDP) (*Jimintoo*), which has been the ruling party since World War II with the exception of a small period in the nineties (Okimoto 1988, p.307; Taira and Wada 1987).[5] The 'Japan, Inc.' interpretation has lost most of its traditional support, although some elements of this view can still be found in relatively recent studies. An interesting example is Upham (1987), which supports the 'ruling-triad' model in the context of explicit reference to the importance of informal relations: it emphasises 'the informal give and take that is the social glue holding the business–bureaucracy–LDP coalition together' and concludes that 'what Japan's tripartite elite had tried to accomplish, and what

---

[4] My classification is supported in various studies, for example Curtis (1999), pp.57ff. Only the main schools will be discussed. No attention will be paid to the corporatist and neo-corporatist interpretations, which are central in Nester (1990), but which are dismissed by several other studies. For other classifications see Richardson 1997; Schwartz 1998.

[5] On 9 August 1993, an eight-party coalition was formed under Prime Minister Morihiro Hosokawa that excluded the LDP, the first time in 38 years that the LDP was not in power. Another sign of the changing political landscape was the establishment of a three-party coalition including the LDP but also their long-term political opponent the Japan Socialist Party in June 1994 (Pempel 1998; Stockwin 1999).

they have in large part succeeded in achieving, is the maintenance of a style of policy formation and implementation that emphasises bureaucratic leadership exercised through informal processes' (Upham 1987, pp.16, 21). This focus on the role of the bureaucracy is the central assumption of the next interpretation of the Japanese political economy, the bureaucracy-led model.

Bureaucracy-led model

This second model of the Japanese political economy stresses the importance of the bureaucracy in Japan's economic development. This school is referred to as the bureaucracy-led, statist, state-led or state-dominant school, and has been the conventional model used for political economy analyses of Japan, in particular during the eighties (Okimoto 1988, p.309; Kosai 1987, p.557). The bureaucracy-led model, with as major representatives Johnson, Pempel and Zysman, stresses the bureaucracy as the main power in Japan (see Johnson 1982, 1995a; Pempel 1982, 1998; Zysman 1983). According to Kosai (1987, p.557), the bureaucracy-led school takes as its main assumptions that 'Japan pursues a single, consistent target (for example, modernisation) and that a consensus on broad goals exists among elitist bureaucrats'. Where the 'Japan, Inc.' school regards power in Japan as being exercised and divided by three more or less equal sectors – big business, the bureaucracy and the LDP – the bureaucracy-led model sees the bureaucracy as by far the most dominant and powerful force with respect to the formulation and implementation of economic policy. This view is also shared by Ramseyer (1985), p.638, where it is noted that 'modern Japan is largely governed by an elite and fundamentally nondemocratic bureaucracy. The ministries rather than the legislature draft the laws and determine basic national policies for the future.'

Pluralistic model

This model stresses the existence and influence of pluralistic interest groups on economic policymaking and consequent policy implementation, similar to interpretations of Western political economies.[6] One such approach has been put forward by Muramatsu and Krauss (1987). According to these authors, the Japanese political economy should not be interpreted as overwhelmingly dominated by the bureaucracy or a ruling triad of bureaucracy, big business and LDP (p.537). Instead, Muramatsu

[6] See, for example, Olson (1982).

and Krauss stress the existence of pluralist elements in the process of Japanese policymaking: this model of so-called patterned pluralism sees Japan as only marginally different from a fully pluralist democracy, with 'the marginal difference (being) the "patterned" element – organised interest groups must observe a more or less formal procedure in presenting their views or making political input through specified channels' (Kosai 1987, p.558). According to Muramatsu and Krauss (1987) and Kosai (1987), the model of patterned pluralism with controlled influence of interest groups fits in pretty well with the contemporary Japanese political economy. The belief that the Japanese political system is more or less comparable with pluralist democracies is shared even more strongly by Tresize and Suzuki (1976, p.782): 'the Japanese political scene is pluralist, competitive, and subject to inherent and effective checks and balances. In essentials, Japanese politics do not differ from politics in other democracies.' Another version of the pluralist interpretation has been introduced in Aoki (1988a), who speaks in terms of administered pluralism, with the government bureaucracy performing the role of administrator in the social bargaining process between various interest groups.[7]

Consensual policy model

A fourth school of the Japanese political economy stresses from a cultural perspective the importance of consensus and consensual policymaking in understanding the political economy of Japan. This view is supported by, among others, Samuels (1987), Haley (1989, 1991, 1992) and Yamamoto (1992), and has been developed into the concept of the societal or network state in Okimoto (1988) and the network society in Kumon (1992), Research Project Team for Japanese Systems (1992) and Gerlach and Lincoln (1998). Okimoto rejects explicitly the 'Japan, Inc.', bureaucracy-led and pluralistic models of the Japanese political economy. Instead, he develops the cultural oriented interpretation of the network state, in which the Japanese political-economic system functions on the basis of consensus and not in accordance with binding rules and laws.[8] According to Okimoto, the Japanese state is characterised by a relatively weak bureaucracy, bound by cultural constraints, which is forced to develop and sustain consensus with involved parties.[9] In his

---

[7] Another study that supports the pluralist interpretation is Hollerman (1988).

[8] The terminology of the network society had been introduced before Okimoto by Imai in the meaning of the information network society (*jōhō nettowaaku shakai*). See Morris-Suzuki (1989), pp.188–191. The role of consensus is somewhat doubted by Schwartz (1998), pp.287–288.

[9] Okimoto (1988), p.313. Haley (1989, 1991) follows an interpretation of an even weaker bureaucracy, which lacks the legal instruments to intervene effectively in all

view, public and private sectors are connected by numerous networks, whose main function is to reach the necessary consensus. In this network state, the separation of public and private sectors is blurred, with 'the exceptional organisation of each side and the highly routinised interaction between public and private actors' greatly facilitating policymaking (Okimoto 1988, p.315). The view of a relatively weak state is shared by Watanabe (1997), where it is asserted that the Japanese state is under control of the corporate sector. Ramseyer and McCall Rosenbluth (1993), using rational choice theory, conclude as well that the Japanese government bureaucracy is relatively weak, because it is being controlled by the political system: in the words of Pempel (1998, p.236), they treat 'bureaucrats simply as agents of the LDP' (see also Curtis 1999, pp.58–59).

Joining Okimoto in developing network interpretations of Japanese society are Kumon (1992) and Research Project Team for Japanese Systems (1992). According to these studies, Japanese society can be interpreted, mainly on cultural grounds, as a network society: 'The distinctive feature in Japan is that network-type social systems . . . are granted social legitimacy; not only have they spread widely, but many segments of them have been institutionalized either formally or informally' (Research Project Team for Japanese Systems 1992, p.79).[10] These so-called societal networks, for example the government bureaucracy and private business, are linked by a wide variety of other formal and informal networks, which facilitate extensive information sharing based on personal relations. This resulting network society establishes a kind of 'insider society' that determines public policymaking and implementation, characterised by substantial informal, non-transparent exchange of information, in order to reach consensus.

Because of the close interdependent relationship between the government bureaucracy and private business in the consensual policy-network state school, Samuels (1987) and Noble (1989) conclude that this school should therefore be interpreted as a 'New Japan, Inc.' school, a revival of the 'Japan, Inc.' school.[11] However, a number of the network state adherents, such as Okimoto and Upham, clearly dissociate from the

circumstances, that is also in cases where consensus has not been achieved. See also Ramseyer and Rosenbluth (1998).

[10] The concept of the network society has gained considerable support in recent years from Castells (1996).

[11] According to Noble (1989), p.54 and pp.69–71, following Samuels (1987), the approach of Okimoto belongs to this 'New Japan, Inc.' school. Noble's analysis of this school includes, among others, Young (1984), Boyd (1987), Samuels (1987), Upham (1987) and Okimoto (1989). The main reason for Noble to use the terminology 'New Japan, Inc.' is that, in his opinion, for its supporters 'informal but intense links between government and business are at the heart of Japanese political economy' (Noble 1989, p.69).

fundamental monolithic characteristics of the 'Japan, Inc.' school, and so the consensual policy-network state interpretation is here classified separately.

Pluralistic network model

The last model to be discussed is an intermediate mode between the pluralistic and network society schools. This model has been developed roughly as the informal organisation approach in Murakami (1987) and culminated in the social exchange model or pluralistic network model of Murakami and Rohlen (1992).[12] This model claims that the 'formal institutional structure of the postwar Japanese political economy is as pluralistic and competitive as those in other advanced industrial countries, but, at the same time, it stresses the importance of inclusive, informal networks as a considerable source of co-ordination, information flows, and patterned choices' (Murakami and Rohlen 1992, p.65). Essential is the concept of social exchange, which is mutual beneficial, based on personal network relations, and long-term and informally oriented. Social exchange, based on co-operative relationships, became a fundamental characteristic of the post-war Japanese political economy as a result of 'a particular cultural legacy and the favorable postwar socio-economic environment' in Japan (Murakami and Rohlen 1992, p.102). Applied to government–business relations, Murakami and Rohlen use social exchange to explain private sector compliance with the government's administrative guidance, as will be explained in section 2.3.

Conclusions

These five models of the Japanese political economy describe five different interpretations of the functioning of the Japanese bureaucratic and the economic-political systems. Opinions regarding these aspects of Japanese society seem deeply embedded in fundamental disagreements about how to interpret the basic cultural, political and social characteristics of Japan. It makes a big difference whether one sees Japan as some kind of pluralistic democracy with influential interest groups or as a country with an almighty government bureaucracy, largely independent from political

---

[12] It has to be mentioned that Murakami, similar to the consensual policy model, also stresses the importance of consensus. According to a 1982 study by Murakami, the most vital aspect of administrative regulation in post-war Japan was 'the building of consensus for voluntary compliance in each industry' (Haley 1991, pp.158–159). However, given the clear evidence of pluralistic elements in Murakami's approach, his contribution is classified separately from the consensual policy school.

influence. Therefore, it is not surprising that the results of a substantial number of political economy studies of Japan yield an impressive number of controversies. As Yamamura and Yasuba (1987, p.2) conclude: 'There exists today no single explanation for the performance of postwar Japan's political economy that a large majority of social scientists accepts as a satisfactory explanation.'[13]

As will be explained in the next section, the various interpretations of the Japanese political economy have strongly influenced the way of thinking regarding the economic system and economic policy in Japan. Furthermore, it will become clear that the lack of clarity which dominates the field of Japanese political economy studies also casts its shadow on studies of the Japanese economic system.

2.3   The Japanese economic system

The impressively high growth figures of the post-war Japanese economy – with the exception of the nineties – resulted in particular in the second half of the eighties and the first half of the nineties in a substantial number of studies investigating the specific characteristics of the Japanese economic system. In the overwhelming majority of these studies, the focus of attention is the role of the Japanese government. Often, the degree of functioning of the market mechanism is discussed, as well as various forms of government intervention and their effectiveness. Especially regarding industrial policy (*sangyō seisaku*) in Japan, many studies have been conducted (Johnson 1982; Eads and Yamamura 1987; Samuels 1987; Suzumura and Okuno-Fujiwara 1987; Uekusa 1987; Friedman 1988; Komiya, Okuno and Suzumura 1988; Okimoto 1989; Nester 1990).

As will become clear, and in accordance with the array of opinions on the Japanese political economy, considerable discussion and controversy exist about the exact nature of the relationship between public and private sectors and the effectiveness of economic policy and its contribution to the 'Japanese economic miracle' – I believe strongly that despite the economic crisis of the nineties it is still justified to use the word 'miracle'. This debate has been referred to in section 2.1 as the contrast between belief in government intervention and faith in the free market.

Within the context of this debate, two established schools – the interventionist and market schools – and two relatively new intermediate

---

[13] According to Johnson (1988): 'The relationship between Japan's political system and its economic achievements is perhaps the most fundamental controversy within the field of Japanese political economy.' More attention is paid to these controversies in Yamamura and Yasuba (1987), Kosai (1987), Okimoto (1988) and Murakami and Rohlen (1992, p.63).

Table 2.1. *Interpretations of the Japanese economic system and their theoretical supporters*

Economic system	Main theoretical supporters
Interventionist school	C.J. Johnson, L.E. Carlile, M. Morishima, T.J. Pempel, U. Schaede, L. Tyson, J. Zysman, M.C. Tilton
Market school	J.O. Haley, R. Komiya, G.W. Noble, H. Odagiri, M. Okuno-Fujiwara, H. Patrick, G. Saxonhouse, K. Suzumura, P.H. Tresize
Consensual policy school	S. Kumon, D. Okimoto, F.K. Upham, Research Project Team for Japanese Systems, R.J. Samuels, O. Watanabe, N. Hiwatari, J.M. Ramseyer, F. McCall Rosenbluth
Pluralistic network school	Y. Murakami, T. Rohlen

or hybrid interpretations can be distinguished (Zysman 1983; Eads and Yamamura 1987; Balassa and Noland 1988; Morris-Suzuki 1989; Noble 1989; Okimoto 1989; Upham 1991; Richardson 1997). This classification joins the World Bank (1993), where three corresponding explanations of the 'East Asian economic miracle' are distinguished: the revisionist, neo-classical and market-friendly views. To keep a clear view of the large number of studies that will be discussed, table 2.1 presents an overview of theoretical schools and their leading proponents. Furthermore, the various interpretations of the Japanese economic system and their accompanying approaches of the Japanese political economy are summarised in table 2.2 (follows partly Noble 1989).

The interventionist school

The first school to be discussed is closely associated with the bureaucracy-led interpretation of the Japanese political economy and stresses the existence of substantial and major government intervention in the Japanese economic system. In this school, for convenience called the interventionist school, the free working of the market mechanism and market forces are minor factors; substantial or overriding importance is assigned to industrial policy.[14] Japanese supporters are found, not surprisingly, mainly among former staff members of the central organisation in Japan for industrial policy, the Ministry of International Trade and Industry (MITI) (Tsūsanshō), supplemented by a mere handful of Japanese academics

[14] Eads and Yamamura (1987), p.423. For the specific forms of government intervention, which will be not discussed here, see Johnson (1978) and Okimoto (1989).

Table 2.2. *Interpretations of the Japanese political economy and economic system*

Political economy	Economic system	Public–private sector relationship
Bureaucracy-led model	Interventionist school: economic system is competitive but within parameters set by government	Strong Japanese state: government leads economic development Industrial policy very successful
'Japan, Inc.' model	In its traditional version no longer relevant	
Pluralistic model	Market school: economic system is a competitive market system	Market leads economic development Industrial policy not successful
Consensual policy model (network state model)	Separation of public and private sectors is blurred: economic system is competitive within parameters set by business; bureaucracy co-ordinates and enforces if necessary	Relatively weak Japanese state: intensive communication, consensus-building and negotiation through formal and informal networks support economic development
Pluralistic network model (informal organisation and social exchange)	Informal organisation model: social exchange (i.e. co-operative relationships) is used to correct market outcomes	Informal government intervention in a pluralistic political economy setting contributed to economic development Social exchange and informal networks

such as Morishima (1982). For example, in what has been called 'A Statement Against Free Competition', a MITI-official asserted that:

Free competition provides neither the most suitable scale nor a guarantee of proper prices. Free competition means excessive equipment and low profits... Free competition has a stifling effect on the economy. We must not allow it to be used in distributing the benefits of high growth – prices, wages, profits.[15]

Main early Western representatives of the interventionist school are Johnson (1982, 1995a), Pempel (1982) and Zysman (1983), followed more recently by Schaede (1992), Tyson (1993), Fingleton (1995), Carlile and Tilton (1998a, 1998c) and Tilton (1998).[16] As has been shown in the previous section on the Japanese political economy, these authors focus on the role of the Japanese state, in particular the government bureaucracy,

---

[15] In Johnson (1982, pp.9–10), another MITI staff member states: 'It is an utterly self-centered (businessman's) point of view to think that the government should be concerned with providing only a favorable environment for industries without telling them what to do.'

[16] Carlile and Tilton (1998c), p.210, claim that 'the developmental state model has been alive and well in the implementation of regulatory reform policies in recent years'.

in achieving high rates of economic growth after World War II. Johnson (1982, p.19) develops the concept of the developmental or plan-rational state, in which 'the government will give greatest precedence to industrial policy'. According to his analysis, in states such as Japan that were relatively late to industrialise, the state will lead the industrialisation process, i.e. will exercise developmental functions. Johnson compares the market rationality of the United States economy to the plan rationality of the Japanese economy, with the benefit given to the latter (Johnson 1982, p.18; Okimoto and Rohlen 1988, p.215). In his work, a central position is given to MITI, an institution for which 'Japan should be given the Nobel Prize' (*Tokyo Business Today* 1991, pp.20–23). Pempel (1982) also emphasises the role of the Japanese government bureaucracy in the post-war economic development of Japan (see also Pempel 1998, p.56 and pp.65ff.). He discusses post-war Japanese economic policy in terms of state-led capitalism.[17] Finally, Zysman (1983) analyses government intervention in Japan using the concept of state-led adjustment. His study focuses on the relationship between the structure of the state and the structure of the financial system on the one hand and the state's capacity for intervention in the economy on the other. Based on various classifications of the structural characteristics of state and financial system, Zysman claims that Japan is a favourable candidate for state intervention.[18]

It has to be mentioned that the interventionist school does not view Japan as a socialist command or plan economy.[19] Its supporters acknowledge to some extent the working of competitive forces in Japan, and the need to preserve them, but emphasise that the state leads economic growth and development and uses the market for achieving its industrial policy goals (see also Vogel 1996, p.51). For example, Johnson adopts the terminology of market-conforming methods of state intervention, of which so-called administrative guidance (*gyōsei shidō*) is the single most important. He states (Johnson 1982, pp.317–318) that 'in implementing its industrial policy, the state must take care to preserve competition to as high a degree as is compatible with its priorities'. Also Pempel (1982, p.xvii; 1998, p.56) stresses the relation between government intervention

---

[17] See especially Pempel (1982), pp.46–89. In more recent work, Pempel is moving towards the views of Okimoto and Samuels of a less dirigistic state. See Pempel and Muramatsu (1993), p.2, and also Pempel (1998) for a more nuanced view.

[18] See Zysman (1983), pp.300ff. His view on the contribution of the Japanese financial system to economic development is criticised by Okimoto (1989), p.143 and Hamada and Horiuchi (1987), p.224. For an alternative view see Lapavistas (1998).

[19] For an overview of Japan's experience with so-called national economic plans, which summarise the goals of macro-economic management of the respective cabinets, but do not contain detailed descriptions of the implementation of economic policy, see Kosai (1987).

and competitive forces in Japan. In addition, Zysman (1983) joins the former two with respect to the relationship between the Japanese state and the market, and discusses this relationship in terms of controlled competition.

Thus, according to the interventionist school, based on the bureau-cracy-led interpretation of the Japanese political economy, the Japanese economic system is characterised by a supposedly relatively high degree of successful government intervention. As will become clear in the next section, the market school heavily opposes this view.

The market school

The emphasis on the implementation of a successful industrial policy in Japan and other admirable forms of government intervention in the economy and the strong-state hypothesis of the interventionist school have been strongly criticised. Opponents follow the neo-classical eco-nomic paradigm and to some extent the pluralistic interpretation of the Japanese political economy,[20] and denounce the notion of substantial positive influence of industrial policy and government intervention on Japan's economic development.[21] According to the adherents of this neo-classical or market school, the economic success of Japan resulted mainly from the working of free-market forces. Government intervention has been marginal, often ineffective and consequently has left the market mechanism to operate efficiently (Noble 1989, p.53; Eads and Yama-mura 1987, p.423). For example, Patrick has been quoted (in Johnson 1982, p.9) as saying:

I am of the school which interprets Japanese economic performance as due pri-marily to the actions and efforts of private individuals and enterprises responding to the opportunities provided in quite free markets for commodities and labor. While the government has been supportive and indeed has done much to create the environment for growth, its role has often been exaggerated.

Other Western supporters of the market school include Saxonhouse (1983), Trezise (1983), Haley (1986, 1989, 1991), Horne (1988), Noble (1989), Evans (1990) and Beason and Weinstein (1993). Japanese sup-porters include Kosai and Ogino (1984), Suzumura and Okuno-Fujiwara (1987), Komiya and various other contributors in Komiya, Okuno and

[20] Their belief in the pluralistic model is not always explicitly stated but seems to be as-sumed. See Noble (1989). In Tresize and Suzuki (1976) it is clearly asserted that both economic and political systems in Japan can be interpreted as being competitive and pluralistic.
[21] See Eads and Yamamura (1987), p.423, Noble (1989), pp.60–65, Nester (1990), p.13 and Upham (1991), p.324.

Suzumura (1988), Okuno-Fujiwara (1991) and Odagiri (1992). The supporters of the market school are predominantly economists: according
to Aoki (1988a, p.265), it is mostly journalists and non-Japanese political scientists who adhere to the view that the 'Japanese economy is
a bureaucracy-led coherent system', but economists more often see the
bureaucrat's role as only complementary to the function of the market
mechanism. The view of the Japanese supporters of the market view is well
described by Morris-Suzuki (1989, p.133): 'far from being the outcome of
the planning of a small elite, Japan's high growth rate was achieved only as
the result of the high rate of saving by the people, by their will to work, and
by the vigorous efforts of Japan's entrepreneurs'. Furthermore, the main
conclusion of the elaborate study on post-war Japanese industrial policy,
published in Komiya, Okuno and Suzumura (1988, p.553), states that:

All the participants in this project recognise that, excluding the brief period immediately after the end of the war, the foundation of rapid growth was competition operating through the price mechanism and a flourishing entrepreneurial
spirit . . . it can even be said that the course of the history of industrial policy in
the principal postwar periods . . . has often been that the initiative and vitality of
the private sector undermined the plans of the government authorities to try to
utilize direct intervention in the nature of 'controls'.

Another and final example of the market school is presented in Odagiri
(1992), where the importance of government involvement in the post-war
economic development of Japan is strongly denied: 'It is not government
policies but a management system favouring growth strategies and innovation, and its interaction with intra-firm and inter-firm competition
that have been the central forces behind Japan's economic achievement'
(p.278).

Summary of interventionist and market schools

In brief, the interventionist approach, embedded in the bureaucracy-led
interpretation of the Japanese political economy, emphasises the successful role of industrial policy and government intervention in post-war
Japanese economic growth, paying only minor attention to market forces.
The exact opposite view is held by the market school, focusing on the
market mechanism and denying any substantial contribution of state-led
industrial and other economic policies to economic progress in Japan. This
school interprets the Japanese economic system as being fundamentally
determined by market forces.

The differences between the two schools appear irreconcilable. However, two relatively new approaches, which follow the criticism of the

market school on the strong-state hypothesis of the interventionist school, but stress the effectiveness of Japanese industrial policy and the use of the market-conforming methods of government intervention of the latter, have been developed. These intermediate or hybrid modes of the Japanese economic system are based on the political-economy interpretations of the consensual policy and the pluralistic network models. In general, hybrid interpretations of the economic development in Japan and the East Asian countries have gained considerable support during the nineties (Wade 1990; World Bank 1993; Weiss and Hobson 1995). I shall discuss the two most specific interpretations for Japan in the next sub-section.

Hybrid interpretations

The first intermediate mode between the interventionist and market schools is based on the consensus oriented political economy school characterised by the societal or network state, which has been strongly supported by Daniel Okimoto. In this network school, the strength of the state 'is derived from the convergence of public and private interests and the extensive network of ties binding the two sectors together' (Okimoto 1989, p.145). Networks of communication and negotiation between public and private sectors are here essential to formulate economic policy. That is, the interaction between public and private sectors takes place through a vast network of formal intermediate organisations, such as industrial associations and public corporations, in combination with informal policy networks. According to Okimoto, these formal and informal networks constitute the main intervention route of Japan's central bureaucracies in the economic system and contribute to the relative success of Japanese industrial policy. Within this framework, MITI's industrial policy differs from 'market-oriented models in its emphasis on the mutual interdependence of government and private industry' (Kumon 1992, p.110). This policy differs also from the interventionist school in placing less emphasis on the vision and power of MITI as explanation for the relative success of Japanese industrial policy (Okimoto 1989, p.xv). As mentioned earlier, in Okimoto's analysis the implementation of this policy takes form 'through market-conforming methods of intervention'; i.e., 'Japanese government officials believe that the market should be given as much leeway as possible to function', but with the constraint that it is positively structured 'in ways that improve the likelihood that industry-specific goals will be achieved' (Okimoto 1989, pp.50, 11 and 48).

The concept of the network state has been followed in Kumon (1992), the Research Project Team for Japanese Systems (1992) and Gerlach and Lincoln (1998) to analyse, among other things, the structure of the government–business relationship, whereas Ramseyer and McCall Rosenbluth (1993) and Watanabe (1997) subscribe also to the notion of a relatively weak Japanese state and government bureaucracy. Following the analysis of the consensual policy model in the previous section, the Japanese network society and economy consist of numerous intertwined network organisations and societal networks. Regarding network organisations, individual firms are often members of large informally organised business groups, commonly called *keiretsu*. Other examples of network organisations are alumni associations, associations of people born in the same town and industry associations. Societal networks are the other major components of the Japanese network society. These large networks are composed of various kinds of network organisations. For example, 'manufacturers of synthetic fibres form a network organization called the Association of Synthetic Fibre Manufacturers, which is a member of the Federation of Textile Industries, which, in turn, is a member of the Japan Federation of Economic Organizations (*Keidanren*)' (Kumon 1992, p.125). The different societal networks are connected by a series of formal and informal network organisations, such as the legally established ministerial advisory or deliberation councils (*shingikai*), composed of government officials and representatives of the private sector, and other non-legal based private counselling groups or study groups for ministers.[22] The result is a network system of decentralised network organisations, intertwined with 'unofficial business, political, and bureaucratic circles, informal intra- and inter-industrial networks, and deliberative councils and research groups in central government', predominantly institutionalised on an informal basis (Research Project Team for Japanese Systems 1992, p.103). Finally, Hiwatari (1998) emphasises the importance of co-ordination by the government bureaucracy of various interests in the policymaking process, which was instrumental in avoiding potential conflicts during the post-war economic development of Japan.

The second hybrid model, located between the interventionist and market schools, is based on the political economy interpretation of the pluralistic network school, which is basically more pluralistically oriented than the consensual policy school. This interpretation was initially developed as the informal organisation approach in Murakami (1987).

---

[22] Kumon (1992), p.126, and Research Project Team For Japanese Systems (1992), pp.80–81. World Bank (1993), pp.181–188, values the deliberation councils highly in contributing to Japanese economic growth by facilitating communication and co-operation between public and private sector. The importance of these *shingikai* is also emphasised in Johnson (1978, 1982), Park (1986), Upham (1987), Okimoto (1989) and Schwartz (1998).

According to Murakami, Japanese industrial policy 'is a successful example of how to combine two conflicting principles, competition and intervention, in order to achieve maximum economic growth' (p.51); furthermore, 'all indications show that both the market mechanism and parliamentary democracy have been at work in postwar Japan, bringing about fierce competition and visible conflicts in many parts of society' (p.39). After World War II, the Japanese government managed to keep a delicate balance between regulation and competition. Government intervention was minimal and informal, that is 'not legally enforceable'. This administrative guidance (*gyōsei shidō*) established a framework in which competition could function. Murakami calls this kind of competition 'compartmentalised competition'. In a subsequent study, Murakami developed in close collaboration with Rohlen the social exchange model, in which the government-business relationship in post-war Japan is presented as an example of social exchange (see section 2.2), and consequently can be explained by 'a theory of implicit give-and-take operating in a long-term framework in which both government and private firms get what they want' (Murakami and Rohlen 1992, p.91). In this relationship, the following elements were essential. First, the relationship was informal and long-term, multi-issue based, expressed in effective non-legal governmental administrative guidance. Furthermore, participants shared the belief that 'excessive competition' should be avoided, and therefore accepted this administrative guidance in general. Another essential feature was the intra-group impartiality: member firms of a specific industrial association were treated equally by the government bureaucracy. Finally, to safeguard the consensus reached, entry to this group was also controlled by the use of administrative guidance. The resulting effectiveness of industrial policy depended on a combination of a 'favorable environment of economic cooperation', i.e. consensus between market participants to prevent 'excessive competition', and a particular Japanese cultural tradition based on co-operative collectivism (Murakami and Rohlen 1992, p.95 and pp.82–83).

As has been stated above, the central focus on the importance of consensual policymaking in the network society interpretation of Okimoto is supported by John Haley, who interprets the intervention of the Japanese government in the economic system as consensual management (Haley 1989, 1991, 1992). However, Haley (1991, p.153) is extremely critical of Okimoto's conclusion of the 'apparent' effectiveness of Japanese industrial policy:

What is described today as a successful 'industrial policy' carried out by an elite corps of Japanese technocrats can be more accurately characterized as a series of ad hoc adjustments to immediate economic needs and circumstances by government and business co-operating when their interests coincided, but often in conflict as they pursued their own individual aims.

According to Haley, as a result of the lack of formal, legal powers, the Japanese government bureaucracy was forced to use informal administrative guidance to intervene in the economic system. And this administrative guidance was so weak that the free working of market forces could survive (Haley 1986, p.108):

The predominance of administrative guidance as a regulatory form for government intervention in the economy . . . has helped to preserve a competitive market economy by maximizing the freedom of individual firms over economic decisions although behind the veil of pervasive governmental direction. Japanese postwar economic achievement can thus be credited in part to administrative guidance because it ensured the failure of a bureaucratically set agenda.

A scholar whose approach is relatively difficult to classify is Frank Upham. As mentioned in section 2.2, Upham departs from the 'Japan, Inc.' model. Furthermore, he also refers to the presence of pluralistic elements, i.e. the influence of interest groups: 'Interest groups abound and are enormously successful in Japan in general and in industrial policy in particular' (Upham 1987, p.200). However, in the development of Upham's work, the so-called 'consultative consensual character' of the public–private sector relationship becomes the dominant line. The process of negotiation, the 'close, informal, collaborative relationship between the bureaucracy and business' is, according to Upham, the lifeblood of Japanese industrial policy.[23] The separation between public and private sectors is blurred to such an extent that 'it may be wrong even to think in terms of government intervention in the economy' (Upham 1991, p.342). In this important respect, Upham's work belongs to the consensual policy school. Therefore, he is incorporated in that school.

The various interpretations of the Japanese political economy and economic system have been summarised in table 2.2. The 'Japan, Inc.' interpretation is in its traditional version dismissed by various authors as being no longer relevant for the present Japanese political-economic structure.[24] Furthermore, in the table the approach of Haley, who follows the paradigm of consensus of the consensual policy school but clearly supports the market school conclusions regarding the Japanese economic system, is located between these interpretations.

---

[23] Upham (1987), pp.201–203, Upham (1991), p.342.
[24] Johnson (1982), Kosai (1987) and Okimoto (1988, 1989) criticise 'Japan, Inc.'. See also how globalisation has unravelled 'Japan, Inc.' in Hirsh and Henry (1997).

2.4   Conclusions

The discussion of the literature of the Japanese political economy and economic system leads to the following conclusions.

First, it is clear from the analysis of the interpretations of the Japanese economic system, summarised in table 2.2, that during the 1990s the network approach gained significant popularity. As has been demonstrated, the studies by Okimoto (1988, 1989), Kumon (1992), Murakami and Rohlen (1992) and the Research Project Team for Japanese Systems (1992) all stress the importance of network relations in the Japanese economic structure. Social network analysis has been developed in anthropology and sociology, and saw a major expansion in the 1960s and 1970s when its application was extended to other sciences as well, including economics; it received even more attention in the 1990s with the publication of Manuel Castells' three-volume study '*The Information Age: Economy, Society and Culture*'.[25] One field of Japanese economic studies which has adopted the network approach for its analytical exercises is that of industrial organisation, clear examples being Nakatani (1991), Gerlach (1992) and Imai (1992).[26] Another area where attention to network relations has grown is the study of the relationship between government and private business, as will be demonstrated in the next chapter.

Second, the analysis shows clearly the existence of fundamentally different interpretations of the Japanese economic system, based on accompanying and similar views of the political economy, state and society. These differences, which are basically different views of the role of the government in the development and regulation of economic markets and private business, i.e. of economic policy, result in completely different frameworks for economic analysis. It makes a big difference whether one sees the Japanese economy as part of a developmental state, guided by the economic bureaucracy, or as a market economy, embedded in a pluralistic model, guided by the forces of supply and demand. It makes a big difference whether one presupposes the economic bureaucracy to be endowed with almighty powers and near-perfect foresight as the interventionist school does, or as a relatively powerless bureaucracy, the view

---

[25] Scott (1988), pp.53–54. In economics, the approach of interpreting intercorporate relations as social networks is gaining ever greater support. See for example Scott (1988), Imai (1992) and Castells (1996).

[26] Nakatani (1991) introduced Japan's 'network capitalism', based on two pillars of a '*keiretsuka*' economy and a system of interlocking shareholding (Johnson 1992, p.8). In Gerlach (1992), the attention is focused on informal intercorporate alliances, which have pervaded much of the Japanese economy. Imai (1992) uses the terminology of corporate networks to define the industrial organisations and connections between business firms in modern Japan, culminating in a theory of network industrial organisation.

of the consensual policy school, which has to co-ordinate and negotiate with private industry in order to implement its policies. It makes a big difference whether public and private sectors are diametrically opposed to each other, as the market school believes, or are a symbiotic network system, their borders blurred by interrelated formal and informal networks, as the network state interpretations say. In short, it makes a big difference which specific school one accepts to formulate the basic assumptions of subsequent economic analysis, assumptions that determine its final conclusions.

The interpretation of the market school traditionally and predominantly has been the departing framework in the contributions of economists to Japanese economic studies. However, during the last decade this orientation has been criticised by the interventionist school, and more recently by the network state interpretations, schools that are dominated by political and social scientists, Japanologists and journalists. The interventionist view, propagated in the academic community mainly by Chalmers Johnson and supported in the media by journalists such as Karel van Wolferen and James Fallows and the former Counsellor for Japan Affairs to the US Secretary of Commerce Clyde Prestowitz, collectively named the revisionists, has in particular been extremely critical of the market school.[27] In reaction to the revisionists' claims, adherents of rational choice theory emerged to argue against the idea that the government bureaucracy in Japan is strong and operates independently from the political structure (Ramseyer and McCall Rosenbluth 1993). This led to a counter-attack by Johnson and Keehn (1994) in a provocative essay titled 'A Disaster in the Making: Rational Choice and Asian Studies'. Furthermore, more recently, the East Asian crisis and the sharp downturn of the Japanese economy in the second half of the nineties have resulted in more explicit criticism of the revisionist views and their explanations of the Japanese economic model (see Lindsey and Lukas 1998). All in all, the controversies regarding the basic characteristics of the Japanese economic system have resulted in polarisation and politicisation in the field of Japanese economic studies, sometimes reduced to narrow and simplistic 'pro' or 'contra' Japan classifications. In this sense, the market school is being interpreted as 'pro': the Japanese economic system is basically determined by market forces, there are no 'unfair' government interventions and trade barriers, and consequently Japan should be treated on equal terms. On the other side, the interventionist school and their

---

[27] See also Okimoto (1998) and Stockwin (1999). A summary of their views is presented in *US News & World Report* (1990), pp.54–55. Other examples of revisionist thinking are Fingleton (1995) and Murphy (1996).

revisionist supporters are typified as the 'contra' Japan movement: they argue that Japanese capitalism is basically different from Western capitalist systems, advocate managed trade and industrial policy, and support a tough policy line with regard to Japan. This polarisation is exemplified in a number of statements. For example, Johnson called Columbia University (the alma mater of Hugh Patrick, who is one of the proponents of the market school) the 'Columbia Geisha School of Economics' for its alleged pro-Japanese views.[28] Johnson also cast aspersions on the integrity of his market school opponents by accusing them of being on the Japanese payroll. On the other side, the revisionists are portrayed as a 'Gang of Four' and 'Japan-bashers', and accused of 'McCarthyism'.[29] This polarisation is also present in the political field. Under the George Bush Snr administration, Gary Saxonhouse, one of the leading proponents of the market school, was a member of the Council of Economic Advisers. The first Clinton administration appointed L. D'Andrea Tyson, one of the main defenders of the interventionist line, as head of the Council of Economic Advisers, and, in the line of revisionist recommendations, started to implement a system of managed trade – much against the belief of market school adherents (see Saxonhouse 1998). Against the background of this polarisation and politicisation, most research, my own included, is quite easily labelled either 'pro' or 'contra' Japan. This stigmatisation is highly regrettable, because it obstructs objective research.[30]

Many studies which criticise economics as being unrealistic, in the sense of neglecting important institutional characteristics, emphasise the importance of informal factors. Clear examples are Johnson (1982), Okimoto (1989), Kumon (1992) and Murakami and Rohlen (1992). Therefore, in the next chapter, the presence and relevance of informal factors as institutional characteristics of the public–private sector relationship in Japan will be discussed. The classification of the various interpretations of the Japanese political economy and economic system established in this chapter will form the basis of this analysis.

---

[28] *Tokyo Business Today* (1991), p.21.   [29] See Choate (1990), pp.153–154.

[30] The existence of a 'furious' controversy between revisionists and proponents of the rational choice theory is reported in Stockwin (1999). An excellent overview of the ongoing debate between interventionists and market economists is presented in Yamamura (1990), where the former are referred to as structuralist pessimists, and the latter are divided into market school utopians and market school optimists. See also Katz (1998).

3 Informal aspects of Japanese economic policy

> It appears that the informal structure of transactions in Japan is receiving greater attention as scholars seek to approximate empirical reality more closely.
>
> Y. Murakami and T.P. Rohlen (1992)

> The informal system, the driving force of Japanese activities, is a native Japanese brew, steeped in a unique characteristic of Japanese culture.
>
> C. Nakane (1970)

3.1 Introduction

As has become clear from the analyses of the Japanese political economy and economic system presented in chapter 2, a significant number of scholars stress the importance of informal factors in the public–private sector relationship in Japan. For example, in the previous chapter the informal organisation approach was introduced, which, according to Murakami, 'provides the most useful explanation of the key feature of the postwar Japanese economy' (Murakami 1987, p.55). Upham (1987, p.204), states that 'informality is preferred by every level of government and in all areas of government–citizen contact'. And Haley (1991, p.163) is emphatic regarding the enforcement of government policy:

What distinguishes Japan is the persuasive resort to informal enforcement in contexts that seem to require formal regulations in other industrial states. In Japan informal enforcement is not a process of governing, but has become the process of governing. It is used to implement nearly all bureaucratic policy, whether or not expressed in statute or regulation, at all levels of government and all administrative offices.

With respect to the organisation of the Japanese bureaucracy, Keehn (1990, p.1021), declares that 'the processes of informality and discretion are a good deal more than flexible practices that complement and flesh out formal rules and procedures. They are organizational strategies crucial to the functions and performance of bureaucracy and government

33

in Japan.' Finally, according to Carlile and Tilton (1998b, pp.8–9), 'Japan is notably lacking in procedural constraints that bind administrative decisionmakers, and this contributes to a lack of transparency, high levels of discretion, and a high degree of informality in administrative activities. State regulation of private sector activities extends well beyond that which is stipulated in laws and formally legitimated regulations.'

In the course of my research, moreover, numerous personal interviewees have emphasised the importance of informal aspects in Japan. According to a Dutch banker, 'informal regulation is in Japan the rule rather than the exception'.[1] A Western scholar, long resident in Japan, commented that 'in Japan, informal control is very strong and has been consolidated in recent years'.[2] A Japanese legal scholar also subscribed to this viewpoint: 'Informalities are a very important aspect of Japanese society. Many fields of Japanese society are determined by informal mechanisms.'[3]

These are just a few random examples from a large number of scholars who emphasise from different disciplines and perspectives the importance of informal factors in the relationship between the public and private sectors in Japan, more specifically in the various forms of government–business interaction in the economic system. However, as will become clear, these scholars disagree sharply in their judgement of the actual relevance and importance of these informal factors for economic policies.

The first question to ask is by what criteria is informality determined. According to the literature, the informal part of the public–private sector relationship with respect to the Japanese economic system has two major components: administrative guidance (*gyōsei shidō*) and informal networks. Of course, the government–business relationship has many dimensions and can take many different forms. This is also true for the informal part of this relationship. The limitations to administrative guidance and informal networks are dictated by the frequent and persistent attention given to these two informal components in studies on the Japanese political economy and economic system. In the existing literature, administrative guidance and informal networks are the central elements in analyses of the relevance of informal factors in the Japanese public–private sector economic relationship, or, in other words, in Japanese economic policy.

First, informal government intervention in Japan is often identified with non-legal intervention, that is intervention without explicit legal backing.[4] In the words of Richardson (1997, p.258): 'Informality refers

[1] Personal interview, Tokyo, March 1995.
[2] Personal interview, the Netherlands, March 1991.
[3] Personal interview, Tokyo, September 1992.
[4] This identification of informality with non-legality is supported by, for example, Murakami (1987, p.46): 'that is, not legally enforceable'; Murakami and Rohlen

to behavior that is not prescribed by constitutions, legal frameworks, or formal, purposive aspects of social organisation.' This informal, non-legal intervention has become well known as 'administrative guidance' (*gyōsei shidō*). Administrative guidance officially means that 'government institutions want specific parties to act or not to act in a specific way, within the primary or secondary task of these government institutions, by realising guidance, strong advice, weak advice or other measures without legal coercive power'.[5] The central characteristic of administrative guidance is the non-legal enforceability: compliance by the recipient of the governmental guidance is from a strict legal perspective voluntary – that is, without formal legal coercion. Thus, the criterion whether or not a government action should be typified as administrative guidance is clearly a legal one. Furthermore, administrative guidance is an instrument of government intervention, that is to say is used to implement government policies. (See section 3.3 for an analysis of administrative guidance.)

The other major component of the informal part of the public–private sector relationship comprises informal networks based on personal relations (*jinmyaku*). These personal relationships are links between the government bureaucracy and business executives resulting from common backgrounds (former employer, university, place of birth, family ties, etc.). According to Okimoto (1989, p.236), these 'informal, personal relationships between bureaucrats and business leaders . . . function as channels of communication between the public and private sectors and as mechanisms for bridging the divide between "frame" organizations in Japan'. The criterion to distinguish these personal networks is the sharing of a common background, which establishes specific personal or private relationships. Essential is the non-transparent character of the use of these networks in economic policy. From the perspective of economic policy, their usefulness as mechanisms to reach consensus in the policymaking process is emphasised, whilst some scholars also stress the importance of informal networks for implementing policy. That is, informal personal networks could be used as instruments of government control over the economic system: they may be thought of as proxy variables for the use of administrative guidance. In this sense, the use of informal networks as instruments of economic policy involves the element of non-legal enforceability. Informal networks will be discussed in section 3.4.

(1992, p.91): 'no legal ground for compulsory affiliation'; Kumon (1992, p.126): 'less formal (not established by law)'. See also Upham (1987), p.22.

[5] *Juristo* (1991, p.74): Administrative Procedures Law, Outline of Bill (The first sectional meeting draft, 26 July 1991). Author's translation from original Japanese text *Gyōsei Shidō Tetsuzuki Hō Yōkō An (Dai Ichi Tsugi/Shi Bukai An) (Heisei 3 Nen 7 Gatsu 26 Nichi).*

To conclude, the analysis of informality in economic policy in Japanese (political) economic studies is usually limited to two interrelated components: non-legal intervention and informal networks. The common denominators are the dimensions of non-legality and generally the dimension of non-transparency. In the latter sense, informal is identified with private, the absence of disclosure. This is sometimes negatively interpreted as the existence of a sneaky and secretive bureaucracy that uses informal (in the sense of non-transparent and undisclosed) instruments at its own discretion. However, various studies, for example Upham (1987, pp.167–168) and Okimoto (1989), emphasise the positive aspects of an informal, 'behind the scenes', consultative and consensual policymaking process which includes a small number of participants, an informal consultative and co-operative interdependent relationship that also remains important in the implementation stage of government policies; in the words of Noble (1989, pp.68–70), 'informal but intense links', in the meaning of 'informal, bureaucratically-sponsored negotiation' between government and business are the heart of Japanese economic and social policy.

As will become clear, non-transparency is relevant for the major part of administrative guidance. Of course, it is particularly relevant for, and even is the major characteristic of, informal networks. It is extremely hard to tell if and to what extent personal relationships based on specific common backgrounds are used in the formulation and implementation of economic policy. The aspect of non-transparency is an essential dimension of informality, and frustrates an objective judgement of the issue.

From an economic perspective, the use by the government economic bureaucracy of non-legal and non-transparent instruments can be interpreted as the existence of a government intervention mechanism behind the market mechanism. In other words, if Japanese economic policy is characterised as informal in the meaning of non-legal and non-transparent, an unknown and unspecified part of government intervention in the economic system is hidden from the view of economic markets. In this respect, informal economic intervention could be typified as non-market economic intervention.

Finally, a major problem with informality as a concept in Japanese political-economic studies is the ad-hoc use of different interpretations, sometimes even in the same study, quite often without explication. For example, according to Upham (1987, pp.198ff), the characteristics of informality regarding the Japanese government bureaucracy include aspects such as 'the creation and operation of wide-ranging administrative systems with little or no statutory basis', and a legal environment that results in 'a judicially unaccountable bureaucracy that operates without clear statutory limits', which have a clear legal basis. But is also contains 'frequent informal consultations' between the members of deliberation councils (*shingikai*), that is informal in the meaning of consultations beyond the formal procedural meetings, informal in the sense of 'behind the scenes' unofficial negotiations.

The purpose of this chapter is to present an analysis of the relevance and importance of informal factors in Japanese economic policy, following the various interpretations of the Japanese political economy and economic system which were presented in chapter 2. First, in section 3.2, some reasons for the alleged importance of informal factors in Japan will be presented. Second, the two major alleged informal components of Japanese economic policy will be discussed: administrative guidance in section 3.3 and informal networks in section 3.4. A final section will be devoted to concluding remarks and puts the findings of this chapter in the perspective of monetary policy.

3.2   The alleged importance of informality in Japan

The purpose of this section is to investigate why, according to a significant number of scholars, informal factors are important in the contemporary Japanese economic system. The analysis will be brief, mainly because several explanations are embedded in sociological and anthropological frameworks, which are beyond the scope of this study. It must also be emphasised that this analysis in no way claims that informal factors are a uniquely Japanese phenomenon – contrary to what is claimed by certain scholars such as Nakane. What the analysis in this section does provide is a survey of studies which stress why informal factors in the Japanese political economy and economic system are important, and therefore provides the argument firstly for the inclusion of informal factors in an economic study and secondly for an investigation of the actual relevance and importance of a specific number of informal factors in Japanese economic policy.

The reasons for the alleged importance of informal factors can be classified in two, partly interrelated categories: legal and social-cultural. The legal line of reasoning, related to the legal dimension of informality, has its main supporter in the work of Haley, who emphasises strongly the importance of informal (i.e. not based on legislation) enforcement of government policies in Japan. According to Haley (1991, p.163, 1986), the 'persuasive resort to informal enforcement in Japan is best explained by two factors: the predominance of promotional as opposed to regulatory policies and the weakness of formal law enforcement' (see also Duck 1996; Tilton 1998; Curtis 1999, p.5). In Haley's view, industry in Japan is assisted by promotional government intervention, and is virtually un-hampered by restrictive economic regulation. Furthermore, as a result of 'Japan's peculiar historical experience' and 'the impact of Occupation reforms', the Japanese bureaucracy lacks explicit legal controls, which has resulted in 'the strength of extralegal forms of social and economic ordering' (Haley 1992, p.58). The reforms of the Supreme Commander of Allied Powers (SCAP) during the occupation of Japan after World War II limited the legal powers of the economic bureaucracy significantly (see also Carlile and Tilton 1998c, p.199). As a result, the promotional orientation of economic policy and the lack of formal legal power impelled the bureaucracy to resort to co-operative policymaking and administrative guidance:

These two factors not only force reliance on administrative guidance as an informal means of implementing policy, but also by the same token significantly curtail the autonomy of the bureaucracy in formulating policy. Both the aim of assisting industry and a lack of strong legal sanctions or other forms of formal legal coercion in effect compel officials in Japan to negotiate and compromise with respect to the policies they seek to implement.[6]

To conclude, Haley (1991, p.166) states that 'the avoidance of legal regulation and coercive state control must be viewed as among the most prominent characteristics of governance in postwar Japan'.[7] According to others, mainly Japanese scholars, the lack of explicit legal controls in Japan 'is considered to be a reflection of either traditional attitudes or "deep culture"' (see Haley 1992, p.57). Some Western scholars, in particular Upham and Young, explain the lack of legal means in terms of bureaucratic power: the bureaucracy was able to prevent the development of legal means (such as litigation) and consequently maintained its power by the use of informal policymaking and implementation (Ramseyer 1985; Haley 1992, p.58).

  Social-cultural explanations of the alleged importance of informal factors in Japanese society and its economic system stress the importance of such aspects as consensus, perception of vulnerability, avoidance of conflict and confrontation in public and other social-cultural factors.[8] As was discussed in section 2.2, the consensual policy school puts forward the notion that consensus is the basis of the functioning of the Japanese political-economic system, rather than binding rules and laws.

[6] Haley (1991, p.163, 1992, p.58). See also Johnson (1982), pp.264–265, Haley (1989), pp.130–131, and Haley (1991), p.155 and p.157.
[7] The general and universal character of Japanese laws also amplifies the importance of informal factors. See section 3.3.
[8] See, among others, Davis (1972), pp.9–10, and especially Research Project Team for Japanese Systems (1992).

This socio-cultural preference for consensus and reliance on informal bargaining has been reinforced by 'Japan's perception of vulnerability'.[9] The focus on consensus is also found in discussions on the importance of legal contracts in Japan. According to several studies, not formal contracts but societal norms, based on consensus, in combination with personal, informal negotiations and agreements, structure Japanese society.[10] Furthermore, socio-cultural explanations of informality in Japan's society and economic system emphasise the importance of human relationships (*jinmyaku*) and resulting informal networks. For example Nakane (1970, p.144) notes that 'Japan has no native concept of "organization" or "network" abstracted or divorced from actual man; "organization" is perceived as a kind of succession of direct and concrete relationships between man and man.' According to Pye (1985, p.287), human relationships are central in Japan: 'Patterns of relationship which are never formally institutionalized in a legal sense can become as rigid and firmly entrenched as the formal rules and institutions of the West.'[11] The use of informal networks is also found in the pluralistic network model, which departs from the concept of social exchange, such as discussed in section 2.2 of the previous chapter. Another school, which was discussed in chapter 2 and which focuses strongly on informal networks, is the consensual policy school. According to Okimoto (1989, p.156), the factors behind the importance of informal, personal networks in Japan are a society based on consensus rather than legal codes, the Confucian stress placed on human relations, particularly the emphasis on loyalty and trust, social homogeneity, the logistical convenience of Tokyo as the hub of both political and economic activity and the role of the educational system as the central mechanism for elite selection and social mobility. Okimoto's conclusion is clear: 'This combination of factors appears to make Japan perfectly suited to the informal, non-legalistic policymaking that is a hallmark of its administrative apparatus' (Okimoto 1989, p.156).

In the next sections, the two major alleged informal components of economic policy in Japan – administrative guidance and informal networks – will be discussed. I shall explicitly link these informal phenomena with the various schools of the Japanese political economy and economic system analysed in chapter 2.

---

[9] Okimoto (1989), p.32. See also Pye (1985), p.288, and Johnson (1982), p.274.
[10] Yamamoto (1992), p.49, declares: 'it is not the contract that has binding force. It is extralegal, supracontractual societal norms that keep Japanese in line'. See also: Nakane 1970, pp.62, 79, 82–83; Murakami 1987, pp.35–36; Okimoto 1989, p.159; Haley 1991, p.175; Haley 1992, pp.42ff.; Imai 1992, p.230.
[11] See also Keehn (1990), p.1033, and van Wolferen (1991), pp.188ff.

3.3   Informal aspects I: administrative guidance

One of the most discussed components of government intervention in the Japanese economic system is the vague, sometimes ill-defined set of informal instruments or 'moral suasion' commonly specified as administrative guidance (*gyōsei shidō*). Praised by some as an important explanation of the Japanese economic 'miracle' (Johnson 1982, p.318), and criticised by others as non-legal government intrusion in the private sector,[12] the phrase 'administrative guidance' has been used frequently by government agencies and in the mass media, but was until 1993 not an official legal technical term.[13] According to some estimates – which seem rather subjective – the use of administrative guidance is significant and widespread: Young (1984, p.954) refers to commentators who estimate that administrative guidance 'comprises over eighty percent of Japanese bureaucratic activity', and Schaede (1992, p.9) states that 'informal industry estimates are that this regulatory practice constitutes 60–90% of all regulation of a given industry'; Duck (1996, p.1708) claims that 'the Japanese bureaucracy relies heavily on administrative guidance, the effects of which are felt throughout all aspects of business in Japan'. However, as will become clear, regarding its effectiveness, the opinions differ greatly (see also OECD 1999b).

Definition and classification

To clarify the concept of administrative guidance, figure 3.1 shows the definitions used in some of the major studies in the field. Comparison of these definitions and their underlying literature leads to the following conclusions.

First, most studies accept the legal criterion: administrative guidance is interpreted as government action without formal legal coercion. Compliance with such guidance is, from a strict legal perspective, voluntary, so, legally, the recipients are free to ignore it. This also implies that these regulated parties presumably are 'not forced to perform without consent, nor are they punished if they do not' (Henderson 1973, p.202; see also Narita 1968; Davis 1972; Johnson 1982; Young 1984; Eads and Yamamura 1987; Murakami 1987; Upham 1987; Wakiyama 1987;

---

[12] Personal interviews with former senior executive of the Japan Federation of Business Organisations, Tokyo, January 1993; senior executive city bank, Tokyo, July 1993.

[13] This changed with the introduction of the Administrative Procedures Law (*Gyōsei Tetsuzuki Hō*) in 1993. See also OECD (1999b) and Ramseyer and Nakazato (1999).

Ackley and Ishi (1976, p.236): Administrative guidance involves the use of influence, advice, and persuasion to cause firms or individuals to behave in particular ways that the government believes are desirable.

Davis (1972, p.1): 'Administrative guidance', a simple though by no means perfect definition, would be a request by an administrative body for voluntary cooperation.

Haley (1991, p.160): Administrative guidance is defined quite simply as advice or direction by government officials carried out voluntarily – that is, without formal legal coercion – by the recipient.

Henderson (1973, p.201): ... 'guidance' means action by which administrative agencies influence parties through voluntary, nonauthoritative – as opposed to legally coercive – means to cooperate willingly with the agency's guidance toward what is academically called 'integration of the social order'.

Johnson (1982, p.265): It refers to the authority of the government, contained in the laws establishing the various ministries, to issue directives, requests, suggestions, and encouragements to the enterprises or clients within a particular ministry's jurisdiction ... although it is not based on any explicit law, it cannot violate the law.

***Juristo* (1991, Administrative Procedures Law, Outline of Bill (The first sectional meeting draft, 27 July 1991), p.74):** Under this law, administrative guidance means that government institutions want specific parties to act or not to act in a specific way, within the primary or secondary task of these government institutions, by realising guidance, strong advice, weak/ordinary advice or other measures without legal coercive power [*author's translation*].

Minami (1990, p.99): *Gyōsei shidō* is a guidance that is given to the people by an administrative organ. It is called instruction (*shiji*), recommendation (*kankoku*), warning (*keikoku*), advice (*shiji*), attention (*chui*), guidance (*shidō*), etc. [*author's translation*].

Narita (1968, p.353): Administrative guidance is understood as the action of administrative organs in respect to matters within a certain administrative field, in executing statutes by applying them, and in ordering strong measures against, and otherwise compelling, specific individuals, juristic persons and associations; where there is voluntary compliance and a statutory basis of action, in guiding, suggesting, and advising; and where there is voluntary compliance but no statutory basis of action, in influencing the parties' voluntary cooperation and consensual performance by expressing, as an administrative organ, the expectation and wish that something should exist or be done in certain ways.

Schwartz (1998, p.27): [Administrative guidance] by the persuasion of private actors to cooperate on matters over which an agency has broad jurisdictional competence even if no specific statutory authority.

Figure 3.1 Definitions of administrative guidance

Stockwin (1999, p.239): [Administrative guidance] involves a variety of informal (not legally sanctioned but not necessarily illegal) techniques whereby public officials put pressure on companies and other organizations to follow policies desired by their ministries.

Trezise and Suzuki (1976, p.784): . . . administrative guidance, under which an official or an agency, without having specific legal authority to do so, might direct or induce private persons to take or refrain from certain actions.

Wakiyama (1987, p.211): Administrative guidance is defined as an administrative action, without any coercive legal effect, which encourages related parties to act in a specific way in order to realize some administrative aim.

Young (1984, p.923): Administrative guidance occurs when administrators take action of no coercive legal effect that encourages regulated parties to act in a specific way in order to realize some administrative aim.

Figure 3.1 *(cont.)*

Kitagawa 1989; Okimoto 1989; Minami 1990; Uekusa 1990; Haley 1991; *Juristo* 1991; Schwartz 1998; OECD 1999b; Stockwin 1999). As will be discussed below, the question is if compliance is from a practical point of view really 'voluntary'. Second, the government agency does not need specific statutory authority to use its guidance. However, it must not act beyond its specific field of administrative concern (Henderson 1973, pp.200–201; see also Narita 1968; Haitani 1976; Tresize and Suzuki 1976; Johnson 1982; Minami 1990; *Juristo* 1991). Third, administrative guidance is given by government agencies to regulated parties with the aim of modifying their behaviour in a specific way (Young 1984, p.932; see also Narita 1968; Ackley and Ishi 1976; Haitani 1976; Tresize and Suzuki 1987; Wakiyama 1987; Minami 1990; Uekusa 1990; *Juristo* 1991; Shindo 1992). Finally, the government agency uses only expressions of expectations or wishes, and not legal directives. In this sense, administrative guidance can be interpreted as a form of 'moral suasion' (Henderson 1973, p.201; see also Narita 1968; Davis 1972; Ackley and Ishi 1976; Young 1984; Upham 1987; Wakiyama 1987; Haley 1991; *Juristo* 1991).

The use of administrative guidance is in some studies perceived as unique to Japan, an informal form of government intervention that would not work in Western countries such as the United States.[14] For example, Johnson (1993, pp.56–57) quotes S. Hoshino, former vice-minister of the Economic Planning Agency, who declares that 'non-transparent methods such as the Japanese government's administrative guidance would have been regarded as "unfair" outside of Japan . . . and most likely could not

---

[14] Okimoto (1989), p.94. Supported by various interviews, 1992–1993.

function in the United States'. Others, such as Narita (1968), Young (1984), Wilson (1988), Haley (1991) and Ramseyer (2000), take the view that in Western countries similar intervention modes exist. For example, Haley (1991, p.162) states that 'administrative guidance is not peculiarly Japanese. Informal enforcement . . . is indeed the most common form of law enforcement.'

According to its purpose, administrative guidance can be classified in at least three different categories.[15] First, promotional administrative guidance is given to assist recipients and to promote their interests: the government as a 'good father' (*josei shidō*). Second, administrative guidance is used as an arbitrage mechanism to solve conflicts between parties (*chōsei shidō*). Third, administrative guidance is used to regulate the conduct of specific parties in a specific way: regulatory administrative guidance (*kissei shidō*). This kind of guidance retains the character of advice, but is used as a substitute for legal compulsion. In general, when administrative guidance is being discussed, it is mostly interpreted as regulatory guidance.

Administrative guidance is practically conducted through directions (*shiji*), requests (*yōbō*), warnings (*keikoku*), suggestions (*kankoku*) and encouragement (*kanshō*) (Narita 1968, p.355; Henderson 1973, p.202; Johnson 1982, p.265; Minami 1990, p.99; Katayama 2000, p.284). These measures are partly implemented through circulars or notifications (*tsūtatsu*), which are often published, and through other formalities and written statements (Narita 1968, p.365). In the case of the Ministry of Finance – at least until 1998 – *tsūtatsu* have been used quite extensively to regulate the activities of financial institutions. According to the Federation of Bankers Associations of Japan (1994, p. 35), these circulars are used to explain laws and ordinances and to give guidance on their practical application. However, a significant part of the administrative guidance is given orally, and some observers include even body language of government bureaucrats.[16] This non-transparent form of administrative guidance is said to include the most important guidance, is the breeding ground for rumours and unspecified claims regarding its effectiveness, and gives administrative guidance its delicate and illustrious connotation.[17] A number of interviewees did not regard even published

---

[15] This classification is based on Minami (1990), p.100, Matsushita and Schoenbaum (1989), p.32, Narita (1968), p.371, and various interviews with legal scholars, Tokyo, September, October and November 1992 and July 1993.

[16] Personal interviews Western scholar, Tokyo, September 1992; Japanese legal scholars, Tokyo, September and October 1992; former high-ranking official Bank of Japan, Tokyo, January 1993.

[17] Personal interviews leading Western and Japanese journalists, Tokyo, June, July and September 1992; Western and Japanese economic scholars, Tokyo, September 1992; Japanese legal scholars, Tokyo, September, October and November 1992. See also Yamamura (1990), p.59.

tsūtatsu as administrative guidance: the dimension of non-transparency was for them an essential criterion to classify government actions as administrative guidance.[18] This interpretation of administrative guidance can also be found in most discussions in the media and empirical studies.

Whether or not *tsūtatsu* are part of administrative guidance remains unclear. According to some Japanese legal scholars and government bureaucrats, the public and general character of *tsūtatsu* disqualifies them as administrative guidance: 'real' administrative guidance is never written down and is very directly oriented at a specific party.[19] Others include the *tsūtatsu* in administrative guidance, because from a legal perspective the affected parties are not obliged to follow them.[20] This interpretation coincides with the definition of administrative guidance followed in this study, and therefore *tsūtatsu* will be classified as administrative guidance. To stress its transparent character, *tsūtatsu* will be referred to as published administrative guidance. The non-transparent guidance is typified as unpublished administrative guidance.

The use of administrative guidance by the Japanese government bureaucracy is intertwined with the basic structure of the Japanese legal system. Japanese laws are usually short and very general, and drafted in vague and ambiguous language: the actual interpretation is left to the discretion of government bureaucrats.[21] In the words of one interviewee: 'In Japan, the law is empty, the bureaucracy is king.'[22] According to certain Japanese legal scholars, Japan uses 'administration through law interpreted by bureaucrats *(hōritsu ni yoru gyōsei)* rather than rule of law *(hōchi-shugi)*' (OECD 1999b, p.159). The lack of clear, explicit formal laws gives rise to discretionary bureaucratic guidance: it has been left to the bureaucracy to interpret and implement the law. According to some scholars, this discretionary authority of the government bureaucracy is the most positive aspect of administrative guidance: firstly, the bureaucracy can

[18] Personal interviews high-ranking staff member Ministry of Finance, Tokyo, September 1992; Japanese legal scholars, Tokyo, September and November 1992 and June 1993; former high-ranking staff member Bank of Japan, Tokyo, January 1993.

[19] Personal interviews Japanese legal scholar, Tokyo, September 1992; senior staff Ministry of Finance, Tokyo, September 1992 and February 1993. According to one legal scholar, *tsūtatsu* are part of administrative law *(gyōsei rippō)* and not of administrative guidance *(gyōsei shidō)*.

[20] Personal interviews Japanese legal scholars, Tokyo, October 1992; senior staff members Ministry of Finance, Tokyo, February 1993. The view that *tsūtatsu* are part of administrative guidance is supported by, among others: Narita 1968; Davis 1972; Eads and Yamamura 1987; Schaede 1992 and 1993; Katayama 1998; OECD 1999b.

[21] Johnson (1982), pp.273, 319; Pempel and Muramatsu (1993), p.37; Milhaupt (1996). Personal interviews Japanese legal scholars, Tokyo, September and November 1992 and June 1993; Japanese banker, Tokyo, December 1992; former MoF official, Tokyo, May 1993.

[22] Personal interviews Japanese legal scholars, Tokyo, November 1992; similar words repeated by Ministry of Finance staff member in interview, Tokyo, September 1992.

act swiftly and flexibly when confronted with new, unforeseen situations by avoiding red tape and complex and time-consuming legal procedures; secondly, it can provide tailor-made solutions (Ackley and Ishi 1976, p.239; Johnson 1982, pp.273, 318–319; Young 1984, pp.936–938; Wakiyama 1987, pp.214–215; Matsushita and Schoenbaum 1989, p.40; Shindo 1992, pp.82–84; Hayashi 1999, p.24).

Compliance

Since administrative guidance cannot be enforced by legal means, the question arises why should recipients comply with it. The answer is five-fold. First, a large number of studies stress the interactive and interdependent nature of administrative guidance: the bureaucracy does not one-sidedly impose the guidance, but usually the regulated parties are extensively involved in its formulation.[23] Kosai (1987, p.586) puts it as follows: 'consensus formation must precede administrative guidance if it is to achieve its aim'. The informal consultations (or *nemawashi*) between the government bureaucrats and the recipients of administrative guidance make compliance with the guidance more likely: they are even said to be necessary to achieve compliance.[24]

Second, clients of the government bureaucracy sometimes request regulatory guidance. To some extent, this results from a paternalistic relationship between government and society: according to Shindo (1992, pp.79ff.), Japanese citizens and private organisations expect government action in times of trouble. In other cases it is the result of private sector attempts to limit bureaucratic uncertainty or to protect specific interests.[25] In this respect, it should be noted that, according to various interviewees, both in the public and private sphere, guidance is welcomed by private parties as in practice it often functions to officially sanction monopolistic or oligopolistic behaviour, i.e. it preserves the status quo and prohibits the entry of new competitors.[26]

---

[23] Young (1984), p.935. See also: Haitani 1976; Johnson 1978; Murakami 1987; Wakiyama 1987; Ballon and Tomita 1988; Bingham 1989; Okimoto 1989; Upham 1991; Shindo 1992; Schwartz 1998. Also supported by various personal interviews, Tokyo, 1992–1993.

[24] *Nemawashi* can be translated as 'to dig around the root of a tree to prepare it for transplanting'. According to Hollerman (1988), p.178, 'the term refers to groundwork to enlist the support or informal consent of those concerned with a pending matter before asking for a formal decision'. See: Ballon 1990, pp.26–28; Young 1984, pp.947–949; Wakiyama 1987, p.218.

[25] Keehn (1990), p.1030, personal interviews high-ranking staff members Ministry of Finance, Tokyo, July 1992 and February 1993; Western economic scholar, Tokyo, September 1992; Japanese banker, Tokyo, December 1992; former high-ranking staff member Bank of Japan, Tokyo, January 1993.

[26] Personal interviews former high-ranking Bank of Japan official, Tokyo, January 1993; private sector economists, Tokyo, May–June 1993.

A third reason for compliance with administrative guidance is the alleged traditional submissiveness to authority and respect for the Japanese government bureaucracy (Upham 1991, p.325; Johnson 1982, p.266; Ackley and Ishi 1976, p.237; Matsushita and Schoenbaum 1989, p.33; OECD 1999b, p.162). Government bureaucrats are recruited among the best graduates from the most elite universities, and feel highly responsible to promote and serve the interests of their country. According to Johnson (1982, p.266), they even claim to 'speak for the national interest'.

Fourth, regulated parties accept administrative guidance out of fear of government reprisal in case of non-compliance: voluntary compliance should be interpreted as 'voluntary' compliance.[27] Ministries have a wide range of powers and cover a large area of responsibility, and consequently have numerous options for an effective carrot-and-stick strategy. In this sense, their so-called permissive authorisation, such as licensing (*kyoninka*), is important – that is, the Japanese government bureaucracy has a large number of licensing categories at its disposal, which according to some represent the core of its regulatory system (Carlile and Tilton 1998b, p.6; Sohn 1998; Tilton 1998). Thus, if a recipient does not follow the ministerial guidance, the ministry can deny its approval to certain other activities, which are often unrelated to the issue at hand.[28] This idea is captured by the proverb 'enemies in Edo (Tokyo) are taken care of in Nagasaki' (*Edo no ada o Nagasaki se utsu*) (Mouer and Sugimoto 1986, pp.243–244). It is important to note that the relationship between administrative agencies and regulated parties is long term and covers many issues, so it is in the self-interest of recipients of administrative guidance to keep this relationship as good as possible, i.e. to comply (Eads and Yamamura 1987, p.433; Murakami and Rohlen 1992, p.93). However, it also has to be mentioned that the guidance should be impartial if compliance is to be reached: in cases of administrative bias in favour of particular parties or interests, non-compliance occurs (Young 1984, p.949; Murakami and Rohlen 1992, pp.93–94).

The importance of permissive authorisation differs from ministry to ministry: in an industry that traditionally has been heavily regulated, such as the financial services sector, the authoritative power of the relevant ministry (i.e. Ministry of Finance – MoF) has been relatively great.[29] On the other hand, the permissive authorisation of the Ministry of International Trade and Industry (MITI) is said to have been less substantial.

---

[27] See Haitani (1976), p.49, Johnson (1982), p.266, Eads and Yamamura (1987), p.433, Matsushita and Schoenbaum (1989), p.33, and OECD 1999b, p.162. Personal interviews with Japanese legal scholars, Tokyo, September 1992 and June 1993.

[28] Mouer and Sugimoto (1986), p.243. See also Murakami and Rohlen (1992), p.92. Personal interviews Japanese legal scholars, Tokyo, September 1992 and June 1993.

[29] Whether the MoF's permissive authorisation has been affected by the process of financial reform will be discussed in chapter 9.

Consequently, MITI has been implementing its guidance much more by consensus, whereas the MoF has been using administrative guidance more by 'order'.[30] Against the background of fear of reprisal in case of non-compliance, it is questionable to what extent administrative guidance is really voluntary: 'the crux of the matter is whether in any real sense one can say in each instance that compliance was in fact voluntary' (Henderson 1973, p.201).

The aspect of *kyoninka* shows clearly that it is extremely difficult to discuss administrative guidance in general terms. Each administrative agency has its own specific form of administrative guidance, dependent on its statutory authority and legal power base, and the structure of and developments in the specific private industry under its jurisdiction.

A fifth and final reason for compliance with administrative guidance imposed by the national government bureaucracy in particular could lie in the fact that supposedly both the national bureaucracy and the courts are controlled by the dominant political party, i.e. the Liberal Democratic Party or LDP (Ramseyer and McCall Rosenbluth 1993; Ramseyer and Nakazato 1999; Ramseyer 2000). Therefore, it seems in general that recipients of guidance exercised by the national bureaucracy see little point in seeking judicial review and therefore comply – although exceptions to this rule exist.[31] As a matter of fact, examples of private banks that challenged administrative guidance such as *tsūtatsu* in court could not be recalled by various 'inside' interviewees (MoF staff members, January–April 1993; high-ranking staff members Zenginkyō, 1993). As Milhaupt (1996), p.31, puts it regarding the securities industry: 'litigation against MoF in connection with its administration of the securities laws is virtually nonexistent'. A MoF staff member –interviewed in February 1993 – in a rather self-confident response found this behaviour quite understandable:

The banks believe that our line is appropriate. To go to court for banks would be meaningless: they know that it is impossible that a *tsūtatsu* is against the law, because we are the law.

In this respect, of course, it should be emphasised that it is in the interests of banks to maintain a good relationship with the MoF, given its broad authoritative powers, and that this relationship could be jeopardised by litigation.

---

[30] Personal interviews with Japanese legal scholars, Tokyo, June and July 1993.

[31] Upham (1986, pp.285ff.) reports two cases related to the Oil Cartel of the seventies in which the Tokyo High Court found MITI's administrative guidance to have induced illegal private behaviour. However, MITI responded by introducing new legislation that preserved both its informal policy mode and control. See also Okimoto (1989), p.95.

Criticism

Besides the problem that 'it is sometimes easy for administrative agencies to exceed the limits of voluntary action and to engage in actual coercion', administrative guidance has a number of other negative aspects.[32]

First, the lack of transparency of a substantial part of administrative guidance obstructs its supervision and deprives the general public of basic knowledge about the government's policy intentions. It gives rise to suspicions of Japanese society being 'a system in which vital decisions are made more or less in secret by a small coterie of bureaucrats and business leaders (many of them retired bureaucrats) who reflect a narrow range of political, economic, and educational backgrounds and interests' (Ackley and Ishi 1976, p.239). This lack of transparency could result in the protection and promotion of specific interests, at the expense of the interests of the general public.

Second, the lack of transparency and the opaque nature of administrative guidance open the door to bureaucratic mistakes or even to abuse of bureaucratic power. The use of administrative guidance is not circumscribed by very specific limits: the discretionary power of the bureaucracy could result in needless intervention and the implementation of policies without sufficient perspective. Furthermore, the specific content of administrative guidance is often decided at relatively low bureaucratic levels, which obstructs the formulation and implementation of coherent and clear policies, according to one former BoJ staff member interviewed in August 1992.

Third, the opaque nature of administrative guidance provides companies with two incentives to meet frequently with the regulators. Administrative guidance is often considered to be vague and unclear – this is not only the case for its oral component but also for the published administrative guidance. This has resulted in often-repeated complaints by both Japanese and foreign private organisations (Ernst & Young 1989; *Keidanren* 1998; US Embassy Tokyo 1999). Therefore, the receivers of administrative guidance could benefit from frequent personal contact with regulators as a mechanism to clarify bureaucratic guidance. Furthermore, this frequent contact could also be used to acquire prior or inside information or to influence the process of formulation and implementation of administrative guidance. In this respect, many observers have pointed at the close relationship between the MoF and the financial services industry (Vogel 1996; Amyx 1998; Brown 1999). For example, Alletzhauser

---

[32] Narita (1968), p.386. See also: Ackley and Ishi 1976, p.329; Matsushita and Schoenbaum 1989, pp.40–41; Wakiyama 1987, pp.225–226; OECD 1999b, p.162.

(1990) cites a MoF official who declared that Nomura Securities, the most powerful securities firm in Japan, *is*, de facto, the MoF, and that Nomura is consulted in many matters and is even involved in the drawing-up of financial legislation. Thus, the close relationship between regulator and regulated parties is beneficial to both: it enhances the control and access to private market information of the former – at least according to its own view (Vogel 1996, p.172) – and allows direct interest promotion by the latter (see also Brown 1999). As a result of the importance of frequent personal contact, many companies have special officers assigned to various regulatory bodies. In the case of the MoF, this led to the institutionalised system of the so-called 'MoF-*tan*' (shortened from *tantōsha* or the 'person in charge of') or MoF-watchers: relatively high-ranking officials from private financial institutions whose responsibility is closely to monitor the MoF and develop direct personal contacts – often through lavish entertainment of various sorts – with the mid-level bureaucrats who design most of the regulatory infrastructure. The system of the MoF-*tan* has been widely discussed and criticised, in particular in Japan itself (Nihon Keizai Shimbunsha 1992; Toshikawa 1995; Takarajima Sha 1995; Amyx 1998; Hartcher 1998; Brown 1999). As I shall assert in chapters 6 and 9, the MoF-*tan* phenomenon has been at the centre of the many scandals that severely damaged the reputation of the MoF in the 1990s.

It should be noted that, contrary to conventional wisdom, Japanese citizens and companies have the legal right to seek effective judicial review by courts – which, as remarked before, are said to be under LDP control – of administrative guidance imposed upon them (Ramseyer and Nakazato 1999, pp.205ff.; Ramseyer 2000). However, as Ramseyer (2000) demonstrates, such rights are rarely asserted other than with regard to actions by municipal governments, which are much less controlled by the LDP than the national government bureaucracy. Not surprisingly, recipients of administrative guidance exercised by the national government bureaucracy do not often seek the protection of the courts.

To counter the – in particular US – criticism of the non-transparent nature of administrative guidance, the Japanese government introduced in 1993 the Administrative Procedures Law (Ramseyer and Nakazato 1999, p.204; Milhaupt 1996, pp.58ff). According to the Management and Co-ordination Agency (1996, p.16), this law 'covers procedures for dispositions, administrative guidance, notifications and the need to ensure the universality of measures regarding such actions. The Law seeks to advance a guarantee of fairness and progress towards transparency in the administrative process, and thereby to protect the rights and interests of the public.' However, several observers have criticised the law as being not sufficiently strong to curtail the use of administrative guidance and to improve administrative transparency (Japan Economic Institute 1994; Grier 1997; Lake 1998).

Relevance of administrative guidance in theoretical schools

To conclude this section, an assessment of the relevance and effectiveness of administrative guidance will be made. This assessment differs sharply in accordance with the various interpretations of the Japanese economic system, such as presented in chapter 2.

First, the interventionist school emphasises strongly the importance and relevance of the use of administrative guidance by the Japanese government bureaucracy. According to Johnson (1982, p.318), administrative guidance is 'perhaps the most important market-conforming method of intervention', one of the means of government control over the economic system. He presents evidence that 'MITI has on occasion retaliated with force against an enterprise that rejected its advice' (Johnson 1982, p.266), so administrative guidance can be accompanied by bureaucratic retaliation if necessary. Johnson thinks that, as a result of liberalisation, administrative guidance will decline in importance, but that 'it will never disappear completely from the Japanese scene' (Johnson 1982, p.274). The alleged important role of administrative guidance is supported by, among others, Schaede (1992, p.5), where it is stated that 'the operative framework for the influence (of the government bureaucracy) is administrative guidance'. In conclusion, the interventionist school sees administrative guidance as one of the most important instruments of Japanese economic policy and emphasises that compliance can be coerced by carrot-and-stick strategies.

Second, not surprisingly, the adherents of the market school hold the opposite view: according to their interpretation, the absence of formal legal means to force compliance limits severely the effectiveness of administrative guidance. The adherents of the market school doubt that private parties would comply with this guidance unless it were in their own interests (Upham 1991, p.325). The clearest exponent of this view is Haley, whose perception that the use of administrative guidance in the post-war Japanese economic development was so weak and unsuccessful that the market mechanism could survive was presented in section 2.3 of chapter 2. Other studies which cast doubt on the effectiveness of administrative guidance are Suzumura and Okuno-Fujiwara (1987), Komiya, Okuno and Suzumura (1988), Noble (1989) and Weinstein (1992).[33] For

---

[33] Some studies argue that administrative guidance was effective in some specific industries during the fifties and sixties, but that it has become ineffective owing to liberalisation and deregulation (Kosai 1987, p.591; Uekusa 1987, p.476; Horne 1988, pp. 152, 167).

example, Suzumura and Okuno-Fujiwara (1987, p.60) mention that 'the so-called voluntary compliance by private firms to the regulatory objectives could be obtained only when such objectives were largely consistent with private objectives. Even MITI could not force an unwilling horse to drink water.'

The third model of the Japanese economic system, that of the consensual policy school, emphasises the consensual character of administrative guidance: to achieve compliance with administrative guidance, prior consultations and consequent consensus are a prerequisite (Upham 1987; Okimoto 1989). Okimoto (1989, p.95) concludes that administrative guidance 'has receded in functional importance over the years, though it continues to be used as a low-key and informal policy instrument'.

The model of the pluralistic network school, the last presented in chapter 2, accepts administrative guidance as an effective instrument that established a system of so-called compartmentalised competition and consequently contributed significantly to post-war Japanese economic development. As was discussed in section 2.3, the government–business relationship in Japan can be analysed from a social-exchange framework, which explains the compliance of business with administrative guidance in the post-World War II economic development. However, the danger of market instability and the threat posed by foreign competition (the original reasons for the use of administrative guidance), have receded significantly. As a result, 'administrative guidance is no longer legitimated . . . by the environment' (Murakami and Rohlen 1992, p.95).

Inevitably, the final conclusions regarding the effectiveness of administrative guidance must distinguish between specific administrative agencies, specific regulated parties and specific periods of time.[34]

3.4   Informal aspects II: informal networks

In chapter 2 we saw that in a significant number of studies the existence of informal networks based on personal relationships is one of the most notable and essential characteristics of the government–business relationship in Japan. Examples of these studies are Okimoto (1989), Kumon (1992), Murakami and Rohlen (1992) and Research Project Team for Japanese Systems (1992), which all incorporate explicitly elements of the network approach. Other studies emphasising the importance of personal networks are Boyd (1987), Taira and Wada (1987), van Wolferen (1989), Calder (1988, 1993), and the large number of studies focusing on specific personal networks, which will be discussed below. For example, Taira and

[34] Personal interviews with Western economic scholar, Tokyo, September 1992; high-ranking staff member Economic Planning Agency, Tokyo, September 1992.

Wada (1987, p.264), draw the conclusion that 'the personal networks and contacts of public officials and private business leaders render the formal structural distinction of government and business almost meaningless in Japan'. Calder (1993, p.271) concludes: 'Government–business networks in Japan deserve extended study in their own right, particularly at the micropolitical and microeconomic level . . . These networks play a crucial role in determining both policy and private-sector outcomes and information flows.'

Regarding the interpretation and relevance of personal networks, various approaches can be distinguished. One approach departs from the existence of so-called 'factions' in Japanese society: 'influential coalitions predicated on common attributes' (Wiersema and Bird 1993, p.1002; see also Stockwin 1999). According to Kusayanagi, 'all human relations in Japanese society are based on four kinds of "factions" [batsu]: keibatsu (family and matrimonial cliques), kyōdobatsu (clansmen, or persons from the same locality), gakubatsu (school and university classmates), and zaibatsu (factions based on money)'.[35] These personal relationships, based on specific common backgrounds, constitute human networks, of which especially gakubatsu and zaibatsu are said to be of great importance in the government bureaucracy (Johnson 1982, p.55; Hartcher 1998, pp.19ff.).

A somewhat different approach, presented for example in Imai (1992) and Research Project Team for Japanese Systems (1992), follows the view that personal networks in Japan are more institutional than individual oriented. Imai (1992, p.228), notes that 'Japanese networks are built on the experiences people share by working in the same place or attending the same school. Relationships in such a network are linkages mediated through "place" in this sense.' According to the Research Project Team for Japanese Systems (1992, p.42), 'in postwar Japanese society, relationships based on kinship and having the same home town have weakened, and intimate relationships of mutual trust based on frequent contact, that is relations of najimi (familiarity), have come to fulfil an important role. Grouping has been furthered by relations of familiarity centering on occupation and workplace.'

These different approaches are united in the interpretation in Okimoto (1989). Okimoto distinguishes between ascriptive and functional networks based on personal relations. The ascriptive networks can be divided in the above-mentioned keibatsu, kyōdobatsu and gakubatsu, and contacts through mutual friends and school club ties. Functional networks include friendships developed in the course of government–industry contacts,

---

[35] As quoted from Johnson (1982), p.55. The importance of cliques is supported by, among others, Haitani 1976; Kenrick 1988; van Wolferen 1991.

participation in informal study-groups and networks constituted by the post-retirement employment of Japanese government bureaucrats in private business, the so-called 'descending from heaven' (*amakudari*). Okimoto (1989, p.237) focuses in particular on the importance of personal networks in the formulation and implementation of industrial policy in Japan: 'It would be hard to formulate and implement Japanese industrial policy if the labyrinth of personal relationships in the intermediate zone (between public and private sector) did not exist.'

Another network based on personal relations is constituted by the mechanism of *shukkō* (temporary external assignment or on-loan service), which can be defined as the practice of a temporary exchange of employees between public and private organisations.[36] The on-loan employees are assigned as regular staff members of the receiving organisation for periods from two to three years and should not be regarded as mere liaison officers; according to some interpretations, personnel loans are the greatest strength of the Japanese government bureaucracy (Miyamoto 1995, p.51; Haitani 1976, p.46). The mechanism of *shukkō* takes place between the government and the private sector, between private companies and between governmental institutions. For example, Keehn (1990, p.1032), notes that all Japanese ministries exchange posts, in order to 'nurture the ability to solve cross-ministerial issues as well as to increase information flows across organizations'; the importance of *shukkō* is shown by the fact that approximately 80% of all bureau directors in ministries had held *shukkō* positions in other government organisations at some stage of their career. The temporarily movement of private-sector employees into the government bureaucracy also takes place: this *shukkō* is sometimes referred to as 'ascending into heaven' (*ama-agari*).[37] In this case, the salaries are paid or supplemented by their original companies. The transferred employees conduct clerical or other supporting tasks at the lower-ranking levels. The benefits of this *shukkō* for the companies involved are evident: better access to information sources, improved knowledge and understanding of ministerial administrative guidance and the establishment of personal contacts with government bureaucrats.

In the literature, and supported by personal interviews, with regard to the relevance of informal networks in the public-private sector relationship, attention is especially focused on *amakudari* and to a lesser extent on *gakubatsu*. Because of this emphasis, and the fact that objective and historical data on these two specific networks are available, the analysis

---

[36] Based on Haitani (1976), Komiya (1990), pp.386–387, Miyamoto (1995), pp.48–51, and, in particular, Hsu (1994), p.322.

[37] Personal interviews with leading Japanese journalist, December 1992, former senior staff member *Keidanren*, January 1993, and Japanese banker, June 1993. See also Amyx (1998), pp.123ff.

of informal networks here will concentrate on *amakudari* and *gakubatsu*. Given the fact that data on *shukkō* are not publicly available and that consequently it is not possible to construct historical data-series, I shall discuss *shukkō* only in the margin.[38] Furthermore, I shall not pay attention to *informal* networks in the private sphere that could also have some significance for the government–business relationship, such as so-called administrative networks, which are based on relationships between managers in private companies and are particularly large-scale and prevalent in Japan (Lifson 1992).

Amakudari

The mechanism of post-retirement employment of government officials in private business, or *amakudari*, has been discussed in a large number of studies (Johnson 1974, 1978, 1982; Haitani 1976; Blumenthal 1985; Taira and Wada 1987; Aoki 1988b; Ballon and Tomita 1988; Hellmann 1988; Hollerman 1988; Horne 1988; Prestowitz 1988; Calder 1989; Okimoto 1989; van Wolferen 1991; Kuribayashi 1992; Nihon Keizai Shimbunsha 1992; Schaede 1992, 1995; Inoki 1993; Yamori 1994; Okazaki 1995; Takarajima Sha 1995; Toshikawa 1995; Yamori and Fujiwara 1995; Tsutsumi 1996; Fujiwara and Yamori 1997; Hartcher 1998; Yamori 1998; Horiuchi and Shimizu 1998; OECD 1998; Brown 1999; Stockwin 1999). Furthermore, the importance of *amakudari* has been supported in numerous personal interviews with MoF and BoJ officials, former MoF and BoJ officials, Japanese legal journalists, Japanese and Western bankers and other businessmen in Tokyo during the period 1992–1995.

A systematic investigation of *amakudari* is frustrated by the fact that the specific characteristics of its definition often differ among authors. A number of these definitions are presented in figure 3.2. Comparison of the characteristics shows a number of differences and sometimes even inconsistencies. The most remarkable one is the distinction in the nature of the corporations that offer the post-retirement positions: some authors limit their definition to private companies while others include public corporations as well (examples of the former: Johnson 1974; Upham 1987; Hollerman 1988; Okimoto 1988; examples of the latter: Aoki 1988b; Calder 1989; Haitani 1976; Horne 1988; Johnson 1978; Okimoto 1989; Prestowitz 1988). To add to the confusion, Johnson and Okimoto use

---

[38] That is to say, I shall present in chapter 5 an analysis of the organisation of *shukkō* positions at the Ministry of Finance and the Bank of Japan for a limited period of time only.

Aoki (1988b, p.265): ... bureaucrats who quit the bureaucracy after attaining positions higher than that of section director in the administrative hierarchy 'descend from the heaven' (*amakudari*) of the elite bureaucracy ... become available as human resources for national and local politics, business management in private and public corporations, and other consulting activities.

Blumenthal (1985, p.310): ... *amakudari* means 'descent from heaven' and is used to describe the reemployment of government bureaucrats after the termination of their service with the government.

Calder (1989, p.382): [*Amakudari*] involves the widespread movement of national government bureaucrats from the 'heaven' of elite government service to private firms, public corporations, local government, and the *Diet* after retirement from the national bureaucracy at around the age of forty-five to fifty-five.

Haitani (1976, p.44): The practice of higher administrators securing postcareer employment in business and public corporations is commonly known as *amakudari*.

Hollerman (1988, p.175): The government career civil service is alluded to as heaven, from which high officials retire at about age 55 to take senior positions in private business.

Horne (1988, p.163): The retirement system in the government bureaucracy whereby many career bureaucrats retired between the ages of 50 and 55 to LDP Diet membership or to senior executive positions in companies for which their ministry had responsibility ... When bureaucrats took retirement jobs in industry or public companies, this was known as *amakudari* or 'descent from heaven'.

Johnson (1974, p.953): The movement from ministry or agency to a private business is known as 'descent from heaven'.

Johnson (1978, p.5): The practice of employing retired government officials as chief executives or members of boards of directors of public and private corporations.

Okimoto (1988, p.319): The reemployment of higher civil servants in high-level posts within the private sector.

Okimoto (1989, p.161): The interpenetration of public and private is nowhere more graphically illustrated than in the well-known practice called *amakudari*, whereby officials leaving the bureaucracy 'descend from heaven' into high-level posts in public corporations, industrial associations, and private industry.

Figure 3.2 Definitions of *amakudari*

Pempel (1998, p.95): ... *amakudari*, through which retiring bureaucrats would 'descend from heaven' to take high-level, high-paying jobs in firms within areas they once were charged with regulating.

Prestowitz (1988, p.113): ... *amakudari* (literally, 'descent from heaven'). In this case, heaven is the bureaucracy, and the descent is into a posh position in a large bank or corporation, or possibly as head of another public body or a think tank.

Stockwin (1999, p.96): This practice ... involves public officials on their retirement or shortly thereafter, taking positions on the boards of companies or other institutions, usually those related to the area of jurisdiction of their former ministry.

Upham (1987, p.167): When Japanese bureaucrats retire, most take positions in the private sector, many in the very firms they have been dealing with during their bureaucratic career – a process known as *amakudari*, or 'descending from heaven'.

Figure 3.2 *(cont.)*

both definitions at different places.[39] Furthermore, Hollerman (1988) and Horne (1988) mention explicitly the involvement of career bureaucrats only; other studies are more ambiguous about the difference between career and non-career bureaucrats among the *amakudari kanryō* – the former government officials who accepted post-retirement positions. Finally, some publications, for example van Wolferen (1989), Schaede (1992) and Prestowitz (1988), refer to descending into 'leading' or 'large' companies. Other studies, in particular Calder (1989), do not exclude medium and smaller companies explicitly.

Definition and classification of *amakudari*   I shall use the following definition of *amakudari*:

> *In this study, amakudari involves the acceptance of high-level functions by retired bureaucrats from the Ministry of Finance (MoF) (Ōkurashō) and the Bank of Japan (BoJ) (Nihon Ginkō) on the boards of Japanese private banks.*

Although staff members of the BoJ are not real civil servants – the BoJ is a special government corporation and not a conventional public organisation – they are included in this study for two reasons. First, the Japanese government (i.e. the MoF) has a majority stake in the BoJ, which makes the BoJ de facto part of the Japanese government bureaucracy.

---

[39] Compare Johnson (1974) with Johnson (1978), and Okimoto (1988) with Okimoto (1989).

Second, the BoJ is responsible for the implementation of monetary policy and is consequently of great importance for the Japanese banking industry. With respect to the definition of *amakudari*, I shall not distinguish between career and non-career bureaucrats for the following reasons. First, the influence of retired bureaucrats on private business is not significantly different whether they are career or non-career bureaucrats; the presence of either career or non-career bureaucrats on the board of a private company constitutes a channel for government intervention.[40] Second, in practice, this distinction is too difficult to make. I also shall not distinguish between the sizes of the *amakudari*-receiving companies. Furthermore, the limitation to private corporations in my definition of *amakudari* is in accordance with the clear classification of after-retirement employment of Japanese bureaucrats in Johnson (1974) and the requirements of the National Public Service Law (Kokka Kōmuin Hō).

According to Johnson (1974, 1978), the various forms of re-employment of Japanese bureaucrats after their retirement, virtually without exception in their early or mid-fifties, can be classified as follows. First, retired bureaucrats find new employment in private, profit-making companies. This movement is known as *amakudari* in the true sense of the word, and is subject to minor legal restrictions. These restrictions are mentioned in Article 103 of the National Public Service Law, which introduced for retiring bureaucrats a minimum delay of two years between retirement from the bureaucracy and accepting a position in a profit-making company where there exists a close connection between the private company and the previous position of the retired bureaucrat. During these two years, the former government officials usually take temporary positions in unrelated private companies, universities or other non-profit organisations. The National Personnel Authority has the power to waive the two-year waiting period – which reportedly occurs quite often – and has published since 1963 an annual report on the number of retiring bureaucrats and the number of exemptions, called 'Eiri Kigyō e no Shūshoku no Shōnin ni kansuru Nenji Hōkokusho' ('Annual Report Concerning Approvals of Employment in Profit-making Enterprises') (Yamori and Fujiwara 1995, p.2). According to Johnson (1974, 1978), Schaede (1993) and various interviewees, the retiring bureaucrats who are subject to the screening procedure by the National Personnel Authority form the system of *amakudari*.

Second, Japanese bureaucrats move after retirement into so-called special legal entities (*tokushu hōjin*), i.e. enterprises established by law and financed in part from public funds (such as public corporations). This

---

[40] Of course, career bureaucrats will have obtained higher-ranking positions in the government bureaucracy (and thus also, after retirement, in private companies) than non-career bureaucrats, and are therefore more influential.

re-employment is called 'sideslip' (*yokosuberi*), because the retiring bureaucrat keeps a position in the public sector and is not subject to legal restrictions. The special entities are of great importance as *amakudari* landing spots for retired government officials, and attempts in the mid-1990s to reduce their number met with severe resistance – in particular from the MoF (Hartcher 1998, pp.212–215; Carlile 1998, pp.92–93). An overview of the variety of special legal entities is provided in appendix 3.1.

Third, retired bureaucrats also find new employment in the political world, called 'position exploitation' (*chii riyō*). The exploitation refers to the fact that political positions, such as membership of the Diet, are 'usually open only to bureaucrats who served in choice national or regional posts that are particularly suitable for building general political support' (Johnson 1974, p.954). The Japanese Election Law puts forward some minor barriers to such employment (Johnson 1978, p.104).

Fourth, retired government officials accept high-level positions in non-profit oriented trade associations that represent specific industries. This form of post-retirement employment is not subject to legal restrictions (Johnson 1974, p.954).

Fifth, retired bureaucrats move into so-called auxiliary organs (*gaikaku dantai*), i.e. non-profit associations, foundations and institutes that are attached to a ministry and are often research oriented. These entities function frequently as 'waiting rooms' to spend the two-year period before accepting a private-sector position and are sometimes used as a 'last resort' for retiring bureaucrats who are experiencing difficulties in finding a landing spot. Finally, retiring bureaucrats accept positions in prefectural governments (Johnson 1978, pp.102–103).

This whole spectrum of retired government bureaucrats in top positions in private and public corporations, politics, local governments, academics and a motley collection of foundations and associations establishes a many-branched network for each of the major Japanese government organisations, commonly defined as their 'old boy' (OB) network. The OB networks of the economic government bureaucracies, more specific MITI and the MoF, and also that of the BoJ, are extensively covered by very detailed Japanese-language publications – which would seem to indicate their importance. These publications often mention even the hobbies of the OBs, and crucial pieces of information such as their golf handicap. However, most of these elaborate data presentations have not reached the relevant English-language literature. Given the focus of this study on the Japanese banking system and monetary policy, by using Japanese-language sources I shall try in chapters 7 and 8 to clarify the mechanism of *amakudari*, i.e. the private sector part of the OB network, in the Japanese private banking industry.

Structure of the government bureaucracy and *amakudari*   Before discussing several interpretations of the significance of *amakudari* from a broader political-economic perspective, it should be noted that as a consequence of the fundamental structure of the Japanese government bureaucracy, it needs the practice of post-retirement employment (Johnson 1974, pp.958–961, 1978, pp.105–109; Calder 1989, p.382). First of all, the organisation of the bureaucracy is based on strict seniority principles. New career civil servants enter a ministry as members of a specific class, a group of about 25 persons at large ministries such as the MITI and the MoF. When one member of a class reaches the highest bureaucratic position possible, that of administrative vice-minister (*jimu-jikan*), the other members of his class in their early fifties must resign, leaving the vice-minister with absolute seniority. Furthermore, the principle of seniority is also important from the perspective of university background: graduates from a specific year are senior in rank to graduates of later years – the promotion schemes follow these seniority lines closely. This means that in the case of the appointment of a new administrative vice-minister, senior graduates from the same university will have to retire. Second, the relatively low purchasing power of the post-war bureaucratic pay scales and pension system as compared with the private sector forces retiring bureaucrats to obtain post-retirement employment. For example, Rasmeyer and McCall Rosenbluth (1993), pp.116–117, note that 1990 figures show a monthly mean national wage of 357,000 yen, compared with a roughly estimated mean career bureaucratic wage of 318,000 yen. In addition, these figures understate the actual differences: career government bureaucrats are recruited among the brightest graduates of the best universities, and consequently their potential private sector income is much higher than the mean national wage. As has been shown by, for example, Hartcher (1998), the financial rewards of post-retirement employment of government officials can be substantial, in particular for retirees who move from one post-retirement position to another – the so-called *watari-dori* or 'hopping birds' (Colignon and Usui 1999). For example, in the case of Mitsuhide Tsutsumi, former administrative vice-minister of the MoF, the cumulative total of salaries and 'bonus' lump sums that he received after leaving the MoF and during his subsequent employment at two semi-government institutions was estimated at 260 million yen – about $2.4 million (Hartcher 1998, p.36).

Thus, as a consequence of its fundamental structure, the government bureaucracy must find every year a number of landing spots for its retiring members. That is to say, *amakudari* is an institutional bureaucratic phenomenon: the post-retirement positions of individual officials are arranged by the government bureaucracy, dependent on their final position

in the bureaucratic hierarchy.[41] In this respect, *amakudari* differs from
the private sector re-employment of Western civil servants, which is left
to individual initiatives and is not centrally organised. However, it has
to be said that surely the system of post-retirement employment of government officials is not a uniquely Japanese phenomenon. For example,
Drucker (1998, pp.69–70) cites the practice of high-ranking government officials moving into private business after retirement in Austria,
Germany, France, the United Kingdom and the United States (see also
Fruin 1998, p.20). In particular France is a country where large numbers of bureaucrats frequently and consistently accept positions in private
sector industries. This movement is called '*pantouflage*' and is according
to Inoki (1993, p.5) estimated to be about ten times more frequent than
amakudari in Japan.

   Theoretical interpretations of *amakudari*   Theoretical interpretations of the political-economic importance of *amakudari* distinguish
among five views: two stressing *amakudari* as a bureaucratic reward system and three others focusing on its significance for government–business
interaction.

   The first view, explicitly discussed in Inoki (1993) and supported by
Okimoto (1987), Aoki (1988b) and Stockwin (1999), among others, regards *amakudari* as an important incentive mechanism and reward system
within the Japanese government bureaucracy. Against the background of
the potentially high financial rewards of after-retirement private sector
employment mentioned in the previous section, *amakudari* positions 'are
provided as the final prize in the competition among bureaucrats in the
ranking hierarchy' (Aoki 1988b, p.266). These financial rewards can be
considered as 'a form of deferred compensation whose values are determined on the basis of two factors: the officials' actual performance in
ministries, and the rank of prestige of various ministries' (Inoki 1993,
p.8). As a result, from a strictly financial point of view, the government
bureaucracy remains attractive for the best and brightest among the university graduates and maintains the competitiveness of its internal promotion scheme. The interpretation of *amakudari* as a reward system is also
emphasised by Ramseyer and McCall Rosenbluth (1993), but there from
the perspective of political control over the government bureaucracy.

---

[41] Komiya (1990). According to Johnson (1974), p.960, Aoki (1988b), pp.265–266, and
Hartcher (1998), p.9, the finding of new jobs for retirees is the responsibility of the
Minister's Secretariat (Daijin Kanbō), with assistance by the administrative vice-minister
and – in the case of the MoF – by an informal club of about 30 to 40 OBs which meets
every fourth Wednesday and where a high MoF official informs them about the latest
developments (the Fourth Wednesday Group or Yon Sui Kai) (Hartcher 1998, p.39;
interview Western banker, June 1993).

These scholars argue, following basic principal–agent theory, that the leading political party in Japan – the LDP – dominates and guides the bureaucracy (pp.99–120), and also controls the bureaucratic promotion scheme and thus the access to *amakudari* positions in the private sector. Consequently, given that 'bureaucrats potentially earn a large fraction of their lifetime wages in post-bureaucratic jobs' (p.108), government bureaucrats find it hard to ignore LDP preferences. In other words, the LDP leaders can hold these bureaucrats 'hostage': *amakudari* positions are given as rewards for bureaucratic 'good behaviour', for achieving policy outcomes that suit the political interests of the LDP.

Besides these views of *amakudari* as a bureaucratic reward system, three interpretations focus on its importance for the government–business relationship. The first interpretation sees *amakudari* as an instrument for indirect government control or dominance over private industry, as a channel to exercise administrative guidance. This approach, for the sake of convenience defined as the government control interpretation, is part of the interventionist school, and as such it has received not only considerable popular support in the Japanese and Western media, but also especially among Japanese legal scholars (Johnson 1974, 1978; Prestowitz 1988; van Wolferen 1989; Nester 1990; various interviews Japanese legal scholars; Schaede 1992, 1993; Fingleton 1995; Brown 1999; Katayama 2000).[42] The government control interpretation of *amakudari* enlarges the set of potential instruments of economic policy with a network of strategically positioned retired bureaucrats: i.e. *amakudari* as an additional instrument to implement government policy (see also Aoki 1988b).[43] For example, Johnson (1974, pp.964–965) notes that from the point of view of the government, the 'placement of *amakudari* officials has been motivated not only by a desire to secure post-retirement employment for them but also as a matter of positive policy to enhance the effectiveness of administrative guidance': that is, *amakudari* 'is one aspect of their implementation of so-called administrative guidance'. Schaede (1992, p.33) concludes that *amakudari* is one of the primary tools to implement administrative guidance: 'given the scope and relevance of administrative guidance in business regulation on the one hand, and the high

---

[42] Various interviews with leading journalists Tokyo, June 1992; Japanese legal scholars, Tokyo, September and October 1992; Japanese business executives, Tokyo, January–March 1993. In the Japanese media, this view is expressed quite regularly in the left-leaning newspaper *Asahi Shimbun* and critical books written largely by journalists. Also the more conservative *Nihon Keizai Shimbun/Nikkei Weekly* (*Japan Economic Journal*, *JEJ*) and *Tokyo Business Today* (*TBT*) follow this line (see, for example, *JEJ*, 8 September 1990, and *TBT*, July 1988).

[43] The view of *amakudari* being an instrument of government policy is supported by Aoki (1988b) as well, although he is not a clear supporter of the government control interpretation.

number of *amakudari* board members on the other, it is safe to assume that bureaucrats constitute the most decisive factor in shaping day-to-day decisions of corporate Japan'. Finally, Stockwin (1999, p.108) also subscribes to the main assertion of the government control interpretation: 'there is no doubt that *amakudari*, together with other bureaucratic practices such as *gyōsei shidō* (administrative guidance), have led to the emergence of an economy which is unusually highly regulated by government'. The use of the *amakudari* network as a mechanism of government control over private business is also emphasised by various non-journalistic Japanese studies, for example Taira and Wada (1987), Tsujinaka (as quoted in Inoki 1993) and Katayama (2000). The former considers the 'administrative guidance of individual companies to make them conform to industrial policy' one of the 'official duties' of retired civil servants in private industry, and states that 'it is commonly acknowledged that placement strategies and decisions are in part motivated by policy considerations' (Taira and Wada 1987, pp.285–287). Tsujinaka notes that, 'denied the path to a strong state based on hierarchical centralization and control under a statist ideology, the state bureaucracy turned toward the osmotic network system whereby more sophisticated and indirect means of control could be developed and systematized' (Inoki 1993, p.4.). In his opinion, *amakudari* is one of these indirect means of control (along with administrative guidance, advisory councils and the like). It has to be mentioned, as various studies of the government control school recognise, that the kind of potential government control exercised through *amakudari* must be subtle and cautious: it is to some extent limited by the need of the bureaucracy to maintain good relations with its private sector constituency, in the sense of exchanging information, and to ensure and safeguard future *amakudari* positions.[44] Nevertheless, the bottom line of the government control interpretation of *amakudari* is that it provides the government bureaucracy with an additional instrument to implement government policies. In other words, this approach emphasises the viewpoint of the government, i.e. the supply-side of *amakudari*, and the implementation of its policies. The government control interpretation implies also the existence of a relatively powerful government bureaucracy, which implicitly and/or explicitly can force private business to accept retired civil servants, in line with the assumptions of the interventionist school.

A second school regarding the importance of *amakudari* in the government–business interrelationship is the equalising school, introduced in Calder (1989) and supported in Aoki (1988b) and Stockwin

[44] Johnson (1978), p.113, and Taira and Wada (1987), p.287. Personal interviews with Japanese legal scholars, Tokyo, September 1992. These possible limitations to the use of *amakudari* as an instrument of government control are defended in Okimoto (1987), p.165.

(1999). This school interprets *amakudari* as a mechanism to equalise differences in access to bureaucratic information resulting from differences in corporate power and status between companies. In more negative wording, this school could be said to subscribe to a 'buying influence' hypothesis. For example, 'smaller firms in Japan have stronger incentives for wanting ex-bureaucrats and are willing to pay relatively more' because 'economically strategic information is much more frequently unavailable from public sources in Japan than in Europe and the U.S' (Calder 1989, p.395). Differences between companies as regards corporate power and status are reflected in having less developed connections with the government bureaucracy. Calder (1989, p.399) finds that 'bureaucrats move with greatest frequency to relatively small, non-Tokyo-based, non-*keiretsu* affiliated firms with relatively small proportions of elite Tokyo University graduates in top management'. That is, the largest firms in Japan value secrecy more, have their own channels for gathering non-public information and consequently do not need and even do not want retired bureaucrats. In the words of a board member of a leading Japanese bank: 'If you don't need them, you don't want them' (personal interview, Tokyo, January 1993). Furthermore, ex-bureaucrats who are employed by private business fulfil an equalising role in the sense of promoting the interests of their constituency.

The equalising school concentrates on the demand-side of *amakudari* and sees a relatively balanced relation between private and public sectors in the sense that private companies follow their own interests when considering whether or not to accept former bureaucrats.[45] On the whole, '*amakudari* thus operates to *broaden* the access of the less-connected portion of the corporate world to government information, and frequently to *co-opt* and to *undermine* bureaucratic efforts at strategic dirigisme. It often constrains the bureaucrats, and thus complicates rather than reinforces their struggle for strategy' (Calder 1993, p.69). In this sense, one can classify the equalising view of *amakudari* as belonging to the market school interpretation of the Japanese economic system: *amakudari* improves the working of the market mechanism by equalising information disadvantages between private companies and obstructing government intervention.

Third, the supporters of the consensual policy school stress the importance of *amakudari* as a general mechanism for informal consultations and consensus building between public and private sectors. Examples of this interpretation are Okimoto (1989) and Upham (1987). Okimoto defines *amakudari* as a so-called informal policy network, i.e. networks 'based on

---

[45] It has to be mentioned that inside recruitment for the leading positions at private firms is commonly preferred to outside appointments. See Odagiri (1992), p.43.

personal relationships which bring government officials and leaders from the private sector together to formulate public policy' (Okimoto 1989, p.152). The personal relations existing between retired and present civil servants, embodied in the system of *amakudari*, facilitate the process of consensus building between public and private sectors; consensus that is a necessary condition for government policies to be effective in the societal or network state. In this approach, *amakudari* is especially instrumental in the process of policymaking: the continual informal consultations and negotiations generate consensus regarding government policies, which are then relatively easy to implement. Upham (1987) also stresses the importance of *amakudari* in reaching consensus between public and private sectors. He describes this as follows (p.167):

The economic bureaucrats and their business counterparts come from similar educational backgrounds, advance at approximately similar speeds, and rotate in and out of jobs having direct contact with each other's institutions. This contact is furthered by an informal, consultative policymaking process that encourages the formation of personal relationships across institutional boundaries. What cements the relationship is a congruence of interests among public and private elites. When Japanese bureaucrats retire, most take positions in the private sector, many in the very firms they have been dealing with during their bureaucratic career – a process known as *amakudari*, or 'descending from heaven'.

In the consensual policy interpretation, *amakudari* is not used to implement administrative guidance or to equalise relative corporate power imbalances, but to formulate government policies in a continuous public–private sector interactive process. Okimoto (1987, pp.164–165) subscribes to the notion that the importance of *amakudari* from the perspective of government control over private business should not be overstated. The ex-bureaucrat in his new business environment will quite likely be regarded suspiciously as an outsider, favoured above the regular staff for a leading executive position, contrary to the tendency of Japanese companies to recruit executives internally. Or even worse, the retired bureaucrat could be suspected of being an instrument of government control, a possible executor of administrative guidance. Consequently, he has to operate carefully and has to show his dedication and loyalty to the company to obtain the confidence of his new colleagues. The governmental organisations which send their retirees into *amakudari* positions face constraints as well: any attempt to exercise substantial and excessive control through their former staff members would be likely to endanger future *amakudari* positions in these companies. These behavioural constraints seem, according to Okimoto (1989), to limit the extent or possibility to which the former bureaucrat is used as an executive body of strong administrative guidance by his former employer. Other interpretations that see *amakudari* as an informal policy network between the public and private sectors have been put forward in Schaede (1995) and Hollerman (1988). Schaede interprets the 'old boy' phenomenon and *amakudari* as having importance as a 'management of (non-transparent) regulation' system, in which the former government officials operate as intermediaries to lobby for regulatory adjustments on behalf of their new employer and to monitor existing regulation on behalf of their former employer – the government bureaucracy. In the view of Hollerman (1988), the private sector regards *amakudari* as an instrument to clarify government instructions. For example, in the case of the financial industry, the written guidelines of MoF (*tsūtatsu*) and the oral component of its administrative guidance are often regarded vague and unclear. Consequently, according to Hollerman, private banks are using their government retirees or *amakudari kanryō* to find out what the real intentions of MoF's policies are; this clarification of informal policies allows for a more effective implementation of those policies.

Gakubatsu   In addition to *amakudari*, the personal network based on common university backgrounds or *gakubatsu* is said to be of importance in the public–private sector relationship in Japan. According to Nakane (1970, p.117), the existence of university cliques is in Japan 'so well developed that they may indeed sometimes have a function comparable to that of a caste group in India, in terms of a monopoly of certain privileges through mobilizing, in a helpful fashion, friendships and relationships that are able to cut across departmental and institutional divisions'. The significance of these university cliques is based on a strong sense of group consciousness, resulting from sharing the experiences and status of the same university. This strong consciousness of one's academic background establishes a mutual support system both within and between Japanese organisations. The importance of *gakubatsu* is a direct consequence of the structure of the university system. The Japanese education system is highly competitive, the ultimate goal being a position at one of the most prestigious universities (Rohlen 1988, p.28, 1992, p.334). The prestige of the university attended is so important because it is decisive for one's future career: as will be explained below, the most prestigious government organisations and private companies recruit from an extremely small number of universities. In other words, if you pass the entrance examination of one of these universities, you have guaranteed a successful future. The importance of university prestige is put aptly by Wiersema and Bird (1993, p.1007): it 'is a strong indicator of social class in Japanese society', and 'is likely to influence not only the organization joined but also the career trajectory within the organization'. The consciousness of prestige develops strong bonds between graduates from the same universities and has a significant influence on relationships not only between individuals inside and outside organisations but also between organisations: the 'hierarchical ranking of Japanese universities in terms of prestige influences interfirm and intrafirm relations, shaping patterns of association, affiliation, and group formation'.[46]

The most famous *gakubatsu* are based on the University of Tokyo, which is considered the top university of Japan, and four other prestigious universities, two public (Kyoto and Hitotsubashi) and two private (Keio and Waseda), which together comprise the 'Big Five'.[47] Generally, common university backgrounds are said to be important from two perspectives.[48] First, a significant number of large Japanese organisations limit their recruitment of new college graduates to specific universities.[49] That is, if one really wants to make a career in these organisations, one has to graduate from one of those universities. The reasons for this specific orientation of recruitment seem to be, firstly, to use prestige consciousness to build a coherent and homogeneous organisation and, secondly, that the best students are located in the small number of most prestigious universities at the top of the tertiary education system. The graduates of these specific universities are, of course, much sought after by any organisation in Japan. The most famous example of the orientation on specific universities when recruiting new university graduates is the recruitment practice of the government bureaucracy. A large number of the career government bureaucrats in Japan have graduated from the University of Tokyo (Tōdai), with the graduates from its Faculty of Law in particular moving into the most prestigious positions in the top-ranking ministries. Looking at the results of the examinations which serve as the basis for all significant bureaucratic recruitment, Pempel and Muramatsu

---

[46] Clark (1979), as quoted from Wiersema and Bird (1993), p.1007. For a more elaborate discussion see Nakane (1970), pp.133–135.

[47] See Ursacki (1994), p.646, for an overview of the 'Big Five' university background of the executives of the leading Japanese private companies. These figures show that the share of the top three public universities has decreased to the benefit of the share of the top two private universities. However, to grasp the real significance of these shares, one has to take into account the total number of graduates from these universities. The importance that the Japanese attach to these figures is shown by the fact that various newspapers and magazines publish them on a regular basis (see for example *Sunday Mainichi* 1992, p.147).

[48] Nakane 1970; Johnson 1974, 1982; Haitani 1976; Taira and Wada 1987; Hollerman 1988; Calder 1989; Okimoto 1989; van Wolferen 1991; Wiersema and Bird 1993; Schaede 1993; Snider and Bird 1994; Ursacki 1994; personal interviews with Western Japanologist and journalists, Japanese legal scholars, staff members and retirees from the Ministry of Finance and Bank of Japan, and Japanese bankers, Tokyo, 1992–1995.

[49] Wiersema and Bird (1993), p.1007. See also Nakane (1970), p.104.

(1993, p.21) note that 'although there has been some reduction in the dominance of the civil service by University of Tokyo graduates, roughly 35–40 per cent of the successful applicants continue to be Tokyo graduates'.[50] Other (semi) public organisations heavily dominated by Tōdai graduates are, for example, the (former) Japan Development Bank and Japan Export–Import Bank, and the Bank of Japan with 80.0%, 87.5% and even 92.9% of their directors being graduates from the University of Tokyo (Toyo Keizai Shinposha 1992, p.1623). The limitation of recruitment to specific universities when hiring new high-level staff members is also present among private sector companies. Wiersema and Bird (1993), p.1007, present the example of Mitsukoshi, a large retail company; about 60% of its college graduates are from two private universities, Keio and Waseda. Another example is S&B Foods, 88.2% of whose directors are from Waseda University (Ursacki 1994, p.638). The importance of networks in the market for university graduates in Japan has been documented in Rebick (2000), where it is shown that almost 60% of hiring in the private sector can be attributed to persistence in hiring by employers from a number of specific faculties at certain universities.

Second, common university backgrounds are important in the sense that they establish informal networks for exchanging information, consultation and co-ordination of policies between various organisations and segments of society. This aspect of *gakubatsu* receives the most attention in Japanese economic studies, in particular in the interventionist, consensual policy and 'Japan, Inc.' schools. The interpretation of *gakubatsu* in the various schools of the Japanese economic system can be described as follows.[51]

First, Chalmers Johnson, one of the main representatives of the interventionist school, concludes that *gakubatsu* 'forms the most pervasive "old boy" network throughout the society as a whole' (Johnson 1982, p.57). Johnson focuses explicitly on the university clique based on the University of Tokyo, the *Tōdaibatsu*. The main reason for him to do so lies in the fact that Tōdai graduates are positioned in the highest levels of public and private sectors, which facilitates communication between

---

[50] When looking only at Class I examinations (Category I bureaucrats), which select the likely future candidates for the top positions, University of Tokyo graduates comprised in 1991 just over 50% of successful applicants, with Waseda and Kyoto Universities placed second and third (11.8 and 7% respectively) (Pempel and Muramatsu 1993, pp.21–22). They also conclude that 'usually only 15 or so of Japan's 460-odd universities see 10 or more of their graduates succeed in the exams'.

[51] The pluralistic network school (see section 2.3 of chapter 2), which stresses the importance of informal networks in Japan without explicitly naming them, will not be discussed.

government and private business. And in Johnson's view, perhaps more important, 'the *Tōdai* connection means that both government offices and boardrooms are staffed by men who share a common outlook', based on the specific education at the University of Tokyo, which results in a 'homogenization of views' (Johnson 1982, pp.60–62). In this sense, *Tōdaibatsu* is instrumental in the process of economic policy and contributes to the effectiveness of administrative guidance.[52] Ulrike Schaede, an adherent of the interventionist school, has a more nuanced view: in Schaede (1993, p.15) it is stated that 'while one should not generalize and exaggerate the relevance of the university relation, in individual cases it can be very important'.

Second, the consensual policy school sees *gakubatsu* as one of the informal policy networks, which are used to bring public and private sectors together to formulate economic policies. This opinion has been put forward especially in Okimoto (1989, p.156), where the importance of the *Tōdaibatsu* is also emphasised, Boyd (1987, p.67) and Upham (1987, p.167).

Finally, the 'Japan, Inc.' interpretation of the Japanese political economy sees the *Tōdaibatsu* as a powerful elite which runs the Japanese economy. A clear example of this interpretation is Taira and Wada (1987), where it is concluded that the economic system is manipulated and led by the Tōdai–government–business 'complex'. Another example of the power elite model is presented in Hollerman (1988, p.112), where it is stated that there are two elites, that is a premier elite formed by graduates from the University of Tokyo – in particular from its Law Faculty – and a secondary elite formed by graduates of the private Keio University. The *Keiobatsu* has become more influential in the *Keidanren*, the powerful business federation that has been lobbying for many years for administrative reform and less government interference with the economy, and which consequently has been indirectly attacking the *Tōdaibatsu* in a struggle for a more liberalised economic system.

3.5   Summary and conclusions

In this section, I shall provide a summary of the main findings of this chapter as regards the relevance and importance of informal factors in the various schools of the Japanese economic system that have been discussed in this and the previous chapter. Finally, some conclusions will be drawn.

---

[52] Personal interviews, Western scholar, Tokyo, August 1990; Japanese banker (chairman), Tokyo, December 1993.

Table 3.1. *Classification of informal aspects of Japanese economic policy*

	Legal	Non-legal
Transparent		*Tsūtatsu* (published administrative guidance)
Non-Transparent		Personal networks:
		Gakubatsu
		Amakudari
		(*Shukkō*)
		Unpublished administrative guidance

Summary

In this chapter, various aspects of the government–business relationship have been discussed from an informal perspective. As has been discussed in section 3.1, informality applied to studies of the Japanese economic system involves commonly and predominantly two issues: administrative guidance and informal networks, in particular *amakudari* and *gakubatsu*. Table 3.1 presents an overview. It shows that informality has two dimensions. First, informality is basically interpreted from a legal perspective: that is, informal government intervention in the economic system implies the implementation of economic policies, which cannot be enforced by legal means. Second, informality means the existence of non-transparent personal networks, which connect public and private spheres. These networks are based on personal relationships resulting from common university (*gakubatsu*) or common institutional (*amakudari*) backgrounds, and are used in either the formulation or implementation of economic policies. For reasons of completeness, I have in table 3.1 also included the mechanism of *shukkō*, i.e. the temporarily transfer of personnel between organisations. Given that this mechanism is not explicitly discussed in the various schools that have been presented in chapters 2 and 3 it is put between brackets.

Furthermore, in this chapter attention has been paid to the specific interpretation of informality in the various schools of the Japanese economic system, which were discussed in the previous chapter. The views of the interventionist, market, consensual policy and pluralistic network schools on the relevance and importance of informal mechanisms in the Japanese economic policy process are summarised in table 3.2. The economic policy process interprets economic policy as a process consisting of two phases: policymaking and policy implementation (van Rixtel 1991).

Table 3.2. *Informality applied to economic policy as interpreted in the various schools of Japanese economic system*

	Administrative guidance	Informal networks
Interventionist school	In the bureaucracy-led state, administrative guidance is one of the most important instruments to implement economic policy and to control business; it is unilaterally enforced by the government bureaucracy.	In the bureaucracy-led state, *amakudari* provides the government with an additional channel to implement administrative guidance; *gakubatsu* is instrumental in the formulation and implementation of economic policy.
Market school	In a pluralistic society, the government bureaucracy is not powerful enough to control the economic system; the market mechanism dominates, administrative guidance is not effective.	*Amakudari* is not an instrument of economic policy, but is used to promote the interests of the private sector and to equalise relative business positions; no significant place for *gakubatsu*.
Consensual policy/ network state school	In the network state, the reaching of consensus between public and private sectors is a prerequisite for administrative guidance to be effective. Generally, administrative guidance is no longer important.	In the network state, where the government bureaucracy is relatively weak and can operate only when consensus is reached, *amakudari* and *gakubatsu* are informal policy networks, instrumental in reaching consensus and formulating economic policy (policymaking).
'Pluralistic network school	Administrative guidance was an important and effective instrument of economic policy, but has lost much of its appeal and effectiveness.	*Amakudari* and *gakubatsu* are not explicitly referred to; however, this school stresses the importance of informal networks as sources of co-ordination and information exchange (policymaking).
'Japan, Inc.' school	Administrative guidance is not relevant.	*Gakubatsu* important: *Tōdaibatsu* 'runs' the Japanese economy.

In the former phase, policymakers must take a decision regarding the choice of their target variables. This phase involves the interactions of the preferences and personalities of the policy authorities and other government officials with formal and informal institutional structures and the pressures of interest groups and market behaviour (Willett and Keen 1990, p.13). In the latter phase, the results of these interactions have to be implemented by the policy authorities, during which feedback is given to the policymaking stage. In table 3.2 it is shown that, as regards informal aspects, the various schools focus on different stages in the economic policy process. The interventionist school emphasises the importance of informal mechanisms for the implementation of economic policy. In its perception, administrative guidance is one of the most important policy instruments, and informal personal networks, in particular *amakudari*, are used to influence business decisions as well. In other words, the interventionists see informality with respect to government–business relations as a direct control mechanism of the government economic bureaucracy over private business. Against this orientation are the views of the consensual policy and pluralistic network schools, which stress especially the significance of informality in the formulation of economic policy, that is the policymaking stage. Administrative guidance is no longer important, but informal networks like *amakudari* and *gakubatsu* are important channels for co-ordination and negotiation between public and private sectors. Furthermore, the market school, which does not believe that the Japanese government contributed significantly to the 'Japanese miracle' anyway, regards the importance of informal factors as control mechanisms or as any other advantage for the government in its formulation and implementation of economic policy as negligible. Finally, the 'Japan, Inc.' school, which, according to numerous authors, is no longer relevant for the contemporary Japanese economic system, sees the economy managed by the political, bureaucratic and business elites, in other words mainly by the *Tōdaibatsu*.

Conclusions

The analysis of informality with respect to the Japanese economic system can be reduced to two main issues. First, in some part of the literature the proposition has been put forward that the economic system in Japan is not only organised by the market mechanism, but that informal networks behind the market have been established, which function as additional co-ordination mechanisms. From this perspective, some studies emphasise the existence of informal business groups and personal networks, such as the informally organised business groups or *keiretsu* (Gerlach 1992; Imai

1992; Miyashita and Russell 1996) and the theory of social exchange (Murakami and Rohlen 1992). This has led to the view that the Japanese economic system is a specific variant of Western market capitalism, giving rise to interpretations such as alliance capitalism or consultative capitalism (Gerlach 1992; Schaede 1993). Second, and particularly relevant for this study, a number of schools stress the importance of informal factors in the public–private sector economic relationship, i.e. in the intervention of the government in the economic system or economic policy. When following the paradigm of the bureaucracy-led state of the interventionist school, this means the use of informal instruments to implement policies. On the other hand, when following the concept of the network state of the consensual policy school, it means the use of informal networks to reach consensus and formulate policies. These differences in interpretation between the various schools of the Japanese economic system once again show how important it is to define clearly the conceptual framework and basic assumptions that form the starting point of economic analysis. That is, different assumptions regarding the specific relationship between the Japanese government bureaucracy and the private sector generate different conclusions regarding the specific role of informal mechanisms in Japanese economic policy.

Furthermore, this chapter has again showed the fundamental differences between the various schools of the Japanese economic system. More specifically, regarding the relevance of informal factors in Japanese economic policy, the interventionist and network schools criticise the market school and consequently, to a certain extent, also economics as a science for ignoring these factors. In fact, the issue of informality seems to lie at the heart of the controversy between these schools. It has to be mentioned that there are important differences in the opinions of those who support the view that informality is an essential characteristic of the Japanese economic system. For example, van Wolferen, one of the so-called revisionists, sees everything in not only the economy but the whole 'Japanese system' as explained by informal relations: this 'system is what it is by virtue of informal relations that have no basis in the constitution, in any other laws or in any formal rules of the ministries, the LDP, the corporations or any other of the administrator institutions' (van Wolferen 1989, p.109). Other interpretations, for example the consensual policy and pluralistic network schools, have a much more nuanced view.

Given the alleged importance of informal factors in Japanese economic policy in the interventionist and network schools, and given their criticism of mainstream economic explanations and interpretations of the Japanese economic system, this study takes up the gauntlet and focuses explicitly on informal factors in Japanese monetary policy. In the next chapter,

the operational framework of this study that will link informality with
monetary policy will be discussed.

Appendix 3.1 *Japanese* 'special legal entities' *(tokushu hōjin)*

Public corporations (kodan) *13*

Water Resources Development Corporation
Japan Regional Development Corporation
Forest Development Corporation
Japan Agricultural Land Development Agency
Japan National Oil Corporation
Japan Shipbuilding Industry Foundation
Japan Railway Construction Corporation
New Tokyo International Airport Authority
Japan Highway Public Corporation
Metropolitan Expressway Public Corporation
Hanshin Expressway Public Corporation
Honshu–Shikoku Bridge Authority
Housing and Urban Development Corporation

Business corporations (jigyodan) *17*

Research Development Corporation of Japan
Power Reactor and Nuclear Fuel Development Corporation
National Space Development Agency of Japan
Japan Environment Corporation
Japan International Co-operation Agency (JICA)
Social Welfare and Medical Services Corporation
Pension Welfare Service Public Corporation
Livestock Industry Promotion Corporation
Japan Raw Silk and Sugar Price Stabilisation Agency
Metal Mining Agency of Japan
Coal Mine Damage Corporation
Japan Small Business Corporation
Japan National Railway Settlement Corporation
Postal Life Insurance Welfare Corporation
Labour Welfare Corporation
Small Enterprise Retirement Allowance Mutual Aid Corporation
Employment Protection Corporation

Finance corporations (koko) *9*

Hokkaido – Tohoku Development Corporation
Okinawa Development Finance Corporation
People's Finance Corporation
Environmental Sanitation Business Finance Corporation
Agriculture, Forestry and Fisheries Finance Corporation
Japan Finance Corporation for Small Businesses
Small Business Credit Insurance Corporation
Housing Loan Corporation
Japan Finance Corporation for Municipal Enterprises

Finance corporations/special banks (kinko/tokushu ginkō) *3*

Japan Development Bank (JDB)
Export-Import Bank of Japan
The Central Bank for Commercial and Industrial Co-operatives

Corporation (eidan) *1*

Teito Rapid Transit Authority

Special corporations (tokushu gaisha) *12*

Japan Tobacco (JT), Inc.
Electric Power Development Company Ltd.
Kansai International Airport Company Ltd.
Hokkaido Railway Company
East Japan Railway Company
Central Japan Railway Company
West Japan Railway Company
Shikoku Railway Company
Kyushu Railway Company
Japan Freight Railway Company
Kokusai Denshin Denwa Corporation (KDD) Ltd.
Nippon Telegraph and Telephone Company (NTT)

Others (sono hoka) *37*

Northern Territories Issue Association
The Overseas Economic Co-operation Fund (OECF)
Japan Consumer Information Centre
Japan Atomic Research Institute

Japan Information Centre of Science and Technology
Institute of Physical and Chemical Research
Pollution-Related Health Damage Compensation and Prevention
    Association
The Fund for the Promotion and Development of the Amami
    Islands
Japan Foundation
Japan Scholarship Foundation
Mutual Aid Association of Private School Personnel
National Education Centre
Japan Arts Council
Japan Society for the Promotion of Science
Japan Private School Promotion Foundation
University of the Air Foundation
National Stadium and School Health Centre of Japan
Social Insurance Medical Fee Payment Fund
Social Development Research Institute
Association for Welfare of the Mentally and Physically
    Handicapped
Japan Racing Association
Mutual Aid Associations of Agriculture, Forestry and Fisheries
    Corporation Personnel
National Association of Racing
Farmer Pension Fund
Japan Bicycle Racing Association
Japan External Trade Organisation (JETRO)
Institute of Developing Economies
Japan Motorcycle Racing Association
New Energy and Industrial Technology Development
    Organisation
Japan National Tourist Organisation
Maritime Credit Corporation (Foundation)
Railway Development Fund
Nippon Hoso Kyokai
Japan Institute of Labour
Construction, Sake Brewing and Forestry Industry Retirement
    Allowance Mutual Aid Association
Japan Workers' Housing Association
Mutual Aid Fund for Official Casualties and Retirement of
    Volunteer Firemen

Total public corporations as of October 1995: 92

Privatised Public Corporations (7 as of October 1995)

Tokyo Small Business Investment Promotion Company, Inc.
Nagoya Small Business Investment Promotion Company, Inc.
Osaka Small Business Investment Promotion Company, Inc.
Central Co-operative Bank for Agriculture and Forestry
High Pressure Gas Maintenance Association
Japan Electric Meter Standardisation Centre
Japan Fire-fighting Standards Association

The above data are from Amyx (1998).

4 Informality and monetary policy: an operational framework

> Monetary theory is like a Japanese garden. It has esthetic unity born of variety; an apparent simplicity that conceals a sophisticated reality; a surface view that dissolves in ever deeper perspectives.
>
> M. Friedman (1969)

4.1 Introduction

In the previous chapter, various informal aspects of Japanese economic policy were discussed. In general, economic policy can be divided into fiscal policy, monetary policy and various structural policies such as labour-market policy and industrial policy. This chapter presents an operational framework for the analysis of informal aspects of Japanese monetary policy. First, monetary policy and the monetary policy process will be discussed in section 4.2. Second, the main elements of monetary policy will be investigated from an informal perspective (4.3). Finally, these findings will be integrated with the results of the discussion of informal aspects of Japanese economic policy that were presented in chapter 3, and some conclusions will be drawn (4.4).

4.2 Monetary policy

The basic conceptual framework for the analysis of the theory of economic policy and subsequently of the theory of monetary policy is due to Jan Tinbergen and Ragnar Frisch. Their target-instrument approach showed how policymakers could utilise policy instruments in order to achieve certain pre-specified policy targets (Petit 1990, p.5). Policy instruments are 'variables under the command of the government' (Tinbergen 1952, p.7), whereas the targets represent the ultimate goals of the policymakers. Following this framework, monetary policy can be defined as the deliberate manipulation of monetary policy instruments by the monetary policymakers, aimed at the realisation of their policy targets (Burger 1971).

In general, following Goodhart (1995), the monetary authorities are responsible for the operation of two types of monetary policy, macro-and micro-oriented policies. Macro monetary policy is aimed at the realisation of macro-economic policy goals such as price stability or full employment. In most countries this policy is the domain of the central bank. By micro monetary policy is meant the monetary authorities' 'concerns with the structure and stability of the banking system' (Goodhart 1995, p.231). The main elements of micro monetary policy are structural policy and prudential policy, including the regulation of financial institutions and markets (Benston 1998). Structural policy is related to the structure of the financial system, i.e. the whole structure of financial institutions and markets (Wytzes 1978, p.1). Examples of structural policy are policy decisions regarding the kind of business various financial institutions are allowed to perform, such as banking, securities and/or insurance business, and listing procedures at stock exchanges. Prudential policy deals, according to Wessels (1987), p.97, with 'the way financial institutions operate as firms and is ultimately aimed at maintaining the continuity of the banking system'. Important instruments of prudential policy are minimum capital requirements and various restrictions intended to limit the type of risks which a bank may undertake (Flannery 1995, p.281). Both macro and micro monetary policies can be interpreted as policy processes consisting of two phases, policymaking and policy implementation, as discussed in section 3.5 of the previous chapter.

4.3   Informality and monetary policy

In chapter 3, I distinguished between two dimensions of informality in the context of economic policy: non-legality and non-transparency. Within the monetary policy process, informality could be instrumental in the following ways. In the policymaking phase, it seems that the aspect of non-transparency could be *particularly* relevant: the existence of non-transparent networks based on personal relationships could smoothen the formulation of policies by taking into account the opinions of the various parties involved. This could be important particularly for societies that are based on consensus, and for central banks with a relatively low degree of independence. Furthermore, these personal networks could function as channels to gather information, enabling the monetary authorities to remain apprised of the latest economic and other relevant developments. With respect to the implementation of monetary policy, non-transparent instruments with no clear legal backing are appealing to monetary policymakers because of the broad range of initiatives implicit in their use (Chant and Acheson 1986, p.109, one of the very rare studies focusing explicitly on non-transparent or covert instruments of monetary policy). This aspect is particularly beneficial during times of great change and crisis, enabling monetary authorities to operate flexibly and fast. According to Chant and Acheson (1986), pp.109–110, the central bank and other monetary policymakers could, by keeping their powers ill defined, expand their range of authority without having to go through a slow and lengthy legal process or consequent public discussion of the degree and extension of their powers. Of course, the use of non-legal and/or non-transparent instruments raises questions of democratic control and accountability, which are beyond the scope of this study. The following analysis will focus on the relevance and importance of informality for macro and micro monetary policy and concentrate on the implementation of monetary policy. Owing to limitations of time and place, no further attention will be paid to informality in the policymaking phase of monetary policy.

Informality and macro monetary policy

The standard approach to analysing macro monetary policy follows the so-called 'targets and indicators' framework, which has been extensively discussed during the last three decades (Friedman 1975, 1990; Eijffinger 1986). This approach is based on the transmission mechanism of monetary policy, which describes in particular the implementation of macro monetary policy. Given both the uncertainty regarding the ultimate effects and the possibility of lagged effects of policy actions on ultimate goals, the monetary authorities also use additional intermediate variables, i.e. indicators and targets (Dennis 1981, pp.21–22; Suzuki 1987a, p.327). Indicators such as interbank interest rates are under the close control of the central bank and are directly affected by the policy instruments. However, the relationship of the indicators with the ultimate goals is somewhat unstable. Therefore, targets such as monetary aggregates or exchange rates are used as an intermediate objective. Following this framework, the question arises in what way informality could be of importance for the implementation of macro monetary policy. Informality would be significant in this respect if the monetary authorities had at their disposal a set of informal instruments, sometimes collectively typified as 'moral suasion', which they could use in addition to their formal (legal and/or transparent, i.e. market oriented) policy instruments. Some central banks acknowledge that they use (or have used) informal instruments in their macro policy operations when necessary. For example, according to one of its former executive directors writing in 1994, the Netherlands Central Bank may use 'moral suasion in order to induce the banks to adopt a certain course of action, if circumstances so require' (Wellink 1994, p.25).

An official publication of the Bank of Canada referred directly to informal instruments, defining 'moral suasion' as 'a wide range of possible initiatives by the central bank designed to enlist the co-operation of commercial banks or other financial organizations in pursuit of some objective of financial policy' (Chant and Acheson 1986, p.111). Furthermore, according to some well-known scholars in the field of US monetary policy, 'the Federal Reserve used . . . moral suasion to restrain bank lending directly' (Romer and Romer 1993, p.72).

Policymakers often face uncertainty about the impact of their policy instruments on intermediate variables and their ultimate goals (so-called multiplicative uncertainty). Use of additional informal instruments could reduce this uncertainty, enabling policymakers to control intermediate variables more accurately.[1] So, the inclusion by monetary authorities of effective informal instruments in their macro operations, instruments that conventional analyses of monetary policy often neglect but which expand the set of policy tools available, can improve the effectiveness of macro monetary policy.

From the perspective of macro monetary policy, additional informal instruments could be particularly useful in influencing bank lending, forms of 'moral suasion' being of a direct character and aimed at individual bank level. At this micro level, bank lending seems to be the single most important variable for macro monetary policy. Moreover, forms of 'moral suasion', which are of a less rigid nature than more conventional formal instruments and are more flexible, allow for better fine-tuning with respect to developments in bank lending. In practice, numerous central banks have employed informal instruments to influence bank lending. This has been the case also for Japanese macro monetary policy. The Bank of Japan used an additional informal instrument to control the lending of private commercial banks. This instrument was the so-called window guidance (*madoguchi shidō*), in the words of Suzuki (1987a), p.325: 'guidance to the financial institutions to keep the increase in their lending to clients within limits that the Bank of Japan feels to be appropriate'. However, this kind of 'moral suasion' was officially abolished in June 1991 (see chapter 5). In fact, the decline in the reliance on direct controls on bank lending has been observed in a number of countries (Batten et al. 1989; Kneeshaw and van den Berg 1989, p.5). As a result of the process of financial reform – including financial deregulation and internationalisation – which has fundamentally changed the financial system in

---

[1] A formal explanation of this proposition, based on optimal control theory and following Theil (1964), Brainard (1967), Henderson and Turnovsky (1972), Johansen (1973), Chow (1975), Gordon (1976), Petit (1990) and Swank (1990), is presented in van Rixtel (1994d, 1997).

most industrialised countries in the past two decades, most central banks that employed restrictions on bank lending have opted for more market-oriented alternatives such as interest rate based operating procedures and strategies. Short-term interest rates can be controlled perfectly by central banks and an additional set of informal instruments in this respect becomes superfluous (Goodhart 1989, p.216; Macfarlane 1989, p.150). Thus, the role of informal instruments in the implementation of macro monetary policy seems to have diminished in most developed countries and therefore the emphasis in this study will be on the relevance and importance of informality for the implementation of micro monetary policy. Although I shall not present here a formalised and structured analysis of informal aspects of the implementation of macro monetary policy,[2] chapters 5 and 6 will present some empirical evidence of the use of informal instruments by the Japanese monetary authorities in their implementation of macro monetary policy.

Informality and micro monetary policy

Regarding the implementation of micro monetary policy, forms of 'moral suasion' could be beneficial to both structural and prudential policy. In addition to general advantages such as speed and flexibility, informal instruments offer the following benefits for the implementation of micro policy in particular. First, informal instruments such as forms of 'moral suasion' are of a direct nature, close to the micro-economic level of individual bank behaviour at which prudential regulation finds its main focus of attention. The possibility of a major crisis differs from bank to bank; at the specific firm level, advantages such as speed and flexibility are of particular importance in situations of a possible bank run. Second, the non-transparent character of informal instruments offers the advantages of confidentiality and secrecy. When a bank gets into problems, the supervisory authorities will want to keep this fact from the general public and financial markets as long as possible to avoid panic and bank runs. Non-transparent instruments allow the monetary authorities to intervene swiftly and silently in an attempt to solve problems before depositors and other stakeholders become aware of them.

Traditionally, supervisory authorities depended heavily on informal instruments to implement prudential policy in particular. As Smits (1997, p.320), aptly puts it:

In the early days of prudential supervision, central banks would exercise control through informal means (the famous 'nod and wink' from the central bank).

---

[2] This is presented in van Rixtel (1994d, 1997).

Moral suasion was effective for several reasons. Bankers used to be 'gentlemen', belonging to the same club where social contact was close and deviant behaviour easily countered. Banks used to operate locally instead of globally, with hardly any foreign presence in the financial centre which the central bank supervised. Nor was there any major international expansion of domestic banks to cause concerns for the supervisor. Finally, the trend towards 'juridification' of society, with norms being laid down more and more in legal form and the predisposition to litigate over them in case of conflicting views, had not yet taken hold.

As the trend towards more formal supervision and the internationalisation of banking has undermined to some extent the effectiveness of informal prudential policies, however, recent publications show that informal instruments are still of significant importance for the implementation of prudential policy. For example, the Federal Deposit Insurance Corporation openly acknowledges in a 1997 publication that it employs informal actions when it perceives at specific banks problems that have not deteriorated to the point where they warrant formal administrative action. These so-called 'informal corrective procedures', which seem to have the character of final warnings, include the use of memoranda of understanding and the bank's adoption of a board resolution 'indicating the directors' intent to take corrective action and eliminate the problems' (FDIC 1997, p.467). The number of these informal actions is quite substantial: according to FDIC (1997, p.62), 'in a sample of 307 FDIC-supervised problem banks there were 209 with formal actions, 83 with informal actions only and merely 15 with neither formal nor informal actions', that is 28.4% of the FDIC's interventions were of an informal nature.

Although the monetary authorities in some countries apparently use informal instruments for the implementation of structural policy as well, the analysis of the relevance and importance of informality for micro monetary policy will be concentrated on prudential policy.[3] The main reason for this orientation is that the banking problems which several countries experienced at the end of the eighties and the beginning of the nineties renewed the attention for bank regulation and supervision in particular, i.e. prudential policy (Dewatripont and Tirole 1994, p.2; Sawamoto, Nakajima and Taguchi 1995; Sheng 1996). Prudential policy, as has been shown, for example, by the 1986 Cross Report and 1988 Basle Accord, is mainly concerned with the solvency of banks.[4] In addition,

---

[3] For example, the Japanese monetary authorities used in their structural policy 'moral suasion' to establish a separation of the activities of various financial institutions, such as long-term finance versus short-term finance and banking versus trust business (Hall 1993, p.181) – see also section 5.2 of chapter 5.

[4] The Basle Committee on Banking Supervision proposed in 1986 an initial plan (Cross Report) to link minimum capital requirements for international banks to their credit risk exposures. After extensive discussions among the Group of Ten countries consensus was reached, culminating in the Basle Accord of July 1988 (IMF 1992).

concern for liquidity is often included as well (Visser 1987, pp.83–84; De Nederlandsche Bank 1995, pp.128–129).

Academic analyses of prudential policy often include the following aspects. First, recent studies investigate prudential policy from a corporate governance perspective, i.e. prudential policy can be interpreted as the corporate governance conducted by the monetary authorities, who perform monitoring functions on behalf of small depositors in particular ('representation' hypothesis) (Dewatripont and Tirole 1994). In this view, the prudential supervision of banks by the monetary authorities is not different from the control of non-financial companies by private banks. Second, studies distinguish often between ex-ante and ex-post supervision (or regulation) activities (Teranishi 1997; Suzuki 2000). The former include measures to prevent competition, balance sheet regulations, such as capital adequacy guidelines, and direct inspections by the monetary authorities. The latter include the 'lender-of-last resort' role of the central bank and other rescue operations. Suzuki (2000, p.10) separates between 'ex ante intervention style discretionary administration' and 'ex post check-style rules-oriented administration'. These aspects will be discussed in the next section from a Japanese perspective.

Corporate governance and prudential policy: the Japanese context

Studies of corporate governance or corporate control investigate internal and external control mechanisms of corporate management (Berglöf 1994; Prowse 1994; Chew 1997; Balling et al. 1998). It is generally acknowledged that in the major industrialised countries different corporate governance systems exist. For example, in the US, internal and external governance mechanisms such as 'equity ownership by top executives, monitoring by institutional and large shareholders, outside directors on the board and the threat of external takeovers' provide incentives for corporate managers to maximise shareholder wealth (Kang and Shivdasani 1995, p.30). In Japan, as has been pointed out in many studies, similar governance mechanisms exist to a considerably lesser extent (Prowse 1992, 1994; Groenewegen 1994; Kang and Shivdasani 1995; Milhaupt 1996; Moerke 1997; Teranishi 1997; Shleifer and Vishny 1997; Corbett 1998; Gibson 1998; Hanazaki and Horiuchi 1998; Miyajima 1998; Morck and Nakamura 1999a, 1999b; Anderson and Campbell 2000; Katayama 2000). However, according to these studies, other systems for monitoring and disciplining of corporate management do exist in Japan, i.e. the *keiretsu* structure, main bank system and concentrated share ownership – the importance of which is being influenced considerably by the processes of financial and economic reform in Japan, as will be explained in chapter 9. The former two monitoring systems are informal institutional characteristics of the Japanese system of industrial organisation. The Japanese system of corporate governance can be explained as follows.

First, corporate governance in Japan is related to the existence of large informally organised business groups or *keiretsu*. The concept of the *keiretsu* can be defined as 'a group consisting of a bank (with its affiliated financial institutions of other kinds, such as an insurance company and a trust bank) and the companies for which it acts as the main bank (main supplier of funds)' (Odagiri 1992, p.167).[5] *Keiretsu* such as the Mitsui, Mitsubishi and Sumitomo groups are direct informally organised successors to the pre-war *zaibatsu* groups that dominated the Japanese economy during the pre-war and wartime periods; the Fuyō (Yasuda *Zaibatsu*) and Dai-Ichi Kangyō (Furukawa and Kawasaki *Zaibatsu*) groups are informal groupings of firms related to other pre-war *zaibatsu* (within brackets) (Gerlach 1992, p.81). Relatively new *keiretsu* with somewhat less cohesive relations are the industrial groups organised informally around Sanwa Bank and Tokai Bank (Viner 1987, p.149). *Keiretsu* are characterised by extensive reciprocal or cross shareholdings (*kabushiki mochiai*) and intense information sharing (through presidents' clubs or *shachō kai*) among member firms. Managers are monitored by the groups' firms, whereas member firms are monitored by other member firms and the *keiretsu*'s main bank, constituting a governance mechanism to support co-operative behaviour (Berglöf and Perotti 1994; Groenewegen 1994).

Second, regarding the corporate governance of Japanese firms, an important role is played by the so-called main banks: the major Japanese private banks operate informally as monitors – also on behalf of other lenders – of large numbers of commercial firms. Even firms that do not belong to a *keiretsu* normally maintain an informally based relationship with a (large) commercial bank. According to Aoki et al. (1994), the main bank system is composed of three broader elements. First, multitudes of financial, informational and managerial relationships exist between firms and their main banks. For example, the main bank keeps significant equity and loan positions in the firm, provides information and management resources, and monitors and disciplines poor management. Second, another major element of the main bank system is the reciprocal delegation of monitoring functions among banks: a 'city bank is concurrently main bank for some of its customers and for other customers is a member of

---

[5] This definition follows the concept of the financial *keiretsu* (*kinyū keiretsu*), which is commonly used as a definition of the *keiretsu*. For discussions of the *keiretsu* see Gerlach (1992), Imai (1992), Odagiri (1992), Calder (1993), Miyashita and Russell (1996) and Fruin (1998).

a *de facto* syndicate for which another city bank is the main bank' (Aoki et al. 1994, p.24). This integrative monitoring consists of ex-ante monitoring (screening of proposed projects), interim monitoring of on-going business and ex-post monitoring (verifying the financial state of firms and, if necessary, intervening to resolve situations of financial distress). In other words, following the terminology of Diamond (1984), the main bank system functions as a delegated monitor for the Japanese capital market as a whole (see also Krasa and Villamil 1992). This function is especially relevant when firms are in situations of severe financial distress (Sheard 1994, p.86). Third, the final element of the main bank system is formed by relationships between the monetary authorities and the banking industry. The monetary authorities provide the institutional framework that guarantees rents 'for banks which perform the delegated monitoring function properly' and that imposes penalties on banks which shirk main bank obligations (Aoki et al. 1994, p.27).

Third and finally, control in the Japanese corporate governance structure is exercised by major shareholders (i.e. concentrated ownership), which are to a large extent financial institutions: according to the Anti-Monopoly Law, Japanese banks may hold up to 5% of the equity of a single firm, and insurance companies up to 10%. These concentrated (intercorporate) holdings provide Japanese financial institutions with the incentives and the ability to monitor and influence managerial performance (Prowse 1994; Kang and Shivdasani 1995; Osano 1996).

Regarding the governance of Japanese banks, I shall concentrate on the first two elements of the Japanese corporate governance structure, i.e. the *keiretsu* and main bank system, which of course are supplemented by the supervisory role of the monetary authorities. Since in the case of the banking sector main banks are defined as the banks that are the main shareholders of other banks, it is not appropriate to take into account concentrated share-ownership as a separate form of corporate governance of Japanese banks. The definition of main bank that is used for non-financial firms, i.e. the bank that is the largest lender and shareholder of these firms, cannot be used, since the element of largest lender is here not relevant. The aspect of the main bank is, in the case of the banking industry, particularly relevant for the regional and so-called Second Tier regional banks, which usually have large banks as their main shareholders; the latter are here interpreted as being their main banks.

This study puts forward the argument that the *keiretsu* and main bank could have important implications for the governance of the Japanese banking industry, including the form of governance exercised by the Japanese monetary authorities, i.e. prudential policy. It can be argued that, in addition to the monitoring or prudential policy implemented by the monetary authorities, monitoring of Japanese private banks is exercised by *keiretsu* member firms (both financial and non-financial firms) of *keiretsu* banks and by main banks with respect to their client banks (monitoring by the main banks of smaller banks). As a result, based on the existing literature of corporate governance in Japan, this study proposes a model of 'hierarchical delegated monitoring' for the governance of Japanese banks, i.e. for the 'monitoring of the monitors' (see also Krasa and Villamil 1992).

First, small (i.e. non-main) banks that do not belong to a *keiretsu* are monitored by their main banks and by the monetary authorities. This proposition of the monitoring of small banks by large (main) banks has been supported by Kazuo Ueda, who has been a member of the BoJ's Policy Board since April 1998 (Ueda 1992, p.11). In this case, the main bank should be interpreted as the bank that has business ties with the smaller bank, for example international representation and ATM networks, and which maintains major equity positions in its smaller partner. Second, small banks that belong to a *keiretsu* are monitored by non-financial and non-bank financial firms which are member of that *keiretsu*, and by the *keiretsu* main-bank, all of which are major shareholders of the small bank as well. In addition, monitoring functions could be exercised by non-*keiretsu* affiliated main banks, whereas the monetary authorities are ultimately responsible for bank supervision. Third, large banks, which function predominantly as main banks of non-bank firms and small banks and which are often also the main bank of a *keiretsu*, are closely monitored by the MoF and BoJ, given their important role in the Japanese economy and their monitoring functions of affiliated small ('client') banks.

It has to be stressed that the MoF and BoJ, being the representatives of small depositors, will always perform ex-post monitoring functions, i.e. will ultimately intervene on behalf of these stakeholders when necessary ('representation hypothesis') (Dewatripont and Tirole 1994, pp.32ff.). Ex-ante and interim monitoring by the MoF and BoJ will be more important in the case of large (i.e. main) banks than with respect to smaller (i.e. non-main) banks, leaving the ex-ante and interim monitoring of smaller banks to a large extent to their main banks. If the main banks shirk their responsibility of monitoring the smaller banks, MoF and BoJ have sufficient regulatory powers to impose sanctions. The proposed model of hierarchical delegated monitoring largely sees the monetary authorities on the one hand and the main banks and the *keiretsu* on the other as substitutes for implementing ex-ante and interim monitoring functions in particular, and more as complementary institutions regarding ex-post monitoring or intervention. This means that, regarding ex-post monitoring functions, the MoF and BoJ operate together with the main banks and *keiretsu* to solve the problems at their client banks. Thus, the relationship between intervention by the monetary authorities and intervention by the main banks and *keiretsu* should be positive.

To conclude, the proposed model of hierarchical delegated monitoring includes, in addition to the monitoring by the monetary authorities, the exercise of monitoring functions by the informally organised *keiretsu* and main-bank systems. As will be argued in section 4.4, the MoF and BoJ could use their retired staff members on the boards of directors of private banks (*amakudari*) and utilise administrative guidance to implement prudential policy (Teranishi 1997).

4.4   Conclusions

In the previous sections, the relevance of informality for macro and micro monetary policy was investigated. This section discusses the relevance and importance of informality for the implementation of Japanese monetary policy from the perspective of the various schools of the Japanese economic system such as discussed in chapter 3 (see table 3.2, page 70). Table 4.1 presents a summary overview.

With respect to the implementation of monetary policy, the conclusion of the interventionist school would suggest an important role for administrative guidance and *amakudari*. Given the growing attention paid to interventionist ideas in the eighties and nineties, the analysis of the relevance and importance of these instruments for the implementation of Japanese monetary policy should be of particular importance. Regarding the implementation of macro monetary policy, the interventionist school suggests that the Japanese monetary authorities have an additional set

Table 4.1. *Informality and the implementation of monetary policy*

Interventionist school	Administrative guidance is one of the most important instruments to implement monetary policy; *amakudari* is used as a mechanism to implement administrative guidance.
Market school	Administrative guidance and *amakudari* are not relevant for the implementation of monetary policy at all.
Consensual policy or network state school	Administrative guidance and *amakudari* are no longer of particular relevance for the implementation of monetary policy.
Pluralistic network school	Administrative guidance and *amakudari* are no longer of particular relevance for the implementation of monetary policy.
'Japan, Inc.' school	*Gakubatsu* (*Tōdaibatsu*) is of some importance in the implementation of monetary policy.

of informal instruments at their disposal. However, as discussed in section 4.3, the relationship between informality and macro monetary policy will not be analysed in a structured and formalised way in the remaining part of this study, although some empirical evidence will be presented in chapter 5 in particular. With respect to the implementation of Japanese micro monetary policy, in particular the implementation of prudential policy, the interventionists would argue that informal instruments are beneficial as well, in particular administrative guidance. As analysed in section 3.3 of chapter 3, administrative guidance consists of published administrative guidance in the form of circulars (*tsūtatsu*) and unpublished administrative guidance. I shall pay attention to both aspects in the subsequent chapters, in particular chapters 5 and 6. Furthermore, the interventionist school asserts that the maintenance of informal networks such as *amakudari* between the MoF and BoJ on the one hand and the private banking industry on the other could be helpful in exercising ex-ante, interim and ex-post monitoring functions. This aspect will be investigated empirically in chapters 7 and 8. Thus, this study will investigate further the relevance and importance of informality for the implementation of micro monetary policy following the paradigm of the interventionist school. The other school that stresses the importance of informality in the implementation of Japanese economic policy, and consequently monetary policy, the 'Japan, Inc.' school, is marginalized and does not play an important role in the present academic discussion.

Part II

The institutions and their policies

5 Informality, monetary authorities and monetary policy: the pre-1998 reform regime

> A son who wins entry to the MOF's elite track at the age of 22 or 23 earns his family as much distinction as if he had won a Nobel Prize... MOF men truly are Nobel-caliber: brilliant, creative, tenacious, public-spirited. Many of them would probably win Nobel Prizes if they chose careers that tend to catch the eye of the Royal Swedish Academy of Sciences.
>
> E. Fingleton (1995)

5.1 Introduction

In this chapter, the organisation in general and informal policies in particular of the two major monetary authorities in Japan – the Ministry of Finance (MoF) (Ōkurashō) and the Bank of Japan (BoJ) (Nihon Ginkō) – until 1998 will be discussed. The year 1998 is chosen because in my view it was a turning point in the post-war development of the Japanese financial system and monetary policy. In this year the major reform programme dubbed the 'Big Bang' started, a new version of the Bank of Japan Law was adopted, bank supervision was removed from the MoF to a new independent organisation (Financial Supervisory Agency), other important reorganisations of the MoF and BoJ were implemented, the issuance of *tsūtatsu* was restricted and last, but certainly not least, measures were implemented to solve finally the severe banking crisis. In this respect, this chapter serves as a yardstick for the assessment of the post-war informal mode of policy implementation in Japan, which, as I shall assert in subsequent chapters, to a large extent caused the banking problems of the nineties and led to the major reforms that will be discussed in chapter 6. Furthermore, the analysis aims to clarify the institutional framework that forms the basis for further empirical analysis in chapters 7 and 8. More specifically, the relevance and importance of informal instruments, i.e. *tsūtatsu* or published administrative guidance and unpublished administrative guidance (see chapter 3), for the implementation of Japanese monetary policy will be investigated. Attention will also be paid to the informal networks that were analysed in chapter 3, i.e. the networks constituted by *gakubatsu* (common university backgrounds of high-ranking MoF and BoJ staff members), *amakudari* (former MoF and BoJ staff members employed by private organisations) and *shukkō* (temporary transfer of staff between MoF/BoJ and the public/private sector).

In addition to the MoF and BoJ, other ministries and lower governments have supervisory responsibilities for specific financial institutions as well. For example, the Ministry of Agriculture, Forestry and Fisheries (Nōshō), in combination with the MoF and by delegation to local governments, supervises the financial institutions for agriculture (*nōgyō*), forestry (*ringyō*) and fishery (*gyogyō*), whereas the credit co-operatives (*shinyō kumiai*) have been supervised by prefectural governments (delegated by the MoF in June 1951 by the enactment of the Shinkin Bank Law) (Suzuki 1987a, p.225; Nagashima 1997, p.200; Kuroda 1998). Furthermore, the Ministry of Trade and Industry (Tsūsanshō) has been responsible for the supervision of non-banks such as real-estate and leasing companies; likewise, the Ministry of Labour (Sōdōshō) and the Ministry of Posts and Telecommunications (Yuseishō) have been responsible for, respectively, labour credit associations (*rōdō kinko*) and postal savings (*yūbin chokin*). However, this chapter will ignore these ministries and lower government departments, given the dominant positions of the MoF and BoJ. The structure of this chapter is as follows. First, the main characteristics of the 'old' or pre-reform Japanese financial system are described (5.2). These characteristics will be used later on in the chapter to explain why certain informal monetary policies such as administrative guidance were – at least to some extent – effective. No attention will be paid to the process of financial reform that started in the later half of the seventies: this process will be discussed in the context of the 1998 reforms in chapter 6. This is followed in section 5.3 by a description of depository financial institutions in particular because of their relevance for macro and micro monetary policy. Knowledge of these institutions is required in order to understand the macro and micro monetary policies of the MoF and BoJ. Only institutions that are the most relevant for this study will be discussed; other financial institutions are explained in, for example, Suzuki (1987a) and Federation of Bankers Associations of Japan (1994). Third, in section 5.4, the institutional framework and informal policies – through published and unpublished administrative guidance – of the MoF until 1998 will be discussed. Successively, its legal framework, personnel (networks) and in particular informal aspects of its macro and micro monetary policies will be described. Fourth, in section 5.5, the institutional characteristics and informal policies of the

BoJ are put into perspective, also for the post-war period until 1998. The final section summarises and concludes (5.6).

5.2   The post-war financial system

The end of World War II heralded the occupation period in Japan (1945–1952). During this period, the Supreme Commander of Allied Powers (SCAP) introduced several reforms with respect to the structure of the financial system. Some of these reforms were embedded in explicit Western-style laws that would play an important role in structuring the post-war financial framework in Japan, which development has been documented extensively elsewhere (Bank of Japan 1973; Suzuki 1980, 1986, 1987a; Sakakibara and Feldman 1983; Federation of Bankers Associations of Japan 1984, 1994; Teranishi 1986b, 1990, 1993; Tsutsui 1988; McCall Rosenbluth 1989; Calder 1993; Hall 1998a; Beason and James 1999).

The most important legal reform was undoubtedly the enactment of the Securities and Exchange Law in 1948, which established the legal separation of banking and securities business, in particular by Article 65 of that law. The Securities and Exchange Law was partly based on the Glass-Steagall Act that separated banking and securities business in the United States. Article 65 prohibited banks from engaging in securities business unless there was an investment motive or a trust contract. In the pre-war period, there was no legal provision that separated Japanese banking and securities activities. Other legal reforms were the promulgation and the implementation of the Anti-Monopoly Law and the Temporary Interest Rate Adjustment Law in 1947. The Anti-Monopoly Law established a formal anti-trust framework in Japan. Its new version of 1976 restricted the holding of equity of any company by Japanese banks to a maximum of 5% (formerly 10%). The Temporary Interest Rate Adjustment Law placed upper limits (ceilings) on some loan rates and most deposit rates. Examples of other reforms introduced by the SCAP are the dissolution of the pre-war industrial conglomerates (*zaibatsu*), the reorganisation of specialised banks into long-term credit banks and new public financial institutions (Johnson 1982; Sakakibara and Feldman 1983; Viner 1987; Wright and Pauli 1987; Cargill and Royama 1988; Tsutsui 1988; Gerlach 1992; Odagiri 1992; Teranishi 1993; Miyashita and Russell 1996). Furthermore, the establishment of the so-called Dodge Line, i.e. the adoption of a balanced budget policy, in 1949 banned the flotation of government bonds to cover current deficits. The Dodge Line was named after J. Dodge, an American banker who was commissioned by SCAP to assist the Japanese government in its effort to implement economic reforms. It was abolished in 1965 (Johnson 1982; Tsutsui 1988; McCall Rosenbluth 1989; Yoshikawa and Okazaki 1993).

The evolving structure of the post-war financial system was expected to fulfil three important requirements (Teranishi 1990, pp.5–6, 1986a, 1986b, 1993). Firstly and most importantly, the system had to supply sufficient long-term funds to realise economies of scale for developing industries, using borrowed technology (the 'catch-up' process). The second role assigned to the financial system was enhancing the availability of funds in low productivity and traditional areas. Thirdly, the financial system was required to be safe and stable.

The financial system during the post-war period of high economic growth, the so-called 'high growth period' (1953–1972), has been characterised in numerous publications of the BoJ and its staff members by four distinctive features (Bank of Japan 1973; Suzuki 1980, 1987a). The first and dominant characteristic of the Japanese financial system, or more specifically of the Japanese banking system, during the period 1953–1975 was the so-called situation of overloan. This situation can be described as 'the existence of loans and investments funded from sources other than deposits and equity capital, so that reserve assets (taken as the sum of central bank money plus second-line reserve assets minus borrowed funds) are consistently negative' (Suzuki 1980, p.5). Borrowed funds include loans from the central bank and borrowing from the money market. It is important to stress that in the case of Japan overloan did not only exist at the micro level, i.e. a situation of overloan at individual banks, but also at the macro level. The macro-based situation of overloan implied that the banking system as a whole was in debt to the BoJ and depended very much for its funding on central bank credit. A second characteristic of the financial system during the high growth period was the predominance of indirect finance (intermediation), mainly resulting from the underdevelopment of capital markets. The preference for indirect finance can be explained partly by the domination of transactions based on customer relationships rather than on funding through the capital markets (Cargill and Royama 1988, p.44). This emphasis on customer relationships can be found in the main bank system, discussed in section 4.3 of chapter 4. Furthermore, the underdevelopment of capital markets was caused by the low level of issuance of government bonds, the use of interest rate and foreign capital controls, and the reduced level of asset accumulation after World War II. The situation of overborrowing was a third characteristic of the Japanese financial structure during the high growth period. Overborrowing refers to corporate finance and indicates a condition of heavy dependence of the corporate sector on bank borrowing, in Japan resulting from the low level of internal financing and predominance of indirect finance (Suzuki 1980, pp.13–14). The fourth and final characteristic of the financial system during the high growth period was the permanent imbalance of liquidity between financial institutions. One group of financial institutions, the city banks (see section 5.3), was chronically in need of funds, while another group (the regional, *sogo* and *shinkin* banks and other financial institutions) was in surplus of funds.

The classification of the Japanese financial system during the high growth period on the basis of these four characteristics has been questioned in Royama (1988). Royama warns against interpreting these superficially observed characteristics as structural features and questions whether the four characteristics were unique to Japan. For example, the imbalance of bank liquidity has also been observed in the United States since the late sixties. However, this situation has not been explicitly mentioned as a unique characteristic of the US financial system. Calder (1993), p.140, observed that the liquidity imbalances among Japanese banks were less severe than among French financial institutions; in addition, he described that a situation of overloan existed in Germany and France as well, which was in terms of a percentage of liabilities much more significant than in Japan. Furthermore, the predominance of indirect finance in Japan has been doubted by Kuroda and Oritani from an international perspective (Sakakibara and Feldman 1983, p.7). They have pointed out that a more consistent definition of indirect finance and adjustment for different accounting methods in the United States and Japan show more or less equal levels of indirect finance in both countries.

Against the background of these remarks, I will present another classification of the post-war financial system, one mostly based on the regulation of the Japanese financial system. As regarding the structure of regulation, the financial system during the high growth period has been regulated on several points. In total, five kinds of regulations can be distinguished (Teranishi 1986b, 1990; Eijffinger and van Rixtel 1992). First, regulations in the form of explicit laws and administrative guidance existed with respect to the structure and activities of financial institutions (see also Hall 1998a). These regulations established a functional segmentation of financial institutions. I have already discussed the separation of securities and banking business. Furthermore, by formal regulation and informal guidance, in the form of unpublished administrative guidance and the issuance of circulars (*tsūtatsu*), banking and trust business were separated and financial intermediaries established a specialisation of lending. Some financial institutions specialised in long-term finance while others became occupied with short-term lending activities. Moreover, specialisation of lending areas could be found in special financial institutions for small and medium-sized firms and agricultural business. Second, the high growth period was characterised by a system of interest rate regulation. The Temporary Interest Rate Adjustment Law (TIRAL) established upper limits for various deposit interest rates. Since 1970, deposit interest rates have been regulated informally according to guidelines from the BoJ, within the limits of the TIRAL. Furthermore, the TIRAL limited lending interest rates in cases of loans of more than 1 million yen in amount or shorter than one year in term. Below these ceilings, the Federation of Bankers' Associations of Japan voluntarily fixed their maximum lending rates (Royama 1983, p.8; van Rixtel 1988, pp.45ff.). This system was replaced in 1959 by a standard rate system, more or less comparable with the prime rate system in the United States. In 1975 the cartel-like agreement with respect to the establishment of the standard rate was abolished. It has to be mentioned that compensating deposits were used to evade the regulation of lending rates: by raising the amount of required deposits of borrowers, banks were able to increase their effective lending rates. Another aspect of interest rate regulation was the issuing of bonds with prices artificially higher than prevailing market prices, causing issue rationing by the Council for the Regulation of Bond Issues (Kisaikai) and hampering the development of the secondary bond markets (Suzuki 1980, p.51; Viner 1987, pp.109). The specialisation of bank lending activities combined with interest rate regulation has been called the 'artificial low interest rate policy' and can be outlined as follows (Royama 1983, pp.7–11). In certain financial markets, such as the market for bank deposits, the monetary authorities fixed interest rates explicitly. On the contrary, in the market for bank loans and the interbank money market, interest rate regulation was rather weak and took a more implicit form. The 'artificial low interest rate policy' resulted in a so-called 'dual interest rate structure', consisting of relatively free but on average higher interest rates in the interbank markets and strictly regulated and artificial lower interest rates in other markets, such as deposit markets. Third, financial regulation during this period was also extended to entry into financial markets. As was mentioned earlier, the Kisaikai regulated the issuance of bonds. Furthermore, the primary equity market was restricted to large firms. With respect to short-term financial markets, until the rise of the market for bond transactions with repurchase agreements (*gensaki* market) in the early seventies, the money market was not open to non-banks. Strict entry control was also applied to the number of financial institutions that could be established. Fourth, during the high growth period international capital movements to and from Japan were strictly regulated. According to the Foreign Exchange and Foreign Trade Control Act of 1947, all financial transactions with foreign countries were forbidden in principle, with freedom of international financial transactions as the exception (Hollerman 1988, p.25). The regulation of international capital flows enabled the monetary authorities to sustain the structure of the financial system by closing the loopholes of interest rate regulation and controlling the foreign source of monetary growth (Teranishi 1986b, p.161). Finally, the creation of new financial instruments during the high growth period was strictly regulated and thus financial innovations were suppressed. As a result, the variety of financial instruments was very limited. In addition to the five major groups of regulations discussed, the post-war financial system can be characterised by two other factors: a complementary relationship between private and public financial institutions and an accommodating stance of monetary policy (Teranishi 1986b, pp.156–160).

5.3   Depository financial institutions

Financial institutions can be divided into financial intermediaries and other institutions; the intermediaries can be subdivided into depository and non-depository institutions. The major depository institutions are the commercial or ordinary banks (*futsū ginkō*), whose activities are set by the Banking Law (Ginkō Hō) of 1927 (a new Banking Law was promulgated in June 1981 and implemented in 1982). The commercial banks consist of the city banks, regional banks, Second Tier regional banks and foreign banks. The city banks (*toshi ginkō*) are the largest of all commercial banks; their funding consists basically of deposits, direct credit from the BoJ and borrowings from the interbank markets. There is no legal definition of city banks but they are customarily understood to have the following characteristics. First, city banks are based (headquartered) in large cities. Second, they possess extensive branch networks within Japan and have also international business networks. Third, traditionally, the city banks provided the greater part of short-term finance to domestic companies. Fourth, city banks operate as main bank of non-financial firms and smaller banks (see chapter 4). Furthermore, most city banks are the main bank of a *keiretsu*. Finally, the degree of concentration within the group of city banks has been increasing, in particular in the early and mid-nineties. The regional banks (*chihō ginkō*) have their headquarters predominantly throughout the country in smaller cities, and mostly operate in local areas. The different classification of city banks and regional banks is not based on any clear legal or other criterion, but is done only for reasons of 'convenience' (Nippon Finance, 1986). The branch network (number and places) of regional banks has been controlled by administrative guidance, which has made it very difficult for regional banks to compete with other regional banks and city banks. The member banks of the Second Association of Regional Banks (Dai-ni Chihō Ginkō Kyōkai), or the Second Tier regional banks, are former *sogo* or mutual savings banks, all of which were changed in commercial banks pursuant to the Law Concerning Merger and Conversion of Financial Institutions after February 1989. The last *sogo* bank (Toho Sogo Bank) merged with a regional bank (Iyo Bank) in April 1992.

The long-term credit banks (*chōki shinyō ginkō*) or LTCBs have been the most important group within the so-called long-term financial institutions. The three LTCBs (Industrial Bank of Japan, Long-Term Credit Bank of Japan and Nippon Credit Bank) were organised under the Long-Term Credit Bank Law of 1952 to provide long-term finance to domestic manufacturers. They were allowed to finance their activities by issuing debentures, a possibility that was not granted to commercial banks. The trust banks (*shintaku ginkō*) are also long-term financial institutions: these banks numbered originally seven and were, unlike the LTCBs, under the Law Concerning Joint Operation of Ordinary Banking and Trust Operations permitted to conduct both ordinary banking and trust business. Since 1954, the MoF has used administrative guidance to separate commercial from trust banking. However, contrary to this guidance, a number of commercial banks, i.e. Daiwa Bank (a smaller city bank) and two regional banks (Bank of the Ryukyus and Bank of Okinawa), consistently ignored this guidance and performed trust-banking activities.

The city banks, regional banks, Second Tier regional banks, long-term credit banks and trust banks have been organised into 72 regional associations (Zenkoku Chihō Ginkō Kyōkai); the Federation of Bankers Associations of Japan (Zenkoku Ginkō Kyōkai Rengōkai or Zenginkyō) is the umbrella organisation of these associations, and is responsible for matters such as maintaining communication with the monetary authorities.

The financial institutions for small businesses comprise three groups, i.e. credit associations (*shinyō kinko*) or *shinkin* banks and their central institution (Zenkoku Shinyō Kinko Rengokai or Zenshinren Bank), credit co-operatives (*shinyō kumiai*) and their central organisation (Zenkoku Shinyō Kumiai Rengokai or National Federation of Credit Co-operatives), and the Central Co-operative Bank for Commerce and Industry (Shōkō Kumiai Chūō Kinko) or Shōkō Chūkin Bank.

The financial institutions for agriculture (*nōgyō*), forestry (*ringyō*) and fisheries (*gyogyō*) are organised on national, prefectoral and municipal levels. They provide financial services to farmers, foresters and fishermen on a mutual basis. The Nōrinchūkin Bank acts as the umbrella organisation for these institutions. At the prefectoral level, credit federations provide deposit-accepting and loan services for the agricultural and fishery co-operatives. The labour credit associations (*rōdō kinko*) perform financial activities in order to improve the living standards of workers and to promote welfare activities of organisations such as labour unions (Suzuki 1987a, p.228).

The *tanshi* institutions are money market dealers, which are active as specialised transaction intermediaries in the short-term money markets (Suzuki 1987a). The money market operations of the Japanese central bank are performed through these intermediaries. According to Hollerman (1988), a significant number of high level staff members of the *tanshi* are former BoJ officials who are strongly sympathetic to the policies of the Bank; according to de Brouwer (1992), p.2, around 30% of *tanshi* directors are former BoJ staff members.

The most important public financial institution is the Postal Savings System (Yūbin Chokin), one of the largest financial institutions in the world in terms of deposits. Its main objective is to collect funds from small depositors for social infrastructural investments. Most Postal Savings funds are entrusted to the Trust Fund Bureau (Shikin Unyō Bu) of the MoF, which uses them to finance the major part of the investments and loans under the Fiscal Investment and Loan Programme (FILP) or Zaisei Tō Yūshi Keikaku (Zaito). FILP has been a kind of secondary budget under the administration of the MoF's Financial Bureau, which provides funds for public works, public corporations and local governments.

5.4 The Ministry of Finance (MoF)

In this section, the legal framework, personnel, macro monetary policy and micro (i.e. prudential) policy of the MoF will be discussed. The emphasis will be on informal aspects and, as mentioned before, the analysis will focus on the post-war period until 1998.

Legal framework

The post-World War II structure of the Japanese government administration is based on the National Government Organisation Law (Kōkka Gyōsei Soshiki Hō) of 1948. This law, and in particular the Ministry of Finance Establishment Law (MoFEL) (Ōkurashō Setchi Hō) of 1949, determined the functions and organisation of the MoF (Ministry of Finance 1992d, p.1). To the best of my knowledge an official translation of this law does not exist. My own translation of this law (including amendments as of 2 May 1991) is presented in appendix 5.1. Article 3 explained the tasks of the MoF:

The MoF is the administrative organisation which has the responsibility of undertaking the administrative business and operations of the government relating to the following items: finance of the Japanese state, currency, finance, foreign exchange, trade of securities, the undertaking of currency creation and the undertaking of printing.

The tasks of the MoF were explained by Article 4, which showed two things clearly. First, the MoF was responsible for a large number of tasks, explained in no fewer than 129 paragraphs. That is, under the version of the MoFEL that is discussed here, the MoF combined in a single institution a set of responsibilities, which are in many other countries exercised by several different organisations. According to Article 4 of the 2 May 1991 version of this law, the MoF was given the following tasks: the formulation of the budget, the management of tax receipts, the planning and management of various public institutions, the management and investment of the funds of the Trust Fund Bureau, the financial regulatory framework, the supervision of the Bank of Japan, government banks, private commercial banks, other private depository institutions, securities and insurance companies and other public and private financial institutions, international finance and investments, foreign exchange transactions and foreign exchange rate policy (see appendix 5.1). In general, the MoF was the 'administrative organisation with overall responsibility for matters related to the nation's "fiscal and monetary" policies' (Ministry of Finance 1992d, p.5). Second, the paragraphs of Article 4, and consequently the responsibilities of the MoF, were formulated in very general and vague terms. As was explained in chapter 3, it is commonly said that Japanese laws are relatively short and vague. These characteristics also apply to the version of the Ministry's Establishment Law discussed here: it is difficult to judge exactly what the MoF was expected to do, as no details were provided and interpretation was obviously left to the MoF officials. For example, according to Paragraph 4.100 of this law, 'the MoF regulates and supervises the financial institutions in their operation of funds'. However, it is unclear what this meant: was the MoF authorised to give binding commands regarding the specific use of funds by financial institutions or could it only give broad indications and express its wishes? Of course, this issue was strongly related to the authority of the MoF, which was explained by Article 5 of the 2 May 1991 version of the MoFEL. It has to be said that the authorisation paragraphs of this article were equally opaque as the corresponding paragraphs in article 4. For example, the authority assigned to the MoF to conduct the tasks described in Paragraph 4.100 such as mentioned above was given by Paragraph 5.36, which stated that 'the MoF regulates the extension of funds and the interest rates of financial institutions'. Again it is not clear exactly what this meant, for example the range of the authority granted and to what extent compliance could be coerced. This indistinctness left the MoF with substantial discretion to interpret its own authority. The MoFEL was (and is) a minimal law, i.e. it is not clearly stated what is allowed and what is not. Consequently, the scope of MoF's actual authority is limited only by its own interpretation of the vague authority as described by its Establishment Law. The vagueness of the legal framework also applies to more specific laws that fall under the scope of the MoFEL such as the Banking Law or the Insurance Law – for the latter see Lake (1998).

Article 5 of the version of MoF's Establishment Law discussed here states that the MoF has to use its authority under the regulation of the law. In this respect the MoF had at its disposal a number of laws or statutes, which are passed by parliament (Diet) and are related to the specific financial institutions existing in Japan. Examples of these statutes are the Banking Law regarding the commercial or ordinary banks, the Long-Term Credit Bank Law for the long-term credit banks, the Foreign Exchange Bank Law under which the Bank of Tokyo was established as a specialised foreign exchange bank, and the Shinkin Bank Law and the Law for Small Business Co-operatives credit for the *shinkin* banks and the credit co-operatives respectively. Furthermore, the MoF's legal regulatory framework includes so-called orders (*meirei*). These consist of cabinet ordinances (*seirei*), which are used to enforce laws, and so-called ministerial ordinances (*shōrei*) that the MoF can draft within its area of administrative authority to enforce *seirei* and laws (Federation of Bankers Associations of Japan 1994; OECD 1999b, p.245). In addition, the MoF uses detailed regulations regarding the application of a law (*shikō saisoku*), informal circulars (*tsūtatsu* or published administrative guidance), public notices (*kokuji*) and business guidelines (*jimu renraku*), which are circulars issued at director level for routine matters. More specific, the informal circulars and business guidelines were explanations and regulations related to particular ministerial ordinances and public notices.

Personnel: informal networks

In this section, the structure of the personnel organisation of the MoF will be discussed. First, the figures on the number of staff employed by the various bureaus and offices of the MoF and similarities of university backgrounds (*gakubatsu*) of its career officials will be presented. These officials passed the highest class of examinations, which serve as basis for recruitment by the major government organisations; consequently, they occupy the top positions in these organisations (Pempel and Muramatsu

1993, p.21). Next, the general pattern of acceptance of post-retirement positions by high-ranking MoF staff (*amakudari*) is presented. Finally, attention is paid to the presence of the mechanism of *shukkō* inside the MoF; as was described in chapter 3, *shukkō* is the practice of temporarily transferring staff members between Japanese organisations, which results in the establishment of vast informal networks. In this section, the specific recruitment system, training programmes, and the career management and development processes inside the MoF are not discussed (for this see Horne 1985; Komiya 1990; Kawakita 1991; Pempel and Muramatsu 1993).

Regarding the number of staff employed by the MoF before the 1998 reforms, which would remove its supervisory staff to a new body, it has to be said that it was already relatively small, especially at its central organisation. Table 5.1 presents the numbers for the secretariat of the MoF, its seven bureaus (which existed until 1998) and the other institutions and main bodies of the MoF as of October 1996 (an in-depth overview of MoF's organisation until 1998 is presented in appendix 5.2). The numbers are the combined figures of the various classes of civil servants, which are employed by the Ministry. The figures show that MoF's central policy organisation, i.e. the secretariat and internal bureaus, employed only 1,942 officials, a number that remained fairly stable until 1998 and that was very small given the large number of tasks under the MoF's jurisdiction. For example, when the officials at the Insurance Department are not taken into account, as of October 1996 the Banking Bureau employed only 89 staff members charged with the formulation and implementation of general banking policies, tasks that involved hundreds of banks. (Having said that, the Banking Bureau's staff members were assisted by 132 officials at the Financial Inspection Department of the Minister's Secretariat and by a number of officials at the Securities and Exchange Surveillance Commission and regional organisations (i.e. inspection sections of the financial divisions of local finance bureaus), who all conducted 'on-the-spot' inspections.)[1]

With respect to the presence of *gakubatsu*, the personal networks based on common university backgrounds analysed in chapter 3, the universities of graduation of the career officials who occupy the highest functions in the MoF as of end 1991 are shown in table 5.2. In total 169 functions were investigated, as published by Jihyō Sha in *Ōkurashō Meikan* ('Personnel Directory of the MoF'). The analysis is limited to the so-called 'Big Five' universities discussed in chapter 3: the three

---

[1] According to Ōkura Zaimu Kyōkai (1992), Kinyū Shōken Research (1992) and Ishizaka (1992), the total of MoF officials engaged in bank inspection duties in 1992 was around 220.

Table 5.1. *Number of staff members at the MoF as of October 1996*

Minister's Secretariat (of which 132 in Financial Inspection Department)	**603**
Bureaus	**1,339**
Budget Bureau	341
Tax Bureau	97
Customs and Tariff Bureau	170
Financial Bureau	370
Securities Bureau	87
Banking Bureau (of which 42 in Insurance Department)	132
International Finance Bureau	142
Total Secretariat + Bureaus	*1,942*
Other business areas	**77,787**
Securities and Exchange Surveillance Commission	89
Institute of Fiscal and Monetary Policy	57
Other central business areas	84
Mint Bureau	1,488
Printing Bureau	6,048
Local finance bureaus	4,648
Customs houses	8,060
National Tax Administration Agency	603
Regional taxation bureaus	55,171
Other	1,539
Total	*79,729*

Source: Ōkura Zaimu Kyōkai (1997, pp.455–457).

leading public universities (University of Tokyo, Kyoto University and Hitotsubashi University) and the two major private universities (Keio and Waseda); the other universities are grouped under the heading 'Rest'. For the largest public universities, i.e. the University of Tokyo and Kyoto University, the faculties Economics (E) and Law (L) are mentioned, as well as other faculties (O) in the case of the University of Tokyo. The figures show clearly the dominance of graduates from the University of Tokyo (Tōdai) and from its Law Faculty in particular (see also Hartcher 1998, pp.10ff.). All functions at the highest levels, from the level of director-general and upward, were occupied by law graduates from Tōdai. In total, 104 out of the 169 highest functions investigated (i.e. 62%) were held by graduates from this faculty. Including the graduates from its Economics Faculty and other faculties, 127 former students from the University of Tokyo were employed in the 169 top positions, a score of 75%. Clearly, graduation from this university, and from its Law Faculty in particular, was a prerequisite for reaching the top at the Ministry. The other top public universities, Kyoto and Hitotsubashi, had respectively

Table 5.2. *University background of top-MoF officials (169 highest functions; end-1991)*

	Tokyo E	Tokyo L	Tokyo O	Kyoto E	Kyoto L	Hitotsubashi	Keio	Waseda	Rest
Adm. vice-minister, etc.[1]		6							
Director-general[2]		11							
Deputy director-general	2	12			1				1
Director division/dept.[3]	12	43	1	1	2	1			5
Councillor[4]		4							
Counsellor[4]	1	3			1		1		1
Special officer/assistant	5	13			4	4			2
Rest[5]	2	12		2	3	1		3	9
Total[6]	22	104	1	3	11	6	1	3	18

Notes: [1] Administrative Vice-Minister, Vice Minister of Finance for International Affairs, Deputy Vice-Minister, Deputy Vice-Minister for Policy Co-ordination, Representative at Policy Board of the BoJ and Special Advisor to Minister of Finance.
[2] Also Director-General (DG) Tokyo Customs, DG Mint Bureau, DG Printing Bureau and Commissioner National Tax Administration Agency.
[3] Including Divisions of the Finance Training Institute.
[4] The councillor/counsellor distinction appears to be one of semantics only; both perform similar functions.
[5] Includes directors of various offices and the group of Budget Examiners.
[6] Certain facilities, local finance bureaus, regional taxation bureaus, tax offices and custom houses other than Tokyo are not included.
Source: Jihyō Sha (1991).

14 and 6 graduates in the highest executive positions. Finally, the share of the elite private universities was very small: Keio and Waseda graduates held only a total of 4 positions, concentrated at the lower-ranking levels.

Second, another important informal network involving MoF officials is constituted by the mechanism of *amakudari*, the post-retirement employment of government officials in private business (see section 3.4 of chapter 3). As is shown in table 5.3, the MoF has been by far the most important source for *amakudari* positions of all Japanese ministries, accounting for up to a third of all cases annually during the period 1993–1995. However, as the same table also reveals, the number of post-retirement employment cases in the private sector involving MoF officials that were approved by the National Personnel Authority (NPL) – its role was explained in chapter 3 – dropped sharply from 59 in 1995 to 27 in 1996. This was mainly caused by a sharp reduction in the number of cases applied by the MoF, and not by a more restrictive policy on the side of the NPL. In the wake of a series of scandals involving MoF officials, the MoF adopted in June 1996 a voluntary restriction on the acceptance of *amakudari*

Table 5.3. *Number of enterprise employment cases approved by the National Personnel Authority*

	1993	1994	1995	1996	1997	1998
Total,	208	209	190	136	119	91
Of which at						
Ministry of Finance	66	58	59	27	21	10
National Tax Administration Agency	5	12	6	4	7	10
Ministry of Education, Science and Culture	19	13	9	15	10	7
Ministry of Agriculture, Forestry and Fisheries	11	13	16	7	8	2
Ministry of International Trade and Industry	15	27	17	17	17	10
Ministry of Transport	17	16	11	14	7	6
Ministry of Posts and Telecommunications	18	17	13	5	12	12
Ministry of Construction	21	11	16	13	16	7
Other	36	42	43	34	21	27

Source: National Personnel Authority (1999a, p.31, 1999b).

Table 5.4. *MoF* amakudari *positions as of March 1996*[1]

	Total	At private financial institutions	At special legal entities, etc.	At other organisations and companies
Former high-ranking officials from MoF's central organisation[2]	150	53	21	76
Former directors of local finance bureaus, MoF	294	105	39	150
Total	444	158	60	226

Notes: [1] Shows the situation as of March 1996 including nearly all new *amakudari* appointments of the period 1993–1994.
[2] Level of director-general and above.
Source: Tsutsumi (1996, p.17).

positions by its officials (see also chapter 6). First, MoF officials who were employed in the position of director or above of a division/bureau charged with the supervision of the financial industry would not accept an executive position at a private financial institution for five years after resignation from the MoF. Second, other staff in the position of director or above of a division/bureau at the MoF would not accept an executive position at a private financial institution for two years after resignation. As regards the total number of *amakudari* positions related to the MoF, table 5.4 provides an overview of the positions involving former high-ranking MoF officials as of March 1996. It is shown that around one-third of the retirees from the highest positions in both MoF's central organisation and the local finance bureaus moved to private financial institutions, and that a minority entered the so-called special legal entities (*tokushu hōjin*) that are favourite post-retirement landing spots for Japanese government bureaucrats (see section 3.4 of chapter 3). The *amakudari* positions of MoF – and BoJ – retirees in the banking sector will be investigated in depth in chapters 7 and 8.

Finally, I would like to consider the mechanism of *shukkō* or temporary external assignment of staff members at the MoF during the period before 1998. These transfers of personnel seemed to be institutionalised in general, i.e. were long-term in nature, often involved the same companies and were related to specific divisions of certain bureaus. Thus, the number of positions that could be exchanged was relatively fixed. In general, the presence of *shukkō* at the MoF until the mid-nineties consisted of the temporary transfer of personnel between the MoF and BoJ, between the MoF and other government organisations and from private financial institutions to the MoF.[2] First, reportedly, since the early seventies, some five to six staff members of the BoJ were assigned for periods ranging from two to three years to the Research and Planning Division of the Minister's Secretariat, the Banking Bureau, in particular its Co-ordination and Commercial Banks Divisions, the Tax Bureau and sometimes the International Finance Bureau or Financial Bureau. Most of these BoJ officials were relatively junior, although also some mid-level BoJ staff were involved. For example, at least one BoJ staff member was consistently appointed as Deputy-Director of a Division (*kachō hosa*), which was the most senior position of a BoJ *shukkō-sha* – official in a *shukkō* position – at the MoF. Furthermore, a couple of BoJ officials were employed in the position of section chief. The tasks of the assigned BoJ staff members were in the research field: they were not allowed access to confidential matters. In general, the BoJ officials on *shukkō* assignment were to a large extent regarded as regular MoF staff members; during meetings between the MoF and BoJ, these officials sat on the side of the MoF. Conversely, the MoF always sent one staff member to the BoJ's Credit and Market Management Department, the BoJ department that was the most actively engaged in day-to-day macro monetary policy implementation. This MoF official's main task was to gain experience in the functioning of the money markets and the management of these markets by the BoJ. The mechanism of *shukkō* between the MoF and BoJ traditionally aimed to promote mutual understanding and personal

---

[2] Personal ministerial interviews February–March 1993. Reported numbers are as of the first quarter of 1993 (unless otherwise indicated).

relationships (*jinmyaku*), in particular at the junior level, which could improve future policy co-ordination.

Second, officials from various government financial and non-financial institutions and agencies were assigned temporarily to the MoF. For example, one *shukkō-sha* from the Export–Import Bank of Japan was employed in the Commercial Banks Division, and staff members of the Japan Development Bank worked in the Financial Markets Office and the Institute of Fiscal and Monetary Policy. The reverse process existed as well: the MoF lent staff members at various levels to government organisations such as the Prime Minister's Office, Ministry of Foreign Affairs, Ministry of Internal Affairs, Ministry of Justice, MITI, Economic Planning Agency, in particular to its Secretariat, Defence Agency, Environmental Agency and the Fair Trade Commission (Komiya 1990, pp.386–387; personal interviews with MoF staff, February–April 1993).

Third, a number of staff members from various private financial institutions such as banks and securities and insurance companies were transferred for a period of two to three years to the MoF (this is called *ama-agari* or 'ascent to heaven', the reverse process of *amakudari*; see also Amyx 1998). With respect to the actual presence of 'on-loan' staff from the private sector, the situation was as follows (ministerial interviews, first quarter of 1993). During the first quarter of 1993, about eight or nine of these *shukkō-sha* were positioned in the Research and Planning Division of the Minister's Secretariat; according to Hartcher (1998), p.266, this was still the case in 1995. Furthermore, some three to four private sector economists worked in the Research Division of the Banking Bureau; in total in the Banking Bureau about five. At the International Finance Bureau, the Co-ordination Division employed one private sector economist (in February 1993, one person from the Industrial Bank of Japan). According to one staff member, about 10% of the officials at the Development Policy Division of the International Finance Bureau came from private (and public) institutions. Finally, to a large extent, the research tasks of the Institute of Fiscal and Monetary Policy were carried out by economists from city and trust banks and securities and insurance companies, estimated between 20 and 25 persons in total. Conservative estimates of the total presence of *shukkō-sha* from the private sector at MoF's central organisation were in the range of 40 to 50 (about 2.1–2.6% of the total number of officials). A good overview of the presence of private sector economists in 'on loan' positions at the MoF until 1996 is presented in Tsutsumi (1996). This overview, which is reproduced in table 5.5, shows clearly the systematic pattern of temporary employment of private sector economists at specific (i.e. planning and research oriented) divisions of the International Finance Bureau and

Table 5.5. *Positions of private financial institutions* (ama-agari) *at the MoF during 1988–1996*

Industrial Bank of Japan	June 1991–July 1993, July 1993–March 1995: Co-ordination Division, IFB
Long-Term Credit Bank of Japan	July 1989–July 1991, May 1995– : Research Division, IFB July 1993–July 1995: Development Policy Division, IFB
Nippon Credit Bank	July 1988–June 1990: Development Institutions Division, IFB August 1990–June 1992, April 1996– : Planning and Legal Division, CTB August 1993–March 1994: Research Division, IFB
Dai-Ichi Kangyo Bank	July 1989–August 1991: Development Finance Division, IFB September 1991–October 1993, August 1995– : Development Policy Division, IFB
Bank of Tokyo	August 1988–June 1990, August 1990–June 1992: Development Policy Division, IFB July 1992–June 1994, July 1994–March 1995, April 1996– : Development Institutions Division, IFB
Mitsui Bank (Sakura Bank)	July 1989–September 1991: International Affairs and Research Division, CTB September 1991–June 1993: Research Division, IFB August 1994–March 1995: Planning and Legal Division, CTB
Mitsubishi Bank	August 1988–June 1989: Planning and Legal Division, CTB July 1989–July 1991: Development Institutions Division, IFB October 1991–August 1993: Development Finance Division, IFB August 1994–February 1995: International Affairs and Research Division, CTB
Fuji Bank	August 1988–July 1990: Development Policy Division, IFB May 1990–February 1992: Research and Planning Division, Minister's Secretariat August 1990–July 1992: Development Institutions Division, IFB August 1992–June 1994: Development Finance Division, IFB May 1995– : International Affairs and Research Division, CTB July 1995– : Institute of Fiscal and Monetary Policy
Sumitomo Bank	July 1988–July 1990: CTB August 1990–July 1992, August 1992–June 1994: Development Policy Division, IFB July 1995– : Planning and Legal Division, CTB
Daiwa Bank	August 1992–June 1994: International Affairs and Research Division, CTB June 1995– : Development Finance Division, IFB
Sanwa Bank	August 1989–June 1991: Research Division, IFB July 1991–July 1994: Planning and Legal Division, CTB July 1994–February 1995: Development Policy Division, IFB
Tokai Bank	August 1993–March 1994: International Affairs and Research Division, CTB April 1996 – : Development Finance Division, IFB
Mitsubishi Trust & Banking	April 1995– : Corporation Finance Division, Securities Bureau

Table 5.5. (*cont.*)

Nomura Securities	August 1992–July 1993: Planning and Legal Division, CTB
	July 1994–March 1995: Development Finance Division, IFB
Tokyo Marine &	August 1992–February 1994: Treasury Division, Financial
Fire Insurance	Bureau
	May 1995– : Research Division, IFB
Taisho Marine &	October 1989–July 1991: Planning and Legal Division, CTB
Fire Insurance	August 1991–June 1993: International Affairs and Research
	Division, CTB
Yasuda Marine &	October 1989–July 1991, August 1991–June 1993: Corporation
Fire Insurance	Finance Division, Securities Bureau
Nippon Life	October 1989–July 1992, April 1996– : International Affairs
Insurance	and Research Division, CTB
	August 1993–June 1995: Development Finance Division, IFB
Dai–Ichi Mutual	August 1993–August 1995: Planning and Legal Division, CTB
Life Insurance	April 1996– : Development Policy Division, IFB
Norinchukin Bank	May 1989–September 1991, October 1991–August 1993:
	Research Division, Banking Bureau
	September 1993–July 1995, August 1995– : First Insurance
	Division, Banking Bureau

Notes: CTB = Customs and Tariff Bureau; IFB = International Finance Bureau.
Source: Tsutsumi (1996), pp.48–49.

Customs and Tariff Bureau in particular and the large number of private financial institutions involved.

As further characteristics of the private sector *shukkō-sha* at the MoF (or *ama-agari*), the following can be mentioned. First, the 'mother' institutions of the on-loan officers paid their salaries. Furthermore, they had to operate under the public service laws and regulations that govern the conduct of civil servants, and their loan period was limited (no longer than three years). To prevent conflicts of interest, the private sector's officials conducted activities in the supporting staff fields such as research and planning, and not in operational policymaking and implementation. For the rest, however, these officials operated as regular staff members.[3] Certain divisions and sections of the MoF relied heavily on these on-loan staff members: by law, the number of employees in the MoF is limited, and given the wide range of tasks under its jurisdiction, the MoF has always experienced difficulties in covering these activities with just its original staff. The reasons for the private financial institutions to comply with MoF's need for additional staff were obvious: to obtain better access to information, receive possible other benefits or simply avoid the

---

[3] For example, these on-loan officers carried MoF name-cards without any indication of their private sector affiliations.

repercussions of failing to comply with MoF's demands for additional staff. Practically, of course, the system of *ama-agari* eroded to a significant degree the separation between the public and private spheres. In combination with the use of informal instruments and informal networks constituted by *amakudari*, *gakubatsu* and the MoF-*tan* system, it would be responsible for the many scandals that erupted during the nineties and which resulted in major institutional reform and reorganisation of the MoF, as will be discussed in the next chapter.

Macro monetary policy

With the exception of exchange rate policy, the BoJ has been officially in charge of macro monetary policy, which aims through day-to-day adjustments of the money markets to influence interest rates and consequently to achieve the intermediate and ultimate goals of Japanese macro monetary policy. However, the MoF obtained a number of ways to implement policies that affect macro monetary policy variables in a rather direct fashion as well. These actions, which are traditionally not included in investigations of Japanese macro monetary policy, are a consequence of the broad and vaguely defined powers entrusted to the MoF under its Establishment Law. For example, Paragraphs 4.100 and 4.101 of the 2 May 1991 version of this law (see appendix 5.1) state that the MoF regulates and supervises financial institutions in the use of their funds and adjusts their interest rates. According to various former MoF staff members and private bankers it has not been clear exactly what this authority means and what its range is (personal interviews with former MoF staff members and Japanese private bankers February–May 1993). As a result, the interpretation by MoF's officials constitutes a set of rather vague instruments without clear and explicit legal backing. In other words, this interpretation establishes a set of informal instruments: from a legal perspective, compliance of affected parties with these instruments cannot always be coerced clearly. In the words of a former high-ranking MoF staff member, in MoF's Establishment Law 'many grey zones exist. These grey zones play an important role in the implementation of monetary policy' (personal interview senior MoF staff member, April 1993). In my view, besides exchange rate policy, the macro monetary policies of the MoF are those policies aimed at influencing interest rates and bank lending and consequently the development of the overall macro-economic situation. Following this definition, the MoF's macro monetary policies have consisted traditionally of operations in the bond market and the issuance of *tsūtatsu* (published administrative guidance) and unpublished administrative guidance aimed at influencing bank lending and bank lending rates.

The latter two forms of the MoF's macro monetary policy are clearly informal instruments according to the classification presented in table 3.1 on page 69; the former is a direct consequence of the vaguely defined MoF's Establishment Law.

Regarding MoF's interventions in the bond market, over the years its Financial Bureau conducted several types of transactions in the secondary bond market. First, the Financial Bureau on several occasions bought government bonds from the private sector with the purpose of lowering the rates of new government bond issues (various interviews at private investment banks and with BoJ staff, Tokyo, 1992–1993). These transactions were called 'fund adjustment operations' (*seiri kikin no ope*). Although according to an unofficial MoF mimeograph the National Debt Consolidation Fund's (NDCF) operations should not affect interest rate movements (Ministry of Finance 1993b, p.1), bond market participants saw clear evidence of bond market support operations carried out through this Fund's Special Account (NDCFSA). For example, in February 1990, the MoF conducted the first buying operations since 1987 (of about 100 billion yen per operation) using funds from the NDCFSA under the management of its Government Debt Division, which were interpreted by the markets and media as an expression of the MoF's disagreement with the restrictive monetary policy stance of the BoJ.[4] Second, the Trust Fund Bureau (TFB) of the MoF, which is explained in appendix 5.2, has been investing frequently in the bond markets. These investments have included both *gensaki* (i.e. trades with repurchase agreements) type transactions and outright purchases (since January 1993). The transactions of the TFB, which have been implemented by the BoJ as the MoF's agent, are in the official view conducted primarily to invest the Bureau's surplus funds until they are incorporated into the Fiscal Investment and Loan Programme (FILP) and to recycle surplus postal savings, and not to influence long-term interest rates as such. However, the monthly outright purchases of 100 billion yen of government bonds by the Trust Fund Bureau that started on 18 January 1993 resulted in bringing down bond yields in the short term and were seen as deliberate policy intentions by the MoF as part of the August 1992 and April 1993 policy packages aimed at stimulating the economy.[5]

It has to be said that the consequences of the bond market operations by the MoF did not worry the BoJ too much. First, possible monetary

---

[4] *Financial Times*, 27 February 1990, and reports from various Tokyo-based American and English investment banks.
[5] According to private sector financial analysts and BoJ staff, these purchases had a major initial impact in the bond market and led to a flattening of the yield curve in the short term; the immediate impact was estimated to be a drop of 10–15 basis points.

effects were sterilised by the BoJ immediately and completely through its daily money market operations.[6] Second, from the beginning of these operations, the BoJ regarded their impact on long-term interest rates as temporary and short-lived, and believed that fundamentally the movement of these rates was in line with the BoJ's expectations and policy stance as reflected in the movement of short-term money market rates. The major problem of the MoF's Financial Bureau's operations aimed at influencing bond yields was that these operations often created confusion in the financial markets: at times, market participants became confused about the macro monetary policy intentions of Japan's monetary authorities and consequently altered their interest rate expectations. Given the huge amounts of funds under MoF control, the Financial Bureau could easily and possibly unexpectedly give signals to the financial markets that differed from those of the BoJ. This was clearly the case during the first quarter of 1990. Therefore, the BoJ wanted these operations stopped.[7]

A second form of MoF's macro monetary policies was the issuance of *tsūtatsu* or circulars which aim directly at influencing bank lending behaviour and bank lending rates in order to achieve a specific desired economic development. The *tsūtatsu*, which by MoF staff members' own accounts are regarded as 'interpretations of the law', were in section 3.3 of chapter 3 referred to as published administrative guidance. These circulars were issued as general guidelines by the director-general of a bureau in cases of important issues such as structural changes or shocks or as lower-level business contacts [*jimu renraku*] at the director level when more routine matters were involved. The *tsūtatsu* were related to a wide range of topics, and consequently the MoF issued each year a large number of them: until April 1992, the monthly average of *tsūtatsu* issued was about 200–300. Given the large number of divisions in the MoF and the differences in tasks between them, the issuance rate of *tsūtatsu* per bureau and division differed significantly. For example, the Co-ordination division of the Banking Bureau issued only one or two *tsūtatsu* per year, whereas some Divisions in the Securities Bureau issued many more.

---

[6] Interviews with BoJ staff and bond market analysts, Tokyo, 1993. In the Japanese media, the outright purchases by the TFB that started in January 1990 were interpreted as attempts by the MoF to increase the money supply (see *The Daily Yomiuri*, 20 January, 1993, 'Ministry Buys Bonds to Shore up Money Supply'). Regarding the question of sterilisation of the TFB's operations by the BoJ, I have found only one publication that pays attention to this aspect. According to Ueda (1994), p.96, during the post-World War II period, 'The BoJ and the trust fund bureau supplied funds to private banks in the form of BoJ lendings and the bureau purchases of bank debentures'. Hence, Ueda seems to conclude that the TFB's operations were not sterilised by the BoJ.

[7] This opinion was also given by a former high-ranking MoF official, April 1993, who was clearly in favour of stopping these operations because 'they simply do not understand how financial markets operate' and 'they want to give politicians the impression that they are doing something'.

A significant number of the *tsūtatsu* that were sent out were revisions of existing circulars. The Banking Bureau's *tsūtatsu* were published each year in a voluminous appendix to its Annual Review.

Over the years, various types of *tsūtatsu* existed inside the MoF. First, circulars were issued to offices and organisations inside the MoF. These internal *tsūtatsu* could be interpreted as inside administrative rules that were legally binding. Second, the MoF issued circulars to external organisations and institutions under its jurisdiction: in the case of Japanese financial institutions, the major part of the *tsūtatsu* was sent to their umbrella associations, whereas foreign banks located in Japan often received these circulars individually. According to a number of legal scholars and MoF staff members the external *tsūtatsu* were not legally binding and consequently constituted administrative guidance. The major part of the external *tsūtatsu* consisted of notifications that were forms of structural and prudential policy, such as regulations related to new financial instruments and banking activities, and solvency and other financial ratios. The issuance of these micro monetary policy circulars was related to the various laws that governed different types of financial institutions, such as the Banking Law or the Shinkin Bank Law. The micro monetary policy *tsūtatsu* that were interpretations of specific banking laws and Cabinet and ministerial orders (*meirei*) were amended regularly and remained valid for a significant number of years.

A much smaller proportion of the external circulars issued by the MoF were expressions of specific behaviour that it wanted banks to follow in order to achieve a specific desired macro-economic development. That is to say, these circulars could be defined as being forms of moral suasion related to the implementation of MoF's macro monetary policy. The macro policy *tsūtatsu* were much more situational (ad hoc) and reactive than most micro policy *tsūtatsu*, less clearly related to specific laws and in force during much shorter periods of time (and consequently less often revised). As an example of the macro policy circulars that were issued by the MoF I have translated *tsūtatsu* no. 176 of fiscal year 1993, dated 8 February 1993. A provisional translation is presented in figure 5.1. As is clear from figure 5.1, the *tsūtatsu* was issued after the lowering of the official discount rate by the BoJ on 4 February and aimed at facilitating lending to small and medium-sized businesses by, among other things, urging financial institutions to lower their lending rates. According to the MoF, then, banks were reluctant to extend new loans given their difficulties in meeting the required solvency ratios, which affected small and medium-sized companies in particular. The circular was accompanied by a statement ('Kinyū kikan no yūshi taiō ni tsuite no shoken' or 'A way to cope with the extension of funds by financial institutions'), including measures to improve the solvency ratios and asset structure of banks.

No. 176
8 February 1993
Mr Teramura, Director-General, Banking Bureau
To each president of financial organisations' associations

To obtain smooth finance for small and medium-sized companies

It is to be expected that the recent decline in the official discount rate, together with the monetary and fiscal policies implemented so far, will considerably contribute to sustainable growth of our economy.

In order to do so, it is very important that financial institutions efficiently conduct their functions, and provide enough funds, which are necessary for efficient economic activity. In particular, financial institutions should be careful to provide for smooth finance of small and medium-sized companies.

Your organisation has performed very well in financing small and medium-sized enterprises.

However, taking the recent decline of the official discount rate, please let each member of your organisation provide smooth finance to small and medium-sized enterprises, for example in the form of a decline of your lending interest rates.

Figure 5.1 *Tsūtatsu* 'Financing of small and medium-sized businesses'
Note: Translation '*Chūshō kigyō kinyū no enkatsuka ni tsuite*'.

The legal justification of the *tsūtatsu* shown in figure 5.1 seems to lie in Paragraph 4.101 of the version of the Establishment Law discussed in this chapter, which allowed the MoF to adjust the interest rates of financial institutions. However, various interviewees at the MoF were not sure what the specific legal foundation of this macro policy *tsūtatsu* was.

The macro monetary policy *tsūtatsu* of the Banking Bureau were not issued frequently: an investigation of the issues for the years 1991–1995 of the supplement to the Annual Review of the Banking Bureau, which contained the *tsūtatsu* that were in force, revealed few relating to macro policy. Besides the circular mentioned above, the MoF issued, for example, a macro policy *tsūtatsu* on 8 October 1993 to various government financial institutions, such as the Small Business Finance Corporation (Chūshō Kigyō Kinyū Kōko) and the People's Finance Corporation (Kokumin Kinyū Kōko), which was intended to promote their lending to small and medium-sized businesses as well.[8] Another example of a *tsūtatsu* aimed

[8] This move by the MoF was followed 11 days later by an announcement of the Federation of Bankers Associations of Japan (Zenginkyō) that its member banks would provide financial assistance to small and medium-sized companies (*Bank of Japan Quarterly Bulletin*, February 1994, p.68).

at stimulating bank lending was the circular sent out on 22 January 1991 to *shinkin* banks, credit co-operatives and other credit associations which allowed them to provide more funds to non-members.

According to several interviewees the macro policy *tsūtatsu* were often issued because of political pressure, i.e. for the benefit of the LDP. By doing so the LDP could show in a very clear way (the *tsūtatsu* were published and all newspapers reported them) that something was being done to deal with certain macro economic problems in general and the problems of certain politically influential interest groups, in this case small and medium-sized enterprises, in particular. In this respect, the main benefit of the *tsūtatsu* to accommodate the demands and interests of the LDP's constituency lay in the fact that they did not require approval by the Diet and consequently could be implemented quickly and easily. The perception that the macro monetary *tsūtatsu* were often implemented because of political pressure and not because of MoF's own power would support the view put forward in Ramseyer and McCall Rosenbluth (1993) that the Japanese government bureaucracy – the MoF in particular – is under political control from the LDP. Thus, the strong state model such as is supported by the interventionists (see chapter 3) does not find evidence in the use of macro monetary policy *tsūtatsu* by the MoF in the period until 1998.

As regards compliance with the *tsūtatsu* issued by the MoF, this seemed not to accord so much with strict legal procedures, but more with the presence of the two following aspects. First, for compliance to occur, it was important that banks or banking associations were involved in the formulation of the *tsūtatsu*. The issuance of a *tsūtatsu* involved three stages: (1) formulation of a strategy, (2) choice of the specific form in which this strategy would be implemented and (3) the actual implementation. In the first stage, officials in one of the Banking Bureau's divisions would identify a problem or issue, which would be discussed up to the level of deputy-director and director. As a result of these discussions and consequent negotiations, a strategy would be developed, which would then be solidified in the form of a discussion paper. This paper would be send to other divisions and a process of consensus building would start. Dependent on the issue and its importance, in this stage other parties concerned such as other ministries, banking associations and individual banks would be invited to put their views. In a case of strongly opposing views, the Banking Bureau's officials would, again dependent on the issue, arrange a meeting in order to reach a compromise. The *tsūtatsu* that were formulated in this way were generally accepted by the banking industry. (However, in the case of the *tsūtatsu* shown in figure 5.1, involvement of the banking industry seemed to have been fairly limited and thus its effectiveness was questioned). Second, banks were inclined to comply with MoF's *tsūtatsu* only if they saw a clear relationship between these circulars and the specific legal statutes that governed their activities. In the case of the micro policy *tsūtatsu* related to structural and prudential policy, banks saw this relationship quite clearly. However, a significant number of bankers interviewed did not see a clear relationship between the few macro policy *tsūtatsu* that were issued by the MoF in the early nineties on the one hand and specific legal statutes on the other. This was also true in the case of the *tsūtatsu* in figure 5.1. As a result, bankers interpreted this *tsūtatsu* as a request and not a command, and consequently did not feel strongly inclined to comply: they blamed a lack of credit demand by small and medium-sized businesses as the main reason for sluggish credit growth. Furthermore, against their growing amount of non-performing loans (see chapter 6), the banks were reluctant to increase their lending to the potentially risky group of small and medium-sized businesses.

Finally, the implementation of macro monetary policies by the MoF also consisted of the use of unpublished administrative guidance regarding bank lending, bank lending interest rates and other macro policy goals such as real estate and stock prices, the exchange rate and the overall structure of financial markets. This is the non-transparent part of administrative guidance such as described in section 3.3 of chapter 3 and which is the most notorious. Contrary to the *tsūtatsu*, the unpublished administrative guidance is very specific, often aimed at individual banks, extremely non-transparent and highly confidential. As a result, very little information is available that can be verified independently, in particular regarding guidance on lending and lending rates. In a series of interviews, representatives of several long-term credit banks reported strong and successful opposition from the MoF in a number of cases when they wanted to raise their long-term prime rates or the coupon rates on their debentures (personal interviews, Tokyo, May–June 1993). Several of these cases were also widely covered by the Japanese media. It should be noted that the long-term prime rate that banks charged for long-term lending to their prime borrowers was of great interest to politicians, as in Japan's regulated interest rate structure it was closely linked to several government interest rates. Thus also here, political interests could be associated with at least some of MoF's guidance related to macro policy goals. Interviewees from other private financial institutions provided evidence of ministerial guidance on various issues related to bank lending and bank lending rates. One area of MoF's unpublished administrative guidance that has received considerable attention is the guidance related to its so-called 'price keeping operations' (PKOs), i.e. operations to support stock prices, and its guidance of the real estate market. The MoF has a long tradition of stock market support operations; its operations in the wake of the October 1987 crash were rather successful in preventing the market from collapsing as seriously as it did in other countries (Kunze 1994, p.13). However, MoF's PKOs in the nineties, which were conducted mainly to support the solvency ratios of Japanese banks and as such could also be classified as a form of prudential policy, have been highly criticised as being a waste of public money. The PKO could be typified as non-transparent intervention since, as remarked in Wood (1998), p.223, its 'notable feature is that it does not officially exist'. The PKOs implemented by the MoF included direct investments of large amounts of public funds in the stock market and various kinds of (unpublished) administrative guidance such as arbitrary changes in accounting and other rules and guidance aimed at individual banks and institutional investors to prevent them from selling and to urge them to buy stocks (various interviews, Tokyo, May–June 1993 and April–May 1995; Hartcher 1998, pp.103ff.; Wood 1998, pp.221ff.; Beason and James 1999, pp.172ff.). MoF's unpublished administrative guidance related to support for the real estate market, which aimed at supporting banks by maintaining the collateral value of their loan portfolios, consisted mainly of measures aimed at preventing real estate being sold (Hartcher 1998, p.152). Finally, the MoF used – in addition to *tsūtatsu* – unpublished administrative guidance to shape the structure of the Japanese financial system in accordance with its macro policy goals. During most of the post-war period, the MoF extensively used administrative guidance to control the establishment of branch offices, the issuance of certain securities (both domestically and internationally), the introduction of new financial instruments and services, the development of the primary and secondary capital markets and the separation of various types of financial activities (see section 5.2), mostly to maintain the status quo and the dominant position of banks (i.e. indirect finance) (Federation of Bankers Associations of Japan 1984, 1994; Hall 1993, 1998a; Duck 1996; Calder 1997; Miyajima 1998).[9]

Micro monetary policy: prudential policy

The formulation and implementation of micro monetary policy, whose main elements were described in section 4.2 of chapter 4 as structural and prudential policy, were mainly the tasks of the MoF until 1998 – this regards in particular the latter part of micro monetary policy, as in

[9] As regards unpublished administrative guidance related to the exchange rate, which is beyond the scope of this book, some evidence is reported in Komiya and Suda (1991; for example p.331, note 19) and Angel (1991).

1998 a new supervisory authority was established (FSA). The BoJ has certain responsibilities in particular in the field of prudential policy, but according to the legal framework the MoF was the main responsible actor for bank supervision during this period. I shall not pay much attention to structural policy, which is discussed more extensively in, for example, Suzuki (1987a), and Hall (1993, 1998a). This section will investigate the legal framework and specific instruments of MoF's prudential policy such as they existed until 1998. As will be shown, this policy was implemented through the combination of an explicit legal framework and the use of both published and unpublished administrative guidance.

The legal framework of MoF's prudential policy was constituted by its Establishment Law and in more detail by the Banking Law. In the discussion of the legal framework of the MoF at the beginning of section 5.4, I pointed at various paragraphs of Article 4 of the Establishment Law that set out the supervisory tasks of the MoF. The task of general supervision of depository financial institutions was authorised to the MoF by Paragraph 4.90, their licensing and control by Paragraph 4.92 (see appendix 5.1). As regards the banking industry, this general framework was explained more specifically in the Banking Law of 1927. This law, which was amended in 1981 and consequently implemented in 1982, explained in its Chapter IV the supervisory tasks of the MoF, in particular in Articles 24 and 25. The latter authorised the MoF to conduct 'on-the-spot' inspections (*kensa*) of banks (which, since 1992, became mainly the task of the Financial Inspection Department of the Minister's Secretariat, whereas the Banking Bureau remained in charge of general supervision). The MoF conducted its inspection of a specific bank every two to three years. The city and other major banks were inspected by MoF's officials from the main office in Tokyo, whereas the smaller regional banks and *shinkin* banks were inspected by the inspectors and investigators of the local finance bureaus. The inspections took into account aspects such as net worth ratios, asset quality, management control systems, profitability and liquidity (Hall 1993, p.151). Another article in the Banking Law of interest from the perspective of prudential policy was Article 13, which limited the amount of lending to a single borrower. This amount could not be in excess of the product of the total of the bank's net worth and a percentage that was determined by cabinet order (Friesen 1986, p.33). Despite being more detailed than MoFs Establishment Law, the Banking Law did not specify clearly the scope and content of bank supervision: similar to the former, details were left to the discretion of MoF officials and thereby gave rise to the use of administrative guidance. As stated by MoF officials and a MITI official respectively, this was done on purpose (Ueda 1994, p.91; Namiki 1996, pp.12–13):

Enforcement by law should be the last resort. Therefore, it would be better to persuade (banks) as patiently as possible relying only on administrative guidance, but not on law.

In Japan (...) although financial regulations had a general legal foundation, the rules were defined and enforced by administrative decree, notification, and government guidance because Japanese have traditionally regarded compulsion by law to be a last resort and have preferred less coercive measures such as guidance and persuasion.

The emphasis on administrative guidance in the operation of the MoF's prudential policy has also been mentioned explicitly in a report by the United States General Accounting Office (USGAO 1996, p.37):

MoF prefers to rely on administrative guidance as its primary means of enforcement.

All in all, it can be concluded that to a large extent the implementation of prudential policy by the MoF was conducted in the form of issuance of *tsūtatsu* and unpublished administrative guidance. The MoF's prudential policy in general and its use of administrative guidance in particular was greatly facilitated by the existence of the regulated financial system during most of the post-war period, as described in section 5.2. The functional segmentation of financial institutions, the lack of broad and deep capital markets, the regulation of interest rates and other regulations such as entry control limited competition within and between groups of financial institutions, guaranteed state subsidies – i.e. lower interest rates in the regulated 'dual interest rate structure' – and promoted financial stability. This resulted in a so-called 'convoy system' (*gosō sendan hōshiki*), in which the efficient banks followed the slower pace that had been set for the smaller and inefficient banks (Mabuchi 1993, p.4; see in more detail Milhaupt 1999, pp.29ff.; Katayama 2000). In the 'convoy system', as the amount of individual bank lending and the number of branches were restricted, market shares remained stable and thus the status quo was preserved, particularly among the city banks. In addition, entry control limited the number of banks, in particular city banks, and competition as well. The 'convoy system' created rents in the form of oligopolistic rents within the banking industry and savings of monitoring costs (Aoki et al. 1994, p.30; Spiegel 1999). These rents included rewards for the (main) banks, which performed their delegated monitoring function properly (see section 4.3 of chapter 4), in the form of extra branches directly awarded by the MoF or the branch franchise of problem banks that they had taken over. On the other hand, in this strictly regulated system, penalties could be imposed easily on (main) banks that shirked their responsibilities. The MoF used administrative guidance to distribute the rents between the properly and improperly behaving banks (Horiuchi 1996, p.20). Furthermore, in the 'convoy system', the Japanese monetary authorities implicitly guaranteed that no bank would be allowed to go bankrupt. In the case of severe financial distress of an individual bank, this bank would receive financial assistance from its main banks and/or from the BoJ, or would be merged with another bank if the problems were too large (Ueda 1994, p.97). All in all, it is not surprising that Japan during the post-war period has been typified as a 'bankers' kingdom' (Calder 1993, p.136, 1997).

It is clear why the banks by and large complied with the administrative guidance that was instrumental in maintaining this 'kingdom'. It ensured their safety and stability, limited competition and protected markets and market shares, and consequently gave them substantial rents and a rather easy life. The effectiveness of administrative guidance was further due to the situations of overborrowing and overloan (see section 5.2), which ensured the dependency of banks on funds from the BoJ. Furthermore, if banks were reluctant to comply, the MoF had at its disposal a large array of sanctions. It could use its licensing power in general and branch policy in particular to force compliance. Given the strong regulation of interest rates and the limitations imposed on most banks to issue debt securities, branches and their access to deposits were an important tool for banks to achieve growth (Horiuchi and Shimizu 1998, p.8). For example, the MoF refused to grant permission to Mitsui Bank to open three new branches in 1980 when it surpassed the lending limit to an individual borrower (McCall Rosenbluth 1989, p.129) and Daiwa Bank experienced problems in getting approval to open new branches after its refusal to comply with the separation between bank business and trust business – as mentioned in section 5.3 (Vogel 1996, p.171). Finally, the MoF could use its supervisory inspections and its influence in tax matters and tax inspections as sanctions. As regards the latter, it is important to note that the MoF is closely linked to the National Tax Administration Agency, which is a so-called 'external organisation' to the MoF (see appendix 5.2). As such, this agency is discussed extensively in MoF's Establishment Law; their higher-ranking staff are, almost without exception, from the MoF (see for example the yearly publication *Ōkurashō Meikan* by Jihyō Sha).

The actual implementation of prudential policy during the post-war period through the use of *tsūtatsu*, issued mostly for desired sectoral developments, and unpublished administrative guidance, often for more individual cases, can be described as follows. Regarding the establishment of branches, the MoF issued *tsūtatsu* every two years containing guidelines for the establishment (number and type) of new general business offices and various smaller branches.[10] Furthermore, as part of a wider scheme of desirable standards for prudent bank behaviour, the MoF introduced in December 1974 a *tsūtatsu* imposing restrictions on lending to a single borrower that were later included in the new Banking Law of 1981. The MoF also controlled strictly via the issuance of several *tsūtatsu* the so-called 'ancillary and peripheral' business of banks, such as real estate, leasing, consumer finance, investment consulting, venture capital and credit card business, conducted through affiliated companies (Federation of Bankers Associations of Japan 1984, pp.102–103, 1994). An important development in prudential supervision was the introduction in the 1970s of the so-called 'efficiency-oriented' guidance (*kōritsuka gyōsei*), which contained specific targets ('soundness standards') for bank performance (Teranishi 1997; Hanazaki and Horiuchi 1998, p.38). This guidance was explained in detail in *tsūtatsu* no. 901 ('Futsū ginkō no gyōmu un-ei ni kan suru kihon jikō tō' or 'Standard items related to the management of the operation of commercial banks'), abbreviated as the 'Kihon Jikō *tsūtatsu*'. I discuss here the version as of 30 April 1992, which is an amended version of the *tsūtatsu* originally issued on 1 April 1982 (see for example Kinyū Zaisei Jijō Kenkyū Kai 1993, pp.177–204). This *tsūtatsu* listed several explicit targets for various ratios related to the financial position of commercial banks, which can be described as follows.[11] First, internationally operating Japanese banks had to meet the (BIS) solvency requirement of 8%, whereas domestically active banks had to observe a minimum solvency ratio of 4%. It has to be said that the MoF had already introduced capital adequacy guidance in 1954, which stated that broadly defined capital should be higher than 10% of total deposits; smaller banks, in particular *sogo* and *shinkin* banks, were exempted from this guidance (Hanazaki and Horiuchi 1998, p.19). This guidance was later replaced by firstly MoF guidance that required broad capital to be at least 4% of total assets in 1986 and secondly by the BIS solvency requirements introduced in 1987 (Horiuchi 1996). Second, the ratio of current assets to total deposits had to be at least 30%. Third, the ratio of fixed assets for business use to net worth should not exceed 40%. Fourth, to stimulate the formation of reserves, the maximum dividend payout ratio, defined as dividend payments divided by current profits, was set at 40%. Finally,

[10] This regulation was liberalised totally in May 1995, two years after liberalising the branch regulation of regional and *shinkin* banks (see chapter 6).
[11] The Federation of Bankers Associations of Japan published these ratios each year in its annual publication *Zenkoku Ginkō Zaimu Shō Hyō Bunseki* (Analysis of Financial Statements of all Banks, 31 March). An appendix (containing the current *tsūtatsu*) to the Annual Review of the Banking Bureau included a summary of these so-called 'guidance criteria' (*shidō kijun*) for commercial and *shinkin* banks and labour credit associations.

the maximum amount of bank lending, defined as loans and bills discounted, to a single borrower as a percentage of own capital was 20% for commercial banks, 30% for long-term credit and trust banks, and 40% for foreign exchange banks. Furthermore, maximum total credit exposure as percentage of own capital was set at 30% for commercial banks, 38% for long-term credit and trust banks and 45% for the Bank of Tokyo as a specialised foreign exchange bank. According to various staff members of the MoF interviewed during the years 1993 to 1996, compliance with these financial ratios was voluntary, that is banks that did not comply were not penalised. Of course, this is in line with the official interpretation of administrative guidance that compliance cannot be coerced (see chapter 3). In contrast with this view, several bankers gave examples of penalties that were imposed by the MoF in case of non-compliance, for example related to MoF's branch policy (personal interviews, Tokyo 1993–1995). However, in the view of many observers, and given the major banking crisis of the nineties, the general effectiveness of these guidelines is doubtful. Or, as has been concluded by Horiuchi (1996), p.18: 'Bankers did not consider that these official guidelines were to be met at any cost, and the MoF was generous enough to permit some divergence between required and actual figures attained by individual banks.' Furthermore, in addition to the guidelines mentioned above, MoF's prudential policy dealt with lending to risky sectors. In response to the growing exposure of banks to the real-estate industry during the 'bubble' years (see chapter 6), the MoF used, from 1986 on, unpublished administrative guidance to urge banks and life insurance companies to refrain from extensive lending to the real-estate, construction and non-bank financial industries. This non-transparent guidance, which according to reports from the BoJ was not very successful, was changed in published administrative guidance in the form of tsūtatsu no. 555 of 27 March 1990 ('Tochi kanren yūshi no yokosei ni tsuite' or 'On restraining real estate related finance') (see also Milhaupt and Miller 1997, p.39). Under this tsūtatsu, which was issued to various banking associations, the growth of real estate related loans by individual banks was required not to exceed the growth of their total lending portfolio. This restriction was imposed for 21 months until the end of December 1991 (Mera 1998, pp.183–184). Furthermore, financial institutions had to report their loans to three classes of businesses: real estate businesses, construction companies and non-bank financial institutions. According to various interviewees, because of important – most likely politically instigated – loopholes, this tsūtatsu was not very effective. For example, loans from agricultural co-operatives to the real estate sector and real estate loans by mortgage companies (jūsen) were not covered. In addition, foreign currency loans to Japanese residents by

authorised foreign exchange banks (so-called 'impact loans') were not
included. Another form of administrative guidance by the MoF as an
instrument of prudential policy was the flexible use of accounting rules
to assist the banking industry, in particular during the early and mid-
nineties (Shimizu 1994, p.326). These rules were originally issued in a
tsūtatsu in 1967 and have been amended several times since; a new *tsūtatsu*
on bank accounting rules was issued in 1982 (Federation of Bankers
Associations of Japan 1984, p.106, 1994, p.42). Furthermore, the MoF
used administrative guidance to orchestrate the rescue of troubled financial institutions. Under this guidance, large banks that functioned
as the main bank of smaller banks often had to provide financial assistance or even to take the problem bank over. The latter was facilitated
by a revision of the Deposit Insurance Law in 1986, which enhanced
the powers of the MoF to facilitate mergers involving troubled banks
(Hall 1993, p.145). Even if the problem bank had not applied for assistance, the amended law authorised the MoF under so-called 'emergency
merger' provisions to start merger proceedings. The bank that took over
the 'failing' bank could receive financial assistance in the form of money
grants, loans or other arrangements from the Deposit Insurance Corporation (DIC) to facilitate the 'merger', i.e. takeover (Ohara 1995, p.16).
To finance this assistance, the DIC could borrow up to a maximum of 500
billion yen from the BoJ and borrow from financial institutions to repay
the BoJ funds. Finally, MoF's prudential policy included the sending of
its staff to troubled financial institutions as instruments of 'micro, on-the-
spot' administrative guidance, either on a temporary (*shukkō*) or permanent (*amakudari*) basis. *Amakudari* appointments have been typified by
Katayama (2000, p.282) as 'an informal means of banking regulation'.
Quite often, the *amakudari* appointments received considerable attention in the media and seemed to have been used by the MoF as a signal
to restore confidence among deposit- and other stakeholders (signalling
function).

In addition to its inspections and administrative guidance, MoF's prudential policy included measures to establish new institutions that assisted
in solving the bad debts of banks and initiatives to increase bank capital.
These and other policies of the MoF aimed at solving the banking crisis
that started to emerge at the beginning of the nineties, and which were
related to the process of financial reform, will be discussed in chapter 6.

5.5   The Bank of Japan (BoJ)

This section will consider the institutional framework and informal aspects of the macro monetary and prudential policies of the BoJ for the

post-war period until 1998. Successively, its legal framework, personnel, macro monetary policy and prudential policy will be discussed. The focus will be on the analysis of the informal aspects that were investigated in chapter 3. This analysis is not possible for all aspects: for example, *tsūtatsu*, which were of considerable importance for the MoF, have not been issued by the BoJ.

Legal framework

The BoJ was founded with the enactment of the Bank of Japan Act (Nihon Ginkō Jōrei) and started its operations on 10 October 1882 (Shinjo 1962, p.65; Muto and Shirakawa 1993, p.5). Its statutes were modelled on those of the National Bank of Belgium, which was the most recent established central bank at that time; practically, however, the BoJ developed into a very different institution (Goodhart 1988, pp.150–160). From the start, the MoF was heavily involved in the creation of the BoJ. For example, the basic ideas behind the organisation and tasks of the BoJ and the Bank of Japan Act were put forward by Masayoshi Matsukata, who was Administrative Vice-Minister at the MoF. Furthermore, the MoF closely supervised the BoJ: the first Governor and Deputy-Governor of the BoJ were both selected from officials of the MoF. In February 1942 the BoJ was reorganised under the Bank of Japan Law (Nihon Ginkō Hō), which remained in force until 1998. The BoJ Law, which was based on the German 1939 Reichsbank Act – the law that governed the central bank of the Nazi regime – further strengthened the already dominant role of the government and defined the role of the BoJ as an instrument of militarist control (Tsutsui 1988, p.15). The main reason for the introduction of the BoJ Law was to establish an efficient financial system to finance the war effort, and the BoJ's priority shifted from providing funds to the banking industry to the financing of the industrial sector, in particular for the production of military goods (Seisaku Jihō Shuppansha 1991, pp.34–36). The influence of the war period was represented by the nationalistic tone of Article 2, which stated that the 'Bank of Japan shall be managed solely for achievement of national aims' (EHS Law Bulletin Series 1991, p.AA1). Also Article 1, which defined the main tasks of the BoJ, reflected the thinking of that time:

The Bank of Japan has, for its object, the regulation of the currency, the control and facilitation of credit and finance, and the maintenance and fostering of the credit system, pursuant to the national policy, in order that the general economic activities of the nation might adequately be enhanced. (EHS Law Bulletin Series 1991, p.AA1)

Furthermore, the influence of the war on the BoJ Law was also clearly present in various articles that showed the strong influence of the government. First, according to this law, the Governor and Deputy-Governor were appointed by the cabinet; the executive directors, executive auditors and counsellors by the Minister of Finance (Article 16); the Minister of Finance also appointed the Deputy-Governor for International Relations, a function that was not explicitly mentioned in the BoJ Law.[12] Second, the BoJ could make advances to the government without taking any collateral, and could subscribe to or take up government loan issues (Article 22). Third, the BoJ needed approval from the Minister of Finance for conducting business other than that prescribed in the BoJ law (Article 27). For example, the MoF had to approve the participation of the BoJ in BIS-orchestrated credit programmes to debt-problem countries such as Mexico and Brazil (personal interview with former high-ranking BoJ staff member, January 1993). Fourth, the Minister of Finance determined the maximum limit for the issuance of banknotes by the BoJ and the penalty in case of issuance above this ceiling (Articles 30 and 31–2); this article corresponded with Paragraph 4.98 of the Ministry of Finance Establishment Law. The fact that the government could determine the maximum value of banknotes issued was based on a special law of March 1941, which was introduced to allow the smooth financing of the war (Seisaku Jihō Shuppansha 1991, p.34). Fifth, the Minister of Finance had to approve the budget of the BoJ (Articles 37 and 38). Sixth, according to Article 42, the Minister of Finance supervised the BoJ (corresponded with Paragraph 4.88 of MoF's Establishment Law). Seventh, the Minister of Finance could order the BoJ to undertake any necessary business (Article 43). Eighth, the Minister of Finance could without prior notification inspect the BoJ's affairs and books, issue orders or take such actions that were deemed necessary in the exercise of his supervision, and appoint the Comptroller of the BoJ, who could inspect at any time the activities of the BoJ (Articles 44–46). Finally, the cabinet could dismiss the Governor and Deputy-Governor, whereas the Minister of Finance could dismiss the executive directors, executive auditors and counsellors (Article 47).

Under the American occupation (SCAP, see section 5.2), attempts were made to decrease the degree of governmental influence on the BoJ. The BoJ Law was amended in 1949, when the so-called Policy Board was established as the highest decision-making body of the BoJ. SCAP hoped that the establishment of the Policy Board would increase the monetary

---

[12] Nakao and Horii (1991), p.42, state that the Minister of Finance appointed the Deputy-Governor for International Relations and executive directors from those recommended by the Governor.

control powers of the BoJ and establish democratic principles in the determination of monetary policy – however, without much success (Tsutsui
1988, pp.86–87). Further attempts to strengthen the legal independence
of the BoJ from the government were initiated in the late 1950s. Around
that time, two plans were drafted which specified the independence of
the BoJ and which would require revisions of the BoJ Law. However,
these plans were ultimately not adopted (Langdon 1963; Suzuki 1987a,
pp.314–315, 1994, pp.86–89; Cargill 1989, p.30). Thus, during the post-
war period, the MoF was to a large extent in control of the BoJ.

The BoJ Law stipulated as the functions of the BoJ the issuance of banknotes, the conduct of transactions exclusively with commercial financial
institutions, to be the intermediate bank between the government and
the private sector and the operation of monetary policy. The BoJ Law
also determined the structure of the BoJ: the BoJ was organised as a special government corporation, with the government holding 55% of the
outstanding shares; the remaining share was in private hands.

Comparison of the pre-1998 BoJ Law with the MoF's Establishment
Law shows that the former was stated in much clearer terms regarding
issues such as authority and jurisdiction than the latter. The BoJ Law
described rather than detailed the tasks of the BoJ: for example, the responsibilities of the Policy Board and the business of the BoJ were one
by one set out in separate paragraphs. Also the instruments that the BoJ
could use were much more explicitly described in the BoJ Law than was
the case with the instruments of the MoF in that body's Establishment
Law. This difference in clarity could be explained by the fact that the BoJ
did not have at its disposal the *tsūtatsu* that the MoF used to explain its
policy intentions in more detail to the private financial sector. It could also
be the case that, given MoF's legal control of the BoJ, the latter wanted
the tasks and responsibilities of the former to be defined in a clear way.

Personnel: informal networks

In this section the post-war personnel organisation of the BoJ will be
discussed, as earlier for the MoF. Particular attention will be paid to the
university background of the officials in the highest executive positions,
the presence of the mechanism of *shukkō* and the presence of retired MoF
staff members (*amakudari*) in the BoJ's organisation. I shall not discuss
here the *amakudari* positions of former BoJ officials for two reasons. First,
since the BoJ is formally not a government organisation, the National
Personnel Authority did not have to check the BoJ's *amakudari* policy and
consequently no information on the BoJ *amakudari* positions in the total

private sector is available through this source. Second, the information that is available – via private sources – regards the positions in the private banking sector, and this information will be presented in chapter 7. The BoJ employed in total around 6,000 persons, of which about 3,000 were at the head office, with the rest employed by the BoJ's branches, offices and representative offices.

The university background of the 248 highest executives of the BoJ, as reported by Seisaku Jihō Shuppansha as of the end of 1991, is presented in table 5.6. Similar to the situation at the MoF, the top-level positions were filled by graduates from the University of Tokyo's Law Faculty: the Governor, the Senior Deputy-Governor, the Deputy-Governor for International Relations, the executive directors and the five executive auditors all graduated from this faculty. Only the Director of the Governor's Office graduated from another faculty and university, the Economics Faculty of Hitotsubashi University. However, taking all 248 top executives into account, the presence of Tokyo University graduates in general and Tokyo Law graduates in particular was less dominant than at the MoF, particularly with respect to the lower-ranking functions: only 34% of all BoJ's top officials were from Tokyo University, and only 21% from its Law Faculty, whereas the figures for the 169 highest MoF officials were 75% and 62%, respectively. Given that differences in the type of functions and in the total number of executives (248 for the BoJ and 168 for the MoF) could blur the picture, comparison of equivalent lower-ranking functions is more clarifying. For example, looking at the comparable function of director of a division, 45% of the BoJ's 51 'directors of division' graduated from the University of Tokyo, and 26% from its Law Faculty; however, of the MoF's 65 'directors of division', 86% graduated from Tokyo University and 66% from its Law Faculty.[13] Among the BoJ's highest executives, graduates from Kyoto University, Hitotsubashi University and the private Keio University were relatively well represented. For example, economics' graduates from Kyoto University filled four out of 14 'director of department' positions (including the Institute for Monetary and Economic Studies). Graduates from Hitotsubashi University were present in relatively large numbers in the functions of general manager of a branch or office.

The mechanism of *shukkō* – the temporary external assignment of staff members between the MoF and the BoJ – has been discussed already in section 5.4. Furthermore, one *shukkō-sha* from the MoF always worked

---

[13] The figures of the MoF include directors of departments (the departments of the BoJ are comparable with the bureaus of the MoF).

Table 5.6. *University background of top-BoJ officials (248 highest functions; end - 1991)*[1]

	Tokyo E	Tokyo L	Tokyo O	Kyoto E	Kyoto L	Hitotsubashi	Keio	Waseda	Rest
Governor, etc.[2]		3							
Executive director, etc.[3]		11				1			
Director of department, etc.[4]	2	5		4					3
General manager of branches and offices	4	8		3	2	10	5	3	9
Deputy director department, deputy general manager	4	1	1	3	1	3	2	1	16
Director of division (chief manager)	10	13		3	2	5	7	3	8
Bank supervisor[5]	3	4				4	3	2	23
Rest[6]	4	8	4	3	3	1	3		14
Total	27	53	5	16	8	24	20	9	73

Notes: [1] Of the 248 highest executive positions, 13 staff members did not graduate from a university (in particular deputy general managers and directors of divisions at branches and offices).
[2] Governor, Senior Deputy-Governor and Deputy Governor for International Relations.
[3] Executive Director, Executive Auditor and Director Governor's Office.
[4] Including Director, Institute for Monetary and Economic Studies.
[5] Bank supervisors at Bank Supervision Department and branches.
[6] Including advisers, councillors, overseas representatives, directors of divisions at large branches such as Kyoto.
Source: Seisaku Jihō Shuppansha 1991.

in the Credit and Market Management Department of the BoJ. In the case of BoJ staff, temporary assignment to the MoF seems to have been an important prerequisite for becoming a senior executive in the BoJ's important Policy Planning Department. As of November 1991, both the Department's deputy-director and the director of the crucial Planning Division had been previously sent for two years and two and a half years, respectively, to the MoF's Banking Bureau; the director of this Department's Co-ordination Division had been assigned for around two years to MoF's International Finance Bureau (Seisaku Jihō Shuppansha 1991, pp.97–98). Given the importance of the MoF as regards exchange rate policy, for example, the experience that these senior officials obtained at the MoF must have facilitated policy co-ordination and communication. Besides sending officials to the MoF, the BoJ temporarily assigned staff to other government institutions, such as the Research Department of the Economic Planning Agency, the Ministry of Foreign Affairs and the Export–Import Bank of Japan, and to some private banks. The latter *shukkō-sha* kept the BoJ informed about the latest financial innovations and developments in the private banking industry. On the receiving end, the BoJ accepted *shukkō-sha* from government organisations other than the MoF and from private banks. For example, as of December 1992 one staff member from the Ministry of Posts and Telecommunications was assigned to the Market Operations Division of the Credit and Market Management Department, and a *shukkō-sha* from MITI worked at the Capital Markets Division. At the same time, staff members from private banks, in particular city banks, worked at the International Department and the Research and Statistics Department; to avoid possible conflicts of interest, they were not employed in operational positions but in research-type functions (various interviews with senior BoJ staff, December 1992–April 1993). In general, *shukkō-sha* were not that important as additional labour force for the BoJ as they were for the MoF. This is because, compared with the MoF, the BoJ's task burden was lighter, and neither was it legally constrained in hiring new staff, as was the MoF.

Finally, the MoF secured a number of positions for its retired staff members (*amakudari* positions) at the BoJ. First, since the early seventies, the positions of Governor and Senior Deputy-Governor were filled alternately by a BoJ and a former MoF top executive. A BoJ staff member promoted to Governor would previously have been Senior Deputy-Governor; a former MoF official similarly promoted would be a former Administrative Vice-Minister. For example, the last Governor appointed in the post-war period until 1998 (as of December 1994) was Yasuo Matsushita, a former Administrative Vice-Minister of the MoF. The Senior Deputy-Governor who was appointed at that time, Toshihiko Fukui, came from the BoJ's own ranks. But for the scandals of 1998 (see chapter 6), Mr Fukui would certainly have become the next Governor. One retired MoF official occupied one of the BoJ's executive director positions; another retired MoF official was employed as Executive Auditor. And so on. During the pre-1998 period this pattern was very consistent and consequently the MoF exercised substantial influence on the BoJ's day-to-day business.

Macro monetary policy

Predominantly, macro monetary policy implemented in Japan during the post-war period consisted of the macro monetary policy implemented by the BoJ. As discussed in section 5.4, the MoF had certain, mostly informal, instruments at its disposal to affect macro variables as well, but the BoJ was by far the most important actor in this respect. In this section I shall address certain informal instruments that the BoJ used to implement its macro monetary policy. I shall not discuss the post-war operational framework of the BoJ's macro monetary policy, which includes its instruments, indicators, targets and goals (see chapter 4), or the transmission mechanism, and the role of Japanese monetary policy in the deflationary spiral of the nineties. These aspects have been documented extensively elsewhere (Suzuki 1980, 1985, 1986, 1987a, 1989b; Shimamoto 1982; Dotsey 1986; Feldman 1986; Fukui 1986; Hutchison 1988; Cargill and Royama 1988; Suzuki et al. 1988; Batten et al. 1989; Royama 1989; Okabe 1990, 1995; Osugi 1990; Nakao and Horii 1991; Tamura 1991; Bank of Japan 1992; de Brouwer 1992; Eijffinger and van Rixtel 1992; Okina 1993, 1999; Ueda 1993a, 1993b; Yoshikawa 1995; Kasa and Popper 1997; van Rixtel 1997; Morsink and Bayoumi 1999; Bernanke 2000; Mori et al. 2000; Okina et al. 2000).

As regards the use of informal instruments by the BoJ in the operation of its macro monetary policy during the post-war period, it used the following. First, prior to 1978, the BoJ used an informal mechanism, the so-called 'quotation system' (*tatene*), and other forms of administrative guidance to regulate interbank interest rates. These rates were fixed after close consultation between the BoJ and the *tanshi* institutions – money market dealers – and changed only once or twice a month (Dotsey 1986, p.17). The BoJ did have a great influence on the *tanshi*, so that the interbank interest rates could be fixed according to its policy objectives. In June 1978 this informal 'quotation system' was abolished and replaced by a new system (*kehaichi*) in which officially the role of the BoJ was reduced – however in practice it maintained its guidance (Ueda 1993a, p.18). Only after the major reforms of the money markets in November 1998 did this guidance gradually decrease (Kasa and Popper 1997). Second, another additional and informal instrument was used to control the lending by private banks. This instrument, the so-called 'window guidance' (*madoguchi shidō*), was a kind of moral suasion and consisted of quantitative restrictions on bank lending. It has been defined as 'guidance to the financial institutions to keep the increase in their lending to clients within limits that the Bank of Japan feels to be appropriate' (Suzuki 1987a, p.325). As a result of the process of financial reform in general and the development of cross-border yen lending to the Japanese non-bank sector in particular, the effectiveness of this instrument was diluted (Osugi 1990, p.66–67). Consequently, it was officially abolished in June 1991 but some form of 'monitoring' of bank loans has been employed since then (personal interviews former BoJ staff members, 1994–1995). During the creation of the 'bubble' in the second half of the eighties, the BoJ strengthened its 'window guidance':

Until the first quarter of 1987 the BoJ simply monitored the lending policy of commercial banks, but from the second quarter switched to moderate moral suasion urging commercial banks to maintain a 'prudent lending attitude' and gradually strengthened the extent of moral suasion thereafter (Okina et al. 2000, pp.16–17).

Third, the amount of BoJ funds extended to individual banks on a daily basis was completely at the discretion of the BoJ and consequently constituted an important instrument of administrative guidance. This was particularly so given the situations of overloan and the permanent imbalance of liquidity between financial institutions. In chapter 7 I present examples of the discretionary use by the BoJ of its 'discount window' in relation to *amakudari* positions of former BoJ staff at private banks.

More recently, during the first half of the nineties, the BoJ still used certain informal modes of intervention as part of its operational framework, which can be typified as unpublished administrative guidance.[14] First, the BoJ operations in financing bills (*seifu tanki shōken*) or FBs (sales) and its *gensaki* operations (purchases of government bonds with repurchase agreement) were compulsory: for each group of banks, the BoJ decided what share they had to take in the total operation and the rates that applied to the operation. In particular with respect to the FBs operations, a compulsory allocation mechanism was used, based on the market shares of individual banks. Since FBs were not attractive to hold, as their rates were below the level of the official discount rate and therefore the BoJ subscribed almost all FBs issued, administrative guidance from both MoF and the BoJ was used to persuade banks to accept these instruments in the BoJ's selling operations. The guidance of the MoF was also related to the fact that the FBs could be recalled before maturity, and therefore for convenience's sake the MoF wanted to keep the FBs concentrated within the banking industry. Second, regarding the treasury bill (*tanki kokusai*) or TB operations of the BoJ (purchases on the secondary market with repurchase), only a limited number of financial institutions were allowed by the BoJ to participate in the repurchases. For example, foreign banks were excluded. Third, despite the official abolishment of 'window guidance' in June 1991, the BoJ continued to 'advise' through its Relationship Management sections in the Credit and Market Management Department on the development of total lending and lending to specific sectors such as real estate, construction and non-bank financial institutions by individual banks. Furthermore, after the ending of 'window guidance', the BoJ's regional branches and offices became more active in giving guidance to the lending activities of regional banks.

[14] Evidence based on a large number of personal interviews with staff members of *tanshi* companies and money-market dealers of private banks located in Tokyo, 1993–1995.

Finally, the BoJ conducted frequent meetings with individual banks, in which it could express its 'wishes' and policy goals.

Micro monetary policy: prudential policy

In addition to the MoF's prudential policy, the BoJ supervised the banking industry as well. According to Article 1 of the 1942 Bank of Japan Law, the prudential policy of the BoJ aimed to maintain a safe and sound financial system. This responsibility was concretised by its provision of payment services, its monitoring and supervision of private financial institutions and its role as lender of last resort. The supervision of the payment system and prudential behaviour of private financial institutions was the responsibility of the Financial and Payment System Department. The monitoring of daily activities of private financial institutions was conducted by the Bank Relations and Capital Markets Divisions of the Credit and Market Management Department, while the on-the-spot examination (*kōsa*) of major banks was the responsibility of the Bank Supervision Department. The examination of local banks, i.e. regional, Second Tier regional and *shinkin* banks, was carried out by the BoJ's branches and offices. For example, the 12 or 13 *shinkin* banks located in Kyoto were examined by the BoJ's Kyoto branch. In particular the larger branches – Sapporo, Sendai, Kyoto, Osaka, Nagoya, Kobe, Hiroshima and Shizuoka – conducted examination tasks, sometimes assisted by bank supervisors who were attached to these offices or by senior managers transferred from the BoJ's Tokyo head office.

Contrary to the MoF, the BoJ's authority to examine banks was not based on legal statutes such as the Banking Law, but was a consequence of the contract banks signed with the BoJ as they opened an account. The 1942 version of the Bank of Japan Law stated that the BoJ's Policy Board was responsible for 'matters of policy pertaining to ... examination of financial institutions as are entrusted to the Policy Board by virtue of other laws and/or contractual relationships', implying that the Bank of Japan Law by itself did not constitute the legal basis to conduct the supervision of the banking system (EHS Law Bulletin Series 1991, p.AA4). In fact, the 1942 law did not mention bank supervision and the on-site examination of private banks at all among the functions of the BoJ. Consequently, the examination of the BoJ had more the character of giving advice regarding matters such as portfolio allocation and loan positions, whereas the MoF's inspection was focused more on, among other things, checking whether banks were obeying the law. However, in practice it is said that the differences between the BoJ's *kōsa* and the MoF's *kensa* were a matter of nuance. This dual monitoring system, including both the MoF and BoJ as de-facto supervisors, was established after the financial crisis of the 1920s, when the BoJ was granted the right to supervise banks under the idea that 'four eyes see more than only two' (interview with a former high-ranking staff member of the BoJ's Bank Supervision Department, March 1993). Contrary to the inspection by the MoF, the BoJ's examinations had to be announced beforehand. The on-the-spot investigations of individual major banks were conducted by the BoJ and the MoF alternately every 2–3 years, so large banks were inspected on a regular basis every year or so. Of course, if the BoJ suspected that a specific bank was suffering from certain problems, it would depart from this regular scheme. These examinations had to be announced in advance as well. In its examinations the BoJ used a standard guide as a checklist; according to various interviewees at private banks, the BoJ's examinations were much more rigorous than the MoF's inspections.

In addition to its examination of private banks, the BoJ prepared a framework for supervising market risk control. The Institute for Monetary and Economic Studies started to develop expertise in a market specialist's team in 1994. This shows the extent to which the BoJ was able to take over the lead from the MoF whenever technical expertise was required: the MoF merely decided to draw up a list of recognised auditing firms and stated that the banks that were to use 'the internal models' approach to market risk measurement should have their market risk systems audited by these firms and forward the reports to the MoF.

In line with the MoF's prudential policy (see section 5.4), the BoJ started to pay more attention at the end of the eighties to the development of bank lending to the real estate, construction and non-bank financial sectors. Basically, the BoJ tried to limit the growth of this lending by tightening its own lending to the banking industry, and used unpublished administrative guidance to persuade banks to improve their risk-control systems. Furthermore, the BoJ had to fulfil its role of lender of last resort more and more often: most of the rescue packages for troubled banks, which will be discussed in the next chapter, involved extra funds and other financial assistance from the BoJ. Finally, the BoJ sent staff members under the mechanisms of *shukkō* and/or *amakudari* to troubled financial institutions. For example, during the first quarter of 1995, the BoJ sent at least one official on a *shukkō* basis to the troubled Tokyo Kyowa Credit Association.

5.6   Conclusions

In this chapter, I have examined the institutional framework of the Japanese financial system in general and the legal framework, personnel networks, macro and micro monetary policies of the Ministry of Finance and the Bank of Japan in particular during the post-war period until 1998.

Where possible, evidence was presented on informal aspects of the MoF's and BoJ's policies. The major conclusions of this analysis can be summarised as follows. First, the legal framework of the MoF, in particular its Establishment Law, was stated in relatively vague terms, certainly when compared with the BoJ Law. This left MoF staff with substantial discretion to interpret the law and to use published (*tsūtatsu*) and unpublished administrative guidance. Taking into account the relatively small number of officials in the MoF's central organisation and the large number of tasks under their responsibility, individual staff members had relatively great influence on specific policy issues. Second, as regards the macro monetary policy operations of the MoF, the findings in this chapter suggest that the effectiveness of at least some of these policies has to be doubted. For example, MoF's operations in the bond market only led to confusion in the financial markets. Furthermore, the *tsūtatsu* that were related to the implementation of macro monetary policy often seem to have been issued because of political pressure from the leading LDP. In addition, the involvement of the banking industry in the formulation of these *tsūtatsu* was mostly limited and consequently their effectiveness was apparently not that great. Third, the highest executive positions at the MoF and the BoJ were filled by graduates from a very small number of universities and faculties in general and from the University of Tokyo and its Law Faculty in particular. This finding gives evidence to investigate further the importance of the informal networks constituted by university cliques or *gakubatsu*. This will be done in chapter 8. Fourth, the MoF and BoJ established informal networks between themselves and with the private financial sector and other government institutions through the mechanism of *shukkō*, the temporary external assignment of staff members. At the MoF, relatively large numbers of *shukkō-sha*, also referred to as *ama-agari*, from the private sector worked in research-type functions. At the BoJ, most of the executives at the Policy Planning Department were previously assigned on a temporary basis to the MoF. Finally, regarding the implementation of prudential policy, the MoF and BoJ used the mechanisms of *shukkō* and *amakudari* to dispatch staff to troubled financial institutions.

As for the rest of this study, I shall focus in chapters 7 and 8 on the use of *amakudari* by the MoF and BoJ in the operation of their prudential policies and its impact on bank performance in Japan. This choice is made because of the limited number of *tsūtatsu* available that are issued for macro monetary policy purposes, the secrecy surrounding unpublished administrative guidance and the lack of data on *shukkō* from the MoF and BoJ to private banks, which make it extremely difficult or simply impossible to investigate these issues empirically. On the other hand, through private sector sources, data on *amakudari* positions are available and therefore can be used for empirical analysis. Before doing so, I shall in the next chapter analyse the Japanese banking crisis and the related process of financial reform, which had major implications for the informal mode of policy implementation by the Japanese monetary authorities. I shall present evidence that the use of informal instruments such as unpublished administrative guidance and circulars (*tsūtatsu*) and the existence of close and intimate informal networks between the monetary authorities in general and the MoF in particular on the one hand and the banking sector on the other, in the form of *amakudari*, *gakubatsu*, *shukkō* (*amaagari*) and the MoF-*tan* system, played a major role both in the outbreak and development of the banking problems and in their prolonged nature.

Appendix 5.1 The Ministry of Finance Establishment Law (Ōkurashō Setchi Hō)[15]

Translated from Ōkura Zaimu Kyōkai, *Ōkurashō no Kikō 1992 Nempō* (Finance Association, Ministry of Finance, The Organisation of the Ministry of Finance in 1992), pp. 71–96. This version of the Establishment Law includes amendments as of 2 May 1991.

Table of Contents

---

[15] I am highly indebted to Hiroki Nogami for his help in this translation.

CHAPTER 4
Staff of MoF (Articles 23–25)
APPENDIX

Chapter 1
Article 1
The aim of this law is to specify clearly the area and authority of the tasks of the MoF, and to specify the organisation, which is sufficient to conduct efficiently the administrative business and undertakings of the MoF.

Article 2
National Government Organisation Law (1948, article 120). Article 3, Paragraph 2 of this Law is related to the establishment of the post-war MoF. The president of the MoF is the Minister of Finance.

Article 3
The MoF is the administrative organisation, which has the responsibility of undertaking the administrative business and operations of the government relating to the following items:
  A) Finance of the Japanese State
  B) Currency
  C) Finance
  D) Foreign exchange
  E) Trade of securities
  F) Undertaking of currency creation
  G) Undertaking of printing

Article 4
The tasks of the Ministry of Finance regard the following items (Paragraphs):
4.1 Research, making of statistics, collecting of data and delivery, and issuance of publications which relates to the administrative business under control of the MoF.
4.2 The MoF is responsible for the management of tax receipts.
4.3 The MoF is responsible for the issuance and maintenance of revenue stamps.
4.4 The MoF is responsible for the planning and research of public monopoly institutions, and the Tobacco Monopoly Company (the daily operations are controlled by the institutions themselves).
4.5a Monopolised goods other than tobacco (except alcohol and drugs). Administrative business relating to the authorisation of retail prices of monopolised goods (except alcohol and drugs) and tobacco.

4.5b The management of the Japan Tobacco Industry Company.

4.5c Administrative business relating to the management of the Union of Tobacco Farmers.

4.5d Not translated.

4.5e The MoF controls the Government Institute for Research of Biology Technology.

4.6 The MoF conducts the business of research, planning, drafting and unification of activities concerning the budget, the settlement of accounts and accounting of the national government.

4.7 The MoF conducts the business of budget, settlement of accounts and accounting of government organisations.

4.8 The MoF conducts the business of making the budget and settlement of accounts.

4.9 The MoF conducts the business concerning the management of reserve funds.

4.10 The MoF conducts the business concerning the management of funds for economic infrastructure.

4.11 The MoF conducts the business concerning the management of funds for adjustment of the settlement of national accounts.

4.12 The MoF conducts the business concerning the acknowledgement of carrying forward every ministry's and every agency's budget of expenditures to the next fiscal year.

4.13 The MoF conducts the business concerning the acknowledgement of the burden of the deficit that is to be paid in the next fiscal year.

4.14 The MoF conducts the business relating to the acknowledgement of issuance of funds to every ministry and agency before the beginning of the fiscal year.

4.15 The MoF conducts the business relating to the acknowledgement of diverting funds of budget expenditures of every ministry and agency.

4.16 The MoF conducts the business relating to the acknowledgement of conducting the planning and the planning of expenditures of each ministry and agency.

4.17 The MoF conducts the business relating to the acknowledgement of the expenditure actions of each ministry and agency.

4.18 The MoF conducts the business relating to the acknowledgement of the nomination of competition bids, free contracts, advance payments, payments at rough estimate of selling and buying, the lending and borrowing, and the assets and liabilities of each ministry and agency.

4.19 The MoF controls the disbursing of officers and cashiers of each ministry and agency.

4.20 The MoF conducts the business relating to the collecting of reports about the budgetary expenditure plans of the national government, the audit of the budget accounts and the instruction of the budgetary expenditure plan.

4.21 The MoF conducts the business relating to the training of accountants of the national government.

4.22 The MoF controls the business relating to the collection of revenues of each ministry and agency.

4.23 The MoF conducts the business of overviewing the management of real assets of the national government.

4.24 The MoF conducts the business relating to the overview of the management of claims of the national government.

4.25 The MoF controls the lending by the national government.

4.26 The MoF controls the reimbursement system of expenditures, such as travelling expenses, of officers of the national government.

4.27 The MoF controls the system relating to the benefit society for officers of the national government.

4.28 The MoF manages the benefit society of officers of the national government.

4.29 The MoF conducts the business relating to budget expenditures of local public organisations.

4.30 The MoF conducts the business relating to the research and planning of the tax system (excluding import tariffs, tonnage tariffs, but including tax agreements between Japan and other foreign countries).

4.31 The MoF estimates the tax revenues and conducts research about the settlement of accounts.

4.32 The MoF conducts the research, planning and designing of the system of certified tax accountants.

4.33 The MoF conducts the research, planning and design of a union-system of liquor producers.

4.34 The MoF conducts the business relating to the revenues of local public organisations.

4.35 The MoF conducts the business relating to the collection of domestic taxes.

4.36 The MoF controls the production and selling of liquor.

4.37 The MoF conducts the business relating to the licensing of production and selling of alcoholic drinks, and the management of unions and organisations of liquor producers and sellers.

4.38 The MoF conducts the testing, giving of courses and giving of instructions with respect to methods of analysis, judgement and brewing of tax imposed goods, such as alcoholic drinks.

4.39 The MoF conducts the business concerning the setting of prices on alcoholic drinks.

4.40 The MoF conducts the business concerning the collection of extra duties that are provided by Article 20 of the Law of Control of Price Margins and General Prices (Imperial Ordinance no. 118 of 1946).

4.41 The MoF conducts the necessary overview of the business of staff of the National Tax Administration Agency (excluding staff of councils and other establishments of the National Tax Administration Agency, Regional Taxation Bureaus and the Okinawa Regional Taxation Office), and, under the regulation of law, conducts the research of the claims of this staff, that are provided by Paragraph 1 of Article 25 and the necessary dispositions.

4.42 The MoF issues revenue stamps and guards against their imitation.

4.43 The MoF conducts the business concerning certified tax accountants, their union and the Japanese Certified Tax Accountants Union.

4.44 The MoF conducts the research, planning and design of a system concerning the administration of import duties, tonnage tariffs and so forth (including agreements on tariffs between Japan and other foreign countries).

4.45 The MoF conducts the business of imposing and collecting of tariffs, tonnage tariffs, and other special tonnage tariffs.

4.46 The MoF conducts the business concerning the contracts of goods that are imported and exported, ships, aeroplanes and passengers.

4.47 Not translated.

4.48 The MoF conducts the business concerning the permission to operate as custom clearance traders and the control and examination of custom clearance traders.

4.49 The MoF manages the customs clearance information centre.

4.50 The MoF produces customs statistics.

4.51 The MoF conducts the adjustment of the balance of payments of the National Treasury, adjustments between public finance and the financial system, general adjustment of funds that are available for domestic use, and the adjustment between the domestic financial system and the international financial system.

4.52 The MoF conducts the research and planning of the system of the National Treasury.

4.53 The MoF conducts the research and planning of the system of the National Treasury, the system of national bonds and the management system of national assets.

4.54 The MoF controls money and securities in the national government's custody.

4.55 The MoF conducts the business concerning the issuance, repayment, and interest payments of national government bonds.

4.56 The national government owes debt due to bonds it issues and its borrowings, and MoF conducts the business relating to the guarantee of the contracts of this government debt.

4.57 The MoF supervises the business of the Bank of Japan regarding the treatment of money in the National Treasury and national government bonds.

4.58 The MoF conducts the business relating to local government's bonds.

4.59 The MoF produces coins and banknotes, and withdraws and controls them.

4.60 The MoF designs the plan of business of the Bank of Japan regarding the production and design of banknotes by the Bank of Japan.

4.61 The MoF controls negotiable securities that resemble currency.

4.62 The MoF conducts the business relating to the management and investment of funds in the Trust Fund Bureau.

4.63 The MoF adjusts the demand and supply of government loans for industries.

4.64 The MoF conducts the collection of reports, 'on the spot' surveys and suggestions in order to avoid the delay of expenditures due to government's contracts.

4.65 The MoF controls the financial affairs related to funds in foreign countries, and bonds and assets in foreign countries, which needed to be disposed of with the arrival of peace (after World War II).

4.66 The MoF conducts the business regarding the debt of diplomatic establishments abroad.

4.67 The MoF conducts the unification of the control and disposition of the national government's Treasury, and of the accompanying necessary adjustments.

4.68 The MoF clarifies/announces the increases and decreases, the amounts and the actual situation of the national government's Treasury.

4.69 The MoF conducts the business relating to the control and disposition of the national government's Treasury in general.

4.70 The MoF conducts and controls the expenditures by the national government.

4.71 The MoF conducts the business relating to the settlement of lodgings of the staff of the national government (as far as their settlement, management, maintenance and control are concerned) and summarises the business related to the settlements, maintenance and control of lodgings of the staff of the national government.

4.72 The MoF conducts the business relating to the acquisition and disposition of specified national government's treasuries due to the arrangement plan of specified national government's treasuries.

4.73 The MoF conducts the business relating to the Special Accountant Company, closed government institutions and companies in foreign countries.

4.74 The MoF conducts the business relating to the restoration of treasuries of the allied powers (except everything under the control of the Ministry of Transport), disposition of precious metals, and so forth, that were captured from the allied powers, and disposition of other special treasuries after World War II.

4.75 The MoF conducts the business relating to the acquisition of the rights of real estate by foreign governments.

4.76 The MoF conducts the business relating to the Memorial Association of the Japan Exhibition of All Nations.

4.77 The MoF conducts the research, planning and design of securities exchange institutions (stock exchanges, securities houses, and so forth).

4.78 The MoF conducts the business relating to the licensing of settlement by stock exchanges and controls them.

4.79a The MoF conducts the business relating to the licensing and control of securities companies, securities financing companies and securities investment trust companies.

4.79b The MoF conducts the business relating to the registration and control of investment advisory companies (which means investment advisor companies specified by the Law of the Regulation of Securities Investment Advisory Companies of 1986 [Law no. 74]. This is the same with Law no. 45–2 regarding the next paragraph).

4.80a The MoF conducts the business relating to the registration and control of the Securities Dealers Association and the Union of Securities Dealers Associations.

4.80b The MoF conducts the business relating to the supervision of the Association of Securities Investment Advisory Companies and the Union of Associations of Securities Investment Advisory Companies.

4.81 The MoF conducts the business relating to the examination and disposition of reports about the issuance of securities, reports concerning the (open) buying of securities, reports about possession of large amounts of stocks, and reports about securities in general.

4.82 The MoF conducts the business relating to the settlement of standards of company accounts.

4.83 The MoF conducts the business relating to the capital of companies and other finance aspects of companies.

4.84 The MoF conducts the business relating to the control of certified public accountants, assistants of public accountants, auditing corporate bodies, and the Japan Certified Public Accountant Association.

4.85 The MoF conducts the business relating to the legislation of corporate bonds.

4.86 Deleted.

4.87 The MoF conducts the research, planning and design of the financial system.

4.88 The MoF supervises the Bank of Japan.

4.89 The MoF supervises the Shōkō Chūkin Bank, the People's Finance Corporation, the Housing Loan Corporation, the Export–Import Bank of Japan, the Japan Development Bank, the Agriculture, Forestry and Fishery Finance Corporation, the Small Business Finance Corporation, the Hokkaido-Tohoku Development Corporations, the Finance Corporation of Local Public Enterprise, the Small Business Credit Insurance Corporation, the Environmental Sanitation Business Financing Corporation and the Okinawa Development Finance Corporation.

4.90 The MoF supervises the depository and insurance institutions, and the federations of deposit and insurance institutions of agricultural and fishery co-operatives.

4.91 The MoF conducts the business relating to the accommodation of funds for housing of industrial workers, and the insurance of housing-finance.

4.92 The MoF conducts the business relating to the licensing and control of banks, *sogo* banks, trust companies and mutual financing associations.

4.93 The MoF conducts the business relating to the licensing and control of life insurance companies and non-life insurance companies.

4.94 The MoF conducts the business relating to earthquake insurance companies.

4.95 The MoF conducts the business relating to automobile damage insurance.

4.96 The MoF is responsible for the licensing of *shinkin* banks, the Zenshinren Bank, labour credit associations, and the National Federation of Labour Credit Associations; the MoF supervises *shinkin* banks, labour credit associations, federations of credit co-operatives, federations of agricultural co-operatives, federations of fishery co-operatives, the Nōrinchūkin Bank, the Credit Guaranty Association, the Agricultural Credit Fund Association, the Fishery Credit Fund Association, the Agriculture, Forestry and Fishery Credit Fund, the Infrastructure Arrangement Fund, the Communication and Broadcast Satellite Organisation, and other financial operations.

4.97a The MoF registers and supervises a person who conducts the business of lending money.

4.97b The MoF registers and supervises a person who conducts mortgage securities business (which is regulated by the Law of Regulation of

Mortgage Securities Business 1987 [Law no. 114], and this is the same with Law no. 35–2 regarding the next paragraph).

4.97c The MoF conducts the business relating to the specification of the Mortgage Securities Reservation Organisation, and supervises it.

4.97d The MoF conducts the business relating to the supervision of mortgage securities associations.

4.97e The MoF conducts the business relating to the permission of the establishment of financial forward exchange business, and supervises it.

4.97f The MoF conducts the business relating to the permission and supervision of financial forward exchange business (which is regulated by the Law of Financial Forward Exchange 1988 [Law no. 77], and this is the same with Law no. 35–4 regarding the next paragraph).

4.97g The MoF supervises the Financial Forward Exchange Business Association.

4.97h The MoF conducts the business relating to the regulation of advance payment vouchers (which is regulated by the Law of Regulation of Advance Payment Vouchers 1989 [Law no. 92]).

4.97i The MoF conducts the business relating to the permission of commodity investment and selling business (which is regulated by the Law of Regulation and Supervision of Commodity Investment Business 1991 [Law no. 66], and this is the same with Law no. 35–6 concerning the next paragraph).

4.98 The MoF decides the maximum amount of issuance of Bank of Japan notes, and gives permission to issue banknotes above the ceiling.

4.99 The MoF gives permission to the Bank of Japan in its setting, change and abolition of the reserve requirement ratio, reference dates and so forth.

4.100 The MoF regulates and supervises the financial institutions in their operation of funds.

4.101 The MoF regulates and adjusts the interest rates of financial institutions.

4.102 The MoF designs the National Savings Plan and promotes national savings.

4.103 The MoF designs the fundamental policy of promotion of worker's wealth accumulation that relates to workers' savings.

4.104 The MoF collects information about the acceptance of deposits.

4.105 The MoF conducts business relating to the design, planning and research of the general framework of the international financial markets and foreign exchange, which includes agreements with respect to the international financial markets and foreign exchange transactions with other countries.

4.106 The MoF conducts the adjustment of the balance of payment.

4.107 The MoF conducts business relating to the control and operation of the Foreign Exchange Fund.

4.108 The MoF decides and supports the level of the foreign exchange rate.

4.109 The MoF conducts the business relating to the management of currency for foreign exchange, and the setting of the conditions for the settlement of foreign exchange.

4.110 The MoF controls foreign exchange that relates to MoF's business, and regulates the export and import of gold.

4.111 The MoF conducts the business relating to the basic policy of the purchase and selling of gold.

4.112 The MoF conducts the business relating to the setting of the government purchase price of gold.

4.113 The MoF specifies the area of foreign exchange business that is conducted by banks, and supervises their operation.

4.114 The MoF specifies authorised securities companies, which are regulated by the Law of Foreign Exchange Control 1949 [Law no. 228].

4.115 The MoF conducts business relating to the IMF, the International Bank for Reconstruction and Development (World Bank), the International Finance Corporation, the International Development Association, the Asian Development Bank, the Inter-American Development Bank, the American Investment Public Corporation, the European Bank for Reconstruction and Development, the African Development Bank and the African Development Fund.

4.116 The MoF conducts the control and adjustment of technological aid, business and acquisition of equity and other assets of foreign investors.

4.117 The MoF conducts the examination of acquisition of real estate by foreign governments.

4.118 The MoF conducts business relating to Japanese foreign investments.

4.119 The MoF controls assets and liabilities that require disposition as a result of the settlement of World War II.

4.120 The MoF produces statistics relating to foreign exchange and the balance of payments.

4.121 The MoF conducts the examination of business that is regulated by the Foreign Exchange and Foreign Trade Control Law, specified in paragraphs 110, 116 and 118.

4.122 The MoF produces (gold) coins and so forth, issues memorial coins and melts down old coins.

4.123 The MoF conducts the examination of the proof of the production and nature of expensive metals, and analyses gold and other minerals.

4.124 The MoF prints Bank of Japan notes, other notes, national bonds, stamps, postal stamps and cards, and other securities.

4.125 The MoF edits, produces and publishes the publications of the government.

4.126 The MoF provides paper that is necessary for the business of proceeding the items in the two preceding paragraphs.

4.127a The MoF conducts the business relating to the control of the production of paper for banknotes.

4.127b The MoF promotes the use of reclamation resources, which is regulated by the Law of Promotion of the Use of Reclamation Resources 1991 [Law no. 48], in the area of its business.

4.128 The MoF conducts the training of its business in an in-service training institute that is specified by government ordinance.

4.129 In addition to the business that is specified by the preceding paragraphs, the MoF conducts business that is asked for by laws from the MoF.

Article 5 (authority)
The MoF has the authority (jurisdiction or *kengen*), which is regulated by the following paragraphs, in order to conduct the business specified by the preceding articles. However, the MoF must use this authority under the regulation of law.

5.1 The MoF conducts the unification of the government budget, settlement and accounts.

5.2 The MoF makes the national government budget and its settlement.

5.3 The MoF controls the reserve money of the national government.

5.4 The MoF controls funds for the arrangement of the economic infrastructure.

5.5 The MoF controls the funds for the adjustment of settlements.

5.6 The MoF acknowledges the expenditures bearing plan of each ministry and agency, and the MoF also acknowledges the expenditure-conducting plan of each ministry and agency.

5.7 Regarding the conduct of the national government budget expenditures, the MoF conducts the collecting of reports, research and suggestions to ministries and agencies.

5.8 The MoF summarises the business concerning the management of goods of the national government.

5.9 The MoF summarises the business concerning the management of bonds of the national government.

5.10 The MoF provides the training of the national government accountants.

5.11 The MoF conducts the business concerning the adjustment of finance of local public organisations, with special attention for the control of the financial situation of the national government.

5.12 The MoF imposes and collects domestic taxes.

5.13 The MoF conducts the control of the examination of certified tax accountants, the business of certified tax accountants, associations of certified tax accountants and the Japan Certified Tax Accountants Union.

5.14 Under the regulation of law, the MoF investigates crimes of staff members of the National Tax Administration Agency, and conducts necessary dispositions.

5.15 The MoF provides the permission of business of liquor manufacturing and liquor, and controls the producers and sellers of alcoholic drinks, and the union of liquor producers and sellers.

5.16 The MoF imposes tariffs, tonnage tax and the special tonnage tax.

5.17 The MoF controls the export and import of goods, related ships, aeroplanes and passengers under the regulation of tariff laws.

5.18 The MoF provides the permission regarding the business of customs clearance, and controls it. Furthermore, the MoF also conducts the examination of customs officers.

5.19a The MoF controls the right of monopoly (except alcoholic drinks and drugs).

5.19b The MoF registers the wholesale tobacco business and gives permission for the retail sales of tobacco, and controls them.

5.20 The MoF summarises the business concerning the assets of the national government and conducts the collection of reports, research and suggestions.

5.21 The MoF controls and disposes the assets of the national government.

5.22 The MoF provides lodgings for the staff of the national government (as far as the settlement, management, maintenance and control of it is concerned), and the MoF also summarises the business concerning the settlement, maintenance and control of lodging of the staff of the national government.

5.23 The MoF acquires and disposes special assets of the national government under the Law of the Special Government Assets Acquisition Plan.

5.24 The MoF controls the financing of reparation of foreign debt, funds and assets abroad.

5.25 The MoF is responsible for the receipts and disbursements, control and operation of money in the treasury of the national government.

5.26 The MoF issues national government bonds and conducts activities regarding repayments and interest payments.

5.27 The MoF conducts the control and investment of funds in the Trust Fund Bureau.

5.28 As far as the debt with respect to national government bonds and other borrowing of the government is concerned, MoF draws contracts that guarantee the debt of the national government.

5.29 The MoF issues coins and banknotes, and MoF also supervises the issuing of Bank of Japan notes.

5.30 The MoF supervises the operation of the deposit reserve requirement system.

5.31 The MoF provides permission for and supervises banking, mutual banking, trust business, insurance business and mutual finance.

5.32 The MoF supervises the financial institutions that are founded under a special law.

5.33 The MoF supervises the deposit insurance system and the insurance system of deposits of federations of agricultural and fishery co-operatives.

5.34 The MoF conducts the insurance business for earthquakes.

5.35a The MoF provides the acknowledgement of the regulation of the automobile damage reparation system.

5.35b The MoF registers and controls the mortgage securities business.

5.35c The MoF gives permission to and supervises the financial forward exchange institutions.

5.35d The MoF gives permission for and supervises the financial forward exchange business.

5.35e Under the regulation of the law regarding advance payment vouchers, the MoF provides the registration and regulation of a person who issues advance payment vouchers.

5.35f The MoF provides the permission for and supervises the commodity investment selling business.

5.36 The MoF regulates the extension of funds and the interest rates of financial institutions.

5.37 The MoF provides the plan for the worker's assets promotion policy.

5.38 The MoF controls the prices of goods that are under its control.

5.39 The MoF controls and operates government funds for foreign exchange and other funds in foreign currency.

5.40 The MoF sets and maintains the market foreign exchange rate.

5.41 The MoF decides the settlement conditions of exchange accounts with foreign countries.

5.42 The MoF controls foreign exchange that is related to the business of the MoF.

5.43 The MoF adjusts the investments and business activities of foreign investors.

5.44 The MoF provides permission to and supervises stock exchanges.

5.45a The MoF provides permission for and supervises the securities exchange business and securities investment trust companies.

5.45b The MoF registers the investment adviser business and supervises it.

5.46 The MoF registers the Securities Dealers Association and supervises it.

5.47 The MoF conducts the examination of reports concerning the issuance of securities, reports concerning open purchases of securities and reports concerning the holding of stocks. The MoF conducts the necessary dispositions.

5.48 The MoF conducts the examination of certified public accountants and supervises the business of certified public accountants, audit corporations and the Japan Certified Public Accountants Association.

5.49 The MoF issues coins, memorial coins and conducts the melting down of old coins.

5.50 The MoF conducts the examination of the refinement of expensive metals, the proof of the nature of it and the examination of minerals.

5.51 The MoF prints Bank of Japan notes, banknotes, national government bonds, stamps, and other securities and items.

5.52 The MoF edits, prints and issues national government publications, such as the official gazette, and so forth.

5.53 The MoF provides paper that is necessary for the business of the two preceding items.

5.54 The MoF conducts business that it is asked for by law.

The remainder of the document has not been translated.

Appendix 5.2 The pre-1998 organisation of the MoF[16]

The organisational structure of the central MoF during the post-war period until 1998 consisted of the Minister's Secretariat and seven internal bureaus. Furthermore, the MoF included local branch offices, two extraordinary organisations, numerous facilities, councils and an external agency. Figure 5.2 provides an overview of MoF's organisational structure. In Figure 5.3, the bureaus and divisions are presented that are primarily responsible for macro and micro monetary policies. As I have paid and will pay considerable attention to the informal networks of *amakudari* and *gakubatsu*, this overview will also describe various positions and functions at the MoF.

[16] This overview is based on Kawakita (1991), Ministry of Finance (1991, 1992d), Ishizaka (1992), Ōkura Zaimu Kyōkai (1992) and personal interviews with MoF officials (January–April 1993, May–June 1994, February–May 1995 and 1997).

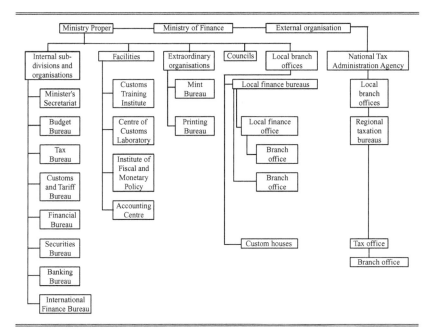

Figure 5.2 The organisation of the Ministry of Finance
Source: Ministry of Finance data.

The Minister of Finance (*Ōkura Daijin*) was assisted by two Parliamentary Vice-Ministers (*seimu jikan*) and one Administrative Vice-Minister
(*jimu jikan*). The Parliamentary Vice-Ministers, who were usually members of parliament, were political appointees and functioned as liaison
officers between the Minister and the parliament and political parties.
The Administrative Vice-Minister was the highest non-political appointee,
i.e. the highest career bureaucrat in the MoF, and handled the leadership
of the daily operation of the MoF. With respect to international financial
policies, a Vice-Minister for International Affairs (*zaimukan*) supported
the vice-ministers. Another top-level function was that of MoF's Representative at the Policy Board of the BoJ (Nihon Ginkō Seisaku Iin), the
highest policymaking body of Japan's central bank. The basis for these
functions lies in statutory laws (*hōritsu*), i.e. the National Government
Organisation Law, the Establishment Law of the MoF and the Bank of
Japan Law.

The organisation of the Minister's Secretariat and the internal bureaus
was determined by Cabinet Order no. 386 (Seirei Dai 386), The Ministry
of Finance Organisation Ordinance (Ōkurashō Soshiki Rei), and Ministry
of Finance Ordinance no. 37 (The Ministry of Finance Organisation

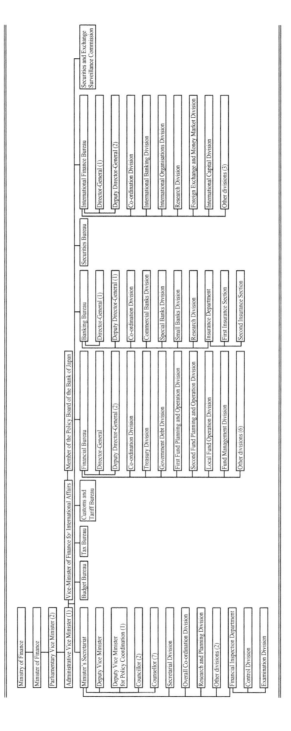

Figure 5.3 MoF bureaus and divisions involved in monetary policy
Source: Ministry of Finance data.

Regulation or Ōkurashō Soshiki Kitei).[17] According to these ordinances the Secretariat and bureaus were given the following responsibilities. The Minister's Secretariat (Daijin Kanbō) was charged with the co-ordination of all administrative functions performed by the MoF, and with advising the Minister and Vice-Ministers (Kawakita 1991, p.5). The Secretariat was put under the leadership of the Deputy Vice-Minister (*kanbōchō*). An important function at the Secretariat was that of Deputy Vice-Minister for Policy Co-ordination (*sōmu shingikan*), who functioned as liaison officer with the BoJ in case of changes in the official discount rate and ensured that the interests of the MoF – in particular those of the Banking and Financial Bureaus – were taken into account (personal interviews MoF officials; Kawakita 1991, p.6). Furthermore, the Secretariat employed a number of so-called counsellors (*sanjikan*) and councillors (*kanbō tantō shingikan*), who functioned as advisors with a special assignment at a level above deputy director; the difference between these functions seems to be a matter of semantics only (interviews with counsellors July 1992 and February 1993). Finally, a number of special officers for clearly specified duties were assigned to the Secretariat.

Traditionally, the most important divisions in the Secretariat were the Secretarial Division (Hisho Ka) and the Overall Co-ordination Division (Bunsho Ka).[18] The Secretarial Division was given the responsibility for career and personnel management, including the organisation of post-retirement employment positions (*amakudari*). The Overall Co-ordination Division functioned as the 'headquarters' division of the MoF: it handled the general co-ordination of policies between the various bureaus and divisions inside the MoF and checked proposed changes in the regulatory framework. Regarding the formulation of macro monetary policy, the Research and Planning Division (Chōsa Kikaku Ka) was important for policy research and analysis. This division was considered to be the most influential research division in the MoF. Its main functions were the making of macro-economic forecasts and long-term economic projections, and to conduct studies on international economic relations. These forecasts and projections, which were made without the use of macro-econometric models, were for internal purposes only; to some extent the MoF's projections were compared – through informal channels – with those made by the BoJ. The Research and Planning Division played also an important role in the decision-making process regarding changes in the official discount rate. The other divisions presented in figure 5.3 are the Accounts Division, which controlled the budget of the MoF, and

---

[17] Ōkura Zaimu Kyōkai (1992), pp.103–172 and pp.173–399, respectively.
[18] The MoF Organisation Ordinance, chapter 1, subsection 1.2.1, Articles 13 and 14 respectively (Ōkura Zaimu Kyōkai 1992, pp.119–120).

the Division Controlling Local Finance Bureaus, which supervised the local finance bureaus of the MoF.

Following the stock-losses compensation scandal of the summer of 1991 involving the largest Japanese securities companies and institutional investors (and the MoF, being both regulator and supervisor), the MoF decided to reorganise its inspection departments and divisions in order to establish a more coherent and effective supervisory system. MoF's organisation was reformed in July 1992; the reforms, which were related to the Minister's Secretariat, were included in Article 19 of MoF's Organisation Ordinance. Basically, these reforms consisted of the following organisational changes (Ishizaka 1992; Kinyū Shōken Research 1992, pp.212–231). First, the Securities and Exchange Surveillance Commission was established, which combined most activities of some erstwhile divisions of the Securities Bureau charged with the inspection of securities trading. Second, and more important from the perspective of the inspection of depository financial institutions, was the establishment in the Minister's Secretariat of the Financial Inspection Department (Kinyū Kensa Bu). This department was given the responsibility for the on-the-spot inspection or monitoring of banks, foreign exchange business and the financial health of securities companies (Ishizaka 1992, p.15). To achieve these tasks, the ex-Banking Inspection Department (Kensa Bu) of the Banking Bureau, consisting of the Control Division (Kanri Ka) and the Examination Division (Shinsa Ka), the Foreign Exchange Inspector's Office (Kawase Kensa Kan Shitsu) of the International Finance Bureau and parts of the Inspection Division of the Securities Bureau were integrated in this new Financial Inspection Department. Consequently, regarding the inspection and examination of banking activities, the Minister's Secretariat became the main supervisory organisation.

As regards the structure of the rest of MoF's central organisation until 1998, the most important elements were its seven internal bureaus: the Budget Bureau (Shukei Kyoku), the Tax Bureau (Shuzei Kyoku), the Customs and Tariff Bureau (Kanzei Kyoku), the Financial Bureau (Rizai Kyoku), the Securities Bureau (Shōken Kyoku), the Banking Bureau (Ginkō Kyoku) and the International Finance Bureau (Kokusai Kinyū Kyoku). The former three bureaus and most divisions of the Financial Bureau were responsible for MoF's fiscal policies; the latter three bureaus and some parts of the Financial Bureau conducted the policies related to the monetary affairs that were under MoF's jurisdiction. There emerged a clear pecking order amongst the bureaus: the Budget and Tax Bureaus have always been the most powerful, whereas the status of the International Finance Bureau has traditionally been relatively low. Furthermore, the rivalry between the bureaus (for example between the

Banking and Securities Bureaus) has been fierce and open: in particular the on-going process of financial reform, such as described in the next chapter, frequently led to the outbreak of intra-ministry conflicts. Consequently, the MoF has been referred to as 'a group of bureaus without a ministry'.[19] The bureaus that were primarily responsible for macro and micro monetary policies related to depository institutions in particular were the Banking Bureau, International Finance Bureau and Financial Bureau.

The Banking Bureau was made responsible for the research, planning and design of the financial system and the licensing and general supervision of depository financial institutions, special government banks and insurance companies. The specific tasks of the Banking Bureau were explained by the 26 paragraphs in Article 10 of the Ministry of Finance Organisation Ordinance (see Ōkura Zaimu Kyōkai 1992, pp.116–117). The Banking Bureau operated under a Director-General (*kyoku chō*) and a Deputy Director-General (*tantō shingikan*). It consisted of the Co-ordination Division (Sōmu Ka), Commercial Banks Division (Ginkō Ka), Special Banks Division (Tokubetsu Kinyū Ka), Small Banks Division (Chūshō Kinyū Ka), Research Division (Chōsa Ka) and the Insurance Department (Hoken Bu).

The Co-ordination Division planned and designed the general policies regarding the financial institutions under the Banking Bureau's jurisdiction, supervised the BoJ, decided the maximum amount of paper money that the BoJ could issue and gave permission to issue banknotes above this ceiling if deemed necessary, and approved the setting, change and abolition of reserve requirement ratios by the BoJ. Furthermore, it regulated and supervised private financial institutions in their operation of funds, adjusted their interest rates, and administered affairs regarding the Interest Rate Adjustment Council (Kinri Chōsei Shingikai).[20] The BoJ section located at the Co-ordination Division was in charge of matters involving the BoJ. In case of issuance of banknotes by the BoJ above the established ceiling and for a period which exceeded sixteen days, the BoJ had to pay an issuance tax of 3% to the MoF. According to some interviewees, the last time the BoJ had to pay this tax was in Fiscal Year 1975. According to a large number of MoF and BoJ staff members, the adjustment of the

---

[19] Examples of inter-bureau rivalries are described in Horne (1985), McCall Rosenbluth (1989) and Brown (1999).

[20] Paragraphs 1, 2, 3, 4, 10, 11 and 15 of Article 66, MoF Organisation Ordinance chapter 1, subsection 1.2.7, described the tasks of the Co-ordination Division (Ōkura Zaimu Kyōkai 1992, p.138). The Interest Rate Adjustment Council was an advisory body to the BoJ's Policy Board charged with handling changes in interest rates. When the MoF wanted to change regulated interest rates, the Minister requested the BoJ to convene the Council, which then issued a recommendation (McCall Rosenbluth 1989, p.41).

ceiling on the issuance of banknotes was in practice just a formality, and the MoF simply followed the requests of the BoJ. Another important section inside the Co-ordination Division was the Financial Markets Office (Kinyū Ichiba Shitsu). This office was in charge of MoF's interest rate policies, particularly on deposit interest rates, and the liberalisation programme of deposit interest rates. The Financial Markets Office watched financial markets closely, including the interbank money markets; according to some interviewees, the money market monitoring activities of this office were aimed at strengthening MoF's leverage over the BoJ.

The Commercial Banks Division conducted the licensing and supervision of the commercial banks (with the exception of the Second Tier regional banks), the long-term credit banks and trust banks. With respect to government banks, the supervision was exercised by the Special Banks Division; the licensing and supervision of Second Tier regional banks, *shinkin* banks, credit co-operatives and other small and medium-sized banks were the responsibility of the Small Banks Division.[21] The Research Division was in charge of the research, planning and design of policies aimed at developing and improving the financial system and the administration of the Financial System Research Council. Finally, the Insurance Department directed the life assurance companies (First Insurance Division) and the non-life insurance companies (Second Insurance Division).

The International Finance Bureau (IFB) was given responsibility for the design, planning and research of the general framework regarding the international financial markets and foreign exchange business, including agreements with respect to the international financial system and foreign exchange transactions with other countries.[22] The Director-General of the IFB was assisted by one Senior Deputy Director-General (*jichō*) and two lower-ranking Deputy Director-Generals (*tantō shingikan*). One of these Junior Deputy Director-Generals was in charge of the International Capital Division (Kokusai Shihon Ka), which carried out general research on international capital markets and the overseas issuance of securities by Japanese companies, and the divisions that formulated and implemented the policies regarding the financing of international economic development projects: the Development Policy Division (Kaihatsu Seisaku Ka), Development Institutions Division (Kaihatsu Kikan Ka) and Development Finance Division (Kaihatsu Kinyū Ka).[23] The other Junior Deputy

---

[21] The functions of these divisions were explained in Articles 67, 68 and 69 of the MoF Organisation Ordinance (Ōkura Zaimu Kyōkai 1992).

[22] Paragraph 1, Article 11, of chapter 1, subsection 1.1, MoF Organisation Ordinance (Ōkura Zaimu Kyōkai 1992).

[23] The specific functions were explained in Articles 79, 80, 81 and 82, chapter 1, subsection 1.2.8, MoF Organisation Ordinance (Ōkura Zaimu Kyōkai 1992, pp.144–145).

Director-General supervised the International Banking Division (Kinyū Gyōmu Ka), the Research Division, the International Organisations Division (*Kokusai Kikō Ka*, responsible for IMF, G7 and OECD affairs) and the Foreign Exchange and Money Market Division (Kawase Shikin Ka). The most important division in the IFB regarding macro monetary policy was the Foreign Exchange and Money Market Division. This division was responsible for the formulation of exchange rate policy, such as set out in Paragraphs 4.107 and 4.108 of the Ministry of Finance Establishment Law discussed in this chapter and in several Paragraphs of the Ministry of Finance Organisation Ordinance. According to Article 78 of this Ordinance, Paragraph 2, the MoF decided and supported the level of the foreign exchange rate. Paragraph 3 stated that the MoF had responsibility for the control and operation of the Foreign Exchange Fund and matters concerning the Foreign Exchange Fund Special Account (Gaikoku Kawase Shikin Tokubetsu Kaisei). This account manages the foreign exchange reserves of the Japanese government. Under the Foreign Exchange Fund Special Account Law, in particular Article 6, the BoJ was charged with the administration of this account's funds and the intervention in the foreign exchange market by using these funds, in both cases operating as agent for the MoF (interviews with MoF staff members, February 1993; Suzuki 1987a, p.312). Finally, the Co-ordination Division was in charge of the control of information and internal and external policy co-ordination.

The Financial Bureau was charged with a wide range of tasks and consequently operated the largest number of divisions (13). In general, the Financial Bureau was established to conduct the administration of fiscal and monetary adjustments and of national property. The former responsibilities were given to the Treasury Division (Kokko Ka), the Government Debt Division (Kokusai Ka) and the various trust fund divisions. The Treasury Division supervised the BoJ's handling of the payments operations and the receipts (including tax receipts) of the Japanese government: in law, the BoJ is responsible for the handling of treasury funds.[24] Furthermore, the Treasury Division controlled the planning of the production and design of banknotes and coins, whose circulation is being conducted by the Bank of Japan.[25] Finally, the Treasury Division was responsible for issues related to financial bills (*seifu tanki shōken*), which are issued to cover temporary shortages of government funds.

The other division in the Financial Bureau that was given responsibility for monetary and fiscal adjustments was the Government Debt Division.

---

[24] Paragraph 6, Article 48, chapter 1, subsection 1.2.5, MoF Organisation Ordinance (Ōkura Zaimu Kyōkai 1992).
[25] Paragraph 9, ibid.

This division became responsible for the administration and formulation of the annual issuance plan for government bonds and treasury bills, research on the issuance system and secondary bond market, compilation of statistics related to government bonds and the management of the National Debt Consolidation Fund Special Account (NDCFSA).[26] Furthermore, it had to supervise the BoJ in its function of fiscal agent of the MoF in all administrative operations concerning government bonds and treasury bills (issuance, redemption, interest payments and registration).[27]

The Trust Fund Divisions were charged with the administration of trust funds, which included the formulation of the Fiscal Investment and Loan Programme (FILP) – under approval of parliament (Diet) – and the management of funds from the Trust Fund Bureau (Shikin Unyō Bu Shikin). In addition to providing funds for the FILP's investments and loans, the Trust Fund Bureau received the authority to invest in treasury bills, government and foreign bonds not related to FILP investments, short-term loans to Special Accounts, and financial bills, bank debentures and *gensaki* operations in government bonds (i.e. buying or selling of government bonds with a reversed transaction later), all without Diet approval.[28] Thus, this authority gave the MoF the opportunity to conduct large-scale financial operations that could potentially have a significant impact on the Japanese capital markets (and also on the macro monetary policy of the BoJ). In practice, the MoF got the discretionary power to use, rather informally, an important set of macro policy instruments. It has to be said that the Trust Fund Bureau (TFB) existed only as an administrative Bureau in MoF's organisation: the following divisions of the Financial Bureau conducted its operations. The First Fund Planning and Operation Division (Shikin Dai-Ichi Ka) was charged with the formulation of the FILP and the management and distribution of the funds from the TFB to some public investment institutions (Paragraphs 1 and 2, Article 50, MoF Organisation Ordinance). The Second Fund Planning and Operation Division (Shikin Dai-Ni Ka) performed the distribution of funds to other institutions, while the Local Fund Operation Division (Chihō Shikin Ka) was charged with underwriting local government bonds and the extension of loans to regional institutions. Finally, the Fund Management Division (Shikin Kanri Ka) conducted the actual management and collection of TFB funds.[29]

[26] Article 49, ibid. The NDCFSA was created to serve and repay government debt by transferring cash from the general account and revenues from the refunding bond issues.
[27] Paragraph 7, ibid; Suzuki 1987a, p.312.
[28] Matsuoka and Rose (1994), p.214; also Suzuki (1987a), p.283.
[29] Ministry of Finance (1992d), p.36, and Kawakita (1991), p.10.

Given the role of the BoJ in the handling and management of treasury funds, the management of the funds of the TFB involved the BoJ in various ways. First, the BoJ operated as the agent for direct transactions of the TFB in the financial markets. Second, certain transactions were conducted between the TFB and the BoJ. According to information based on personal interviews with MoF and BoJ staff members, these transactions, which to a large extent are the result of seasonal effects in the availability of funds to the TFB (i.e. temporary surplus funds), were of the following nature.[30] The BoJ sold financial bills to the TFB with repurchase agreement (*gensaki*), and second, *gensaki* operations in government bonds were conducted. Furthermore, the TFB used outright purchases of financial bills from the BoJ. The transactions involved the Credit and Market Management Department on the side of the BoJ, with its Operations Department functioning as back-office. Seemingly, the BoJ offered to conduct these transactions to avoid direct investments by the TFB in the market, which could have disrupted the interest rate strategy of the BoJ.[31]

Besides the Minister's Secretariat and the internal bureaus, the MoF's organisation included local branch offices such as the local finance bureaus (*zaimu kyoku*) and customs houses (*zeikan*), two extraordinary organisations, namely the Mint Bureau (Zōei Kyoku) and Printing Bureau (Insatsu Kyoku), research facilities such as the Institute of Fiscal and Monetary Policy (Zaisei Kinyū Kenkyūjo), various advisory councils (*shingikai*) and one external organisation, the National Tax Administration Agency (Kukuzei Chō). The local finance bureaus were charged with regional monetary and fiscal matters, with the exception of tax affairs. As part of the July 1992 reform of the inspection tasks of the MoF, large local finance bureaus such as the Kanto (Tokyo area) Finance Bureau established independent financial divisions consisting of several inspection sections, which were primarily occupied with the responsibility of inspecting regional banks and small- and medium-sized banks in particular (Ishizaka 1992, pp.17–20). The Mint Bureau was given the task of producing coins, whereas the Printing Bureau was put in charge of printing items such as banknotes, government bonds and official publications. The Institute of Fiscal and Monetary Policy was established to conduct research on fiscal and monetary affairs, and to train various personnel of the MoF. Finally, the National Tax Administration Agency, an external

---

[30] According to one MoF official, the TFB 'buys only short-term securities from the BoJ when it is deemed necessary from the point of view of the economic situation' (interview April 1993). The transactions between the TFB and the BoJ have been highly confidential and therefore official disclosure has been minimal.
[31] Personal interview with high-ranking BoJ staff member, May 1993.

organisation of the MoF and consequently under the jurisdiction of the Minister of Finance, was charged with the collection of domestic taxes through 11 regional taxation bureaus (*kokuzei kyoku*) and 518 tax offices (*zeimu sho*).

Appendix 5.3 The pre-1998 organisation of the BoJ[32]

After the reorganisation of May 1990, the organisation of the BoJ consisted until 1998 of the Policy Board (Seisaku Iinkai) and its Secretariat (Seisaku Iinkai Shitsu), the Executive Committee, the Governor's Office (Hiji Shitsu), 13 departments (*kyoku*), the Institute for Monetary and Economic Studies (Nihon Ginkō Kinyū Kenkyūjo), 33 branches (*shiten*), 12 offices which are attached to the head-office in Tokyo and some of the branches (*jimusho*), and 6 overseas representatives (*kaigai chūzai sanji*). The organisation of the BoJ is shown in Figure 5.4.

The Policy Board was, according to the law, the highest policymaking body of the BoJ. According to Article 13.2 of the 1942 BoJ Law, the Board had the duty 'to formulate, direct and/or supervise currency regulation, credit control and other basic monetary policies' (EHS Law Bulletin Series 1991, p.AA3). The jurisdiction of the Policy Board covered all major policy instruments such as the official discount rate, interbank and open market operations, reserve requirement ratios and regulation of deposit interest rates. However, as stipulated by Paragraph 4.99 of MoF's Establishment Law, the setting, change and abolition of reserve requirement ratios needed the approval of the Minister of Finance. Furthermore, regarding the setting, change and abolition of the maximum limits on regulated interest rates, the Policy Board could act only after the Minister of Finance made a proposal and the Interest Rate Adjustment Council had been consulted. The Policy Board, whose meetings were usually held twice a week, consisted of seven members: the Governor (*Sōsai*), four representatives of respectively the city banks, the regional banks, commerce and industry, and agriculture, and two representatives of the government who did not have voting rights (from the Ministry of Finance and the Economic Planning Agency; the latter person was actually from MITI). The actual authority of the Policy Board was seriously questioned during the post-war period until 1998, as the Minister of Finance had the right to issue directives to the BoJ (Article 43, BoJ Law). As a result of this, the Policy Board was sometimes referred to as the 'sleeping board' (M. Suzuki 1992, p.2).

[32] This section draws heavily on Suzuki (1987a), Bank of Japan (1988), Kokusai Kyoku Shōgai Gurūpu (1990), Seisaku Jihou Shuppansha (1991), Muto and Shirakawa (1993), and Nihon Ginkō Kinyū Kenkyūjo (1993).

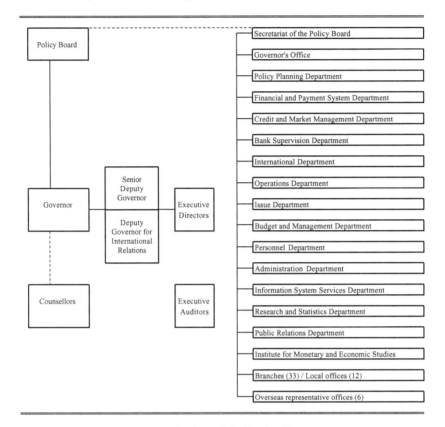

Figure 5.4 The organisation of the Bank of Japan

The Executive Committee or 'round table meeting' (*marutaku*) was actively engaged in the day-to-day monetary policy implementation and management of the BoJ's business. It consisted of the Governor, Senior Deputy-Governor, Deputy Governor for International Relations and six Executive Directors (*riji*). Other high-level executives, who did however not participate in the Executive Committee, were the Counsellors (*san-yo*) and Executive Auditors (*kanji*). The former advised the Governor upon request; the latter audited the Bank's accounts (Nakao and Horii 1991, p.28).

The planning and formulation of macro monetary policy in particular was the main task of the Policy Planning Department (Kikaku Kyoku). When the BoJ considered a change in the official discount rate, this department compiled the material for the discussions in the Policy Board (Bank of Japan 1988, p.6). The Policy Planning Department consisted of the Planning Division (Kikaku Ka), Co-ordination Division (Chōsei Ka) and Press Division (Seisaku Kōhō Ka). The Planning Division was mainly charged with the actual policy planning and the reaching of consensus through negotiations between the various involved parties. This division, which was under supervision of one of the executive directors, was from the very beginning always involved in major policy decisions. The Co-ordination Division conducted the internal co-ordination and examination duties, among others, with the Operations Department, which is in charge of transactions with the banking sector (Seisaku Jihō Shuppansha 1991, p.96). Finally, the Press Division maintained the relations with the press and announced major policy changes such as changes in the official discount rate.

The Financial and Payment System Department (Shinyō Kikō Kyoku) was newly established as a separate department under the major reorganisation of the BoJ in May 1990, with as its main tasks 'maintaining the prudential management of financial institutions and constructing an efficient and stable payment system' (Bank of Japan 1990, p.3). Thus, it was given responsibility for prudential policy. The establishment of this department reflected the concerns of the BoJ regarding the stability of the financial system in an area of financial reform and consequent increased competition between financial institutions. Its policies were implemented by two divisions, the Financial System Division (Shinyō Kikō Ka) and the Payment System Division (Kessai Shisutemu Ka). The former was involved in discussions and analysis of the BIS solvency ratios and financial risk criteria, whereas the latter investigated problems related to the efficiency and stability of the payment system (Seisaku Jihō Shuppansha 1991, p.102).

The Research and Statistics Department (Chōsa Tōkei Kyoku) was given the task of conducting studies on the development and prospects of the domestic and foreign economies in the Current Studies Division (Keizai Chōsa Ka) and General Research and Planning Division (Kikaku Chōsa Ka). Economic and financial statistics were compiled in the Economic Statistics Division (Keizai Tōkei Ka); price statistics and indices were put together by the Price Statistics Division (Bukka Tōkei Ka). The Research and Statistics Department held quarterly meetings with the policy-related departments in order to evaluate the monetary and economic situation and the possible consequences for the formulation of monetary policy (Bank of Japan 1988, p.7). Furthermore, its staff members frequently visited leading private non-financial companies to hear their opinion about the economic situation and their expectations.

Of the group of departments which was responsible for the actual policy implementation and day-to-day operations with the banking industry, the Credit and Market Management Department (Eigyō Kyoku) was the most important. This department was also established as part of the May 1990 reorganisation, and combined the functions of the former Market Operations Department and some monitoring tasks of the former Foreign Department. The concentration of these functions in one department allowed for more effective and coherent monitoring of the activities of financial institutions both at home and abroad. In particular the former separation of the monitoring of domestic and international activities of banks and securities houses was regarded as no longer effective in an area of increased financial globalisation. The Credit and Market Management Department was organised in three divisions (within brackets number of staff members as of 7 December 1992): the Bank Relations Division (Kinyū Ka) (60), the Capital Markets Division (Shōken Ka) (18) and the Market Operations Division (Shijō Ka) (21). The Bank Relations Division, which maintained daily contacts with the banking industry, consisted of six sections. The four main operational sections were the Relationship Management Sections 1 (RM1) (14) and 2 (RM2) (13), the International Finance Section (Kokusai Kinyū) (10) and the Credit Judgement Group (Shinyō Hantei Gurūpu) (7). The RM1 Section was considered the core section of the Bank Relations Division, and maintained the relations with the city and other large banks. The RM2 Section performed the same functions regarding the regional banks, while the International Finance Section was charged with maintaining relationships with foreign banks and monitoring the international activities of Japanese banks. The individual staff members of the RM1, RM2 and International Finance Sections were responsible for a number of specific banks and were in frequent contact with these banks: they developed close long-term functional relations that were beneficial to informal modes of policy implementation. The Credit Judgement Group took decisions regarding the amount of direct credit that the BoJ extended to individual banks. Besides these operational sections, the Bank Relations Division had a Planning and Co-ordination Section (Sōmu) (5), a Special Projects Group (*Purojekuto*) (5) and a Management Team made up of the division General Manager and five Senior Managers. The Capital Markets Division maintained relations with securities houses and monitored their domestic and overseas activities. Finally, the Market Operations Division conducted the daily monetary operations and monitoring of the developments on the money and capital markets. This division also made the forecasts of the daily flow of funds in the money market. In addition to the three divisions, a General Affairs Group (Shōmu Gurūpu) (5) handled clerical affairs. Given the importance of changes in interest rates for the development of foreign exchange rates the Director of the Credit and

Market Management Department met almost daily with the Director of the International Department.

The Bank Supervision Department (Kōsa Kyoku) was given responsibility for implementing the BoJ's prudential policy, in particular its examinations: more specifically, after the establishment of the Financial and Payment System Department in May 1990, the Bank Supervision Department performed exclusively the actual on-the-spot examination (*kōsa*) of banks (Bank of Japan 1990, p.4). The Bank Supervision Division (Kōsa Ka) conducted these investigations: the on-the-spot examination was the task of around 40 banking supervisors (*kōsayaku*), who visited individual banks to examine their management and asset structure. The collected data, together with the reported data, were analysed by the Data Analysis Division (Kanri Ka).

The maintenance of the BoJ's international relations, the research of international economic and financial developments, compilation of balance of payments statistics, and foreign exchange business and interventions were the responsibility of the five divisions of the International Department (Kokusai Kyoku). Under the reorganisation of the BoJ in May 1990, the international research function of the Research and Statistics Department was transferred to the reorganised Foreign Department, which was renamed International Department. As a consequence of the BoJ's role as agent of the MoF, the International Department was given the authorisation to implement the following functions. First, the Market Operations Section (Shijō Kei) of the Foreign Exchange Division (Kawase Ka) conducted the actual foreign exchange interventions in co-ordination (through the department's Planning and Co-ordination Division) with the MoF's Foreign Exchange and Money Market Division: the actual intervention scheme was made at the International Department's Planning and Co-ordination Division (Sōmu Ka). Second, the Balance of Payments Division (Kokusai Shūshi Ka) compiled the balance of payments statistics. Third, the International Investment Division (Tōshi Ka) was agent for the MoF regarding foreign exchange regulation matters under the Foreign Exchange and Foreign Trade Control Law. Regarding the BoJ's foreign exchange market interventions, according to various staff members from the MoF and BoJ, the specific aspects of this function were set out in a confidential circular (*tsūtatsu*) of the MoF. The MoF mostly took the initiative and consulted the BoJ about the timing and amount of the intervention. Then the BoJ would start the actual interventions, using funds from the Foreign Exchange Fund Special Account (i.e. using the MoF's 'money') and report back to the MoF on the reaction in the markets. If more interventions than previously agreed were deemed necessary, consultations at the division level took place. If the division's directors could reach no agreement, the Director of the International Department and the Director-General of the International Finance Bureau would take a decision. In exceptional cases, the BoJ's Deputy-Governor for International Relations and the MoF's Vice-Minister for International Affairs would be involved as well. Administrative tasks related to the foreign exchange market interventions were the responsibility of the Foreign Exchange Division's Reserves Management Section (Unyō Kei) and Government Account Section (Tokubetsu Kaikei Kei).

The Operations Department (Gyōmu Kyoku) was in charge of handling the BoJ's day-to-day financial administration, i.e. the settlement of transactions, and operated as agent for the MoF regarding the management of treasury funds, all the clerical operations concerning government bonds, such as issue, redemption, interest payments and registration, and the transactions of the Trust Fund Bureau (back-office).[33] The last department charged with operational day-to-day transactions was the Issue Department (Hakken Kyoku), which performed the duties of issuing banknotes and the accounting, examination and custody of coins and gold (Bank of Japan, *Annual Review 1994*, p.93). The departments responsible for internal management had to take care of the BoJ's organisation, management, budget and auditing (Budget and Management Department – Keiei Kyoku), administration, training and promotion of personnel (Personnel Department – Jinji Kyoku), matters relating to real estate, supplies, welfare, security, transportation, etc. (Administration Department – Bunsho Kyoku), computer systems and data-base management (Information System Services Department – Densan Jōhō Kyoku), and public relations, library and dissemination of savings information (Public Relations Department – Jōhō Seebisu Kyoku) (Bank of Japan, *Annual Review 1994*, p.93).

The Institute for Monetary and Economic Studies, compared with the research in the Research and Statistics Department, conducted the more theoretical and theoretical-empirical research on macro monetary policy and economic issues (Division I), micro monetary policy issues (Division II) and the history of the Japanese financial system (Division III). The BoJ's 33 branches and 12 offices operated as liaison centres between the Bank and the local financial industry such as regional and Second Tier regional banks, business and governments. One of the responsibilities of the branches was to conduct business transactions with

---

[33] Based on Suzuki (1987a), p.312, and *Bank of Japan Quarterly Bulletin*, November 1993, p.39; the treasury business of the BoJ is described in Bank of Japan (1993).

the financial institutions in the region and to study the economic and financial trends in their respective areas (Bank of Japan 1988, pp.10–11). The results of these studies were reported at quarterly meetings held at the Tokyo head office. Furthermore, whereas the head office was responsible for deciding on the total amount of lending to the specific categories of banks such as city, regional and *shinkin* banks, the branches were given the task of distributing these amounts over the regional banks under their jurisdiction. In addition, the BoJ maintained six overseas representative offices (New York, London, Frankfurt am Main, Washington, DC, Paris and Hong Kong), which served as international liaison offices and information-gathering centres.

6 Informality, banking crisis and financial reform: 1998 and beyond

> Financial regulation and supervision were designed with opaqueness and non-transparency in mind to provide an environment for political favours and concessions to be struck between politicians, government bureaucrats and the business sector.
>
> *T.F. Cargill* (1998)

6.1 Introduction

The structure of the Japanese financial system and monetary authorities as described in chapter 5 came under heavy pressure during the second half of the nineties. This was predominantly the result of the deteriorating situation of the Japanese banking industry, which was caused by the collapse of the so-called 'bubble' economy, the process of financial reform, a general policy of forbearance on the side of the supervisory authorities and, as I shall assert in this and the following chapters, the use of informal instruments and the existence of informal networks between the monetary authorities and banking sector. As regards the latter, informal instruments such as unpublished administrative guidance and transparent guidance in the form of circulars (*tsūtatsu*) often proved to be ineffective, and elaborate informal networks institutionalised by *amakudari, gakubatsu, shukkō* (*ama-agari*) and the MoF-*tan* system persistently blocked the adoption of timely and effective policy measures, as government bureaucrats entangled in these networks tried to protect both their own interests and those of the banking industry. This system of intertwined relations would be largely responsible for a great number of scandals that initiated institutional and organisational reforms at both the MoF and BoJ. In the end, the banking crisis would function as a catalyst for further administrative and financial reforms, affecting financial institutions, financial markets and monetary authorities, culminating in 1998 in the most fundamental changes of the Japanese financial system since the implementation of financial reforms during the American occupation (see section 5.2 of chapter 5). The changed situation of the Japanese banking sector during this period can be described most aptly by two diametrically opposed views put forward in, respectively, Burstein (1988) and Dattel (1994). These views cover a period of six years only but present perceptions of the Japanese banking industry that range from a dominant financial superpower to an inefficient third-rate industry:

In financial services, the world's most strategic economic sector in the next century, Japanese companies are already dominant, even though they are just beginning to develop the global infrastructure to match their domestic strength. (Burstein 1988)

The Japanese financial institutions are no longer the vanguard of a new economic empire. They are no longer a threat nor the source of boundless capital. They are a drain on their own economy, their inefficiencies and spendthrift ways now subsidised by the Japanese people and Japanese manufacturers. (Dattel 1994)

This perception of the rise and fall of Japanese banks seems to some extent exaggerated, but the fact remains that the unfortunate developments in the Japanese banking sector during the nineties threatened not only the stability of the Japanese financial system but also occasionally led to fears about the stability of the international financial system as well.

In this chapter I shall discuss the developments in the Japanese banking sector during the eighties and nineties that resulted in a major banking crisis, the policy responses to this crisis and the administrative and financial reforms that were finally implemented. First, in section 6.2, a short overview of the process of financial reform during the seventies and eighties will be presented. Around the mid-seventies, the Japanese monetary authorities started slowly but steadily to liberalise existing regulations. As will be explained in this chapter, this process was partly responsible for the creation of the 'bubble' economy and the subsequent banking crisis. Second, in section 6.3, attention is paid to the rise of the 'bubble' economy during the second half of the eighties, which was characterised by a speculative boom in asset prices, and its collapse at the beginning of the nineties. The aftermath of the 'bubble', including the severe banking crisis, caused the monetary authorities to introduce important administrative and financial reforms. This policy response is analysed in section 6.4, in which seven phases are distinguished. In general, the policy reaction included elements of delay, forbearance and non-disclosure, but also important administrative and financial reforms, which were often implemented as a result of major scandals involving private banks and monetary authorities. As in the previous chapters, the emphasis will be on the analysis of informal aspects, in particular related to prudential policy. Finally, section 6.5 concludes and puts the Japanese policy reaction to the banking crisis in the perspective of similar experiences of the US supervisory authorities.

6.2   Financial reform: the experience of the seventies and eighties

Until the end of the sixties, the pace of financial reform in Japan was slow. From 1973 this changed owing to the transition to the floating exchange rate system and the rise of inflation throughout the world. Furthermore, the first oil crisis that marked the end of the high growth period in Japan resulted in large issues of government bonds to finance rising public borrowing requirements. The shift to lower economic growth and higher levels of public debt, combined with the increasing accumulation of financial assets by individuals, the growth of internal reserves of Japanese companies and increasing monetary growth, raised the degree of interest rate sensitivity in the private non-financial sector (Suzuki 1987a; van Rixtel 1998c). Furthermore, the Japanese financial structure changed slowly but steadily, as the dependence of non-financial firms on bank borrowing was reduced, and other sources of corporate finance such as internal finance and direct finance became more important (Calder 1993; Horiuchi 1996). As regards the latter, this implied a development towards corporate financing through the money and capital markets, in particular the Eurobond markets, in which the issuance conditions for Japanese companies were significantly less restrictive than in Japan itself.[1] Furthermore, the shift to the floating exchange rate system stimulated the internationalisation and globalisation of finance and resulted in a substantial increase of international capital flows. Finally, the rapid progress of computer and information technology resulted in lower costs of financial innovations and higher profit opportunities for financial institutions.

The process of financial reform resulted in a gradual decrease of the degree of regulation of the Japanese financial system.[2] The traditional segmentation of the activities of financial institutions became increasingly blurred, as banks and securities companies started to operate more and more on each other's business territories. Furthermore, the city and major regional banks diverted their operations towards smaller and

---

[1] Eurobonds are bonds denominated in a currency other than the national currency of the issuer (Barron's 2000, p.165).

[2] For more elaborate analysis of the process of financial reform see: Feldman 1986; Suzuki 1986, 1987a, 1987b, 1989a; Suzuki and Yomo 1986; Cargill and Royama 1988; Pauly 1988; McCall Rosenbluth 1989; Goodhart and Sutija 1990; Eijffinger and van Rixtel 1992; Calder 1993, 1997; Hall 1993, 1998a; van Rixtel 1996, 1997, 1998c; Steenbeek 1996; Vogel 1996; Craig 1998b; Lincoln 1998a; Miyajima 1998; Norville 1998; Beason and James 1999; Harner 2000.

medium-sized companies, forcing the smaller banks and credit co-operatives to look for new business opportunities, as will be explained in the next section. Also the traditional segmentation between short- and long-term lending by, respectively, commercial banks and long-term financial institutions was in practice no longer followed. All in all, the Japanese financial system started to move slowly but steadily towards a universal banking system.[3] In addition, the regulatory authorities embarked on a carefully orchestrated path of abolition of interest rate controls, and also the regulation of the entry of financial markets was gradually lifted. Finally, the degree of international openness of the Japanese financial system was improved, and international capital could move more easily into and out of Japan.

Traditionally, financial reform in Japan has been of a gradual step-by-step character, the aim being to avoid disruption of the status quo in market shares and business territories between various individual financial institutions and groups of financial institutions. This policy strategy was instrumental in maintaining the 'convoy system' and the stability of the financial system during the seventies and eighties. Thus, the initial stage of the process of financial reform resulted in a more market-oriented financial system without causing major problems and crises. Over the years, in the context of the Japanese experience with financial reform, five interrelated sub-processes can be distinguished: financial innovations, financial liberalisation, financial globalisation, concentration of financial institutions and the rebuilding of financial reputation (Eijffinger and van Rixtel 1992; van Rixtel 1997, 1998c). Financial innovations can be described as the introduction of new financial products, processes or markets. The most important financial innovations in Japan were the introduction of certificates of deposits (CDs) in May 1979 and money market certificates (MMCs) in March 1985 by banks, and the creation of so-called *chukoku* funds, which included investments in medium-term government bonds, in January 1980 by securities companies (Suzuki and Yomo 1986). Examples of new financial processes were the increased use of funding instruments with market related interest rates – i.e. liability management – and spread-based lending rates – i.e. asset management – and the introduction of securitisation techniques, which implied the creation of marketable securities, in the banking sector (Suzuki 1984; Kanda 1990, p.1). New markets that were introduced were the market for purchases of government bonds with repurchase agreement – or *gensaki* market – in the early

---

[3] Various reports of the Financial System Research Council, which was affiliated with the Banking Bureau, and the Securities and Exchange Council, which was linked to the Securities Bureau, discussed this de-segmentation process extensively. See Federation of Bankers Associations of Japan (1988, 1990a).

seventies, the market for banker's acceptances in June 1985, which however became de facto defunct in November 1989 owing to too stringent conditions, the market for financial bills (*seifu tanki shōken*), the market for treasury bills (*tanki kokusai*) in February 1986, the Japan Offshore market in December 1986 and the market for commercial paper (*shōgyō tegata*) in November 1987 (Feldman 1986; Foundation for Advanced Information and Research 1991; de Brouwer 1992; Federation of Bankers Associations of Japan 1994).

Financial liberalisation is here interpreted as the easing or lifting of existing financial regulation. The process of financial liberalisation changed the regulatory structure of the Japanese financial system drastically. At first this meant a gradual relaxation and abolition of interest rate regulations for large bank deposits. Hence, interest rates for deposits of three months' to two years' maturity with a minimum amount of 1 billion yen were fully liberalised in October 1985. Furthermore, this minimum for large time deposits was gradually reduced to 10 million yen in October 1990. With respect to liberalisation of lending interest rates, the introduction in January 1989 of a new short-term prime rate system was a major step in the move towards more market-oriented interest rates (Kuroda 1989, p.10). Under this system, interest rates were related to market developments and determined by a weighted average of funding costs. Also the long-term prime rate system, i.e. interest rates on loans with a maturity longer than one year to most preferred customers, was changed: from April 1991, the long-term prime rate was linked to the short-term prime rate by adding a certain spread.

The third sub-process of financial reform that is distinguished here is financial globalisation, which can be defined as the increasing development of international financial relations, including the opening of national financial markets to non-residents. In Japan this process was promoted by, in particular, the enactment of a new Foreign Exchange and Foreign Trade Control Law in December 1980, which provided freedom of international transactions unless explicitly prohibited (freedom in principle). With respect to the money markets, the process of financial globalisation in Japan has been stimulated by two important reforms. First, the removal in June 1984 of the so-called swap limits or yen conversion limits, which restricted the amount of foreign currency that could be converted into yen by financial institutions, increased arbitrage between interbank markets and the Euroyen-markets – the financial markets outside Japan where instruments denominated in yen are traded. Second, the internationalisation of Japanese money markets was stimulated by the abolition in April 1984 of the so-called real demand doctrine, which allowed forward exchange transaction only for trade (or real) finance. As a result of the globalisation of the Japanese financial system and the development of the Japanese economy, Japanese financial institutions advanced into the ranks of the world's largest banks and securities houses (Wright and Pauli 1987; Düser 1990). Instrumental to this development were the protected domestic financial markets, de facto largely closed to foreign financial institutions. Furthermore, because of existing regulations, foreign institutions seldom raised funds in the Japanese financial markets and residents often preferred to use overseas capital markets (Takeda and Turner 1992, p.94). Also the liberal attitude of the Japanese monetary authorities with respect to the international financial activities of Japanese financial institutions supported their international advance. For example, Japanese banks were allowed to operate as universal banks in various countries with universal banking systems and consequently could conduct various activities such as securities business through securities subsidiaries, which were not permitted in Japan. By using low-spread/high-volume strategies aimed at gaining market share and acquiring established institutions in global financial centres, Japanese financial institutions became major players in the international financial markets, in particular in the Euromarkets. These markets gained increasing importance for the issuance of debt securities and equity-linked products by Japanese corporations (Düser 1990; Takeda and Turner 1992; van Rixtel 1997).

Furthermore, financial reform in Japan became increasingly shaped by an increase in financial concentration, i.e. a decrease in the number of financial institutions. In 1971 Dai-Ichi Kangyo Bank was established as a result of the merger between Dai-Ichi Bank and the Nippon Kangyo Bank, followed in 1973 by the merger between Taiyo Bank and Bank of Kobe in Taiyo-Kobe Bank. At the beginning of the nineties, Mitsui Bank and Taiyo-Kobe Bank merged in Mitsui Taiyo-Kobe Bank (1 April 1990), and Kyowa Bank and Saitama Bank became Kyowa Saitama Bank as of 1 April 1991; their names were later changed to Sakura Bank and Asahi Bank, respectively. Finally, towards the end of the eighties, financial reform, in particular reform of the organisational structure of the monetary authorities, was increasingly instigated by the need to restore Japan's financial reputation in the aftermath of a rapidly growing number of financial scandals. As will be shown in the following sections, this became even more so the case in the nineties.

6.3   The rise and collapse of the 'bubble' economy

Japan experienced a strong surge in asset prices during the eighties, in particular in the second half. The Nikkei 225 stock-index rose from a level of 13,000 at the end of 1985 to a maximum of 38,915 on the last trading day of 1989. During the 1985–1990 period, property prices surged, rising on average by 22% compared with a year earlier; in 1989 it was calculated that the property value of metropolitan Tokyo exceeded the value of the entire United States (Werner 1992, p.22). This situation of excessive asset price inflation gave rise to the terminology of the 'bubble' economy. It is generally believed that the following factors were behind the surge in asset prices (Takeda and Turner 1992; Ministry of Finance 1993a; Hamada 1995; Nakajima and Taguchi 1995; Lincoln 1998b; Okina et al. 2000). First, the process of financial reform increased competition not only among banks but between banks and other private financial institutions such as securities companies and insurance companies as well. The increased competition put heavy pressure on the banks' profit margins. As a result, banks started to look for more profitable, less traditional, but riskier projects: they expanded their lending to real estate and construction companies and non-bank financial institutions such as consumer credit institutions and leasing companies. Because of existing regulations, these institutions were virtually denied access to the open financial markets, and therefore relied heavily on bank credit (Takeda and Turner 1992, p.61). The figures show this development clearly: according to Nakajima and Taguchi (1995), p.59, 'between 1985 and 1992, bank loans to the real estate industry grew 13.7 percent annually, compared with 6.6 percent for total bank lending, and the share of such loans in total bank lending rose from 7.5 percent in 1985 to 12.1 percent in 1992'. In addition, 'lending to "non-banks" also grew rapidly, from 10.4 percent to 14.0 percent of total bank lending'. It has to be mentioned that a number of these institutions were established by the banks themselves or were members of the same *keiretsu* or industrial grouping, thereby increasing the exposure of banks to these risky sectors. Furthermore, Japanese banks extended considerable amounts of credit to the corporate sector for investment in stocks and other financial assets. This development of financial investments by non-financial private companies was called 'financial engineering' (*zaitech* or *zaiteku*), which means, literally, know-how in the management of financial assets (Hsu 1994, p.406). For many non-financial firms, this became a major profit-generating activity. In addition, lending by so-called housing loan companies or *jūsen*, which had been established at the end of the seventies under the guidance of the MoF and often in affiliation with large banks, grew rapidly (Rosenbluth and Thies 1999). In the end, Japan experienced a rather classic credit-induced real estate boom and financial assets' bubble, fuelled by a vicious spiral of rising asset prices, higher collateral value and increasing bank credit. This development was certainly not a unique Japanese experience, but occurred in a significant number of other developed and developing countries as well (Borio et al. 1994; Demetriades 1999; Herring and Wachter 1999). Second, an important explanation of the creation of the 'bubble' is related to the use of informal policy instruments and the existence of informal networks between the monetary authorities and banks. In general, the use of the former often turned out not to be effective, and the existence of the latter on numerous occasions prevented the use of prudent and stringent measures. For example, as will be asserted in this chapter, MoF's administrative guidance regarding the *jūsen*'s lending policy was not very effective, most likely owing to a combination of political factors and the large presence of MoF retirees on their boards. Also the informal guidance of bank lending by the BoJ, its so-called 'window guidance' (*madoguchi shidō*), proved to be ineffective and was even abolished in 1991 (see chapter 5). Third, in personal interviews former staff members from the MoF and BoJ noted that one of the reasons for the rise of the 'bubble' could lie in the fact that the BoJ was in control of the short-term financial markets, but that the capital markets were mainly the domain of the MoF, and that co-ordination between the two was less than perfect. As a matter of fact, as was described in the previous chapter, the MoF used several and predominantly informal macro monetary policy instruments that primarily affect capital market developments, sometimes contrary to the policy objectives of the BoJ. Furthermore, arbitrage deficiencies between money market and capital market interest rates and the existence of the 'dual interest rate structure' (see section 5.2 of chapter 5) hampered the pass-through of changes in policy rates to long-term interest rates. Fourth, the 'bubble' was fuelled by the accommodative stance of Japanese macro monetary policy, partly caused by international exchange rate considerations and related pressure from the MoF (Hamada 1995, p.277; Hartcher 1998, p.85; Okina et al. 2000, p.14; Ueda 2000, p.16; Cargill 2000, p.12; personal interviews with former high-ranking BoJ staff members). This protracted monetary easing has been more or less acknowledged by the BoJ in its monthly report (*Nippon Ginkō Geppo*) of April 1990, which has been interpreted as a self-critique of the Bank's policy stance during 1987–1989, and later in several other publications as well (Ito 1992, p.48; Okina et al. 2000, pp.8ff.). The Louvre Accord of February 1987 aimed to stabilise the dollar and prevent a further depreciation against other major currencies. Consequently, the BoJ eased its policies: in February the official discount rate was reduced to an (at that time) historic low of 2.5%. It remained at that level until the end of May 1989. The low-interest-rate policy resulted in the creation of excess liquidity, and enabled the banking industry to keep the asset price boom going. It also has to be emphasised that the BoJ was in the difficult situation where asset prices surged, but actual

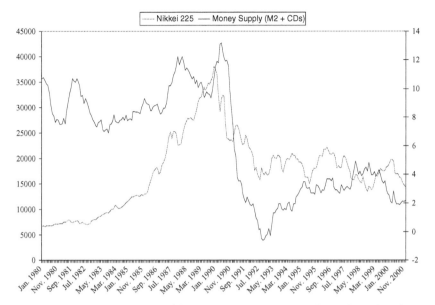

Figure 6.1 The 'bubble' economy: money supply and stock prices
(January 1980–January 2001)
Note: Left-hand scale: Nikkei 225 stock-index level; right-hand scale:
% annual growth of broad money (M2 + CDs)

inflation and inflationary expectations seemed not to require a change of
its monetary policy stance. The co-existence of asset price 'bubbles' and
price stability is indeed one of the most complex issues in monetary policy
assessment, as has been noted by several observers (for example: Borio
et al. 1994; Gertler et al. 1998; Federal Reserve Bank of Kansas City
1999; Cecchetti et al. 2000; Okina et al. 2000). In addition, the position
of the BoJ was further complicated by the fact that the MoF was unwilling
to boost public spending given its concern for the budgetary situation,
so the BoJ had to provide the economic stimulation (Ueda 2000, p.18).
The accommodative policy stance during the middle and latter half of
the eighties is clearly reflected in the high yearly monetary growth rates
such as shown in figure 6.1, which also depicts the sharp increase in the
Nikkei 225 stock index during the 'bubble' years. Figure 6.2 shows a
similar development in the prices of commercial land in Tokyo, such as
measured by surveys at the end of March and September.

Finally, during the creation of the 'bubble', Mr Satoshi Sumita, a former high-ranking MoF official, was serving as Governor of the BoJ. Since
the early seventies – and until the appointment of Mr Masaru Hayami
in April 1998 – the positions of Governor and Senior Deputy-Governor

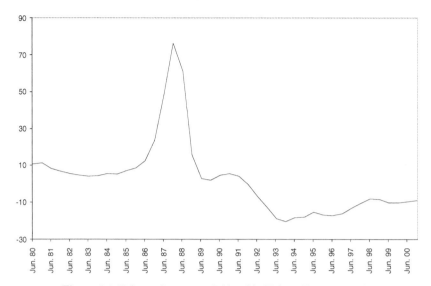

Figure 6.2 Prices of commercial land in Tokyo (June 1980–June 2000)
(% change over two semesters)
Note: Percentage change in commercial land prices in Tokyo area as
published by the National Land Agency in March and by local governments in September.
Source: Bank for International Settlements.

of the BoJ have been filled alternately by BoJ and former MoF top executives (in the case of the MoF, a former Administrative Vice-Minister).
Furthermore, one retired MoF official occupied one of the BoJ's executive director positions, and another retired MoF official was employed
as Executive Auditor (see chapter 5). The presence of these retired MoF
officials in the highest executive positions of the BoJ, predominantly the
consequence of MoF's need to find post-retirement positions for its staff
in the private sector (*amakudari*), could have been instrumental in the
implementation of the relatively loose monetary policy stance during this
period.

   However, as inflationary pressures started to mount, the BoJ changed
its policy stance and began to tighten its policy in May 1989. This change
would mark the start of the collapse of the 'bubble'. After some delay, the
rise in interest rates deflated the value of assets such as land, real estate
and stocks. Asset prices came down sharply. From its peak of around
39,000 in 1989, the Nikkei 225 dropped to the 14,000 range in August
1992; a similar development took place in real estate and land prices (see
figure 6.1). The bursting of the 'bubble' caused severe problems for the

Japanese banking industry (Takeda and Turner 1992; Hamada 1995). First, a significant number of real estate companies and other non-banks found it increasingly difficult to service loans. Furthermore, the decline of asset prices diminished the value of the collateral of extended loans, in many cases below those of the loans they secured. Consequently, banks became saddled with non-performing loans, classified by the MoF as loans on which interest had not been paid for six months or more. Second, the collapse of the 'bubble' and the subsequent deflation of asset prices caused problems in meeting the BIS solvency requirements. According to the 1988 Basle Accord, international operating banks would, by the end of 1992, have to meet a capital to weighted assets ratio of 8%. The MoF interpreted this date as the end of Fiscal Year 1992, i.e. the end of March 1993. The capital taken into consideration consisted of core or Tier I capital, that is equity and disclosed reserves, and supplementary or Tier II capital, i.e. subordinated debt and revaluation reserves. In the case of Japan, up to 45% of banks' latent gains on securities holdings were allowed to be counted as Tier II capital. According to the Anti-Monopoly Law, Japanese banks were allowed to hold up to 5% of the equity of a single firm. Given the rise in share prices during the 'bubble' period, these cross-shareholdings embodied substantial revaluation reserves, and consequently the unrealised gains on these securities holdings were included in Tier II capital (Frankel and Morgan 1992, p.588). However, the burst of the 'bubble' and the sharp drop in stock prices eroded this part of Japanese banks' Tier II capital, causing concern among Japanese and international supervisory authorities. The erosion of the revaluation reserves of the major Japanese banks at the beginning of the nineties is presented in table 6.1. From 1991 to 1992 the reservation reserves were halved, resulting in a significant worsening of the solvency position of the Japanese banking sector. Table 6.1 also shows the rise in the issue of subordinated debt, which was issued to compensate for the decline in Tier II capital that resulted from the decline in revaluation reserves.

6.4   The policy response: forbearance
and financial reform

The collapse of the 'bubble' and the resulting problems in the Japanese banking industry prompted the Japanese supervisory authorities to take action, which, however, was often 'too little, too late'.[4] Their response

---

[4] This section draws on the following publications: *Asahi Shimbun*, Bank of Japan (Annual Review), Bank of Japan (Nihon Ginkō Kinyū Kenkyūjo, *Nihon Kinyū Nenpyō*), *Bank of Japan Quarterly Bulletin*, *Daily Yomiuri*, *The Economist*, Federation of Bankers Associations of Japan (*Japanese Banks*), *Financial Regulation Report*, *Financial Times*, International

Table 6.1. *Revaluation reserves and subordinated debt of major banks (trillion yen)*

	Revaluation reserves			Subordinated debt		
	1991[1]	1992[1]	1993[1]	1991[1]	1992[1]	1993[1]
City banks	22.2	10.8	10.9	3.9	6.0	8.3
Long-term credit banks	6.4	3.4	3.6	0.8	1.0	1.6
Trust banks	6.4	3.1	3.2	–	0.1	0.6
Total	35.0	17.3	17.8	4.7	7.1	10.6

Note: [1] As of the end of March.
Source: International Monetary Fund (1993), p.11.

can be typified as a combination of regulatory forbearance, policy failures, cover up, manipulation of (stock) markets, case-by-case intervention and careful financial reform, often hoping that the problems would disappear by themselves, and has been the focus of broad academic scrutiny (van Rixtel 1996, 1998c; Schaede 1996; Yamawaki 1996; Nagashima 1997; Cargill et al. 1998; Craig 1998a; Fukao 1998; Gibney 1998b; Hall 1998a; Hanazaki and Horiuchi 1998; Japan Economic Institute 1998; Kitami 1998; Kuroda 1998; Lincoln 1998b, 1998c; OECD 1998, 1999a, 2000; Patrick 1998; Pempel 1998; Posen 1998; Wood 1998; Beason and James 1999; Brown 1999; Corbett 1999, 2000; Curtis 1999; Hoshi and Kashyap 1999; Hutchison et al. 1999; Milhaupt 1999; Nakaso 1999; Cargill 2000; Hoshi 2000; Hoshi and Patrick 2000b; Ito 2000; Kanaya and Woo 2000; Mori et al. 2000; Saito and Shiratsuka 2000; Ueda 2000). Initially, in order to avoid an outbreak of financial panic, to mask supervisory failure and to protect various interests including their own, the supervisory authorities – in particular the MoF – often denied that there was a crisis, stuck to non-disclosure and non-transparency, preserved the status quo and 'convoy system' and failed to address the moral hazard risk from private banks under this system. They were also particularly keen to preserve and guard the symbiotic system of informal relations and networks with the private banking sector. Extensive informal networks established by *amakudari, gakubatsu, shukkō (ama-agari)* and

Monetary Fund (Staff Country Reports – Japan), International Monetary Fund (*International Capital Markets*), *Japan Economic Journal*, Japan Economic Institute Reports, *Japan Times*, Kinyū Shōken Research, Ministry of Finance (*Monthly Finance Review*), Ministry of Finance (Ōkurashō Ginkō Kyoku, *Ginkō Kyoku Kinyū Nenpō*), Moody's Investors Service, *Nihon Keizai Shimbun, Nikkei Weekly*, Nippon Finance, OECD (*Economic Surveys – Japan*), Capital Markets Research Institute *Review* (Japan), *The Wall Street Journal, Tokyo Business Today* and *Zenginkyō Financial Review*.

the MoF-*tan* (and similar BoJ-*tan*) system blurred the already weak separation of the public and private sectors even further, and seem to have prevented prompt and adequate intervention on numerous occasions. Thus, I put forward the proposition that the element of regulatory forbearance was to a significant degree related to the existence of strong and intimate informal network relations between the monetary authorities and private banks. In some cases, as I shall assert in chapter 8, they were even directly responsible for the development of major problems at specific banks. As has been asserted by Kanaya and Woo (2000), p.27, forbearance was also linked to the use of administrative guidance: 'Regulatory forbearance was possible also in part because of the system of informal administrative guidance prevailing at the time.' Furthermore, the use of certain informal policy instruments such as administrative guidance directed at the stock market and the lending behaviour of banks and discretionary changes in accounting rules often proved to be ineffective and even counterproductive. However, the inadequate policy response was also the result of a paralysed political system, in which government and opposition parties lacked the courage and flexibility to really tackle the issues and implement a public bailout programme. Also, for a long time, the large banks especially yielded sufficient political influence to resist public-funds injections and the inherent government conditions and control attached; owing to weak corporate governance, banks were also not pressured to change their policies. Later on, often after major scandals involving the monetary authorities, some reform measures were implemented, but it would not be until 1998, when the international financial community increasingly feared a breakdown of the Japanese financial system, that somewhat more effective and substantial measures were adopted.

The aspect of forbearance as implemented in Japan would cast a deep shadow on the reputation and credibility of the monetary authorities and has been identified as one of the major characteristics of the policy response to the banking crisis in Japan (see for example: Yamawaki 1996; Cargill et al. 1998; Kanaya and Woo 2000; Ueda 2000). It has to be acknowledged that sometimes forbearance can be a rational policy (Eisenbeis and Horvitz 1993). In this interpretation, the supervisory authorities permit a bank to 'operate without meeting established safety-and-soundness standards for a limited period of time while taking remedial actions to reduce risk exposure and correct other weaknesses' (FDIC 1997). In other words, it could be interpreted as a kind of 'buying-time' policy, implemented in order to avoid the outbreak of a systemic financial crisis (Mori et al. 2000). Furthermore, as has been suggested by Charles Lindblom (1959), 'muddling through', which contains certain aspects of forbearance in the Japanese context, can be the best strategy to follow as regards the implementation of public policy. However, when forbearance leads to the situation where many insolvent banks are allowed to remain operational and it becomes increasingly costly to solve the problems, crises can evolve almost beyond control. This is what essentially happened in Japan, as has been more or less acknowledged by the BoJ itself (see Mori et al. 2000).

The second crucial aspect of the policy response to the banking crisis has been financial reform. In the context of the orientation in this study on informality, financial reform is separated into administrative reform (*gyōsei kaikaku*) and financial reform in its strict sense (*kinyū no jiyūka*). The former includes, for example, the reform of the MoF, the establishment of the Financial Supervisory Agency (Kinyū Kantoku Chō) and Financial Services Agency (Kinyū Chō), review of the use of administrative guidance and moves towards more disclosure of governmental information (rule based instead of discretionary policies), the end of the MoF-*tan* (and BoJ-*tan*) system, the abolishment of most circulars issued by the MoF (*tsūtatsu*) and the adoption of new guidelines for the acceptance of post-retirement positions by former high-ranking MoF bureaucrats in the private sector (*amakudari*). Financial reform in its strict sense takes into account reorganisations of the Bank of Japan and the programme for the liberalisation of financial markets and institutions in Japan ('Big Bang'), including the introduction of a new Bank of Japan Law.[5] A detailed analysis of the complete 'Big Bang' programme is beyond the scope of this book (see for example: Financial System Research Council 1997b; IMF 1997, 1998, 1999b; Matsushita 1997a; Mikuni 1997; Ministry of Finance 1997a, 2000a, 2000b; Securities and Exchange Council 1997; Craig 1998b; Hall 1998a; Hamada 1998; Katayama and Makov 1998; Norville 1998; van Rixtel 1998c; Watanabe and Sudo 1998; Financial System Council 1999a; Ito and Melvin 1999; Harner 2000). However, certain elements of this programme related to the monetary authorities will be discussed. As regards both administrative and financial (in its strict sense) reform, it will become clear that these processes were often driven by scandals, and that on many occasions lukewarm and half-hearted reforms were implemented to create the impression that certain problems were really being tackled – until the next scandal came along (Keehn 1998, pp.207ff.).

The development of the banking crisis and bad loans in Japan is shown in tables 6.2 and 6.3. In general, it is rather difficult to assess the amount of bad loans in an economy. However, in Japan, additional problems in

---

[5] The BoJ is not a government organisation, and therefore not subjected to administrative reform.

Table 6.2. *Bad loans of 'all deposit-taking financial institutions' in Japan (trillion yen and as a percentage of GDP)*[1]

	Amount of bad loans		Amount of bad loans	
	('Self-assessment')[2]	Related loan losses[3]	('Risk management loans')[4,6]	Related loan losses[5,6]
End March 1992	7–8 (1.5%–1.7%)	–	–	–
End March 1993	8.4 (1.8%)	–	12.8 (2.7%)	1.6 (0.3%)
End March 1994	10.5 (2.2%)	–	13.6 (2.8%)	3.9 (0.8%)
End March 1995	11.6 (2.4%)	–	12.5 (2.6%)	5.2 (1.1%)
End March 1996	34.8 (6.9%)	8.3 (1.7%)	28.5 (5.7%)	13.4 (2.7%)
End March 1997	27.9 (5.5%)	4.7 (0.9%)	21.8 (4.3%)	7.8 (1.5%)
End March 1998	87.1 (17.5%)	18.9 (3.8%)^{OP}	38.0 (7.6%)[7]	13.3 (2.7%)
End March 1999	80.6 (16.3%)	15.9 (3.2%)^{OP}	38.7 (7.8%)[7]	13.6 (2.7%)
End March 2000	81.8 (15.3%)	15.9 (3.0%)^{OP}	41.4 (7.8%)[7]	6.9 (1.3%)

Notes: ^{OP} Own projections.

[1] City banks, regional banks, long-term credit banks, trust banks and co-operative type financial institutions (*shinkin* banks, credit co-operatives, etc.). For end-March 1992, 1993, 1994 and 1995 city banks, long-term credit banks and trust banks only. GDP figures are calendar-year figures.

[2] Figures for 1992–1997 are projections from the MoF, as reported in Hall (1998a), p.30. Source for 1998–2000 is the Financial Supervisory Agency (http://www.fsa.go.jp), following the 'self-assessment results of asset quality' for Category II ('grey area' or 'substandard') and Category III ('doubtful') loans. Failed institutions are not included. For example, the figures as of end-March 2000 do not include Nippon Credit Bank, Kokumin Bank, Kofuku Bank, Tokyo Sowa Bank, Namihaya Bank, Niigata Chuo Bank and co-operative type institutions that declared their own bankruptcy.

[3] For 1996–1997, figures are based on MoF estimates as reported by Hall (1998a), p.30. Figures for 1998–2000 are own projections (OP) based on uncollectable rates of respectively 17% and 75% for Category II (questionable) and III (doubtful) loans, such as projected by the BoJ (Hoshi and Kashyap 1999, p.29).

[4] As reported by the Financial Supervisory Agency as of the end of March 2000. For 1992–1994, risk management loans include loans to borrowers in legal bankruptcy plus past due loans. For 1995–1996, these loans include loans to borrowers in legal bankruptcy, past due loans plus restructured loans.

[5] Losses on the disposal of bad loans as reported by the FSA (http://www.fsa.go.jp).

[6] Figures for risk management loans and losses on the disposal of bad loans are for banks only, as they are reported by the banks themselves (i.e. city, long-term credit, trust, regional and Second Tier regional banks). Hokkaido Takushoku, Tokuyo City, Kyoto Kyoei, Naniwa, Fukutoku and Midori Bank are excluded as of end-March 1998. The Long-Term Credit Bank of Japan, Nippon Credit Bank, Kokumin, Kofuku and Tokyo Sowa Bank are excluded as of end-March 1999. Namihaya Bank and Niigata Chuo Bank are excluded as from end-March 2000.

[7] All banks plus co-operative type financial institutions (*shinkin* banks, credit co-operatives, etc.), thus all depository financial institutions.

this respect were caused by widespread mutual stakes of financial institutions in each other's affiliates, which became apparent in the bankruptcy of Japan Leasing in 1998,[6] and which also often made it possible to hide bad loans relatively easily from supervisory inspections, as was shown in the 1998 failure of the Long-Term Credit Bank of Japan. Despite these caveats, table 6.2 provides an overview of the development of bad loans and related loan losses of Japanese depository institutions according to two definitions, firstly projections by the public supervisory authorities (MoF and FSA) – from 1998 based on the so-called 'self-assessment' results of banks – and secondly 'risk management loans', which are published by individual banks in their financial statements.[7] The Financial Supervisory Authority started to publish bad loans according to the 'self-assessment' results of banks in April 1998 within the framework of the so-called 'prompt corrective action' (PCA) scheme, which distinguishes loans into four categories including 'grey area' loans (Category II, of which the major part should be recoverable) and 'doubtful' loans (Category III, of which only a minor part is recoverable). It has to be said that, owing to differences in coverage of financial institutions and frequent adjustments of the definitions of bad loans, the figures presented in table 6.2 are difficult to compare (Hall 1998a; Moody's Investors Service 1998; Hoshi and Kashyap 1999; IMF 1999b; Hoshi and Patrick 2000b; Ueda 2000). For example, as regards risk management loans, only the figures for the years 1998, 1999 and 2000 include co-operative type financial institutions as well; the figures on the losses of the disposal of risk management loans do not include these financial co-operatives at all. Furthermore, frequent changes in the definitions of bad loans over the years have blurred a coherent and complete overview of the banking problems considerably. For example, at end-September 1995 MoF's definition of bad loans included for the first time so-called 'reduced interest loans', which are loans on which interest has been reduced or waived. The introduction of this new definition could be largely responsible for the substantial increase in the amount of bad loans at end-March 1996 compared with previous years.

According to the projections by the public supervisory authorities, the amount of bad loans increased from 7–8 trillion yen (1.5–1.7% of

---

[6] Japan Leasing was affiliated with the Long-Term Credit Bank of Japan and collapsed in September 1998, leaving 2.2 trillion yen in liabilities behind, a post-war record at that time. The LTCB was subsequently nationalised in October.

[7] In Japan, three classifications of bad loans are used ('risk management loans' of the banks themselves following guidelines from the Federation of Bankers Associations, the bad loans definition in the context of the October 1998 Financial Revitalisation Legislation and the classification of bad loans following the banks' 'self-assessment' results). For detailed explanations see Hoshi and Kashyap (1999), IMF (1999a, 1999b), Bank of Japan (2000), Hoshi and Patrick (2000b).

GDP) at end-March 1992 to a maximum of 87.3 trillion yen (17.5% of GDP) at end-March 1998, which was around 11% of total private lending. The big jump in the figures for 1998 is to a large extent caused by the shift to the definition of bad loans based on 'self-assessment' results. In terms of risk management loans, the maximum amount of bad loans was 41.4 trillion yen (7.8% of GDP) at end-March 2000, which is around half the 81.8 trillion yen (15.3% of GDP) of bad loans according to the 'self-assessment' definition in the same year. However, it has to be noted that possibly a significant part of the 'grey area' or Category II loans, which are included in the bad loan definition based on the 'self-assessment results', should ultimately not be classified as non-performing.[8] According to a 1997 study by the BoJ, 83% of Category II loans and 25% of Category III loans could be recovered within three years, for example by the sale of collateral (Hoshi and Kashyap 1999, p.29). Thus, the 'actual' difference between the two definitions of bad loans as reported in table 6.2 should be significantly smaller, in particular for the years 1998–2000 when 'self-assessment' figures were used, owing to the fact that the majority of Category II loans will not generate actual losses. This is reflected in the figures for loan losses presented in table 6.2. Their differences are much smaller than those between the figures for the two definitions of bad loans: as a percentage of GDP, loan losses projected by the MoF and FSA ('self-assessment' figures, from 1998 onwards including co-operative financial institutions) varied between 0.9% of GDP and 3.8% of GDP, whereas the losses on the disposal of bad loans in terms of risk management loans (for major banks only) ranged from 0.3% of GDP to 2.7% of GDP.

Not surprisingly, the bad loan figures published by the supervisory authorities and banks were significantly below a substantial number of estimates from independent international organisations and private sector institutions, in particular for the year 1998 when the banking crisis reached its peak in terms of bad loans following the 'self-assessment' definition. According to the IMF, the total size of problem loans in the financial industry in 1998 was almost 60 trillion yen higher (12% of GDP) than the official government figures. Estimates by several American and European investment banks of the amount of bad loans at the major Japanese banks were almost double the official figures; Moody's projected the amount of bad loans in the Japanese financial sector to be around 150 trillion yen or 30% of GDP. However, some observers also played down the magnitude of the banking crisis, as not all problem loans

---

[8] However, several private rating agencies have been much less optimistic. For example, Moody's Investors Service (1998), p.14, stated that 'Category II include exposures which, in Moody's opinion, may result in significant losses in the relatively near future'.

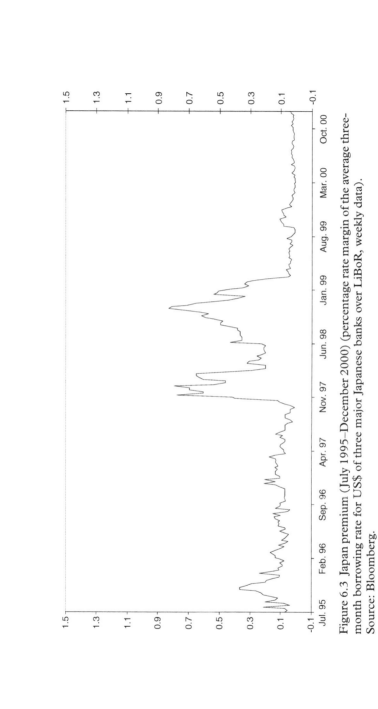

Figure 6.3 Japan premium (July 1995–December 2000) (percentage rate margin of the average three-month borrowing rate for US$ of three major Japanese banks over LiBoR, weekly data).
Source: Bloomberg.

Table 6.3. *International comparison of bad loans (peak years of crisis)*

	Non-performing loans		Restructured loans		Net unprovisioned problem loans
	as % of loans	as % of assets	as % of loans	as % of assets	as % of Tier I of capital
USA (peak 1991)	3.7	2.2	0.5	0.3	13.9
Norway	11.5	9.3	–	–	99.5
Finland	12.9	7.7	1.0	0.6	141.0
Sweden	13.4	8.3	3.9	2.4	145.4
Japan all banks (March 1998)	3.7	2.1	1.6	0.9	78.0

Source: Corbett (2000), p.155.

were actually written off – for example in the case of the Category II loans discussed above – and were backed by collateral that could be liquidated. Beason and James (1999, p.84) asserted that the amount of actual non-performing loans for the banking sector peaked at 40 trillion yen (8% of GDP) – including bad loans of non-bank affiliates – in September 1995, and that the major banks should have solved their bad loan problems rather easily by 2002. Given the varying estimates of the amount of bad loans in Japan, these figures are, in table 6.3, compared with the bad loan figures of other countries that experienced banking problems. This international comparison shows that at the peak of the Japanese banking crisis – following 'self-assessment' results – the amounts of non-performing loans as percentage of total loans and assets were comparable to those at the peak of the US banking crisis, whereas in terms of restructured loans the problems in Japan were about three times larger than in the USA. The Scandinavian bank crises, however, were considerably more severe compared with the situation in both Japan and the USA.[9]

Given the difficulties in assessing the amount of bad loans, an alternative way to investigate the development of the Japanese banking crisis is by analysing the trend in the so-called 'Japan premium'. This premium is the difference between the interest rates paid by major Japanese banks for their interbank Eurodollar and Euroyen borrowing and those paid by large American and European banks (Peek and Rosengren 1998, p.1; Ito and Harada 2000; Saito and Shiratsuka 2000, p.3). As is shown in figure 6.3, the 'Japan premium' increased in the course of 1995, and since then it has always been positive. It peaked during the last months

[9] For an elaborate discussion of the Japanese banking crisis from an international perspective see Hutchison et al. (1999) and Corbett (2000).

Table 6.4. *The policy reaction to the banking crisis*

Phase I (1990–June 1996)	The initial policy response
Phase II (June 1996–January 1997)	Administrative and financial reform
Phase III (January 1997–January 1998)	The end of 'too big to fail'
Phase IV (January 1998–June 1998)	Scandals, public funds and financial reform
Phase V (June 1998–October 1998)	Administrative reform and intensifying crisis
Phase VI (October 1998–July 2000)	Financial revitalisation: The end of the crisis?
Phase VII (July 2000–)	Consolidation of prudential policy

of 1997, when various large Japanese financial institutions collapsed, and was also particularly large towards the end of 1998. Clearly, for a significant part of the nineties, interbank funds obtained on the Euromoney markets were more expensive for all Japanese banks than for other major international banks. Furthermore, the differences between Japanese banks were quite small compared to the spreads vis-à-vis major European or US banks. This supports the assessment that the spreads were related to the whole Japanese banking sector, and not so much to individual institutions. Thus, the emergence and increase of the 'Japan premium' were a clear indication of the severe nature and magnitude of the Japanese banking crisis, and showed the damaged confidence of the international financial community in the Japanese banking sector. The spreads, which are shown in figure 6.3, reveal that it became increasingly difficult for Japanese banks to maintain profitable international wholesale activities. In fact, Japanese banks retreated en masse from the international lending markets: according to figures from the BIS, their outstanding international lending declined by US $170 billion during 1998 alone.[10]

In this section, the policy response to the banking crisis will be separated in seven phases (see table 6.4). During the first phase, which lasted from the collapse of the 'bubble' economy until the enactment of six so-called financial reform laws in June 1996, the monetary authorities often denied that there were significant problems in the banking sector and maintained a general policy of non-disclosure, but implemented some measures to solve the bad loan situation and related collateral problems. The second phase, which ended around the end of 1996, was characterised by the implementation of reform legislation, which aimed in particular at the bailout of the collapsed housing loan companies (*jūsen* resolution package) and strengthening of the Deposit Insurance Corporation

---

[10] The Japanese banking problems also affected other national banking sectors: for example, Peek and Rosengren (1997) present evidence that the contraction in Japanese bank lending was transmitted to the credit markets in the USA through the US branches of Japanese banks.

(Yokin Hoken Kikō), and the related establishment of public institutions such as the Resolution and Collection Bank (Seiri Kaishū Ginkō). The third phase started after the administrative reform proposals adopted by the Hashimoto administration in December 1996 that began the process of breaking up the Ministry of Finance. In June 1997 the Diet passed a new Bank of Japan Law that increased the independence of the Japanese central bank substantially. At the end of the same year a number of major financial institutions collapsed, which could be interpreted as the end of the 'too big to fail' policy and as the first erosion of the 'convoy system'. During the fourth phase – from January to June 1998 – initial developments in the Japanese financial system were dominated by major scandals, implicating both the MoF and BoJ. Later on, some public funds were injected in the banking sector and major financial reforms such as the revised Bank of Japan Law and so-called 'Big Bang' deregulation measures were implemented. Furthermore, following major scandals involving officials from both the MoF and BoJ, the use of informal instruments and the existence of informal networks between policymakers and banks were increasingly criticised and prompted louder demands for administrative reforms, including an attempt to limit *amakudari*. The next phase (June–October 1998) was characterised by the establishment of a new supervisory authority, the Financial Supervisory Agency (Kinyū Kantoku Chō) (FSA), the enactment of a major administrative reform bill and the announcement by the MoF of a substantial decrease in the number of its informal circulars (*tsūtatsu*). However, this phase also showed embarrassing signs of political impotence to adopt adequate measures, which resulted in a near collapse of national and international confidence in the Japanese banking sector. In the sixth phase, important legislation aimed at solving the banking problems was implemented, including the establishment of the Financial Reconstruction Commission (Kinyū Saisei Iinkai) (FRC), and at least some degree of stabilisation and control of the crisis was achieved. This phase also saw further attention paid to problems resulting from certain aspects of informality in Japanese public policy, in particular regarding the monetary authorities. In the seventh and final phase, further consolidation of bank supervision was achieved by integrating the FSA and MoF's Financial System Planning Bureau into the Financial Services Agency (Kinyū Chō) (FSEA) in July 2000.

Phase I (1990–June 1996): initial policy response

The collapse of the 'bubble' economy and the growing problems for the Japanese banking industry forced the monetary authorities to take action, which, however, was predominantly half-hearted and contained elements of forbearance in its worst form. Their response can be typified as a slow, step-by-step intervention, often hoping that the problems would disappear by themselves, for example as a result of improvements in bank profitability and asset structure. As part of the reaction of the monetary authorities, various financial regulations were liberalised and new financial institutions created, which aimed at solving the bad loan situation and related collateral problems. In general, the initial measures taken by the MoF consisted of improving the solvency of banks by enlarging their capital base and introducing new methods to dispose of non-performing or bad loans. Furthermore, MoF's response to the problems consisted of an expansion of the safety net, in the form of expanded deposit insurance arrangements and enhancement of its powers to arrange mergers involving troubled financial institutions, tougher capital requirements and somewhat strengthened – but still relatively lax – supervision of private financial intermediaries (Hall 1993, p.144). The MoF also regularly published reports containing outlines of its policy reaction to the crisis, for example in August 1992 and February 1994 (Ministry of Finance 1992c, 1994). However, these attempts to stabilise the financial crisis often proved counterproductive, as the MoF regularly played down the scale of the banking problems. Furthermore, the initial policy response included a gradual decrease (in nine steps) of the official discount rate by the Bank of Japan from a high of 6% in August 1990 to a level of 0.5% from September 1995 onwards (see figure 6.4). This policy, which resembled the lowering of short-term interest rates by the Federal Reserve in the aftermath of the savings and loan associations débâcle, enabled banks to improve their earnings by acquiring cheap funds and investing them in higher-yielding assets ('riding the yield-curve'). In addition to an accommodative monetary policy, the authorities also implemented expansionary fiscal policies in the form of stimulus packages and supplementary budgets.

As a way of enlarging banks' Tier II capital, the MoF for the first time permitted banks to issue subordinated bonds with maturity over five years in June 1990. This resulted in a sharp increase of the amount of subordinated debt issued by private banks, as was shown in table 6.1. Reportedly, the MoF employed administrative guidance to order insurance companies to absorb most of this debt (Hanazaki and Horiuchi 1998, p.8). In August 1992 the MoF issued a memorandum regarding its stance on prudential policy and announced measures to secure the stability of the financial system (Ministry of Finance 1992c). Part of the announced policy package was the promise to assist banks in developing additional measures to raise capital, including perpetual subordinated bonds. Furthermore, in February 1993 the MoF announced measures to make it easier for

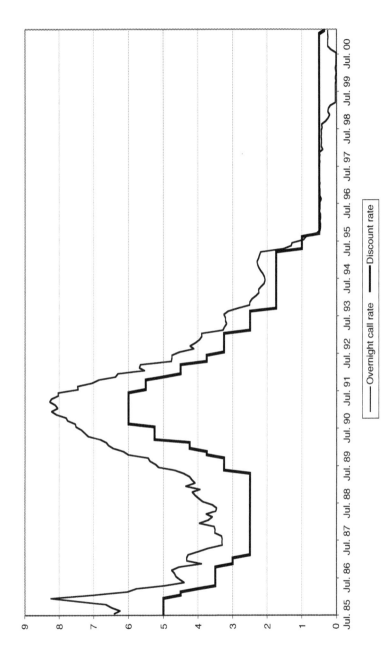

Figure 6.4 Overnight call rate and official discount rate (1985–2000)
Source: Bank of Japan.

banks to issue preferred stock. As part of further financial reform measures aimed at improving capital adequacy ratios against the background of the BIS requirements, the MoF allowed banks to securitise various assets and thereby reduce their asset exposure. Banks were permitted to securitise housing loans, loans for municipal governments and corporate loans. In December 1992 the MoF issued a *tsūtatsu* authorizing the liquidation of loans by transferring them to loan trusts. In March 1994 the MoF issued a revised *tsūtatsu* that allowed companies, which were capitalised by financial institutions, to purchase real-estate backed assets from financial institutions beyond the maximum credit limit.

Besides these new methods of raising Tier II capital and securitisation of bank loans, the MoF initiated the introduction of new institutions which would make it easier for Japanese banks to handle problem loans. Basically, these institutions aimed at disposing of non-performing loans secured by real estate and of so-called reduced interest loans – loans on which interest has been reduced or waived, excluding rescheduled loans (Ohara 1995; *Zenginkyo Financial Review* and *Nihon Ginkō Kinyū Kenkyūjo*, various issues). The first of these institutions was the Co-operative Credit Purchasing Company (Kyōdō Saiken Kaitori Kikō) (CCPC), jointly established by 162 private financial institutions in January 1993. The purpose of the CCPC was to buy non-performing loans secured by real estate, to promote sales of such real estate and to provide information on real estate transactions. Participating financial institutions sold their collateral to the CCPC, which then would attempt to recover the original debt or to sell the real estate. Furthermore, in June 1994 the MoF approved the establishment of bank subsidiaries (realty companies), which could buy real estate that functioned as collateral of non-performing loans, with the aim of selling this real estate in the future at a higher price. The problem with both the CCPC and the realty companies was that because of the big slump in the real estate market the demand for property was very weak. Consequently, these institutions encountered great difficulties in disposing of their holdings. Furthermore, the main benefit of the CCPC was to allow banks to achieve tax deductions on bad loans; it did not really result in an effective reduction of problem loans (Packer 1994; Wood 1998, p.228; Kanaya and Woo 2000, p.11). To assist banks in writing off their reduced interest loans, the MoF approved in January 1994 the creation of so-called 'special purpose companies' (*tokubetsu mokuteki kaisha*) to acquire these loans from their parent banks. It was estimated at that time that the amount of these reduced interest loans, which were not included in the official definition of bad loans until end-September 1995, was around the amount of officially declared bad loans.

In addition to these measures, in order to stimulate the disposal of bad loans, the MoF eased provisions for banks to qualify for tax-exempt write-offs of non-performing loans (Nagashima 1997, p.195). Furthermore, it also exercised great discretion from August 1992 in applying existing accounting rules on reporting stock-portfolio losses to banks, which enabled them to 'temporarily' defer these losses to the end of the fiscal year instead to their interim results (Cargill et al. 1998; Ito 2000, p.3). In both 1992 and 1993, changes in the accounting rules and the definition of non-performing loans generated a more optimistic outlook of the health of the Japanese banking industry than was warranted by the actual situation (Shimizu 1994). In general, it has been concluded that during the period 1989–1996 the discretionary accounting behaviour of Japanese banks was instrumental in enabling them to comply with the BIS capital adequacy rules (Shrieves and Dahl 1998). To a significant extent, this should have been the result of MoF administrative guidance, as after all, it must have been the MoF that allowed them to do so. Thus, and as will be shown on numerous occasions, the MoF actively engaged in promoting non-disclosure and non-transparency by using administrative guidance to hide the real magnitude of the bad-loan problems and banking crisis from the public. Reportedly, it even allowed certain financial institutions such as Musashino Shinkin Bank to engage in 'window dressing' behaviour and submit inaccurate statements (Horiuchi 1996, p.31). Also local and prefectural governments, which were responsible for the supervision of the credit co-operatives, assisted troubled financial institutions in concealing their problems, for example the Tokyo Metropolitan government in the case of Cosmo Credit Co-operative (Horiuchi 1996, p.9). Finally, the MoF started to use administrative guidance in various forms to support the stock market ('price keeping operations' or PKOs), in order to try to preserve the amount of banks' Tier II capital (see also section 5.4 of chapter 5).

Meanwhile, the situation in the banking sector deteriorated further, in particular as regards the smallest financial institutions such as *shinkin* banks and credit co-operatives – some of these institutions even experienced panic runs. Slowly but steadily and on an ad-hoc basis, the MoF started to allow the closure of the worst affected institutions. In December 1994, Tokyo Kyowa Credit Co-operative and Anzen Credit Co-operative, two major credit co-operatives, went bankrupt, and in doing so revealed close connections between politicians, MoF officials and private bankers which led to strong opposition to use public funds. Because of the political scandals and subsequent public outcry, the involvement of the BoJ was scaled down; however, it was the first time since the rescue of Yamaichi Securities in the sixties that the BoJ had used emergency loans following

Article 25 of the BoJ Law (Horiuchi 1996, p.8). The increasing aware-ness of ordinary Japanese citizens of widespread connections and informal networks between the political, government and business spheres would become one of the most important impediments to large-scale injections of public funds in the banking industry. With assistance from the Deposit Insurance Corporation (DIC), Tokyo Kyodo Bank was established to continue the activities of the two failed credit co-operatives in January 1995, and later – after deposit runs – also the activities of the collapsed Cosmo and Kizu Credit Co-operatives in, respectively, July and August 1995 (Nagashima 1997, p.217; Corbett 1999). In the early nineties – the first time in 1991 – by using administrative guidance the MoF had already arranged a number of rescue operations (i.e. takeovers and mergers) in-volving financial support from the DIC, which led to an increasing role for the latter in the stabilisation of the banking crisis.[11] These operations were mostly part of a larger emergency package, involving support from the BoJ, banking associations and individual 'main' banks, i.e. banks that maintained the largest equity stake in the problem bank (see section 4.3 of chapter 4). For example, the establishment of Tokyo Kyodo Bank was made possible by 20 billion yen in financial support – after a 'voluntary' request from the MoF – from the Long-Term Credit Bank of Japan, the main bank of the failed Tokyo Kyowa Credit Association, which was far more than was given by any other private financial institution.

The problems in the Japanese banking industry became even more apparent when Sumitomo Bank reported an overall loss for fiscal year 1994 as a result of substantial provisions for bad loans, the first Japanese bank to do so in 50 years. This move was followed by large write-offs of bad loans by more than a dozen of the biggest banks in fiscal year 1995, which consequently also reported major losses (Wood 1998, p.226).

The crisis intensified after the collapse of Hyogo Bank, which was the largest Second Tier regional bank and heavily manned by former MoF and BoJ high-ranking staff members on its board, in August 1995. It was the first collapse of a Japanese bank in post-war Japan. As is shown in figure 6.3, the 'Japan premium' rose to almost 20 basis points. In December 1992, the monetary authorities had already organised an

---

[11] For example the takeovers of Toho Sogo Bank by Iyo Bank – the first time that financial assistance by the DIC was extended – and Toyo Shinkin Bank by Sanwa Bank in 1992 and Kamaishi Shinkin Bank by Bank of Iwate in 1993, the merger of Osaka Fumin Credit Co-operative with Osaka Koyo Credit Co-operative in 1993, and the takeover of the credit co-operative Gifu Shogin by Kansai Shogin in March 1995 (Kitami 1998, p.11). Also the disposal of the business of Yuai Credit Co-operative (failed in February 1995), Fukui-ken Daiichi Credit Co-operative (failed in November 1995), Osaka Credit Co-operative (failed in December 1995), Sanyo Credit Co-operative and Kenmin Yamato Credit Co-operative (both failed in April 1996) involved financial assistance by the DIC.

assistance operation that involved Hyogo's three top shareholders (Sumitomo Bank, Industrial Bank of Japan and Long-Term Credit Bank of Japan), apparently without much success. The bankruptcy of Hyogo Bank resulted for the first time in more elaborate discussions in the media on the relationship between *amakudari* and bank performance (various issues *Nihon Keizai Shimbun* and *Asahi Shimbun* 1995; Yamori 1994; see also Fujiwara and Yamori 1997). The activities of the failed Hyogo Bank were in October 1995 concentrated in a new bank, Midori Bank, which later assumed a role in reorganisations and failures of Second Tier regional banks. Furthermore, seven housing loan companies (*jūsen*) were liquidated in September 1995, which led to a surge in the 'Japan premium' to almost 40 basis points (see figure 6.3) (Rosenbluth and Thies 1999). This liquidation happened after the publication of a report by the MoF and the establishment of a joint task force by the three ruling coalition parties in June (Mori et al. 2000, p.36). The *jūsen* débâcle led to the approval of resolution measures by the Murayama administration in December 1995, which included for the first time the injection of public money; a special bill in this respect was adopted by the new Hashimoto cabinet in February 1996.[12] The sharp increase in the 'Japan premium' was intensified by an emerging scandal involving the US branch of Daiwa Bank, which was forced by the Federal Reserve Board, Federal Deposit Insurance Corporation and various state supervisory authorities to terminate its operations after fraudulent non-reported activities of some of its employees were discovered (FDIC 1995; *International Currency Review* 1995). The incident raised international doubts about the disclosure policy of Japanese banks and the willingness of Japan's prudential supervisors to co-operate with their international counterparts in case of the outbreak of a crisis, as the US supervisory authorities were informed too late about certain malpractices at Daiwa Bank, of which, according to media reports, the MoF was aware.[13] In combination with the collapse of the credit co-operatives and Hyogo Bank and the *jūsen* débâcle in the same year, the incident seriously undermined national and international confidence in the Japanese financial system and its supervisors. In reaction to the Daiwa Bank scandal, the MoF tried to restore confidence by announcing measures in December 1995 to improve its supervision of the banking sector in general and inspections in particular and establish better co-operation and co-ordination with foreign supervisors. Another

---

[12] The Murayama cabinet lasted from June 1994 to January 1996, and was replaced by the Hashimoto administration, headed by the former finance minister Ryutaro Hashimoto.

[13] Daiwa's New York branch incurred heavy losses in bond trading which were hidden from the US supervisory authorities, apparently with the full knowledge of the MoF's Banking Bureau (*Nikkei Weekly* 1995; Hall 1998b, p.175).

major Second Tier regional bank, Taiheiyo Bank, collapsed in March 1996. This also happened after support from its 'main' banks: its four largest shareholders, Sakura Bank, Fuji Bank, Tokai Bank and Sanwa Bank, provided in May 1992 in total 229 billion yen in low-interest loans for a period of 10 years, of which 110 billion was borrowed from the BoJ – again without lasting success. These main banks were involved in setting up (with DIC financial assistance) Wakashio Bank, which took over the business of Taiheiyo.

It became increasingly apparent that the strategy of forbearance in the form of 'muddling through' by strengthening the solvency position of banks and closing the worst problem banks involving BoJ and DIC assistance was not sustainable, as, for example, the funds of the latter were almost exhausted. Furthermore, the traditional concept of orchestrating emergency 'mergers' of troubled financial institutions with healthier banks increasingly faced resistance by the latter, which resulted in several failed rescue operations despite administrative guidance by the MoF aimed at rewarding banks that collaborated with such rescue attempts.

The period of the initial policy response to the collapse of the 'bubble' and the emerging banking problems also included major administrative reforms, in particular regarding the financial supervisory framework. In 1991, the MoF increased its regulatory leverage over the non-bank sector, which includes consumer credit institutions and leasing companies. A new bill that was introduced by the Ministry of International Trade and Industry (MITI) in 1992 gave the MoF an important role in the regulation of non-banks (Vogel 1996, p.191). Furthermore, as a result of the stock-loss compensation scandals and other scandals in 1991 (see Shindo 1992; Wood 1993), the MoF established in July 1992 the Securities and Exchange Surveillance Commission (Shōken Torihiki Tō Kanshi Iinkai), whose primary objective was to supervise compliance with market rules by stock-market participants, and changed its internal organisation to improve the supervision of depository financial institutions (see appendix 5.2 of chapter 5). Despite strong political pressure and public outcry over various scandals involving the MoF, it succeeded in thwarting attempts to establish an independent organisation for the supervision of financial markets (Vogel 1996, pp.187ff.; Keehn 1998, pp.205ff.).[14] Further administrative reforms were decided in December 1995, including measures

---

[14] Finance Minister Ryutaro Hashimoto announced that he preferred to keep the supervision of securities companies in the Ministry of Finance instead of establishing a new independent supervisory body. Against the background of this statement, it is somewhat ironic – and a sign of the changing political climate – that under Hashimoto's leadership in 1998 the new and more independent Financial Supervisory Agency was established.

to streamline and reform special public corporations, which have been important landing spots for retired bureaucrats.

The handling of the banking crisis by the MoF and its policy of forbearance were increasingly criticised, in particular after the decision to use public money to resolve the *jūsen* crisis (see, for example, Stockwin 1999, p.104). But also the large number of tasks under its jurisdiction, its use of non-transparent policy instruments, its internal bureaucratic system and autocratic management style became increasingly the topic of political and public debate (Hall 1998b, p.175). In February 1996, the Hashimoto administration initiated a government study to investigate possible ways to break up the MoF and limit its powers.

Finally, during the period 1990–June 1996 the process of financial reform continued to change the basic structure of the Japanese financial system. For example, the liberalisation of interest rates on demand and time deposits was completed in 1994, when the MoF liberalised the interest rates of demand deposits excluding current accounts. A complete liberalisation of all deposit interest rates had been hampered by the existence of attractive savings accounts with the non-profit oriented postal savings system. However, study groups from the MoF and the Ministry of Posts and Telecommunications (MPT) reached an agreement on the deregulation of interest rates in December 1992 (Ministry of Finance 1992b). According to this agreement, the determination by the MPT of interest rates on specific Postal Savings deposits would be consequently in line with interest rates on similar deposits offered by private financial institutions. In April 1994, further agreement was reached on the interest rate setting on ordinary postal savings deposits and the liberalisation of interest rates on demand deposits.

The most important financial reform measure was the enactment and promulgation by parliament of the Law Concerning the Realignment of Relevant Laws for the Reform of the Financial System and the Securities Trading System, abbreviated as the Financial System Reform Act, which became effective on 1 April 1993. The aim of this law was the breaking up of the functional segmentation of Japanese financial institutions, i.e. enabling mutual entry into each other's traditional areas of business activity through the establishment of subsidiaries (Semkow 1993, p.435). Thus, under the Financial System Reform Act, commercial and long-term credit banks could establish securities and trust subsidiaries and securities companies were given the permission to engage in trust banking business. Regarding the entry of financial institutions into each other's traditional business area, the MoF adopted a step-by-step approach to ensure a balanced process: that is, the weaker financial institutions were allowed to enter first the business areas of other types of financial institutions.

As the result of the process of financial reform and fundamental changes in the financial structure, the regulation of the number and type of branch offices was liberalised totally in June 1995, two years after liberalising the branch regulation of regional and *shinkin* banks. This was an important development regarding the use of administrative guidance by the MoF, as traditionally its branch regulation was instrumental in forcing banks to comply with its informal policies. It seemed to imply that the MoF had increased its leverage over the banking industry through other means, for example its licensing policy related to the establishment of subsidiaries in new business areas or its assistance to troubled banks, and therefore no longer needed branch regulation as a 'stick' (see also Vogel 1996, pp.192–193). Apparently, it did not imply that, because of the changing structure of the Japanese financial system, the MoF had concluded that administrative guidance has lost its effectiveness and thus regulations could be lifted. As the further policy initiatives of the MoF would prove, it continued to use administrative guidance as an important policy instrument in its reaction to the banking problems.

Phase II (June 1996–January 1997): administrative and financial reform

In June 1996, a package of six laws was enacted that aimed in particular at solving the crisis of the housing loan companies (*jūsen*), strengthening the Deposit Insurance Corporation and implementing a new supervisory system similar to the 'prompt corrective action' framework (PCA) adopted by the US supervisory authorities (IMF 1997; Nagashima 1997; OECD 1997). The resolution of the *jūsen* débâcle was of great importance, as for the first time substantial amounts of public funds were allocated by the government to mitigate bad-loan problems. It also revealed the close connections between the ruling Liberal Democratic Party (LDP) and the agricultural sector and related preferential supervisory treatment by the MoF, and led to accusations that public money was being used because of political connections and favouritism (Schaede 1996; Hartcher 1998; Brown 1999; Rosenbluth and Thies 1999). In particular the agricultural co-operatives, whose support was critical for the LDP to stay in power, invested heavily in the *jūsen* – and therefore their public bailout was of major interest to the LDP. A clear example of preferential regulatory treatment by the MoF was the exemption of the *jūsen* from MoF's April 1990 administrative guidance aimed at restricting lending to the real estate sector (Cargill et al. 1997, p.121). In this respect, it should be noted that large commercial banks and securities companies established the *jūsen* in the seventies with active support from the MoF and that they had become a favourite landing spot for large numbers of retired high-ranking MoF officials (*amakudari kanryō*). From the start, retired MoF officials were appointed in the highest executive positions: in fact, seven out of eight housing lenders started with a former MoF official in one of the highest executive positions (van Rixtel 1996; Schaede 1996; Milhaupt 1999). MoF retirees were also present in relatively large numbers when the *jūsen* moved into the risky real estate sector. There has been no sector in the Japanese financial system where former MoF officials were so heavily involved as the housing loan companies; it may be just a coincidence, but no other sector has ever experienced such a high percentage of failures. All in all, the suspicion that political motives and bureaucratic interests were behind the injection of public funds in the *jūsen* and the subsequent public outcry would seriously hamper new initiatives for public bailouts of the banking sector in the years to come.

The legislation to solve the *jūsen* crisis included 685 billion yen in public funds and the establishment in July of the Housing Loan Administration Corporation (Jūtaku Kinyū Saiken Kanri Kikō) (HLAC), which had to take over the assets of the collapsed *jūsen*. The HLAC was established as a subsidiary of the Deposit Insurance Corporation (DIC) and funded by private financial institutions and the Bank of Japan. The June legal package also widened the role of the DIC in the resolution of failed banks, which would allow for a faster resolution of bank failures, through amendments of the Deposit Insurance Law. It included permanent measures such as allowing the DIC to purchase deposits from failed institutions and the establishment of a temporary facility to protect all depositors of failed banks until the end of March 2001 under a 'special account'. To strengthen the financial position of the DIC, which was severely depleted by the large number of bank failures, its borrowing limit was increased and bridge finance from the BoJ was made available. Finally, the Diet passed legislation in June which aimed at improving the transparency of bank supervision through the introduction of so-called 'prompt corrective actions' (PCA), following similar initiatives by the US supervisory authorities in the early nineties (Nagashima 1997; Katayama and Makov 1998). The PCA framework was based on the capital adequacy ratios of banks, and led to automatic corrective actions were these ratios to fall below certain published norms; however, the Japanese PCA framework offered supervisors more discretion than the US system (IMF 1997, p.140). In December 1996, the Banking Bureau published more explicit regulatory guidelines that were based on the capital ratios of banks. The new PCA system would become effective as of 1 April 1998.

In addition to the legal package enacted by the Diet aimed at solving the banking problems, the MoF amended in June (and again in November) administrative guidance related to the operational procedures of commercial banks, which gave attention to market risk management and internal auditing. Furthermore, various *tsūtatsu* were changed to improve the disclosure of derivatives transactions by financial and non-financial firms. The MoF issued administrative guidance in September requiring banks to meet certain management criteria or otherwise submit plans to meet these criteria. Thus, the MoF followed its old habit of actively using and renewing informal regulation in order to adjust the behaviour of financial institutions in general and banks in particular. As regards other informal aspects of the MoF's policies, it announced in June the voluntarily restriction of the number of its *amakudari* positions (as discussed in section 5.4 of chapter 5).

After the revision of the Deposit Insurance Law, Tokyo Kyodo Bank was reorganised in September as the Resolution and Collection Bank (Seiri Kaishū Ginkō) (RCB) – similar to the Resolution Trust Corporation in the USA which was established to manage and resolve insolvent savings and loan institutions in the early nineties (Mishkin and Eakins 2000, p.498). Its main function was to restructure and continue the activities of failed credit co-operatives and *shinkin* banks. In relation to the establishment of the RCB, the government also created a special fund for financial assistance ('new financial stabilisation fund'). The new framework to resolve bank failures, established under the legislation that passed parliament in June, was adopted for the first time with the failure of Hanwa Bank in November. Contrary to the past, the MoF did not attempt to arrange a 'rescue merger' with a healthier organisation but simply ordered Hanwa to close. Its losses were covered by the DIC, and the RCB was made responsible for the administration and collection of its assets. The RCB was also involved with the resolution of the failed Sanpuku Credit Co-operative in November.

The run-up to the October elections resulted in a large number of initiatives for further administrative reform (*gyōsei kaikaku*) and financial reform (*kinyū no jiyūka*) submitted by various advisory committees and project teams, in particular by those related to the government. Without doubt, the ruling cabinet wanted to convince the Japanese electorate that the continuing banking problems and apparent bureaucratic impotence to tackle these would be resolved under a new administration. The government study on the possible break-up of the MoF, supported by the three coalition parties (LDP, Social Democratic Party and Sakigake), was released in September 1996 and suggested the implementation of major organisational reforms of the MoF and the establishment of an independent Financial Supervisory Agency (Kinyū Kantoku Chō) (FSA) (Bank of Japan, *Annual Review 1997*, p.152; Ministry of Finance 1996). As a result of the mounting bad-loan problems and the many scandals in the Japanese financial system, the financial supervisory framework was increasingly being criticised as being ineffective, politically influenced and dispersed among too many organisations. By proposing the establishment of a new supervisory body outside the MoF, and indirectly putting all the blame for the crisis on MoF's shoulders, the politicians tried to divert the attention from their own inability to handle the banking problems promptly and effectively. Thus, the LDP in particular prioritised political opportunism above its traditional strong support for the ministry. It was also agreed that the Banking Bureau and Securities Bureau of the MoF would be merged into a new Finance Bureau (later changed to Financial System Planning Bureau or Kinyū Kikaku Kyoku). Furthermore, the Administrative Reform Council (Gyōsei Kaikaku Kaigi) (ARC), established by Prime Minister Ryutaro Hashimoto, would investigate the separation between the fiscal and financial functions of the MoF. The ARC had been conducting an investigation of six reform areas including administrative and financial reform (Carlile 1998, p.101). Finally, it was proposed to review the Bank of Japan Law and to improve substantially the independence of Japan's central bank. A committee from another advisory council to the Prime Minister – the Economic Council – promoted in October initiatives to reform and vitalise the Japanese financial system, which incorporated a review of the regulatory and supervisory system.[15] In addition, a MoF study group released recommendations for improvements in the financial system, including improvements in the structure of financial administration and disclosure by financial institutions.

The process of financial reform received a major boost with the announcement of Prime Minister Ryutaro Hashimoto of the 'Big Bang' financial reform package in November, which would be implemented during a three-year period from April 1998 until March 2001 (Financial System Research Council 1997b; Matsushita 1997a; Ministry of Finance 1997a; Securities and Exchange Council 1997; Hall 1998a; Hamada 1998; van Rixtel 1998b, 1998c; Watanabe and Sudo 1998). The main goal of the 'Big Bang' was to establish 'free, fair and global' financial markets, including further deregulation of financial activities, improved competition, transparent rules and the introduction of legal, accounting and supervisory frameworks that could meet international standards.

---

[15] The so-called Action Plan Committee of the Economic Council was established under the programme for structural reform that was decided by the cabinet in December 1995 (Bank of Japan, *Annual Review 1997*, p.154). The ARC and Economic Council published follow-up reports on financial and administrative reform in December.

Thus, an important aspect of the 'Big Bang' was the abolition of certain non-transparent practices and the intention to move towards more rule-based regulation instead of discretionary or informal regulation such as administrative guidance. In the view of Ito and Melvin (1999), the 'Big Bang' may have been a political response to the criticism of the MoF in relation to its handling of the banking problems and the scandals involving some of its staff.

Also in November and related to the 'Big Bang' initiative was a report issued by the Central Bank Study Group (CBSG), which was established in April as an advisory panel to the Prime Minister to investigate the reform of the Bank of Japan Law, that aimed at strengthening the independence, transparency and accountability of the Japanese central bank (Financial System Research Council 1997a; Hall 1998b; van Rixtel 1998c). For a long time the BoJ had been advocating reforms of its old-fashioned legal framework, which was discussed in chapter 5.[16] The recommendations of the CBSG were a substantial improvement of the 'old law' in terms of independence and transparency and met to a considerable extent the demands of the BoJ.

In December 1996, the second Hashimoto cabinet decided to implement an overall programme of administrative reform that included reform of the central government's ministries and agencies, reorganisation of the administrative structure, further easing of government regulations in various areas and promotion of disclosure by various administrative organisations (Bank of Japan, *Annual Review 1997*, p.161).[17] It followed to a large extent the recommendations of the government study on the break-up of the MoF. Given the huge impact of this decision on the future structure of bank supervision in Japan and the resolution of the banking problems, it marked the move to a new phase in the policy reaction to the financial crisis. The mounting political and public criticism of MoF's reaction to the deteriorating situation in the banking sector convinced the government that certain reforms of the financial system and supervisory framework could no longer be avoided. That is, the political establishment could no longer hide behind its strategy of blaming the bureaucrats

[16] For example, the BoJ expressed in a written statement in January 1994, which was drafted for discussions in the British Parliament on the independence of the Bank of England, its wish to become legally more independent from the government and the consequent need of revision of the BoJ Law (*Nihon Keizai Shimbun*, January 1994). Furthermore, Yoshio Suzuki, former Executive Director of the BoJ, called the BoJ Law in a publication 'outdated and vague' and 'based on fascist ideology and wartime conditions' (Suzuki 1994, p.86). Finally, former Governor of the BoJ Yasushi Mieno emphasised the need to revise the BoJ Law in a public speech in November 1994 and at his last press conference as Governor in December 1994.

[17] The second Hashimoto administration consisted of the LDP only but was supported by the previous coalition parties, the Social Democratic Party and Sakigake.

for all the things that went wrong in the financial system ('bureaucrat bashing'), but had to take action itself (Curtis 1999, p.231). As will become clear from the discussion of the next phase, it would turn out not to have been sufficient.

Phase III (January 1997–January 1998): the end of 'too big to fail'

Owing to a lack of funds, organisation and political determination, however, the banking problems were still not addressed vigorously and fundamentally. As a result, the situation at more banks deteriorated. In April 1997, Nippon Credit Bank, one of the three long-term credit banks, and Hokkaido Takushoku Bank, one of the smaller city banks, and both former government banks, announced major restructuring plans which included financial support from various private financial institutions and even the BoJ. However, an announced merger of the latter with Hokkaido Bank was postponed in September. Also in April, a major financial institution, Nissan Mutual Life Insurance, was ordered by the MoF to halt its operations. It was seen as a first signal of a possible end to the post-war 'convoy system'. The MoF continued to be involved in minor and major scandals, which were related to close and intimate informal network relations between some of its staff and the ruling LDP and certain private financial institutions. For example, in January 1997 two high-ranking MoF officials were reprimanded for accepting gifts from a business executive and a LDP politician (and former finance minister). A major scandal erupted in July 1997 when 11 MoF officials were 'warned' for accepting favours from the Dai-Ichi Kangyo Bank, one of the largest city banks. They included two banking inspectors who were in charge of supervising DKB. The incident raised doubts about the impartiality of MoF's inspections and the existence of collusive behaviour between banking supervisors and banks:

> Some industry sources said that they suspected the Dai-Ichi Kangyo inspections were not strict enough because the inspectors were entertained by the bank. More seriously, such action may not be limited to one bank. Bank sources said it was a usual practice to entertain Finance Ministry inspectors in order to obtain inspection-related information, such as the timing and branches to be checked. (*Nikkei Weekly*, 4 August 1997, p.4)

The improper behaviour of these MoF officials seems to have been a direct consequence of the existence of close informal networks between the monetary authorities and private financial institutions. In this respect, the system of the MoF-*tan* or MoF-watchers – from private banks in particular – was increasingly questioned, as in particular the involved 'wining and dining' raised concerns about too cosy relations between supervisors and banks (see section 3.3 of chapter 3). It has often been asserted that because of the opaque nature of administrative guidance the banks needed the MoF-*tan* system, since without the close contacts with MoF officials at the dining table they would not be able to understand MoF's informal policies (see section 3.3 of chapter 3). In an apparent reaction to the scandals, the MoF announced in August 1997 a review of its use of informal regulations such as the *tsūtatsu*. The move was her-alded as an improvement of the transparency of its policies and a shift from discretionary to rule-based regulation (*Japan Times*, August 1997). Furthermore, the Diet passed a bill in December to impose stricter penal-ties on financial institutions for improper behaviour such as evasion of supervisory inspections and to amend existing financial legislation ac-cordingly. However, the bill did not manage to bring around a culture shift at the supervisory authorities, as would become clear at the be-ginning of 1998. In a clear reaction to the scandals involving MoF of-ficials, the Management and Co-ordination Agency (Sōmu Chō) stated in a report that the MoF and other government offices should overhaul inspection procedures for financial institutions by introducing more ef-fective on-the-spot checks. In the meantime, further scandals continued to undermine the already tarnished reputation of Japan's financial ser-vices industry. The MoF imposed sanctions on Dai-Ichi Kangyo Bank and Nomura Securities in July – and again in December on two other major securities companies – for paying illegal funds to a notorious stock racketeer or *sokaiya*.[18]

The MoF also continued to use administrative guidance in its efforts to mitigate the effects of the evolving banking crisis. It allowed banks to transfer bad loans to special purpose companies, which employed them for securitisation purposes (Katayama and Makov 1998, p.130). The policy move made it easier to remove bad loans from the banks' balance sheets and improve their capital adequacy ratios. Furthermore, banks re-ceived permission in July to exempt from taxes their losses on the writing off of bad loans without asking explicit approval from the MoF. How-ever, these measures had no significant impact on the actual situation in the banking sector. In October, Kyoto Kyoei Bank, a small Second Tier regional bank, announced that it would start liquidation procedures and that its business would be transferred to Kofuku Bank.

---

[18] *Sokaiya* are sharcholder-extortionists who extort money from companies by threatening to disrupt companies' annual shareholders' meetings by revealing sensitive information about the company (Hsu 1994, p.327).

Table 6.5. *Reserve positions of Japanese banks (yen 100 million), 1997*

	Reserves of financial institutions subject to reserve requirement system		
	Actual reserves (A)	Required reserves (B)	Excess reserves (A) – (B)
April	1,009,800	1,007,940	1,860
May	1,049,722	1,045,413	4,309
June	1,023,960	1,021,050	2,910
July	1,063,734	1,061,998	1,736
August	1,066,555	1,064,230	2,325
September	1,029,180	1,026,090	3,090
October	1,063,362	1,054,713	8,649
November	1,085,790	1,042,050	43,740
December	1,116,899	1,101,678	15,221

Source: Bank of Japan.

The magnitude of the banking crisis was revealed to the general public and international financial community in 'Black' November, when two banks and two securities houses collapsed. Despite the restructuring attempts earlier in the year, Hokkaido Takushoku Bank announced its failure on 17 November, the first city bank to shut its doors since the end of World War II. The announcement was widely interpreted as the end of the 'too big to fail' policy by the Japanese monetary authorities, which in previous years allowed only the smaller financial institutions to close down. It was followed later by Tokuyo City Bank, a mid-size Second Tier regional bank. The shock intensified when a crying chairman of one of the 'Big Four' securities houses, Yamaichi Securities, declared its bankruptcy on national television. This came after the failure of Sanyo Securities, a smaller securities firm, at the beginning of the month. The reaction of the international financial markets was rapid and intense. The 'Japan premium' jumped to almost 80 basis points to an all-time high (see figure 6.3).[19] In Japan itself, the amount of excess reserves – the difference between actual and required reserves – in the Japanese banking sector increased more than tenfold compared with the highest level in the previous months (see table 6.5). This was an indication of both emergency liquidity injections by the BoJ and the fact that Japanese banks increasingly lost faith in their own banking system, i.e. they preferred to hold non-interest-bearing deposits at the BoJ instead of lending them to other

---

[19] According to Peek and Rosengren (1998) the largest movements in the 'Japan premium' were associated with announcements of large previously undisclosed losses. These were particularly important as regards the failure of Yamaichi Securities, and not so much for Hokkaido Takushoku Bank.

Japanese banks. The Minister of Finance and the Governor of the BoJ were forced to declare in a joint and unprecedented statement that they would take all possible measures to ensure the stability of the financial system. However, it became clear that the end of the 'too big to fail' policy did not also imply an immediate and definite end to the 'convoy system'. Finance Minister Mitsuzuka publicly stated that the government did not intend to consider the implementation of a new framework for using public funds to restore the stability of the financial system. In other words, it was clear that the government was not yet ready for massive injections of public money. The MoF considered the existing framework including DIC financial assistance and rescue mergers to be sufficient to handle the situation, in line with the general rationale of the 'convoy system'. To strengthen the existing framework, the Diet passed in December a bill to amend the Deposit Insurance Law that allowed the DIC to extend its financial assistance to banks established through rescue mergers. This revision of the DIC's legal framework would pave the way for a first round of small capital injections involving the major banks in 1998. In addition, the MoF announced a package of new stabilisation measures (Ministry of Finance 1997b; IMF 1998). First, the 'prompt corrective action' scheme, to be implemented as of April 1998, would be implemented flexibly for non-internationally operating banks and suspended for one year. This measure was instigated by the fear of 'too many to fail' instead of 'too big to fail' (Corbett 1999, p.207). Second, the MoF changed – again – the accounting standards, in particular for the valuation of banks' equity holdings, effectively postponing the move towards accounting based on market prices.[20] The change allowed banks to avoid reporting potential capital losses (Hoshi and Patrick 2000b). Third, the MoF announced the establishment of credit guarantees and a new lending facility by government financial institutions, which aimed at mitigating possible 'credit crunch' type problems for non-financial corporations. From its side, the BoJ provided emergency assistance by extending special loans based on Article 25 of the Bank of Japan Law to the collapsed financial institutions and the use of various market operations to provide sufficient liquidity to the financial markets (see also IMF 1998).

The year 1997 also saw some major administrative and financial reforms. In June the Diet passed both a bill to establish the Financial Supervisory Agency (FSA) in 1998 and a substantially revised Bank of Japan Law that would become effective as from fiscal year 1998.[21] Furthermore, the MoF issued ordinances to revise parts of the Banking

[20] Banks were permitted to value securities at cost prices instead of the minimum of cost and market prices (IMF 1998, p.114).

[21] I shall present an overview of the major changes in the Bank of Japan Law regarding prudential policy in the next subsection.

Law that allowed for the introduction of the 'prompt corrective action' scheme in April 1998, in particular for internationally operating banks. In September the BoJ announced revisions of its organisation, to take effect as of April 1998 in combination with the effectuation of the new BoJ Law (Bank of Japan 1997). Its organisation was to be scaled down from 13 departments, two offices and one institute to 10 departments, five offices and one institute. The planning and formulation of monetary policy would be concentrated in the new Policy Planning Office (Kikaku Shitsu), based on three divisions (i.e. Planning Division 1 (Kikaku Dai 1 Ka), Planning Division 2 (Kikaku Dai 2 Ka) and the Policy Research Division (Seisaku Chōsa Ka)). Furthermore, the important Credit and Market Management Department was renamed Financial Markets Department (Kinyū Shijō Kyoku), consisting of the Money and Capital Markets Division (Kinyū Shijō Ka) and Open Market Operations Division (Kinyū Chōsetsu Ka), and parts of its functions were transferred to the new Financial and Payment System Office (Shinyō Kikō Shitsu) and the Bank Supervision Department. This office would consist of a Financial System Division (Shinyō Kikō Ka) and a Payment System Division (Kessai 'System' Ka) and replace the previous Financial and Payment System Department, to be abolished as of 1 April 1998. The reorganisation concentrated both on-site examinations and off-site monitoring at the Bank Supervision Department. In relation to its improved independence, the BoJ strengthened the position of the secretariat of the Policy Board. Furthermore, the BoJ decided to consolidate housing facilities for staff and to reduce its holdings of golf course memberships.

As regards the organisation of the central government, the Administrative Reform Council (ARC) recommended in its final report the reorganisation of the government's 22 ministries and agencies into 12 ministries and a strengthened Cabinet Office, which would be partially responsible for economic and budgetary matters (Administrative Reform Council 1997; Carlile 1998, pp.102–103). Furthermore, it was suggested that all supervisory functions related to the financial system, at that time under the co-jurisdiction of various ministries, be concentrated in an independent Finance Agency around the end of the century (including those of the Financial Supervisory Agency that was yet to be established in 1998). As regards the MoF, the ARC proposed to rename it the Ministry of the Treasury (Zaimusho); its jurisdiction over the planning and drafting of policy measures to cope with financial institutions' bankruptcies and financial crises was not addressed clearly, as it was considered politically to be too sensitive an issue. The National Tax Administration Agency was not touched upon either, thus maintaining the strong influence of the MoF over tax matters. However, the Fiscal Investment and Loan Programme (FILP) or Zaito, a kind of secondary budget that was more or less controlled by the MoF and gave it considerable powers (see section 5.3 of chapter 5), was to be reformed drastically. Finally, the ARC suggested changing the system of public administration through directives, thus proposing a move towards a more rule-based and transparent system of government policy. In reaction to the ARC report, the ruling LDP could not reach agreement with its two allies in the Diet – the Social Democratic Party and Sakigake – on the reorganisation of the MoF, as the latter two were in favour of more stringent reforms such as a clear separation between the financial and fiscal functions of the MoF.

Finally, in an apparent attempt to mitigate growing criticism of the vast informal networks between the public and private spheres involving former high-ranking government bureaucrats, a working group of the LDP released a report that recommended to cut the number of staff at the so-called 'special legal entities' (*tokushu hōjin*; see appendix 3.1 of chapter 3) by 10%, and that fewer than half of the executive positions at these institutions should be reserved for retired government officials. Executive positions at these public institutions had been favourite landing spots for high-ranking ex-bureaucrats to overcome the two-year waiting period stipulated by the National Public Service Law before accepting private sector or *amakudari* positions in businesses related to their previous working areas (see section 3.4 of chapter 3). The LDP panel also proposed limiting the custom of retired civil servants moving from one post-retirement position to another – the so-called *watari-dori* or 'hopping birds' (Colignon and Usui 1999). However, the proposals to curtail the post-retirement employment of government bureaucrats remained rather vague and failed to meet demands from opposition parties for more substantial revisions.

Phase IV (January 1998–June 1998): scandals, injection of public funds and financial reform

The publication of the ARC report on administrative reform and the amendment of the DIC Law that made it easier to provide DIC assistance to specific problem banks marked a move towards a new phase in policy reaction to the banking crisis. In January 1998 the Hashimoto administration drafted legislation based on the ARC proposals to restructure the government bureaucracy in 2001, including the establishment of the new Finance Agency and the restructured MoF. A compromise was reached between the LDP and its non-cabinet allies – the Social Democratic Party and Sakigake – that for the foreseeable future the monetary and fiscal functions of the MoF would not be separated, and that the MoF would maintain responsibility for financial crisis management.

Thus the LDP, the staunchest defender of the MoF when deemed politically opportune, did not give in to demands from its political allies for
more stringent reforms.

Then, in January 1998, a series of scandals erupted which involved
various types of informal networks and led to one of the most severe
crises in the history of both the MoF and BoJ. It started with the arrest of Takehiko Isaka, an executive director at the Japan Highway Public
Corporation (one of the 'special legal entities' or *tokushu hōjin*) and
former Director-General of MoF's Mint Bureau, for accepting bribes
from Nomura Securities in return for preferential treatment regarding the
leadership of bond issues.[22] Another former high-ranking MoF official
and Lower House member of the LDP, Shokei Arai, was accused of having received substantial profits from a non-disclosed securities account at
one of the 'Big Four' securities houses, which most likely was established
when he was still in active service at the MoF. The biggest blow to the
prestige of the MoF, in the view of many the most powerful institute in
Japan, came when, in an unprecedented move, its head office in Kasumi-
gaseki (downtown Tokyo) was raided by officials from the Tokyo District
Public Prosecutor's Office. Two financial inspectors from the Financial
Inspection Department (see appendix 5.2 of chapter 5) were arrested
on corruption charges. They were accused of revealing bank inspection
plans, passing on confidential information about specific banks to their
competitors and destroying incriminating evidence, in return for monetary bribes, entertainment and discounts on the purchase of real estate.
This all came after a long series of scandals over the years involving MoF
officials and only six months after a similar incident implicated MoF's
bank supervisors, which led to accusations in the Japanese media of collusive behaviour between supervisors and banks and explicit promises
by the MoF that this would never happen again.[23] Not surprisingly, this
time public outrage was even more immense, and the media published detailed accusations of lax and even fraudulent inspections and revelations
of close and informal connections between the MoF and the private banking sector (see also Lincoln 1998b, pp.359–360).[24] In an attempt to calm

---

[22] Later also the elite Industrial Bank of Japan was accused of providing lavish entertainment in return for receiving certain favours.

[23] In this respect it should be noted that in relation to certain scandals, the MoF had already
issued a prohibition on accepting entertainment from private companies in December
1996. However, this prohibition was non-binding, an indication of MoF's seriousness
and sense of urgency in coping with situations that could implicate its staff, and, not
surprisingly, ineffective (*Nikkei Weekly*, 26 January 1998, p.4).

[24] According to the *Nikkei Weekly*, 2 February 1998, p.3: 'An official at a major bank
asserted in an interview: "We knew two or three months ahead of time which month
the inspectors would be coming". Because a special format had to be used for MoF's
inspections, the bank could fix its books to ensure a smooth inspection after being tipped

things down, the chairman of the Federation of Bankers Associations of Japan proposed to abolish the MoF-*tan* system, arguing that it also was no longer needed because of the 'increased' transparency of financial regulation in recent years. Thus, he publicly supported the view that the system of informal networks between the MoF and the private banking sector, of which the MoF-*tan* phenomenon was a prominent element, was intrinsically intertwined with the structure of bank regulation and supervision. The scandal prompted the resignation of Finance Minister Mitsuzuka, followed by the resignation of the Administrative Vice-Minister, and led to the suicide of several MoF officials.[25] All this came just three months after the collapse of a number of major financial institutions, amid increasing signs of a worsening financial crisis. However, the tragedy was not over yet. In February, a former head of MoF's Securities Bureau who had descended after retirement into an association of regional banks, was questioned for his handling of a cover-up of losses accumulated through certain stock-trading activities at the failed Yamaichi Securities. In March, two MoF officials responsible for the regulation of the securities industry were arrested on suspicion of accepting bribes in exchange for granting certain favours to a number of securities companies. Furthermore, three former executives of Yamaichi Securities were arrested on charges of window-dressing activities, which effectively gave a much rosier impression of Yamaichi's financial situation. In the view of many observers, they could not have done this without the explicit consent of the MoF. All in all, a general picture emerged of a close network of informal relations between the MoF and the financial services industry, aimed at protecting respective and mutual interests by any means. Further evidence of this picture was provided by the submission of MoF reports to parliament containing the results of its inspections of four banks involved in the bribery scandal (Hokkaido Takushoku Bank, Dai-Ichi Kangyo Bank, Asahi Bank and Sanwa Bank), which clearly showed that the MoF was well aware of certain problems at these banks but did not act and allowed them to hide the real magnitude of the problems (*Nikkei Weekly*, 23 March 1998, p.12).

In reaction to the scandals involving MoF officials, the media started to report on the alleged lavish entertainment of BoJ officials by private sector

some months in advance.' Furthermore, one publication quoted some insiders as saying that banks allocated up to $800,000 in wining and dining expenses for each high-ranking MoF official (*Asiaweek* 1998). In the words of Lincoln (1998c), the issue of problem loans is 'further complicated by the complicity of the MoF in condoning, encouraging, or even recommending unethical and illegal actions by the banking sector'.

25 Later the Director-General of the Securities Bureau and Deputy Director-General of the Banking Bureau would also resign. In the end, the MoF would punish 112 of its staff implicated in one way or another by the scandals.

banks in exchange for sensitive information on interest rates; for the first time, extensive discussions about the existence of a BoJ-*tan* system were published. These and other accusations led to a raid on the BoJ's head office by public prosecutors. The similarity with the MoF was striking: two of the most prestigious institutions in Japan were implicated in scandals pointing at fraudulent behaviour of their staff, sending shockwaves to both the Japanese public and the international financial community. The BoJ started an internal investigation into possible illegal behaviour of its staff; ultimately, around a hundred of them would be disciplined. A senior manager of the Capital Markets Division of the Credit and Market Management Department was arrested on bribery charges, which included the leaking of confidential information related to the BoJ's market operations and lending policy to various financial institutions. Governor Matsushita and Senior Deputy-Governor Fukui resigned in March. A new Governor, Masaru Hayami, was appointed, a former Executive Director at the BoJ and *amakudari kanryō* at a non-financial company, and by exception not a graduate from the University of Tokyo but from the Tokyo University of Commerce (the present Hitotsubashi University). One of Hayami's first moves was to announce publicly that the worst was over as regards the instability of the Japanese financial system. In a remarkable effort to restore credibility and open up to the outside world, Sakuya Fujiwara, an independent editorial writer at Jiji Press, was hired to occupy a new second deputy-governor position, in addition to Deputy-Governor Yutaka Yamaguchi who came from the BoJ's own rank and file. Thus, in a span of a couple of months and as a result of scandals, Japan's complete financial leadership was replaced. The BoJ also adopted a code of conduct that established rules on the ethical discipline and relations of its staff with the private sector and restricted *amakudari* movements, particularly of its higher-ranking staff.[26] According to media reports, as of 1 April 1998 the Bank prohibited its executives from accepting a position at any private financial institution for two years after resignation; in the case of bank supervisors the waiting period was extended to five years. Both restrictions were in line with similar guidelines adopted by the MoF in June 1996 (see section 5.4 of chapter 5). Thus, the BoJ explicitly linked the existence of informal relations and mechanisms such as *amakudari* to the improper behaviour of some of its staff members. Furthermore, the BoJ announced that it would review all its internal rules and abolish many that left too much discretion to officials in order to ensure more transparency and efficiency. It became increasingly apparent that the informal

---

[26] In March, it was revealed that as of end-September 1997, 96 former BoJ officials were employed by financial institutions, which compared with 164 retired MoF staff members as of March 1997 (Kyodo World Service, 12 March 1998).

mode of policymaking in Japan was reaching its limits, and that policy by opaque discretion had serious shortcomings compared with policy by clear, equal and transparent rules.

In a reaction to the arrest of MoF's 'old boy' at the Japan Highway Public Corporation on corruption charges, the Hashimoto administration announced in January that it would start a critical review of the post-retirement employment of government officials in the public and private sector, of which the latter is typified in this study as *amakudari*. The Cabinet Secretariat, the Management and Co-ordination Agency and the National Personnel Authority were asked to draft a proposal aimed at improving the situation. Expectations of substantial improvements, how-ever, were low: in the past, similar government efforts had failed owing to strong opposition from bureaucrats. And, after all, as has already been discussed, the MoF had already implemented 'significant' restrictions on *amakudari* in June 1996 (see section 5.4 of chapter 5). Apparently, they had not been restrictive enough. From its side, the Management and Co-ordination Agency, one of the most reform-minded government or-ganisations, recommended that administrative vice-ministers should not resign before the age of 62, resulting in a lesser need of *amakudari* positions as an institutionalised aspect of the employment system of the Japanese government bureaucracy (see section 3.4 of chapter 3). Forced by the opposition, the MoF published a list of its retirees (*amakudari kanryō*) employed by private financial institutions, which included only the high-est executive positions at the major banks, securities and insurance com-panies. It showed that 117 MoF retirees had descended into executive positions at banks – one at a city bank, three at long-term credit banks, two at trust banks and 111 at regional and Second Tier regional banks – 25 at securities companies and 22 at insurance companies.[27] To silence some of the public criticism on *amakudari*, a new system intended to introduce more transparency and checks and balances was put in place as of the beginning of the new fiscal year 1998 (i.e. 1 April). The sys-tem tightened restrictions on the acceptance of private sector jobs by the highest-ranking government officials and on the re-employment of gov-ernment officials in executive positions at private companies under the jurisdiction of the respective ministry or government agency (National Personnel Authority 1999a, p.30). The new rules stipulated that if pri-vate corporations wanted to hire former bureaucrats they would have to submit a request to the National Personnel Authority through the Japan Federation of Employers' Associations (Nikkeiren). It was clear that the

---

[27] As of end-June 1997 for banks and the beginning of August 1997 for insurance companies.

intention of the new system was to show that individual companies took the initiative in hiring former government officials and that they were not forced to do so by the respective ministry. From the perspective of the MoF, the new system gave it some kind of alibi as regards the movement of its retired staff into *amakudari* positions, as from now on its could be argued that the receiving companies had asked for these respected former bureaucrats themselves. The new rules did not apply to civil servants who were accepting private sector jobs two years after retirement, which was the waiting period stipulated by the National Public Service Law for retired bureaucrats who moved into private sector positions that were closely related to their previous job in the government bureaucracy – for example a retired bank inspector who entered a private bank. Thus, the new system did not cover the most sensitive and delicate *amakudari* appointments that could most easily lead to possible conflicts of interest.

Meanwhile, the problematic situation in the banking sector continued to drag on. In January, the MoF published a figure of 76.7 trillion yen in bad loans based on the banks' 'self-assessment' results. However, despite the mounting scandals implicating the monetary authorities, a situation of complete policy paralysis was avoided. The ministry announced measures to support the stock market ('price keeping operations', see chapter 5), which included the use of administrative guidance. The government introduced in February 1998, still within the general framework of the 'convoy system' that did not allow for the failure of major financial institutions, another package of emergency measures for stabilising the financial system that included for the first time substantial injections of public money into the major banks. Funds in total of 30 trillion yen (6% of GDP) were to be distributed through the DIC; its expanded role in financial crisis management and the widened safety net were made possible after the amended Deposit Insurance Act and other legislation passed the Diet in February (Ministry of Finance 1998a). The measures included the establishment of a 13 trillion yen 'account for financial crisis management', which aimed at injecting public money into viable banks to strengthen their capital base, and the broadening of the financial basis of the DIC with 17 trillion yen by establishing one unified 'special account', which would have to ensure the full protection of deposits and could be used to finance the consolidation of the banking industry. The scope of the Resolution and Collection Bank (RCB) was expanded so that it could take over the financial business of not only credit co-operatives and *shinkin* banks but of other collapsed financial institutions as well. A Financial Crisis Management Committee (Kinyū Kiki Kanri Iinkai) was established within the DIC, which formulated and published criteria for banks applying for public funds (Hoshi and Patrick 2000b). Under the proposals, the banks would issue preferred stocks and subordinated bonds or apply for subordinated loans, which would be purchased or provided by the RCB, based on funds received from the DIC. By March 1998, however, only 1.8 trillion of the 13 trillion yen had been distributed to 18 major and three regional banks, mainly because of the strict restructuring conditions attached and the stigma of taking public support. It was clear that the major banks preferred to abstain from public capital injections out of fear of losing their independence and having to accept some form of government control. Apparently, the large banks were still powerful enough to resist confidence-building attempts of the government simply because they did not like the price they had to pay in return, which possibly could be explained by the longstanding tradition of financial support from the banking sector to the LDP, the ruling party in Japan, and the LDP's dominance over the MoF (Ramseyer and McCall Rosenbluth 1993; Rosenbluth and Thies 1999; see also section 3.3 of chapter 3 and chapter 9). Most likely, the prudential supervisors also did not pressure the banks too much, given their close and intimate relations with the banking sector. All in all, it can be concluded that this recapitalisation attempt failed (OECD 1998; Fukao 1999).

Owing to its enhanced role in the financial safety net, the role of the DIC in handling failed financial institutions continued to grow. By the end of April 1998, the DIC had been involved in 24 failures of financial institutions, and provided financial assistance worth 2.6 trillion yen in funds and 0.4 trillion yen in asset purchases (Kitami 1998, p.3). Meanwhile, more and particularly smaller banks announced rescue attempts and the start of bankruptcy proceedings. In March 1998, Hokkaido Bank was ordered to restructure its activities. In May, resolution measures involving 22 credit co-operatives were published. In its attempts to stabilise the situation, the MoF used its complete arsenal of informal policy instruments, such as price keeping operations aimed at the stock market, which involved administrative guidance towards financial institutions to prevent them from selling shares, and discretionary changes in the accounting rules (Craig 1998a, p.16; Lincoln 1998b, pp.366ff.). A more constructive solution was provided by the trend of increasing securitisation of bad loans, predominantly through Western investment banks, which effectively improved the bad-loan situation of the involved Japanese banks. Furthermore, in March, based on 'advice' from the MoF, the Federation of Bankers Associations of Japan decided to revise the uniform disclosure guidelines for the preparation of financial statements, including widening the definition of non-performing loans following the standards of the US Securities and Exchange Commission and amending the report form for the disclosure of capital adequacy ratios. The changes were aimed at improving transparency and thus showing that the banking industry was finally willing to reveal the 'real' size of the bad-loan problems, a move intended to boost national and international confidence in the determination of the Japanese banks to solve their problems at last (Hanazaki and Horiuchi 1998, p.8; Craig 1998a, p.16). The call for more transparency was reflected in recommendations published by the Corporate Accounting Council in March that proposed a new disclosure system and standards for interim accounting. In addition, as from April, the 'prompt corrective action' (PCA) scheme became effective for the larger international Japanese banks. Within the PCA scheme, financial institutions were required to submit a report on their self-assessment of loan portfolios, based on four categories of loans, with external audit provided by certified accountants.[28]

As regards the process of financial reform, in March a package of four bills related to the 'Big Bang' programme (that would formally begin the following April) was agreed upon by the Hashimoto administration, which, among other things, allowed for the re-establishment of financial holding companies that were abolished by the American occupation forces after World War II in their attempt to dissolve the powerful *zaibatsu* industrial conglomerates (see section 5.2 of chapter 5). This was an important step in the further gradual removal of the remaining barriers that still existed between various financial activities. The most important financial reform was undoubtedly the introduction of the new Bank of Japan Law in April that enhanced significantly the independence, transparency and accountability of Japan's central bank. As the amended BoJ Law has been discussed extensively elsewhere, I shall concentrate on the implications for prudential policy in particular (see for example: Financial System Research Council 1997a; Matsushita 1997b; Martin and Truedsson 1998; van Rixtel 1998b, 1998c; OECD 1997, 1998; Cargill et al. 2000). Contrary to the 1942 Bank of Japan Law, the new law established an explicit statutory basis for the BoJ's bank supervision, particularly of its on-site bank examinations. Article 44 states that the Bank may enter into contracts with financial institutions in order to conduct on-site examinations. However, it is made clear that the BoJ's examinations are not a separate or independent task, but a direct consequence of other tasks, in particular to conduct or prepare the provision of temporary loans (Article 37), to implement business contributing to the maintenance of an orderly financial system (Article 38) and to conduct business

---

[28] These categories are (in MoF and BoJ terminology respectively): 'good' or 'non-classified' (Category I), 'grey-area' or 'substandard' (Category II), 'probably bad' or 'doubtful' (Category III) and 'bad' or 'loss' (Category IV).

contributing to the smooth settlement of funds (Article 39) (see figure 6.5). In other words, the amended BoJ Law shows clearly that the Japanese government remains the main body responsible for the supervision of the banking industry. This is in line with the recommendations set out in the report issued in November 1996 by the Central Bank Study Group, which emphasised that the BoJ's examinations should be carried out in support of other functions such as maintaining a stable payments and settlements system. The dominant position of the government is clearly stated in Articles 38 and 39 of the revised BoJ Law, and to a certain extent in Article 37 as well. For example, Article 38 empowers the Prime Minister and the Minister of Finance to request the BoJ to provide extra liquidity to the banking system to maintain orderly conditions in the financial system. Based on the revised Bank of Japan Law, the BoJ announced in March that it would focus its prudential policy on the further strengthening and promotion of the examination of banks based on their risk management systems and the improvement of the efficiency and flexibility of its on-site examinations. In relation to the introduction of the PCA Scheme based on 'self assessment', the BoJ promoted a specific asset management method that supported financial institutions to maximise the use of their own assessments of asset-liabilities structures and loan losses as management tools (Bank of Japan 1998a). Furthermore, the BoJ announced that it would increase its on-site examinations of overseas branches of Japanese financial institutions located in Asia – this in response to the worsening Asian crisis – and would try to reduce the reporting burden of financial institutions.[29]

Phase V (June 1998–October 1998): administrative reform and intensifying crisis

The fifth phase in the policy reaction to the banking crisis, which started in June 1998 and ended in October, was characterised by the establishment of a new supervisory body outside the MoF and further reforms aimed at formally reducing the importance of informal policy instruments. As has been discussed above, in an attempt to silence the growing criticism of its handling of the banking problems, the LDP-led government proposed in 1996 the establishment of a new supervisory body, the Financial Supervisory Agency (Kinyū Kantoku Chō) (FSA), which would operate independently from the MoF and take over its inspection and supervision

---

[29] In correspondence with the revised BoJ Law that enhanced the BoJ's independence from the MoF, Paragraph 88 of the Ministry of Finance Establishment Law (Ōkurashō Setchi Hō) (October 1998 version) was amended to clarify that the MoF did no longer supervise (kantoku suru) the BoJ, but that it was only related (kan suru) to the central bank.

Article 37:
The bank of Japan [...] may provide uncollaterlised loans to financial institutions [...] and other financial business entities prescribed by a Cabinet Order [...] for a period within that prescribed by a Cabinet Order when they unexpectedly experience a temporary shortage of funds for payment due to accidental causes [...] whereby the business operations of the financial institutions may be seriously hampered if the shortage is not recovered swiftly [...]

Article 38:
The Prime Minister and the Minister of Finance may request that the Bank of Japan conduct the business necessary to maintain an orderly financial system, including provision of loans, when it is believed to be especially necessary for the maintenance of an orderly financial system including the case where it is judged, after consultation [...] that a serious problem in an orderly financial system may arise.
2. At the request of the Prime Minister and the Minister of Finance as prescribed by the preceding Paragraph, the Bank may conduct business necessary to maintain an orderly financial system, including provision of loans under special conditions [...]

Article 39:
The Bank of Japan [...] may [...] conduct business, upon the authorisation from the Prime Minister and the Minister of Finance, which is deemed to contribute to the smooth settlement of funds among financial institutions [...]

Article 44:
The Bank of Japan may, for the purpose of appropriately conducting or preparing to conduct business prescribed by Article 37 through 39, enter into a contract with financial institutions which become the correspondents in such business [...] regarding on-site examination [... Such contract must contain the clauses required by a Cabinet Order including, that requiring the Bank to notify correspondent financial institutions and obtain prior consent from them when conducting on-site examinations].
2. The Bank shall consider the administrative burden incurred by financial institutions when conducting on-site examinations.
3. At the request of the Commissioner of the Financial Supervisory Agency, the Bank may submit the results of on-site examinations or other information to the Commissioner, or provide them for his staff for their perusal.

Figure 6.5 Articles of the revised BoJ Law related to prudential policy
Source: Bank of Japan 1998. Since its enforcement, the Law has been amended in June and December 1998 (to adjust for the establishment of respectively the Financial Supervisory Agency and Financial Reconstruction Commission) and in April and July 2000 (to adjust for the establishment of the Financial Services Agency).

responsibilities regarding individual financial institutions in particular. The FSA was established on 22 June as a governmental organisation under the Prime Minister's Office (Sōri Fu) with the authority to inspect and supervise private financial institutions, including private banks, securities and insurance companies, labour credit associations, agricultural financial co-operatives and non-bank financial institutions (IMF 1998; Ministry of Finance 1998c; Kinyū Kantoku Chō 1999). The inspection and supervision of the latter three categories of financial institutions would be shared with the competent respective ministries, i.e. the Ministry of Labour, the Ministry of Agriculture, Forestry and Fisheries and the Ministry of International Trade and Industry. The creation of the FSA was a considerable drain on MoF's resources (within brackets number of MoF staff transferred to FSA): the staff of its Financial Inspection Department of the Minister's Secretariat (150), the Securities and Exchange Surveillance Commission (91) and the sections in the Banking Bureau (77) and the Securities Bureau (30) responsible for supervising private financial institutions were all transferred to the FSA, in total around a sixth of its policy staff at central headquarters (see table 6.6).[30] The remaining parts of the Banking Bureau and Securities Bureau were merged into a new Financial System Planning Bureau (Kinyū Kikaku Kyoku), with a total staff of 98.[31] Furthermore, the International Finance Bureau lost certain functions as well and was renamed International Bureau (Kokusai Kyoku).[32] In total, the FSA initially received 403 staff, of which 373 (or almost 80%) came from the MoF and four from other public organisations; only 26 new staff members were recruited. Thus, it can be asserted without doubt that the MoF yielded considerable influence on the FSA's policies and organisation. In addition, it was agreed that lower and mid-level staff in particular would be allowed to return to the MoF, effectively resulting in temporarily assignments or *shukkō* between the MoF and FSA. Furthermore, the FSA would also use MoF's local finance bureaus for the inspection and supervision of regional private financial institutions. Consequently, the MoF maintained at least some degree of influence over the politically important small and medium-sized banks, which traditionally provided considerable support to the LDP and have

[30] After the establishment of the FSA and reorganisation of the MoF, the combined number of staff at the Minister's Secretariat and the six policy bureaus totalled 1,679, compared with 1,942 two years earlier (Minister's Secretariat and seven policy bureaus), a decrease of 13.5% (Ōkura Zaimu Kyōkai 1997, 1999).

[31] The Financial System Planning Bureau consisted of four divisions (Co-ordination Division (Sōmu Ka), Planning and Legal Division (Kikaku Ka), Market Division (Shijō Ka) and Credit System Division (Shinyō Ka)) and three offices (Research Office (Chōsa Shitsu), Investment Services Office (Tōshi 'Saabisu' Shitsu) and Credit System Stabilisation Office (Shinyō Kikō Shitsu)), compared with a combined total of 11 divisions and several offices at the Banking and Securities Bureaus.

[32] For example, its responsibility for overseeing trade in currency futures at financial futures exchanges was transferred to the Financial System Planning Bureau (Ministry of Finance 1998c).

Table 6.6. *Staff at the FSA and the MoF*

Transferred from the MoF	To FSA	To Financial System Planning Bureau	To International Bureau	To Minister's Secretariat, etc.
Minister's Secretariat (175)				
From Financial Inspection Department	150			
Others	25			
Securities Bureau (87)	30	46		11
Banking Bureau (134)	77	41		16
Securities and Exchange Surveillance Commission (91)	91			
International Finance Bureau (144)		10	134	
Other staff (32)	30[1]	1	1	
Total (663)	403[2]	98	135	27

Notes: [1] Of which one staff member each from the Ministry of Agriculture, Forestry and Fisheries, Ministry of International Trade and Industry, National Police Agency and Public Prosecutor's Office. Furthermore, the FSA announced in June 1998 that it would start recruiting a small number of certified public accountants.
[2] Of which 151 permanent Inspectors at the FSA's headquarters. Furthermore, the FSA could employ 420 permanent Inspectors at the MoF's Local Finance Bureaus (Jarrett 1998, p.29).
Source: Ministry of Finance (1998c) and Kinyū Kantoku Chō (1999).

become more important in this respect (see McCall Rosenbluth 1989). With the publicly announced removal of its inspection and supervision tasks, the MoF became responsible for the planning and research of the financial system, in particular the legal framework, and the supervision of the DIC and securities markets. Basically, the MoF was now the planning authority for the financial system, including involvement in financial crisis management, and controlled the legal framework, whereas the FSA was given the task of enforcing financial supervision. Furthermore, it was formally agreed that the MoF could systematically 'interact' with the FSA, for example to obtain information about certain financial issues. Specifically, this would take the form of guidance to the FSA on matters related to the co-ordination of overall strategies to handle major financial crises or concrete financial assistance from the DIC to finance rescue mergers. All in all, the close personnel relations between the MoF and FSA, MoF's involvement in financial system planning and financial crisis management and its control of the legal framework showed the substantial influence of the MoF on the FSA and caused many observers to question the FSA's real 'independence' (see for example: *Handelsblatt* 1998; Japan Economic Institute 1998, p.3–4; OECD 1998, p.131; Norville 1998; Brown 1999, p.224; IMF 1999a, p.47).

The establishment of the FSA had also major repercussions for the financial system's legal framework. In total, 59 laws were amended, including the Banking Law and the Securities and Exchange Law. For example, the responsibilities of the MoF in the field of financial system planning and crisis management were reflected in its right to request information from financial institutions and other parties. Also the Ministry of Finance Establishment Law (Ōkurashō Setchi Hō) was adjusted, and various paragraphs were abrogated, for example Paragraph 4.100 which stated that the MoF was responsible for the regulation and supervision of financial institutions in their operation of funds, and that possibly could have led to the use of administrative guidance in the past (see section 5.4 of chapter 5).[33] However, Paragraph 4.101 which could have been related to the use of administrative guidance as well, i.e. forcing financial institutions to change their interest rates whenever the MoF deemed necessary, for example given the status of the economy, remained unchanged. Furthermore, neither was Paragraph 4.90 amended, which provided the MoF with the right to supervise (*kantoku suru*) depository and insurance institutions. Thus, despite the establishment of an independent FSA, the law that governed the MoF explicitly stated that the ministry was still maintaining responsibilities for the supervision of financial institutions. Despite the fact that the FSA was from now on in charge of the supervision and inspection of individual financial institutions, MoF's legal framework still authorised it to operate as financial supervisor.

In addition to the start of the FSA, the release of two reports in June and July that contained outlines for a 'total plan' to cope with the crisis provided important input for the discussion on supervisory policy reform and the ways to solve the banking problems (Government Ruling Party Conference 1998a, 1998b). In particular the first report included proposals for the disposition of bad loans through debt forgiveness, which would reduce the debt burden of the real estate and construction sectors and increase liquidity in the property market. A Temporary Council for Co-ordinating Real Estate-Related Rights would be established to settle claims and liabilities regarding bad loans with real estate collateral. Most of these proposals, however, which were widely interpreted as effective solutions to reduce the amount of bad debts, disappeared from the second report. According to some sources, this happened owing to strong

[33] Analysis based on the version of MoF's Establishment Law from 16 October 1998, as included in Ōkura Zaimu Kyōkai 1999.

resistance and even substantial financial donations by the banking industry to the LDP in advance of the 12 July elections (personal interviews,
November 1998, Tokyo). This was another example of the significant
political influence of the banking sector. The banks preferred to keep the
bad loans on their balance sheets, which they could finance almost against
zero costs owing to the ample liquidity provided by the BoJ, instead of selling the related collateral against large discounts or writing off substantial
numbers of loans. Instead, the idea of public 'bridge banks' was introduced (Ministry of Finance 1998e). Under the bridge bank scheme, the
FSA would conduct regular inspections and formulate critera to decide
which banks were insolvent and should be placed under public administration. A detailed examination of bank portfolios would distinguish the
bad loan portfolios – to be taken over by the Resolution and Collection
Bank (RCB) – from the 'healthy' ones. The latter would be either directly
sold to private receiver banks or to public bridge banks, with the necessary funding provided by the DIC. The bridge banks scheme was received
rather critically by neutral observers, as it did not contain elements of debt
forgiveness and would be generally used for relatively small failed banks
only; the remaining large banks were still not allowed to go bankrupt
but instead would be kept alive artificially through 'convoy system'-style
rescue mergers (*The Banker* 1998; Goldman Sachs 1998; Neuffer 1998;
Ohara 1998). Thus, the fundamental concepts of the 'convoy system'
were still very much alive, which became clear after statements from the
newly elected Prime Minister Keizo Obuchi and Finance Minister Kiichi
Miyazawa that it should be preferred to treat the bad-loans problems
'delicately' rather than closing unsound banks. This policy line was also
followed in public statements from FSA's Commissioner Masaharu Hino
and the Governor of the BoJ Masaru Hayami (*Japan Times*, various issues, July–August 1998). An interesting development was a public rift
between the BoJ and the government (i.e. MoF) regarding the disclosure
of information about the banks' bad-loans portfolios, as the former –
supported by the FSA – urged banks to reveal more than was welcomed
by the latter (*Wall Street Journal Europe*, 23 June 1998). Prime Minister
Obuchi refused to publish the results of an audit into the country's
largest banks because it might undermine 'market order'. In the meantime it became clear that the Long-Term Credit Bank of Japan (LTCB),
the second largest long-term credit bank, needed substantial financial
assistance. Merger talks with Sumitomo Trust & Banking, one of the
largest trust banks, were started, with full support from the government.
Finance Minister Kiichi Miyazawa declared that public funds should
be used; however, the opposition opposed a government plan involving
substantial capital injections into the LTCB in August.

In the context of the process of administrative reform, the MoF announced in June major revisions of its use of informal circulars or *tsūtatsu* and business guidelines (*jimu renraku*), of which the former have been typified in this study as published administrative guidance (see chapter 3).[34] These revisions had been promised by the minister in August 1997 after several MoF staff members were reprimanded for improper behaviour. In addition, the use of informal policy instruments such as the *tsūtatsu* was also considered in relation to the existence of informal networks including the MoF-*tan* system and the outbreak of the scandals at the beginning of 1998. Under the revisions, 382 of the around 400 *tsūtatsu* and 234 of the 243 business guidelines notices were formally abolished (*Bank of Japan Quarterly Bulletin*, August 1998, p.133; OECD 1999b, p.56). As regards the Banking Bureau, 236 of its 259 *tsūtatsu* and 178 of its 184 business guidelines, plus one 'newspaper announcement' (*shinbun happyō*) were discontinued (Ōkurashō Ginkō Kyoku 1998).[35] However, the regulations that were considered to be indispensable were simply put in another legal format or incorporated in other existing *jimu* guidelines: according to OECD (1998), p.132, about 60 *tsūtatsu* and *jimu renraku* were upgraded to the level of ministerial ordinances (*shōrei*) and public notices (*kokuji*).[36] In addition, the MoF still had the option of using unpublished administrative guidance, thus replacing one form of informal regulation by another. From the document published by MoF's Banking Bureau, it is not clear into which specific new format the regulations that remained in force were changed, leading in my view to considerably less transparency than before (Ōkurashō Ginkō Kyoku 1998). All in all, a number of *tsūtatsu* were transformed into other forms of financial regulation and effectively maintained, implying that some of the revisions were merely cosmetic. For example, the 'Kihon Jikō' *tsūtatsu*, which contained specific targets for bank performance,[37] was split into various public notices or *kokuji* under the jurisdiction of the FSA, for example as regards the solvency requirements and targets for the maximum amounts of bank lending to a single borrower; certain rules on accounting practices included in this *tsūtatsu* were put in a circular of the Japanese

---

[34] As was discussed in chapter 5, certain MoF officials considered the *jimu renraku* to be a specific form of *tsūtatsu*.

[35] The newspaper announcement was related to the participation of foreign banks in trust business activities ('Gaikoku ginkō no shintaku gyōmu sannyū ni tsuite').

[36] The legal arsenal of the MoF included several other detailed regulations such as *shokō saisoku* (detailed regulations regarding the application of a law) and *kokuji* (public notices), in addition to *tsūtatsu* and *jimu* guidelines. Thus, it had plenty of formal legal alternatives to replace or substitute the abolished regulations.

[37] This was *tsūtatsu* no. 901 ('Futsū ginkō no gyōmu un-ei ni kan suru kihon jikō tō' or 'Standard items related to the management of the operation of commercial banks'). See section 5.4 of chapter 5.

Bankers Association (Zenginkyō) (personal correspondence with private bankers, Tokyo, 1999). It should be emphasised that MoF's revision of its use of *tsūtatsu* and business guidelines coincided with the start of the FSA, which maybe was more than just a coincidence. As a large part of MoF's *tsūtatsu* were related to the implementation of micro monetary policy, in particular prudential policy (see chapter 5), the establishment of the FSA implied almost automatically that the MoF would no longer be responsible for these circulars, and even would no longer need most of them. By announcing their abolition in order to improve the 'transparency' of its policies, the MoF obtained relatively easily some much-needed goodwill. Furthermore, the macro monetary policy *tsūtatsu* issued by the MoF were, as was asserted in chapter 5, often instigated because of political interests of the ruling LDP. Their abolition could have been beneficial to increase MoF's independence from political pressure and interests, although possibly also here the circulars could have been simply replaced by other regulations.

As part of the general process of administrative reform, the Diet passed in June 1998 the Administrative Reform Bill that was drafted by the Hashimoto administration in January on the reorganisation of the general structure of the Japanese government. It was agreed that a government panel would work out the specific details and prepare legislation to be submitted to parliament in 1999. In July 1998, the so-called 'Council on the Ministry of Finance's Administration' published a report that contained recommendations to avoid unethical actions of MoF staff, reduce the use of administrative guidance and improve its personnel policy, aimed at mitigating the dominance of graduates from specific universities and faculties (*gakubatsu*), in particular from the University of Tokyo (*Tōdaibatsu*) (Ministry of Finance 1998d). The Council suggested that 'administration by discretion' and the hiring of elite (Category I) bureaucrats should be adjusted and become more diversified:

Further measures to promote transparent and fair administration based on clear rules must be promoted. The overall review of financial administrative guidance is a good precedent for such changes.

To avoid having too many Category I employees at the Ministry be graduates of a particular university, recruitment activities should be done at various activities, and the National Personnel Agency should be asked to admit a substantially larger number of applicants to the appointment examination for national public officials. (Ministry of Finance 1998d).

As is shown in table 6.7, the attention of the Council on the university background of the highest MoF officials was certainly justified. Compared with the situation at end-1991 (see table 5.2, page 104), the dominance of graduates from the University of Tokyo actually increased as

Table 6.7. *University background of top MoF officials (149 highest functions; September 1998)*

	Tokyo E	Tokyo L	Tokyo O	Kyoto	Hitotsubashi	Keio	Waseda	Rest
Adm. vice-minister, etc.[1]	2	3						
Director-general[2]	2	7	1					
Deputy director-general	2	9		1				1
Director division	6	30	2	5	3		3	3
Councillor[3]		3		1				
Counsellor[3]	5	1						
Special officer, senior officer, special assistant	3	20						1
Rest[4]	3	18		1	1			12
Total[5]	23	91	3	8	4		3	17

Notes: [1] Administrative vice-minister, Vice-Minister of Finance for International Affairs, Deputy Vice-Minister, Deputy Vice-Minister for Policy Co-ordination and Special Advisor to Minister of Finance. With the revision of the BoJ Law, the MoF lost its representative at the BoJ's Policy Board.
[2] Including Director-General (DG) Tokyo Customs, DG Mint Bureau, DG Printing Bureau and Commissioner National Tax Administration Agency.
[3] The councillor/counsellor distinction appears to be one of semantics only; both perform similar functions.
[4] Includes directors of various offices and budget examiners.
[5] Facilities, such as the Customs Training Institute and the Institute of Fiscal and Monetary Policy, local finance bureaus, regional taxation bureaus, other local tax offices and custom houses other than Tokyo Customs are not included.
Source: Jihyō Sha 1998.

of September 1998. Although the MoF was reorganised in 1998 – owing to the establishment of the FSA – and consequently the total number of top-level positions decreased and is not fully comparable with 1991, in percentage terms the importance of Tōdai graduates increased from 75% (i.e. 127 out of a total of 169 positions) at end-1991 to around 79% (i.e. 117 out of 149) as of September 1998. Despite a slight decrease in the share of graduates from the University of Tokyo's Law Faculty, from 62% in 1991 to 61% in 1998, the share of graduates from its Economics Faculty and other faculties increased from 14% to almost 18%. Furthermore, compared with seven years earlier, the share of the latter increased in particular among the highest positions such as Director-General. An interesting development was the significantly larger number of Tōdai graduates among the Special Officers and Senior Officers in 1998 compared with 1991, possibly due to the reorganisation of the MoF and consequent re-allocation of positions. The figures also show that certain functions were presumably predestined for graduates with a specific university background and thus out of reach for others. For example, the prestigious positions of Councillor and Special Officer for Research and Planning at the Minister's Secretariat (10 in total) were all occupied by graduates from Tōdai's Law Faculty, whereas five of the six Counsellors at the Secretariat graduated from its Economics Faculty.[38]

Turning to the reaction to the banking crisis, the BoJ continued from its side to monitor closely the deteriorating situation in the banking industry.[39] It conducted extensive on-site examinations in collaboration with the FSA and provided the markets with ample liquidity as it became increasingly worried about the banking problems and systemic risk.[40] In September, the Policy Board of the BoJ decided to further ease the stance of monetary policy and to allow its policy interest rate – the uncollateralised overnight call rate – to move on average around 0.25% (see figure 6.4). It also announced the provision of more ample funds if judged necessary to maintain the stability of the financial markets (Bank of Japan, September 1998, http://www.boj.or.jp/). In order to maintain close and effective co-ordination between the various bodies involved with bank supervision and financial crisis management after the regulatory changes in June, the FSA, BoJ, MoF and DIC agreed to establish a liaison council.

Despite the policy initiatives of the MoF, FSA and BoJ, however, the situation in the banking sector failed to improve. The merger between Long-Term Credit Bank of Japan and Sumitomo Trust & Banking was definitely cancelled. In September Japan Leasing, the largest of three leasing companies affiliated with LTCB, applied for court protection. National and international confidence in Japan's financial system dropped significantly, as reflected in the rise of the 'Japan premium' to almost 90 basis points (see figure 6.3). This was to a large extent also due to the incredible lack of political willingness and sense of urgency among both ruling and opposition parties to compromise on a plan to inject public funds in the ailing banking industry. One proposal after another was rejected, without any clear prospect of a deal. It was politics at its worst, a dangerous and irresponsible political soap-opera that increasingly started to threaten not

[38] Two new counsellors were added to the Minister's Secretariat to oversee the Financial System Planning Bureau when it was established in June 1998 (Ministry of Finance 1998c).

[39] Unfortunately, the source of information on the university background of BoJ executives in chapter 5 (table 5.6) ceased publication and therefore no direct comparison between 1991 and 1998 is possible.

[40] In Fiscal Year 1998 (April 1998–March 1999), the BoJ would examine 62 banks, of which 48 in collaboration with the FSA, 65 *shinkin* banks and 12 other financial institutions (including securities companies and Japanese branches of foreign banks) (Bank of Japan 1999).

only the stability of the Japanese financial system but that of the international financial markets and institutions as well. Commentators could only express their abhorrence on developments in Japan, finding more and more evidence of a system gripped by political and policy paralysis (see, for example, Abrahams 1998; *The Economist* 1998). The IMF stated that the main risk to the world economy now was that Japan 'will not move promptly and resolutely to address its financial-sector problems while ensuring adequate domestic demand [...] Speed is becoming increasingly critical' (Reuters, September 1998).

Phase VI (October 1998–June 2000): financial revitalisation – the end of the crisis?

Finally, after months of indecisiveness and political uncertainty, the government and opposition reached an agreement in October 1998 on the injection of substantial amounts of public money in the banking industry and the establishment of several new institutions aimed at solving Japan's banking problems once and for all, of which the Financial Reconstruction Commission (Kinyū Saisei Iinkai) (FRC) was the single most important (Ministry of Finance 1998f, 1998g; IMF 1999a, 1999b; OECD 1998, 1999a; Milhaupt 1999; Nakaso 1999; Kanaya and Woo 2000). This new supervisory body was established legally on 12 October 1998, when a package of laws known collectively as Financial Revitalisation Legislation passed parliament, which set up the framework for dealing with failed or insolvent financial institutions, and contained elements of the bridge bank scheme. Furthermore, on 16 October the Financial Function Early Strengthening Law was enacted, which developed measures to strengthen weak but in principle healthy financial institutions in order to save them from bankruptcy (see figure 6.6).

The new FRC was established as the main body responsible for the supervision of private financial institutions and the resolution of failed financial institutions, with, however, a very limited staff in its Secretariat of just 38 (see figure 6.7). The FSA was put under the jurisdiction of the FRC as its so-called external agency; the FRC would provide guidance to the FSA regarding the latter's preventive inspections of private financial institutions and decide how failures of these institutions would be dealt with. Thus, the FRC took over some responsibilities that were given to the MoF when the FSA had been established just a couple of months earlier. It was further agreed that the FRC (in particular its Financial Crisis Management Division) would share with the MoF the research, planning and formulation of financial resolution schemes and financial crisis management, thus maintaining MoF's considerable leeway

---

Financial Revitalisation Legislation (12 October 1998):

In total four laws, i.e the Law Concerning Emergency Measures for the Revitalisation of the Functions of the Financial System (set out the basic framework), Amendment of the Deposit Insurance Law (established the Resolution and Collection Organisation), the Law for the Establishment of the Financial Reconstruction Committee (FRC) and the Law for the Preparation of Related Laws for the Implementation of the FRC Establishment Law.
Main elements:
- Establishment of the FRC.
- This Committee could choose among three methods for dealing with failed banks:
  - appointment of financial administrators and transfer of business to a private successor bank
  - appointment of financial administrators and transfer of business to a public bridge bank
  - temporary nationalisation under special public management.
- Merger of the Resolution and Collection Bank and the Housing Loan Administration Corporation into the Resolution and Collection Organisation (RCO), which until 31 March 2001 would be able to purchase bad loans from failed financial institutions.
- Establishment of an 18 trillion yen (3.6% of GDP) 'financial revitalisation account' at the DIC to be used for financing successor banks, public bridge banks and nationalised banks.

Financial Function Early Strengthening Law (16 October 1998):

Based on the level of solvency ratios, the FRC could approve capital injections in weak banks. Establishment of a 'financial function early strengthening account' (or 'prompt correction account') of 25 trillion yen (5% of GDP) at the DIC.

Figure 6.6 Financial reform laws, October 1998
Source: Ministry of Finance 1998f and 1998g.

to influence the financial revitalisation process. The lasting influence of the MoF on various issues regarding the financial system and prudential policy was explicitly incorporated in several articles of a new version of the Banking Law that came into force in December 1998 (Japanese Bankers Association 1998):

Article 14-2: The Financial Reconstruction Commission and the Minister of Finance may, in order to contribute to sound management of banking business, set forth the [following] criteria [or other criteria] to be used as criteria to judge the soundness of bank management.

Article 57-2: The Financial Reconstruction Commission shall consult in advance with the Minister of Finance on measures required to maintain the credit order

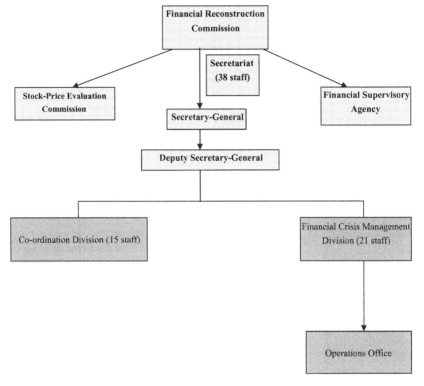

Figure 6.7 The organisation of the FRC
Source: Financial Reconstruction Commission.

when it deems it likely that (the following) dispositions taken in regard to a bank could have a serious effect on the maintenance of the credit order.

Article 57-4: The Minister of Finance may, when he or she deems necessary for the research, planning, or drafting of systems related to banks, request the submission of necessary materials from the Financial Reconstruction Commission. 2. The Minister of Finance may, to the extent he or she deems especially necessary for the research, planning, or drafting of systems related to banks, request the submission of materials, furnishing of explanations, and other cooperation from banks, bank holding companies, and other related parties.

Furthermore, the MoF maintained its legal responsibilities such as the drafting of legislation with respect to the financial system and thus controlled to a large extent the legal environment of the FRC (and FSA). Various activities such as the subordinated business of banks plus other matters (accounting, suspension of banking business and issues related

to bank holding companies) were to be determined by ordinances of
the Prime Minister's Office (*seirei/sōrifurei*) and the MoF (*shōrei*). Thus,
many legal matters concerning the FRC and FSA were decided by or
jointly with the MoF, which questioned their legal independence. For example, the revision of regulations relative to the application of the Banking Law (Ginkō Hō Sekōkisoku) carried the names of ordinances from
both the Prime Minister's Office and the MoF (private correspondence,
Japanese banker, November 1999). As an example of the legal complexity
of the intertwined financial regulatory structure in Japan involving various bodies, I shall present the set of regulations that was used by the FSA
at the end of 1999. Its regulatory framework consisted of approximately
30 cabinet ordinances (*seirei*), of which one was related to the Banking
Law, 50 ministerial ordinances (*shōrei*) (also one related to Banking Law),
120 public notices (*kokuji*) (14 related to Banking Law) and four types
of *jimu* guidelines for, respectively, depository financial institutions, insurance companies, securities companies and finance companies. The
influence of the MoF was the most clearly present as regards the *shōrei*,
which it issued and managed jointly with the FSA.

The nature of the relationship of the BoJ with the FRC was not explained clearly, but in practice the BoJ would continue to implement its
supervisory duties parallel to those of and in co-ordination with the FSA.
The FRC received a temporary mandate (until 31 March 2001) and was
put under the leadership of a board consisting of a chairman (Minister of
State in charge of Financial Affairs) and four other members. It started
work on 15 December 1998, headed by Hakuo Yanagisawa, a former
Director for Corporate Income-Tax Policy at the MoF (*Nikkei Weekly*,
1 December 2000, p.6).

The framework of the FRC allowed for the use of three alternative
methods to deal with failed financial institutions. First, it was given the
authority to appoint financial administrators who would take over management and organise a private sector solution through the transfer of
business to a private successor bank, which would receive financial support from the DIC. This was basically the same strategy that financial
supervisors followed in the past of organising rescue mergers between
weak or failed financial institutions and healthy ones. Second, if no private sector solution could be found, the business of the failed institution
would be transferred to a public bridge bank, established by the DIC.
Third, in the case of a failure of a major financial institution that threatened the stability of the financial system, the Committee could decide to
put the failed institution temporarily under special public management
(temporary nationalisation). The DIC would purchase the shares of the
failed institution against a price decided by the Stock Price Evaluation

Commission (see figure 6.7). In any case, the FRC would decide which of the three methods would be used. Given the problematic situation of the Japanese banking sector, a private rescue operation (option 1) was no longer deemed to be a realistic option. Also the usefulness of public bridge banks (option 2) was questioned, as FSA officials doubted whether it would be feasible to establish bridge banks of sufficient size to take over the activities of failed institutions; in these circumstances bridge banks would probably be used only for smaller regional banks. As a result, temporary nationalisation (option 3) appeared to be the most realistic option. To finance successor banks, public bridge banks and nationalised banks, the Diet approved the establishment of a 'financial revitalisation account' of 18 trillion yen (3.6% of GDP) at the DIC.

Finally, the Financial Revitalisation Legislation established a Resolution and Collection Organisation (Seiri Kaishū Kikō) (RCO) as of April 1999 by merging the Resolution and Collection Bank (RCB) and the Housing Loan Administration Corporation (HLAC), which was established to handle the bad debt of the failed housing loan companies (*jūsen*). The RCO could not only purchase bad loans from failed banks, but also directly from sound financial institutions. This was considered to be a major improvement compared with the previous resolution framework and safety net, as it could improve the situation of relatively sound banks.

The second part of the legislation that passed parliament in October was The Financial Function Early Strengthening Law, which provided a framework for the recapitalisation of weak banks through the purchase of stocks by the RCO, using funds provided by the DIC. For this purpose, a new 'financial function early strengthening account' of 25 trillion yen (5% of GDP) was established at the DIC. Dependent on the level of the solvency ratios, which were distinguished into four categories (0 to 2%, 2 to 4%, 4 to 8%, 8% and above), the FRC would attach more severe conditions to the injection of public money, such as the reduction of the number of directors, staff and branches, abolition of international operations and the suspension of dividend payments. In combination with the 17 trillion yen 'special account' established in February 1998, the DIC had now at its disposal a total of 60 trillion yen (12% of GDP) of public money in three accounts to solve the bad-loan problems. In addition to these public funds, as of October 1998 a total of 40 trillion yen in public credit guarantees was made available through credit-guarantee associations of local governments and central government organisations to avoid a 'credit crunch' of small and medium-sized companies. From its side, the BoJ established in November a 'temporary lending facility' to facilitate borrowing by the corporate sector and mitigate credit crunch concerns, and initiated reforms regarding money market operations in commercial paper and a new lending mechanism for financial institutions collateralised by corporate debt (IMF 1999b; OECD 1999a). Furthermore, the MoF and FSA announced that banks would have to report the performance of companies in which they held significant holdings, in order to get a clearer picture of their risk exposure.

The decision by the Japanese government and parliament to provide substantial amounts of public funds to support the banking industry was greeted with great enthusiasm by the financial markets, as was shown in the rapid decline of the 'Japan premium' (see figure 6.3). It was clear that without large injections of public money it would have been impossible to make a start on restructuring the Japanese banking sector and disposing of the huge amounts of bad loans. However, several observers, who had experienced years of forbearance and 'muddling through' on the side of Japanese policymakers, maintained their doubts about developments in Japan, as a number of uncertainties regarding the specifics of the reform laws remained. First, the proposals for the disposition of bad loans through debt forgiveness and loan workout programmes incorporated in the first report of the so-called Government Ruling Party Conference to Promote the Comprehensive Plan for Financial Revitalisation, published in June 1998, were not taken over in the Financial Reform Laws.[41] According to various banking analysts, these proposals were key to the revitalisation of the markets for loan collateral and would have established significant land and real estate liquidations that could have diminished the bad-loan problems considerably (see also OECD 1999a, p.81). Second, the conditions attached to the injections of public money were not made very clear, which could pose moral hazard problems (Jarrett 1998, p.18). Furthermore, certain conditions such as an increase of lending to small and medium-sized enterprises in return for public capital injections seemed rather odd and politically motivated. This element of killing two birds with one stone – rescuing banks and small businesses – seemed to be logically inconsistent. Fourth, doubts remained whether the 60 trillion yen package would be sufficient to cover all costs of the banking crisis, including the problems at public financial institutions and in the insurance sector, and whether the funds could be used effectively. Finally, despite the perceived credit crunch situation, lending by private banks to the construction and real estate sectors was rising. As discussed in section 6.3, these sectors were among the riskiest in the Japanese economy and largely responsible for the creation of the banking problems in the first place. This development gave rise to suspicions of political interference regarding the lending behaviour of banks, as the

---

[41] For this report see Government Ruling Party Conference (1998a).

construction and real estate sectors were known to be closely related to the governing LDP, and thus the danger was perceived that public funds would be used to support the political interests of the LDP as well.[42]

Despite the prevailing scepticism in certain circles about the effectiveness of the October legislation, it is fair to say that the supervisory authorities finally adopted a tougher policy stance and allowed the closure of insolvent institutions. The old policy line under the 'convoy system' of artificially keeping failed banks alive by rescue mergers and DIC support seemed to have been abolished. The method of temporary nationalisation was used for the first time in October in the case of the failed Long-Term Credit Bank of Japan (LTCB). Its failure illustrated the general lack of disclosure and transparency in the Japanese financial system and the danger of structural underreporting of the amounts of bad loans under the 'self-assessment' framework that contained certain elements of arbitrariness: at the end of September, the bad loans of the LTCB were estimated at 4.3 trillion yen, nearly double what it admitted to in August based on its self-assessment (Jarrett 1998, p.18; Ohara 1998, pp.7–9). It was followed by the insolvency and subsequent temporary nationalisation of Nippon Credit Bank (NCB), another long-term credit bank, in December. The supervisory authorities also started to negotiate with the healthier banks on the injection of public funds to strengthen their capital base using the funds made available under the 'financial function early strengthening account'. After initial reluctance, 15 of the largest banks – 8 city banks, 5 trust banks, the Industrial Bank of Japan and Yokohama Bank, the largest regional bank – agreed in March 1999 to accept 7.46 trillion yen of public funds that included the issuance of preferred shares (Fukao 1999; IMF 1999a; OECD 1999a). In return, they started to cut back on their operations in the form of limiting the number of staff and withdrawing from overseas operations, and promised to increase their lending to small and medium-sized enterprises;[43] however, incumbent management was largely left in place.[44] All in all, a general sense of careful optimism began to emerge in the first months of 1999, as was shown by a further decrease of the 'Japan premium' to close to zero (see figure 6.3). The

---

[42] The seriousness of the financial crisis in Japan was highlighted by reports that Western banks reduced their yen deposit rates to below zero, as depositors, including Japanese banks, were increasingly unwilling to hold their funds denominated in yen at Japanese banks, owing to fears about their declining creditworthiness (*Financial Times* 1998).

[43] According to the *Japan Times*, the 15 banks increased their lending to small and medium-sized enterprises by a total of 4.25 trillion yen in FY 1999, which was much more than the 2.99 trillion yen they pledged when accepting the public money (*Japan Times* Online, 9 June 2000).

[44] On the other hand, criminal charges (suspicion of fraud) were brought in 1999 against several former executives of the failed Hokkaido Takushoku Bank and Nippon Credit Bank, which served as a clear warning to the banking industry's leadership.

policy line that was adopted by the FRC and FSA, which included an official end to the delay of the strict enforcement of the 'prompt corrective action' framework that was announced at the end of 1997, was generally assessed in more and more positive terms by private sector analysts and international organisation (see for example: Fiorillo 1999a; IMF 1999a, 1999b, pp.82ff., 2000a; Moody's Investors Service 1999a; OECD 1999a; see also Bank of Japan 2000).[45] After having stabilised the situation at the largest banks, the supervisory authorities now turned to the regional and Second Tier regional banks and other smaller financial institutions, followed by the foreign banks and the Japanese insurance industry. First, as regards the smaller Japanese commercial banks, the situation at numerous Second Tier regional banks was particularly problematic (Moody's Investors Service 1999a, 1999b). In October 1998, the failed Fukutoku Bank and Bank of Naniwa merged into Namihaya Bank, which ultimately collapsed in August 1999; in November, Hanshin Bank took over the collapsed Midori Bank. In January 1999, Moody's Investors Service downgraded the ratings of five regional banks. Kokumin Bank, a medium-size Second Tier regional bank, was put under FRC control in April; one of the larger Second Tier regional banks, Kofuku Bank, announced in May that it would request about 60 billion yen in public funds after the FSA applied the 'prompt corrective action' scheme, followed by the bankruptcies of Tokyo Sowa Bank (June) and Niigata Chuo Bank (October), and public money requests from Kumamoto Family Bank in December. Based on its inspections, which were partly conducted in collaboration with the BoJ,[46] the FSA announced in September that the remaining Second Tier regional banks had significantly understated the amount of their problem loan, which were about 22% higher than indicated by their 'self-assessment' results. In relation to the FSA's inspection results of the regional banks, the FRC decided to inject 260 billion yen into three regional banks (Ashikaga Bank, Hokuriku Bank and Bank of the Ryukyus) and one Second Tier regional bank (Hiroshima-Sogo Bank).[47] Several banks were recapitalised using private money from their 'main banks', including Kanto Bank and Chiba Kogyo Bank. In December 1999, Shonai Bank and Shokusan Bank announced their intention to merge. As regards other small financial institutions, the FSA ordered in October 1999 the prefectures, which still maintained supervisory responsibilities, to inspect about 100 credit co-operatives.

[45] A survey by the *Nikkei Weekly* published in May 1999 showed that many institutional investors and analysts had a high opinion of the FSA and FRC.

[46] The BoJ examined during fiscal year 1998 62 banks (48 jointly with the FSA), of which 43 were regional and Second Tier regional banks (Bank of Japan 1999).

[47] Some of these banks received also financial assistance from their 'main banks', i.e. banks that were their main shareholders (see section 4.3 of chapter 4).

The problematic situation of these financial institutions was shown by their rising bankruptcies, from 13 in 1998 to 20 in the first half of 1999 (Standard & Poor's Rating Services 2000, p.11; see also IMF 1998, pp.117–118).[48] Second, in 1999 the supervisory authorities also shifted their focus towards the foreign banks, including Crédit Suisse, Lehman Brothers and Deutsche Bank. In particular the case of Credit Suisse received considerable attention. The FSA started an investigation in January, based on accusations that CSFB helped Japanese financial institutions to illegally hide losses through complex financial constructions, and later penalised the foreign bank.[49] However, in the view of many Western bankers it was simply a backlash against foreign banks; they argued that the MoF had been fully aware of these constructions and condoned them, as they had been instrumental in concealing the magnitude of the banking problems (*Financial Times*, 21 May 1999). The incident illustrated the continuing discretionary and vague nature of prudential policy in Japan, as supervisors interpreted regulations as they saw fit, permitting certain activities one day and banning them the next (*The Economist*, 17 July 1999, pp.74–75 *Euromoney* 1999b; *Wall Street Journal*, 30 July 1999).[50] Third, in addition to the regional, Second Tier regional and foreign banks, the FSA also became increasingly involved with the Japanese insurance industry, which was widely seen as facing considerable problems (see, for example, IMF 1998, 1999b, pp.93–94, 2000a). It announced in January that it would start to examine the asset quality of insurance companies; measures following the 'prompt corrective action' scheme that was introduced for the banking sector were adopted for insurance companies in April 1999. That the FSA's concerns were justified was shown by the collapse of Toho Mutual Life Insurance Co. in June. The orientation of the FSA towards smaller financial institutions and insurance companies was publicly laid down in its yearly policy plan that aimed for the inspection of a total of 445 financial institutions during the period July 1999–June 2000, including 220 *shinkin* banks and 20 life assurance companies (Financial Supervisory Agency 1999). The FSA also unveiled a financial-examination manual, which would be used as a guide to be followed by financial institutions in its inspections. The human resources available to the FSA, which were put under considerable strain by the problems in

---

[48] According to the BoJ, 20 credit co-operatives and 9 *shinkin* banks failed during FY1999 (Bank of Japan 2000, p.71).
[49] Also Deutsche Securities, the securities subsidiary of Deutsche Bank, and BNP Paribas were both punished in the course of 2000 for providing services to help clients to hide losses.
[50] In a reaction to the incident, in July 1999 both Western and Japanese bankers urged the supervisory authorities to adopt more transparency in the regulatory process (*Financial Times*, 16 July 1999).

the financial services industry, received a major boost in December 1999
when the government announced funding for 300 additional banking inspectors in Fiscal Year 2000, which would boost the numbers to around
1,000 inspectors nationwide (including the local finance bureaus of the
MoF) by April 2000 (Nikkei Net, December 1999).[51] The increase was
needed because the FSA would take over the supervisory responsibility
for the credit co-operatives from the prefectures as of that date, which
would actually be performed by MoF's local finance bureaus.

As regards the use of informal policy instruments, in the course of
1999 more information became available on the specific policies that the
MoF had adopted to stave off the bankruptcy of Nippon Credit Bank.
According to various reports, it used administrative guidance in 1997
to 'persuade' 34 private financial institutions to provide 210 billion yen
in financial support to NCB in return for equity stakes, in addition to
80 billion yen from the BoJ. Despite this support, the bank collapsed and
was put under temporary nationalisation in December 1998, leaving the
private investors empty-handed. Various executives of the private financial institutions that injected emergency funds in NCB accused the MoF
of having given them incorrect and even false information about the deplorable situation of the bank.[52] The incident showed that the MoF was
still capable of putting considerable pressure on the financial industry
and that despite the formal process of administrative reform and deregulation its use of administrative guidance was still active and alive; however,
its effectiveness seemed to have become more uncertain, as the ultimate
collapse of NCB showed. A similar conflict on the provision of financial assistance instigated by the MoF erupted in the summer of 1999,
as the BoJ wanted to be repaid by the MoF for a special loan it had extended to the failed Yamaichi Securities in November 1997. At the same
time, more details about the opaque and discretionary nature of MoF's
prudential policy became publicly known. According to media reports,
the leadership of MoF's Banking Bureau instructed its bank inspectors
in April 1997 not to conduct strict inspections of NCB, after receiving
complaints from the ailing bank that these were too severe (*Japan Times*,
21 June 1999). A Western magazine published in June 1999 a report
that showed that the MoF had been fully aware of, and had even actively

---

[51] In Japan, the fiscal year runs from 1 April to 31 March.
[52] For example, in public testimonies, both the president of Tokyo Marine & Fire Insurance
and the vice-president of Nippon Life Insurance accused the MoF of having strongly
'persuaded' them to provide financial support to NCB. As discussed in chapter 3, administrative guidance consists of government actions without formal legal coercion; therefore
the euphemism 'persuasion' is often used. Furthermore, the president of NCB claimed
that the MoF had misled financial institutions that provided financial assistance about
the size of its bad loans (*Financial Times*, 26 February 1999).

encouraged, the hiding of losses on financial transactions by a specific Japanese financial institution some years earlier (*Euromoney* 1999a). The criticism of MoF's past supervisory practices forced Finance Minister Kiichi Miyazawa to admit publicly that the ministry's bank inspections had been opaque and ineffective.

The growing confidence in the Japanese supervisory framework in general and the policies of the FRC and FSA in particular received a considerable blow from political developments in October 1999. In a new cabinet formed by Prime Minister Obuchi, the respected and reform-oriented chairman of the FRC Hakuo Yanagisawa was replaced by the traditional LDP-politician Michio Ochi, also a former MoF bureaucrat (Director of the Research Division, Budget Bureau).[53] The move was interpreted by certain Western bankers as 'madness' (Financial Regulation Report, October 1999). Only a week later, it was revealed that his political support organisation had received 92.75 million yen in soft loans from various financial institutions. Again, as had happened so often before, scandals implicating supervisory officials and revealing close and intimate relations between financial bureaucrats and private financial institutions undermined the credibility of prudential policy in Japan. Ochi was ultimately forced to resign in February 2000, when it became known that he had suggested at a closed meeting showing consideration for certain problem banks. He was succeeded by Sadakazu Tanigaki, a former parliamentary vice-minister of the MoF (*NRC Handelsblad*, 31 July 2000; *Nikkei Weekly*, 6 March 2000). Another development that according to some observers was detrimental to the FRC's reputation and prestige was the decision by the ruling coalition parties in December 1999 to extend the special and temporary measures to protect depositors of failed institutions by one year until March 2002 (Financial System Council 1999b; JP Morgan 2000a).[54] This decision was interpreted in certain circles as possibly encouraging moral hazard in banks, delaying necessary reorganisations of the banking industry and giving in by the ruling LDP to pressure from the smaller banks in particular, although some reports played down these concerns, stating confidence in the FRC's determination to inspect strictly those institutions that received public money (for the former see: Fiorillo 2000a; Hoshi and Kashyap 2000; OECD 2000, p.89;

---

[53] Ochi, when head of the LDP's Investigation Committee for the Finance and Banking Systems, had said that 'an 8% equity ratio is too high a hurdle for credit associations and co-operatives' (which was a reaction to the FRC's new policy that regional banks that received public money should raise their equity ratios from 4% to 8%). He also seemed to be less keen on promoting financial deregulation and internationalisation than his predecessor (*Japan Times*, 24 October 1999).

[54] At the same time, Finance Minister Miyazawa announced that the amount of public funds available for financial assistance to the financial services industry would be raised to 70 trillion yen (14% of GDP) (Mori et al. 2000, p.36).

an example of the latter is JP Morgan 2000a). In addition to the policies of the FRC, MoF and FSA that aimed at restoring confidence in the Japanese financial system, the BoJ continued to provide ample liquidity to the banking industry. The central bank introduced in February 1999 a 'zero interest rate policy' consisting of maintaining the overnight call (policy) rate around zero (see figure 6.4). However, as the economy failed to show clear signs of a structural recovery, political pressure started to mount on the BoJ to do more, such as conducting outright purchases of government bonds. In October, the BoJ's Policy Board decided to broaden its money market operations in order to achieve a smoother distribution of liquidity through the financial system, including outright purchases of short-term government securities (OECD 1999a).

The problems in the financial system and the related demands for more transparency in public policy, the rationalisation of government and the establishment of arm's-length relations between the public and private spheres continued to fuel the processes of administrative and financial reform. In February 1999 the cabinet decided to introduce legislation that would merge six government financial institutions into three, which, however, did not effectively reduce the number of landing spots for retiring bureaucrats. Furthermore, in March a three-year deregulation programme was approved that involved the lifting of barriers between the banking and insurance industries and regulations on brokerage commissions. The cabinet also announced a revision of its use of administrative guidance in order 'to shift emphasis in public administration from ex ante facto regulations to ex post facto monitoring of compliance with general rules'. (Cabinet Decision 1999; Economic Strategy Council of Japan 1999). Thus, the Japanese government publicly admitted that administrative guidance was still an important instrument of public policy, including economic policy. Part of the revision of the use of administrative guidance involved efforts to improve its transparency, in accordance with the Administrative Procedures Law (see section 3.3 of chapter 3). The general policy of trying to improve the transparency of government action was reflected in the enactment of a freedom of information law in May (Law Concerning Access to Information Held by Administrative Organs). Finally, in July 1999 the Upper House of the Diet passed 17 bills that concreticised the principles of the Administrative Reform Bill, enacted one year earlier, and reorganised the 22 existing government bodies into 10 ministries, two agencies and a new cabinet office (OECD 1999a, p.117; IMF 2000c, pp.96ff.). It was decided that the new system would be established as of 1 January 2001. The MoF (Ōkurashō) would be renamed Zaimusho or Ministry of the Treasury; the FRC, FSA and most functions of the MoF related to the financial system would be incorporated in the new Finance Agency – later called Financial Services Agency – which would be responsible for all duties related to the domestic financial system, including drafting legislation. However, the new MoF would, in joint responsibility with the new agency, still maintain certain powers regarding policy planning for bank failures and financial crisis management such as the injection of public funds. A new Financial Council (later renamed the Conference for Financial Crisis) headed by the Prime Minister, would be established as of January 2001 to co-ordinate financial crisis management and assess systemic risk implications of bank failures. The reorganised MoF would remain responsible for the supervision of public finance, the international financial system, including exhange rate policy, relations with the BoJ and the Fiscal Investment and Loan Programme. An important step in the process of financial reform involving the banking sector was the start of a bank straight bond market in October. Previously, only the long-term credit banks and the Bank of Tokyo(-Mitsubishi) had been allowed to issue bank debentures; one year after its inception, the market for straight bonds issued by banks ranked fourth among the other markets for corporate bonds (JP Morgan 2000b). As regards reforms involving the BoJ, the central bank announced in January 1999 the streamlining of housing and recreation facilities for its staff, followed in October by the announcement that 500 jobs would be cut by the end of March 2004, based on recommendations from McKinsey.

After the renewed optimism that had characterised the start of 1999, the general atmosphere at the start of 2000 was once again increasingly pessimistic. Evidence mounted that the real amounts of bad loans in the banking sector were substantially larger than the official figures showed and that they were still not fully recognised and provisioned, that the governing LDP was increasingly reluctant to pursue further financial reform and to support the 'arm's-length' supervisory policies of the FRC and FSA and that the problems in the banking and insurance industries could exacerbate each other in the years to come (Fiorillo 1999b, 2000a; Deutsche Bank 2000; Goldman Sachs 2000; IMF 2000a; Standard & Poor's Ratings Services 2000). In other words, the hard fought credibility and prestige of the new Japanese financial supervisors was put under increasing pressure. In the course of 2000 a number of developments would underline the renewed sense of urgency and concern about the situation in the Japanese financial system.

First, the credibility of Japan's supervisory authorities was damaged for the umpteenth time by a scandal that led to the resignation of the head of the FRC, Kimitaka Kuze, in July.[55] He was succeeded by Hideyuki

---

[55] Kuze was forced to resign when it was revealed that he had accepted money from several companies, including 230 million yen from Mitsubishi Trust & Banking Corp. (*Japan Times*, 1 August 2000).

Aizawa, a former administrative vice-minister of the MoF, who was the fourth person at the helm of Japan's major supervisory body in 2000. The appointment of Aizawa was criticised by many, because it was widely known that he maintained close connections with the banking industry and was not supportive of further financial reforms (*NRC Handelsblad*, 31 July 2000; *Japan Times*, 1 August 2000; Nikkei Net, 7 August 2000).[56]

Second, as regards the development of the bad-loans situation, figures published in March 2000 for all deposit-taking financial institutions, following both the 'self-assessment' and 'risk management loans' definitions, were higher than the March 1999 figures (see table 6.2); figures published in September 2000 for the banks only were higher than the corresponding figures for March 2000. Thus, despite the capital injections and substantial write-offs that reduced the stock of bad loans, the sluggish economy and the increasing amounts of liabilities involved in corporate bankruptcies (see figure 6.8) led to a continuing flow of new bad loans which more than offset that reduction.[57] As a matter of fact, during the period April–September 2000, the bad loans of eight major Japanese banks increased, despite substantial write-offs (*The Banker* 2001a).

Particularly during the second half of 2000, a number of bankruptcies and near-collapses involving large companies such as the department-store operator Sogo, the retail chain operator Daiei and the construction company Kumagai Gumi highlighted the debt overhang in the corporate sector and the important implications for the bad-loan situation of balance-sheet restructuring and rising bankruptcies in the private non-financial sector (see also: IMF 1999a, 1999b and 2000c, p.73; OECD 2000).[58] According to figures from Teikoku Databank, the amount of liabilities involved in corporate bankruptcies in 2000 was 77% higher

[56] Aizawa was one of the key advocates of the extension of the deposit insurance measures until March 2002; according to a financial report released by his own office, he received 1.2 million yen in donations from financial institutions during the years 1997–1998, which were according to himself within the limits set by the law (*Asahi Shimbun*, 31 July 2000).

[57] The rise in the number of bankruptcies was partly due to the introduction in April 2000 of the 'Civil Rehabilitation Law' (sometimes called Financial Rehabilitation Law), under which troubled companies could file much more easily for protection (*Nikkei Weekly*, 30 October 2000, p.18; IMF 2000a). For an excellent discussion see Levy (1999).

[58] The bankruptcy of Sogo left 1.87 trillion yen (0.4% of GDP) in debts, which were predominantly owned by small *shinkin* banks and credit co-operatives (*The Economist*, 15 July 2000, p.89; IMF 2000b). It came after a controversial bailout programme, involving huge amounts of public money, was abandoned. Kumagai Gumi announced in September that it had asked banks to waive 450 billion yen (0.1% of GDP) in loans. As will be discussed in chapter 8, the company employed a number of *amakudari kanryō* from the Construction Ministry on its board. The increasing number of bankruptcies involving construction companies was of major concern, given the considerable exposure of the banking sector to these firms.

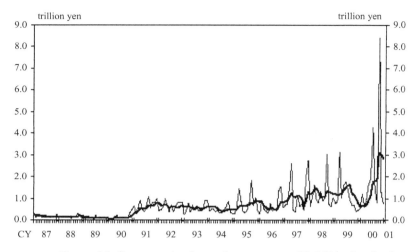

Figure 6.8 Corporate bankruptcies: amounts of liabilities involved
Note: The bold line is the six-month moving average of the flow of
liabilities registered in corporate bankruptcies. For comparison: GDP
in 1999 was around Yen 500 tm.
Source: Tokyo Shoko Research Ltd., 'Tosan Geppo' (Monthly Review
of Corporate Bankruptcies) (from: Bank of Japan 2001)

than in 1999, aggravating without doubt the bad-loan situation (Teikoku
Databank 2001). The worrying condition of the corporate sector also provided further evidence that banks continued to understate the amount
of their bad loans, as for example was shown in the case of the exposure of Sumitomo Bank to the problems at Kumagai Gumi;[59] one Western investment bank estimated in December 2000 that the additional
amount of problem loans 'hidden' on the banks' balance sheets could
be around 18 trillion yen (3.6% of GDP) (Fiorillo 2000f). The IMF also
expressed its concern over 'overly optimistic loan classification, especially
with regard to the impact of corporate restructuring on loan quality' (IMF
2000c, p.79; see also Hoshi and Kashyap 1999). Further disposal of bad
loans was being hampered by the small market for securitised assets and
cumbersome bankruptcy proceedings, and, as already mentioned, banks
seemed still to adopt a 'wait and see' attitude, hoping that the real estate prices of their collateral would recover (OECD 2000, p.91).[60] The
BoJ estimated that the 136 largest banks (city, long-term credit, trust,

[59] Sumitomo Bank reported that it had only 265 billion yen of problem loans to the construction sector as a whole. However, to save Kumagai Gumi from bankruptcy, the bank
had to write off almost the same amount, i.e. 260 billion yen (*The Economist* 2001b, p.73).
[60] The disposal of bad loans and debt workouts were stimulated to some extent by various measures (IMF 1999b, pp.92–93). First, the securitisation of assets was propagated
by the enactment of a new securitisation law in June 1998 that facilitated the use of

regional and Second-Tier regional banks) had disposed of only 60% of the non-performing loans that were created during the period March 1991–March 2000 (*Nihon Keizai Shimbun*, 1 September 2000). The seriousness of the situation was highlighted by the deteriorating outlook for the economy towards the end of the year: at the beginning of 2001 the revised annualised GDP growth rate for the third quarter of 2000 showed a decline of 2.4%.

Third, the problems at Japanese banks were also reflected in the continuing decline of their lending, in particular by the banking sectors that were the hardest hit by the collapse of the 'bubble' economy (i.e. the long-term credit banks, trust banks and Second Tier regional banks). That this was not only due to a lack of demand for loans was shown by the significant increases in the annual growth rates of lending by foreign banks, which on average were in much better shape than their Japanese counterparts, during the last months of 2000 (see table 6.8).[61] The table shows that in particular the long-term credit banks, trust banks and Second Tier regional banks experienced significant declines in their annual lending growth rates. Furthermore, the year-on-year growth rates of deposits at Japanese private banks continued to decline as well, with the exception of the regional banks, of which a number of solvent and well-performing institutions in particular managed to attract savings (see table 6.9). The withdrawal of deposits at the city, long-term credit, trust and Second Tier regional banks – the banks which were among the hardest-hit financial institutions in Japan in the aftermath of the collapse of the 'bubble' economy – seemed to be a sign of lacking confidence among Japanese savers in the long-term viability of at least some of these banks, in particular after it had become clear that emergency measures to protect deposits would be terminated in the next few years. Furthermore, the figures presented in tables 6.8 and 6.9 do not include the credit co-operatives and other small financial institutions, whose problems still have to be addressed (IMF 2000b, 2000c; OECD 2000, p.88; *The Economist*, 4 March 2000, p.89). Fourth, doubts were raised about the quality of the banks' capital (IMF 1999a, 1999b, 2000a, p.195, 2000c, pp.79–82; *Nikkei Weekly*,

---

special purpose vehicles for securitisation purposes. Second, the tax code was changed to make it easier to introduce debt workout agreements. Third, the October 1998 legislation stimulated the use of private loan collection companies for bad-loan disposal purposes. However, all in all, these measures were still deemed insufficient in the view of several observers; somewhat more was expected from financial innovations, such as the introduction of commercial mortgage-backed securities and real estate investment trusts (*The Economist*, 29 July 2000, pp.78–79).

[61] According the IMF (2000c), p.69, the decline in bank lending was due to both demand and supply factors and the increasing importance of securities-based or direct finance (dis-intermediation).

Table 6.8. *Loans and discounts by banks located in Japan*
(Percent changes in average amounts outstanding from previous year, 10 billion yen)

	2000 July–Sep.	Oct.–Dec.	2000 Oct.	Nov.	Dec.	Average amounts outstanding (December)
Total	−4.3	−3.9	−4.0	−4.0	−3.8	46,041
City banks	−3.3	−3.4	−3.1	−3.4	−3.7	21,071
Long-term credit banks	−20.0	−15.4	−18.2	−16.1	−11.6	2,851
Trust banks	−5.2	−5.8	−5.5	−5.9	−6.1	4,020
Regional banks	−0.3	−0.4	−0.4	−0.4	−0.4	13,342
Regional banks II	−7.0	−6.4	−6.8	−6.4	−6.0	4,757
Foreign banks	−11.1	8.2	1.0	8.1	16.0	805

Note: Figures for foreign banks include yen-denominated loans on domestic accounts only.
Source: Bank of Japan.

Table 6.9. *Deposits and certificates of deposits at Japanese banks*
(Percent changes in average amounts outstanding from previous year, 10 billion yen)

	2000 July–Sep.	Oct.–Dec.	2000 Oct.	Nov.	Dec.	Average amounts outstanding (December)
Total	−0.4	−0.9	−1.0	−1.0	−0.7	46,559
City banks	−1.2	−2.6	−2.7	−2.6	−2.5	23,056
Regional banks	2.5	2.5	2.4	2.3	2.9	17,723
Regional banks II	−5.4	−4.3	−4.5	−4.3	−4.1	5,780

Note: Unsettled bills and cheques are excluded.
Source: Bank of Japan.

4 September 2000, p.13; *The Economist* 2001b). For example, it was observed that only a minor part consisted of Tier I or core capital, i.e. retained earnings, common stock and general loan-loss reserves. Furthermore, the capital injected by the government, which added on average aound 3% to the solvency ratios of the major banks, would have to be repaid one day in the future, and a significant share of the subordinated debt would mature within two years. In addition, as stock prices continued to drop in the course of 2000 (see figure 6.1), concerns were raised

about the impact of this development on bank capital. In particular, it is generally accepted that the solvency ratios of Japanese banks are vulnerable to shifts in stock prices in two ways. As was explained in section 6.3, up to 45% of Japanese banks' unrealised profits on securities holdings could be counted as Tier II capital. Although the FSA announced plans in June 2000 to limit the extent to which banks could count these latent gains as capital, the fall in stock prices eroded at least to some extent banks' Tier II capital. Furthermore, a decline in stock prices that would result in unrealised losses on banks' equity portfolios would, under the new accounting system of mark-to-market accounting (to be introduced in April 2001), directly affect bank capital. The IMF calculated that a fall of 30% in stock prices would reduce the amount of Tier I capital by about 50% (IMF 2000c, p.82). Furthermore, as banks became increasingly risk averse in their lending behaviour and shifted their asset structure from loans towards government bonds, a possible rise in long-term interest rates and a decline in bond prices could lead to substantial capital losses with detrimental effects on bank capital as well (IMF 2000c; OECD 2000, p.93). All in all, it was seen as increasingly likely that capital adequacy ratios could once again fall well below 8% (*The Economist* 2001b, p.74).[62] Market analysts expected that if stock prices fell below a level of 13,000 for the Nikkei 225 Stock Index, most banks would incur (non-realised or paper) losses on their stock portfolios. As Japanese stock prices continued to drop, almost reaching this level at the end of 2000, the head of the FRC, Hideyuki Aizawa, publicly asked banks not to unwind their cross-shareholdings, despite the fact that the FRC had approved these stock sales earlier as part of restructuring plans that banks had to implement as one of the conditions to receive public capital injections. Although he stated that the government should not use administrative guidance to support the stock market, Aizawa's earlier remarks were interpreted as attempts in the same direction and brought back memories of the government's 'price keeping operations' (*Nikkei Weekly*, 4 December 2000).[63] More worryingly, it showed that despite the large number of councils, task forces and reports committed to administrative reform and transparency during the nineties, apparently the Japanese government

---

[62] Experience has shown that care should be taken in interpreting the capital adequacy ratios of Japanese banks. Illustrative was the case of the Long-Term Credit Bank of Japan, which 'reported a capital adequacy ratio of 10.3% for March 1998, but was subsequently found to have negative net worth of Yen 2.7 trillion (equivalent to 15.3% of risk assets) as of October 1998' (IMF 1999a, p.33).

[63] Apparently, the government considered using administrative guidance to limit the unwinding of cross-shareholdings and postponing the introduction of mark-to-market accounting, i.e. the same discretionary and opaque policy measures that had been used without much success in the past (*Nihon Keizai Shimbun*, 27 November 2000).

would not hesitate to adopt the 'old' market-rigging practices and informal policies of the past if deemed necessary. In any case, it was seen as being detrimental to the banks' creditworthiness (JP Morgan 2000c).

Fifth, the protracted fall in land and real estate prices continued to erode the collateral values of the banks' loan-portfolios (see figure 6.2). Standard & Poor's (2000, p.2) estimated that a 10% decline in collateral values would force banks to make 1 trillion yen in additional provisions.

Sixth, the magnitude of the problems in the insurance sector were brought to full light by the bankruptcies of Daiichi Mutual Fire & Marine Insurance Co., Daihyaku Mutual Life Insurance Co. (both in May 2000), Taisho Life Insurance (August), Chiyoda Mutual Life Insurance Co. and Kyoei Life Insurance Co. (both in October); another signal of the problematic situation was the large number of announcements of tie-ups and mergers in the course of 2000.[64] The problems in the insurance industry were also a major embarrassment for the FSA, which seemed to have been overwhelmed by the situation; it also raised doubts about its inspection policy, as the performance indicators of several insurers, such as their solvency margins, did not signal significant problems.[65] Given the widespread custom of mutual share- and debt-holdings between various (financial) companies belonging to the same industrial group or *keiretsu* (see section 4.3 of chapter 4), these bankruptcies most likely negatively affected the banking industry situation. It also increased concerns whether the amount of public funds available for financial assistance were still sufficiently large to cope with the problems in the financial system.[66]

Seventh, concerns about the development of the economy, fiscal situation and financial system led Moody's Investors Service to downgrade the sovereign debt rating of Japan from Aa1 to Aa2 in September 2000.

Finally, Western banks in particular increasingly questioned certain elements of Japanese prudential policy. For example, as was shown by the Crédit Suisse experience, interpretations of existing regulations tended to change when deemed necessary. This was partly due to the custom that, with the exception of certain basic rules, few regulations were written down explicitly, leaving much to the interpretation and discretion of

---

[64] The amounts of debt left behind were staggering: the bankruptcies of Chiyoda and Kyoei Life alone involved liabilities totalling 7.4 trillion yen (1.5% of GDP). The bankruptcy of Chiyoda also saw the resurgence of 'old' supervisory policies, as the FSA pressed Tokai Bank, Chiyoda's largest creditor, to provide substantial financial assistance, which it refused to do (*The Economist*, 14 October 2000, p.109).

[65] After the collapse of Kyoei Life Insurance, the FRC's head Hideyuki Aizawa publicly said: 'We never imagined that the situation would deteriorate so quickly. It was simply beyond our expectations' (*Nikkei Weekly*, 30 October 2000, p.18).

[66] To cope with the increasing problems in the insurance industry, the government submitted a bill to parliament in order to enhance the safety net for life insurance companies (Bank of Japan 2000, pp.75–76).

the FSA's officials.[67] As was extensively discussed in chapters 3 and 5, Japanese legislation such as the Ministry of Finance Establishment Law and various regulations were said to be rather vague and not very specific, leaving considerable room for the use of various forms of administrative guidance. Apparently, such leeway still existed after many administrative reforms and the establishment of the FSA.[68] Furthermore, reports started to emerge that questioned the will of Japan's financial regulators to implement further financial reforms, and that instead the traditional participants in the financial services industry were being increasingly protected, often at the expense of foreign investors (*The Economist* 2000; *The Banker* 2001b). Some even asserted that there were signs of a rebirth of the 'convoy system' (Hoshi and Kashyap 2000).

The renewed concerns about the stability of the Japanese financial system were reflected in the bill to extend the special and temporary deposit insurance measures that was submitted to the Diet in February 2000, which went beyond the agreement reached between the coalition parties in December 1999. The most important elements of the bill can be summarised as follows (Bank of Japan 2000, p.74; JP Morgan 2000a; IMF 2000c pp.78–79; Ministry of Finance 2000c). First, the protection of deposits, bank debentures purchased by individuals and interest was extended by one year to March 2002. After this date, no more than 10 million yen in deposits and interest would be guaranteed per depositor. Second, the concerns about the condition of the smallest financial institutions led to the extension by one year of possible capital injections by the government to credit co-operatives only.[69] Third, additional public money in the amount of 6 trillion yen was put in the DIC's 'special account' to be used in the case of bank failures until March 2002. Fourth, the new Conference for Financial Crisis, to be established in January 2001, could decide to implement emergency measures where a bankruptcy of a financial institution was deemed to have major systemic risk implications ('exceptional treatment'). These measures could take the form of capital subscription by the DIC, provision of financial

---

[67] A Western banker referred to the vagueness of Japanese financial regulation as follows: 'an environment where the regulation is complex, and where the language in which it is written is not necessarily day-to-day Japanese – even when you are Japanese it can be read and interpreted in different ways' (*Euromoney* 2000).

[68] A more favourable view is put forward in IMF (2000c), p.76, where it is asserted that considerable progress has been made in improving the quality of bank supervision in Japan.

[69] This possibility was created by the enactment of the Financial Function Early Strengthening Law in October 1998. The concerns for the credit co-operatives were also shown by the inspection plans of the FSA for the period July 2000–June 2001 that revealed its intention to inspect 255 credit co-operatives, compared with only seven in the previous programme year (Financial Services Agency 2000).

assistance exceeding the payoff costs of the bankruptcy or special crisis management. A new 'prevention of financial crisis account' at the DIC would be established to finance operations related to financial crises involving systemic risk implications. Finally, when the costs of the failure of a financial institution could not be borne by the financial services industry, the government could consider the use of public money. In total, for Fiscal Year 2000 the government made available a total nominal amount of 70 trillion yen (14% of GDP) in various accounts at the DIC for deposit insurance and financial assistance: 4 trillion at the 'general account' (in the form of government guarantees), 23 trillion at the 'special account' (13 trillion in subsidised government bonds plus 10 trillion in government guarantees), 18 trillion at the 'financial revitalisation account' (government guarantees) and 25 trillion at the 'financial function early strengthening account' (government guarantees) (Ministry of Finance 2000d). In total, an extra 10 trillion yen (4 trillion at the 'general account' and 6 trillion at the 'special account') were added to the 60 trillion yen that was allocated to the DIC in relation to the financial support measures adopted in 1998. However, the amounts of public funds available were effectively lower, as large sums of money had been used already in the previous years, in particular for the nationalisation of the LTCB and NCB, which total costs were estimated at around 7 trillion yen (IMF 2000c; Ministry of Finance 2000d).

In the course of 2000, the supervisory authorities continued to inject public funds into the banking system. A total of 170 billion yen in financial assistance was provided to four regional banks, and 240 billion yen was injected into the failed but reprivatised Long-Term Credit Bank of Japan (renamed Shinsei Bank), followed by 260 billion yen into Nippon Credit Bank (reprivatised and renamed Aozora Bank).[70] As regards other policy initiatives taken by the monetary authorities, the BoJ announced in January 2000 its intention to end the extension of unsecured special loans to failed financial institutions from April 2002. Furthermore, the BoJ ended in August its 'zero interest rate' policy and set a new target for its policy rate of 0.25% (see figure 6.4), a move heavily criticised by the government and various political parties.[71] In May, the BoJ implemented reorganisations involving its Financial Markets and International Departments. In the field of administrative reform, no major new initiatives were taken in the course of 2000, except for the establishment of the Financial

[70] The LTCB was bought by a consortium led by Ripplewood Holdings from the USA in March 2000; NCB was taken over by a group of investors under the leadership of Softbank, the leading e-commerce company in Japan, in September 2000.

[71] For example, the head of the FRC, Hideyuki Aizawa, publicly said prior to the BoJ's decision that it would be wrong for the BoJ to end the 'zero interest rate' policy (*Nihon Keizai Shimbun*, 10 August 2000).

Services Agency in July (see next section) and measures to curb the move-ment of retired government bureaucrats into public and private corpo-rations (*amakudari*). In February, the government announced that as of September 2000 it would start to publish annually information on retired high-level civil servants employed by both public and private corporations (Kyodo World Service, 15 February 2000). In March, a new law became effective that covered personnel exchanges between the public and private sectors (*Japan Times* Online, 30 March 2000). An interesting announce-ment was made by a reform council established by the three ruling parties in the summer – around the time of the elections – to introduce a proposal that would impose a ban on the practice of *amakudari* by 2005 (Japan Press Network 2000). The abolition of *amakudari* would be compen-sated by extending the retirement age of government bureaucrats, so that they could actually retire from civil service in the true sense of the word and would no longer have to 'retire' and then accept a job in the private sector. However, to many observers it was not clear how seriously this proposal should be taken. Furthermore, in the summer of 2000 a govern-ment panel developed guidelines that would require public corporations as from April 2001 to disclose data on the inflow of retired government officials on to their boards (*Nihon Keizai Shimbun*, 29 June 2000).

Phase VII (July 2000–): further administrative reform – consolidation of prudential policy

According to the Administrative Reform Bill that passed parliament in June 1998 and the follow-up legal package of 17 bills that was approved by the Upper House in July 1999, prudential policy in Japan would be concentrated in a new agency, at the latest in March 2001, when the tem-porary mandate of the FRC would end. In anticipation of the reorganisa-tion of the government bureaucracy in January 2001, the new Financial Services Agency (Kinyū Chō) (FSEA) was established in July 2000 by merging the Financial Supervisory Agency (Kinyū Kantoku Chō) (FSA) with MoF's Financial System Planning Bureau (Kinyū Kikaku Kyoku) (Financial Services Agency 2000). Thus, the legal powers of the MoF regarding the financial system were integrated with the prudential policy responsibilities of the FSA. In this respect, the new agency received pol-icymaking responsibilities and thus would become more involved in the political process than the former FSA, as the drafting of new legislation re-quired consultations and negotiations with political parties, and political support was needed to ensure that new laws would pass parliament in the end. This also implied that most likely the FSEA would encounter more political interference than the FSA, as politicians would attempt to modify proposed legislation in accordance with the interests of their constituency. Thus, the biggest threat to an independent formulation and implementation of prudential policy in Japan was perceived not to come so much from the MoF, whose last remaining separate bureau on financial system matters was integrated with the FSA, but much more from the political world (Fiorillo 2000c; see also *Japan Economic Institute Report*, 30 April 1999, p.5). The new Financial Services Agency, however, still had to share the responsibility for financial crisis management and public funds injections with the MoF, as the latter would have to bear the fiscal consequences of such measures. To this end, the Ministry's Secretariat took over certain responsibilities of the former Financial System Planning Bureau. For example, the MoF retained the Credit System Stabilisation Office of the former Financial System Planning Bureau as a separate division (Shinyō Kikō Ka) in its Secretariat (*Nihon Keizai Shimbun*, 30 June 2000); further policy issues regarding financial matters were taken care of by the Policy and Finance Division (Seisaku Kinyū Ka). In addition, former high-ranking MoF officials became the heads of the FSEA's Inspection Department (Kensa Bu) and Supervisory Department (Kantoku Bu).[72] The establishment of FSEA led to an increase of the number of banking inspectors at the FSA from 249 to 319 (*Japan Times* Online, 24 June 2000; IMF 2000c, p.76). In total, the FSEA was allocated a staff of 733.

In January 2001 further consolidation of prudential policy in Japan was achieved by merging the FSEA with the FRC, establishing one unified prudential supervisory agency in Japan with a total staff of 766 (see figure 6.9). The enlarged FSEA was placed under the new Cabinet Office (Naikaku Fu), supervised by the State Minister for Financial Affairs. It was headed by Shoji Mori, the Secretary-General of the FRC, who reported to 'old-hand' Hakuo Yanagisawa (the first chairman of the FRC in December 1998) as the new State Minister. Although both men were former high-ranking officials at the MoF, the appointments were deemed by some not to jeopardise the independence of the new agency (Fiorillo 2000e).[73] However, it may be too early to draw any conclusion in this respect.[74] Furthermore, it seemed that in general the climate for further financial and regulatory reform had turned more negative, which could frustrate the policies of the new FSEA (*Financial Times* 2000;

---

[72] Kazuto Nishikawa, the former head of the Tokyo Regional Taxation Bureau, was appointed as head of the Inspection Department; the head of the Supervisory Department became Shokichi Takagi, who was a former counsellor of the Ministry's Secretariat (*Nikkei Weekly*, 3 July 2000).

[73] Mori was the Deputy Director-General of the Securities Bureau and later the Director-General of the General Affairs Department, Tokyo Regional Taxation Bureau (Fiorillo 2000e, p.2).

[74] See also *The New York Times* (2001).

State Minister for Financial Affairs
Senior Vice Minister
Commissioner
Planning and Co-ordination Bureau (203 staff)
    General Co-ordination Division
    Communications and Policy Division
    International Affairs Division
    Planning and Legal Division
    Financial Markets Division
    Director for Corporate Accounting and Disclosure
    Credit System Division
Inspection Bureau (319 staff)
    Inspection Co-ordination Division
    Inspection Administrator
    Evaluation Division
Supervisory Bureau (131 staff)
    Supervisory Co-ordination Division
    Banks Division I
    Banks Division II
    Insurance Business Division
    Securities Business Division
Securities and Exchange Surveillance Commission (112 staff)
    Executive Bureau

Figure 6.9 The organisation of the Financial Services Agency
(January 2001)
Source: Financial Services Agency.

The Economist 2001a). The integration of the functions of financial inspection, policymaking and the ownership of failed banks into one body could also generate possible conflicts of interest (OECD 2000, p.87). Finally, it was concluded that the FSEA was still suffering from a shortage of human resources and also expertise in complex financial transactions (*Euromoney* 2000, p.35; IMF 2000b, p.33).

Furthermore, as part of the reorganisation of the Japanese government administration in general and of Japanese prudential policy in particular the Conference for Financial Crisis (Kinyū Kiki Taiō Kaigi) was established in January 2001 as well. According to Article 42 of the Cabinet Office Establishment Law (Naikaku Fu Setchi Hō), the Conference can be called together on the initiative of the Prime Minister (as chairman) in the event of a financial crisis that could have significant implications for financial stability (systemic risk concerns).[75] It may decide to provide

[75] The Conference is classified as a special institution (*tokubetsu no kikan*) under the Cabinet Office. As regards the role of the Prime Minister, in reaction to questions in parliament the Administrative Vice-Minister of the MoF answered that it is completely up to the Prime Minister to decide when the Conference will be convened.

public financial assistance to individual financial institutions, using funds from the new 'prevention of financial crisis account' of 15 trillion yen at the DIC. The funds for this new account came from both the 'financial revitalisation account' (from 18 to 10 trillion yen) and the 'financial function early strengthening account' (from 25 to 16 trillion yen); the remaining 2 trillion yen were transferred to the DIC's 'general account' (Nikkei Net 2000). In total, a nominal amount of 70 trillion yen (14% of GDP) remained available for financial assistance. In addition to the Prime Minister, the Conference consists of the Secretary-General of the Cabinet, the State Minister for Financial Affairs, the Minister of Finance, the head of the Financial Services Agency and the Governor of the Bank of Japan. Thus, the conference is dominated by politicians, which could lead to pressure on the BoJ to provide emergency liquidity support in its role as lender of last resort to bail out political interests of the ruling political parties, with detrimental consequences for monetary policy. All in all, first assessments of the Conference and the inherent politicisation of Japanese prudential policy in the media were rather critical (*The Economist* 2001b, p.79). An overview of the reorganisations of prudential policy in Japan during the years 1998–2001 is presented in table 6.10.

Further reforms introduced under the reorganisation of the government administration in January 2001 affected the MoF (Ōkurashō), which was renamed Zaimushō or Ministry of the Treasury, although in English the official name Ministry of Finance was retained (see also *Euromoney* 2001). The most important change was the establishment under the Cabinet Office of the Council on Economic and Fiscal Policy (Keizai Zaisei Shimon Kaigi), whose members included the Governor of the BoJ and which was given the right to draft the outline of the national budget. However, its role was questioned, as in July 2000 the government had already set up a fiscal-policy committee headed by the Prime Minister and consisting of other key political figures. It was claimed that the MoF initiated the creation of this committee in order to retain its control over the budgetary process (*Nikkei Weekly*, 4 December 2000).

6.5   Conclusions

This chapter has discussed the Japanese banking crisis of the nineties and the policy response of the monetary and supervisory authorities. The central elements in the authorities' reaction were regulatory forbearance and financial and administrative reforms, which were often implemented hastily in reaction to major scandals involving regulators and private banks. To a significant degree, the slow reaction to the banking problems

Table 6.10. *Reorganisations of prudential policy in Japan*[1]

Function	June 1998	October 1998	July 2000	January 2001
Planning and formulation of legal system	MoF	MoF	FSEA	FSEA
Planning of resolution scheme and crisis management	MoF/FSA	FRC/MoF	FRC/MoF	FSEA/MoF
Resolutions and capital injections based on October 1998 legislation	–	FRC	FRC	FSEA (authority expires in March 2002)
Resolutions/capital injections based on revised DIC Law in event of systemic risk concerns	–	–	–	Conference for Financial Crisis
Inspection and supervision	FSA/BoJ[2]	FSA/BoJ	FSEA/BoJ	FSEA/BoJ
Oversight of Deposit Insurance Corporation	MoF	FRC/MoF	FRC/MoF	FSEA/MoF
Oversight of Securities and Exchange Surveillance Com.	FSA	FSA	FSEA	FSEA
Lender of last resort function (emergency liquidity injections)	BoJ (MoF)	BoJ (MoF/FRC)	BoJ (MoF/FRC)	BoJ (MoF/FSEA/Conference for Financial Crisis)

Note: [1] FSA = Financial Supervisory Agency, FSEA = Financial Services Agency.
[2] The BoJ's role in prudential policy was legally established in the new BoJ Law.
Source: IMF (2000a), p.195, and own assessments.

seemed to be related to the existence of intimate and extensive informal relations between public and private spheres. As a result, the banks could adopt a 'wait and see' attitude that delayed an effective and fast resolution of the bad-loans problem. This inherent protection of mutual interests between bureaucrats and private bankers could prosper in the context of a paralysed political system whose main exponent – the LDP – proved for many years to be a close ally of the banking sector.

As regards the relevance and importance of the previously discussed various informal instruments and networks for the policy reaction to the banking crisis in general and during the 1998–2000 period in particular, the following can be concluded. In general, many of the informal mechanisms analysed in chapter 5 came under increasing pressure, resulting in the abolition of some of them; however, others were simply maintained or changed into another format. First, despite the formal process of administrative reform that aimed at improving transparency and establishing rules-based regulation, the MoF continued to use various forms of (unpublished) administrative guidance, often with detrimental effects. Second, due to the growing criticism of its informal policies, the MoF to a large extent abolished its informal circulars or *tsūtatsu* (published administrative guidance); however, many were simply transferred in other regulations. Third, the MoF-*tan* and similar BoJ-*tan* systems lost much of their importance after the scandals in the first months of 1998. The existence of these informal networks between bureaucrats and private bankers played an important role in the delayed policy reaction to the banking problems (regulatory forbearance). Fourth, as described in this chapter, the practice of *amakudari* became the target of many attempts to curtail its use. In reaction to the scandal that forced the resignation of its highest executives, the BoJ adopted restrictions on the acceptance of private sector jobs by its retired officials, similar to these enforced two years earlier by the MoF. Furthermore, in conjunction with the enactment of the new BoJ Law, in 1998 the BoJ seemed no longer to employ an *amakudari kanryō* from the MoF in the position of executive director; however, one of its executive auditors still came from the MoF (Nippon Kinyū Tsushinsha 1999). According to figures from the National Personnel Authority, the number of retired former high-ranking MoF staff members that accepted private sector positions increased to 12 in 1999 from 10 in 1998; including retirees from the National Tax Administration, the number remained constant at 20. The system of *amakudari* at the MoF and BoJ and its role in the banking crisis will be investigated in depth in the next two chapters. Fifth, I demonstrated that the importance of *gakubatsu* or university cliques at the MoF actually increased during the nineties, despite explicit promises to achieve the opposite result: the relative presence of graduates from the University of Tokyo in the highest positions at the MoF increased from 75% at end-1991 to around 79% at end-September 1998. Unfortunately, owing to lack of data, the similar analysis conducted for the BoJ in chapter 5 could not be repeated. Sixth, as regards the importance of *shukkō* or *ama-agari* (temporary assignments from private companies) at both the MoF and the BoJ, apparently this decreased considerably after the 1998 scandals, although no objective information is available. According to media reports, as of 15 August 1999 the official total number of *ama-agari* movements from the private sector to the central government was 329, of which only 10 to the MoF (*Japan Times* Online, 30 March 2000). Reportedly, none of the *ama-agari* officials to the MoF came from private financial institutions. However, it was also reported that of the total *ama-agari* officials to the central government, 144 (44%) came from 36 private financial institutions.[76] Thus, the financial services industry continued to maintain extensive informal networks with various branches of the central administration. Finally, as regards the operations by the MoF in the bond market that were discussed in chapter 5, the MoF announced that its Trust Fund Bureau would stop purchasing a specific amount of bonds each month, which resulted from the reform of the Fiscal Investment and Loan Programme (Zaito) that took effect as of April 2001 (*Nikkei Weekly*, 11 December 2000, p.13).[77] However, the MoF also announced that it might start buying bonds again in order to neutralise demand–supply imbalances that would lead to higher long-term interest rates.

The banking crisis of the nineties had a severe impact on the structure of the Japanese banking industry. As a result of the bad-loan problems, not only small and medium-sized banks but also even the largest banks have been looking increasingly for partners to strengthen their position, resulting in a major consolidation of the banking sector (see for example: *Japan Economic Institute Report*, 29 January 1999, pp.4ff., 23 October 1998, pp.3ff.; Group of Ten 2001). After the merger between the Bank of Tokyo and Mitsubishi Bank in April 1996, in recent years some of the largest banks announced mergers and tie-ups. Chuo Trust & Banking

[76] These included 11 staff members from both Fuji Bank and Sakura Bank, nine from Nippon Life Insurance Co. and eight from both the Bank of Tokyo-Mitsubishi and Tokyo Marine & Fire Insurance Co. (*Japan Times* Online, 3 April 2000).

[77] The reform of Zaito would require government-affiliated financial institutions and agencies to take recourse to the capital markets for their funding. Furthermore, the Postal Savings System and pension systems would no longer be required to transfer their deposits to the MoF's Trust Fund Bureau (see chapter 5). Instead, the government could issue special *zaito* bonds to obtain the necessary funding (IMF 2000c, p.54).

Table 6.11. *Number of financial institutions in Japan (end of fiscal year)*

	1990	1995	1999	Change since 1990
City banks	12	11	9	−3
Long-term credit banks[1]	3	3	3	0
Trust banks	7	7	7	0
Regional banks	64	64	64	0
Second-Tier regional banks	68	65	60	−8
All major banks	*154*	*150*	*143*	*−11*
Shinkin banks	451	416	392	−59
Credit co-operatives	407	368	298	−109
Agriculture and forestry co-operatives	3,634	2,461	1,606	−2,028
Insurance companies[2]	50	55	80	30
Securities companies	272	285	288	16

Notes: [1] Long-Term Credit Bank of Japan and Nippon Credit Bank were nationalised in 1998 and subsequently transferred their business to other institutions.
[2] Largely due to foreign institutions.
Source: Group of Ten (2001).

and Mitsui Trust & Banking merged in April 2000. Dai-Ichi Kangyo Bank, Fuji Bank and the Industrial Bank of Japan (new name Mizuho Financial Group) established a holding company in September 2000. Sakura Bank and Sumitomo Bank (new name Sumitomo Mitsui Banking Co.) announced a merger in April 2001. As of the same date, the Bank of Tokyo-Mitsubishi, Mitsubishi Trust and Nippon Trust (new name Mitsubishi-Tokyo Financial Group) and Sanwa Bank, Tokai Bank and Toyo Trust (new name United Financial of Japan) will establish holding companies. In addition, smaller banks were hit by the ongoing process of financial reform, with interest rate liberalisation narrowing interest margins and larger financial institutions taking away their traditional business. All in all, the Japanese financial system has experienced since 1990 a severe rationalisation process, in particular as regards the smaller financial institutions (see table 6.11).

Finally, I shall discuss the analysis presented in this chapter from the perspective of the response of the US supervisory authorities to the savings and loan and other banking crises in the United States during the eighties and early nineties. With the benefit of hindsight, it is regrettable that Japan's prudential authorities did not draw lessons from the experiences of their American counterparts. As a matter of fact, the similarities in the policy responses are striking (Eisenbeis and Horvitz 1993; FDIC 1997; Herring 1998, pp.21ff.; see also Kane 1993). First, the American supervisors also initially used the method of promoting mergers between healthy and problem banks, for example in the mutual savings bank crisis during the first half of the eighties. Second, just like their Japanese colleagues, the US supervisory authorities responded to crisis situations by 'instituting laxer set of accounting principles' (Herring 1998, pp.15–16); they too 'engaged in a series of accounting and related gimmicks' (Eisenbeis and Horvitz 1993). Thus here too discretionary changes in accounting standards were accepted policy instruments. Third, also the banking supervisors in the USA lacked sufficient numbers of well-trained staff. Furthermore, supervision was often inadequate, and banking inspectors were on numerous occasions instructed to be lenient (FDIC 1997; Herring 1998). Fifth, the political climate was strongly against injecting large amounts of public funds. In addition, the political allies of problem banks in both the administration and Congress tried to obstruct and delay more strict intervention by the supervisory authorities.[78] Sixth, many of the banks that failed during the eighties and early nineties in the USA were heavily exposed to regional real estate market bubbles, which would also turn out to be the case in Japan. Finally, it was generally concluded that the policy of regulatory forbearance in the USA had been costly and that the prompt closure of insolvent banks would have saved taxpayers large sums of money. As a matter of fact, based on the experiences with the savings and loan associations and the policies of the Federal Savings and Loan Insurance Corporation (FSLIC), E.J. Kane had already warned Japanese policymakers in 1993 about the costs of a policy of forbearance: 'If the economic insolvency of individual banks is tolerated for extensive periods of time, odds are that Japanese taxpayers and the strongest members of the Japanese banking industry will pay a heavy price' (Kane 1993, p.354).

However, the main difference between the Japanese and American policy experiences with the banking crises seem to lie in the presence of extensive informal networks between the supervisory authorities and private banks in Japan, which most likely were instrumental in postponing adequate intervention by the supervisory authorities. Thus, even compared with the experience of regulatory forbearance in the USA, the Japanese experience stands out for its policy inaction, the recurrence of major scandals implicating supervisors, which were often linked to the informal dimension in the relationship between supervisory authorities

---

[78] For example, supervisors were accused of having become 'Gestapo-like' and 'heavy handed' (FDIC 1997, p.180). In this respect, the story of corruption and political interference involving C.H. Keating Jr. and the Lincoln Savings and Loan Association around the mid-eighties was more than telling (Mishkin and Eakins 2000, pp.496ff.).

and private banks such as the use of informal policy instruments, and the long-term existence of elaborate informal networks that may have been responsible for creating agency problems related to the implementation of prudential policy. The relationship of the most famous of these networks – *amakudari* – to Japan's banking problems and their resolution will be investigated empirically in the two next chapters.

Part III

Empirical evidence

7 *Amakudari* in the private banking industry: an empirical investigation

> By far the most notorious aspect of public corporate practice in Japan.
> C. Johnson (1978)

7.1 Introduction

The practice of *amakudari* or 'descending from heaven' refers to the post-retirement employment of Japanese government bureaucrats in private business. According to various studies, which were discussed in chapter 3, the informal network constituted by *amakudari* is said to be an important aspect of the relationship between the public and private sectors in Japan. Against the background of this claim, it is rather surprising that empirical analyses of this mechanism are few and far between. Therefore, I shall investigate in this chapter the situation of *amakudari* in the private banking industry. More specifically, the purpose of this chapter is to present a data-analysis of the positions of former MoF and BoJ staff members on the boards of directors of the major Japanese private banks and to confront these data with the theoretical interpretations of *amakudari* such as presented in section 3.4 of chapter 3 (see van Rixtel 1994a, 1995).

The structure of this chapter is as follows. First, the various data sources existing on *amakudari* and the specific choice for one of these sources in this study are discussed. Second, section 7.3 will focus on an empirical analysis of the positions of former MoF and BoJ staff members on the boards of city, long-term credit, trust, regional and Second Tier regional banks. As will become clear, the picture is a differentiated one: most of the biggest city banks, especially the ones belonging to a *keiretsu*, did not employ many former MoF or BoJ staff members as high-ranking executives, whereas at the group of regional and Second Tier regional banks a relatively significant number of board members were former MoF/BoJ officials. Furthermore, the various theories on *amakudari* that were presented in chapter 3 will be compared against the reported data. It will be shown that the movement of former MoF and BoJ staff members into the private banking sector cannot be explained convincingly by these general

255

theories, and that the presence of MoF and BoJ *amakudari kanryō*, the Japanese expression for retired bureaucrats working in the private sector, on the boards of Japanese private banks has to be investigated at the firm level. Third, an alternative explanation of *amakudari* will be presented in section 7.4, which involves the elements of patterned equalisation, bureaucratic intervention and career management. Fourth, section 7.5 will compare the results from the empirical analysis with some of the latest figures on *amakudari* available. The final section will conclude. It will be argued that, despite the enormous changes during the past decades in the Japanese financial system, the movement of former MoF and BoJ staff members into the boards of private banks showed a specific pattern of continuity.

7.2   Data sources on *amakudari*

An empirical investigation of the phenomenon of *amakudari* is hampered by several difficulties. First, its 'human dimension' complicates objective and independent research. In several interviews, especially those with active staff members of the MoF and BoJ, the interviewees were quite reluctant to discuss the issue. At neither the MoF nor the BoJ was it possible to obtain data on their *amakudari kanryō* positions through the official channels.[1] *Amakudari* is a delicate topic: the acceptance of highly paid jobs after retirement by former government bureaucrats raises suspicious feelings among the general public and media of possible conflicts of interests and collusive practices.[2] To put it more bluntly: according to the 'man in the street', *amakudari* could be interpreted as the existence of a small and privileged group of former civil servants who line their pockets by cashing in on relations established during public service. Or,

---

[1] In a personal interview, October 1992, a Japanese political scholar mentioned a similar experience: with rare exceptions, he did not manage to get the information on *amakudari* positions at industrial federations through the official channels. He stated that 'our Japanese scholars do not have information regarding *amakudari*'.

[2] The delicate nature of *amakudari* even forces one author to avoid using the word. In his excellent study of the Japanese financial system, James Horne states: 'The Japanese often use the phrase *amakudari*...I have avoided use of the word in line with this book's aim of producing an analysis understandable to the non-Japanese specialist but also because the word is often used with pejorative connotations' (Horne 1985, p.263). A good example of the suspicious feelings surrounding *amakudari* can be found in Johnson (1974), p.955. Regarding the report on *amakudari* published by the National Personnel Authority, Johnson mentions that in the media it 'provoked bitter comments: it raised suspicions that bureaucrats on active duty but looking ahead to retirement, as well as those already retired, might be more interested in protecting the interests of businesses than of the public'. Furthermore, in February 1995, an independent satirical quarterly called the *Amakudari Shimbun* (*Amakudari newspaper*) was launched, which ridiculed the practice of *amakudari*.

as Komiya (1999, p.86), puts it: 'The word (*amakudari*) carries a sarcastic or even biting nuance, so that it is not openly used by those who are directly concerned.' Against the background of these feelings, it is not surprising that directly involved persons and institutions are reluctant to discuss the issue. Second, as was shown in section 3.4 of chapter 3, various studies follow different definitions of *amakudari*. These differences obstruct comparative studies and the interpretation of data.

These difficulties seem to explain why for many years empirical studies on *amakudari* hardly existed. On many occasions, claims regarding the importance and relevance of *amakudari* for specific industries and statements about specific numbers of *amakudari kanryō* were not backed by presentations and analyses of the relevant data.[3] Consequently, these claims were often not precise. For example, Prestowitz (1988, p.113), van Wolferen (1989, p.114) and Schaede (1992, p.10) state that Japanese bureaucrats accept positions 'in a large bank', 'as executive of a large ... bank' and 'in the board of a leading bank' respectively. As will be shown in the subsequent analysis, these statements are not accurate. Since the mid-nineties, however, more empirical and institutional analyses of *amakudari* have become available (van Rixtel 1994a, 1995; Yamori 1994, 1997, 1998; Okazaki 1995; Schaede 1995; Yamori and Fujiwara 1995; van Rixtel and Hassink 1996a, 1996b; Tsutsumi 1996; Fujiwara and Yamori 1997; Moerke 1997; Amyx 1998; Horiuchi and Shimizu 1998; Nakano 1998; Colignon and Usui 1999).

The best-known and most quoted data sources on *amakudari* are published by government-related institutions. Examples are publications such as *Amakudari Hakusho* (*Amakudari* White Paper), which is published annually by Seirōkyō (Labour Union of Government-Related Institutes), *Eiri Kigyō e no Shūshoku no Shōnin ni kansuru Nenji Hōkokusho* (Annual Report Concerning Approvals of Employment in Profitmaking Enterprises), which is an annual publication of Jinji In (National Personnel Authority), and *Kōmuin Hakusho* (White Paper on Government Employees), which is also published annually by Jinji In. Furthermore, *Ōkura Yōran* (Ministry of Finance Survey), which is published by Ōkura Yōran Shuppansha (Ministry of Finance Survey Publisher) that is affiliated with the MoF, contains a chapter that lists all the MoF's 'old boys'. However, these sources are not especially suitable for this study. First and most importantly, given the fact that from a strict legal perspective the BoJ is not a public organisation (see chapters 3 and 5), the aforementioned publications do not include the *amakudari* positions of retired

---

[3] Early exceptions are Johnson (1974), Blumenthal (1985), Calder (1989) and Inoki (1993).

BoJ staff members. Secondly, these publications do not cover all *amaku-dari kanryō* of the MoF as well. For example, *Eiri kigyō*...does not give details of bureaucrats who 'serve their ministries as advisors before entering the private sector or enter sectors unrelated to their previous duties where National Personnel Authority authorization is not required' (Calder 1989, p.401). Third, retired MoF staff members who first go to other ministries or public organisations and from there to private sector institutions – the so-called *watari-dori* or 'hopping birds' (see chapter 3) – are often not included in these sources (Blumenthal 1985, p.314; various interviews, Tokyo, November–December 1992).

Besides the public sector publications, private companies have started to publish surveys of *amakudari* positions as well. Some of the most de-tailed data-sources available on MoF's and BoJ's retirees in the private sector are Seisaku Jihō Sha (1992) and Seisaku Jihō Shuppansha (1991). Unfortunately, I was able to find the most recent issues only; further-more, the latter publication has ceased to exist. Another publication, the booklet *Yakuin Shiki Ho* (Board of Directors Information) published by Toyo Keizai Shinposha, started to include information on *amakudari* positions from the beginning of the nineties only. Furthermore, since 1991 Teikoku Databank has published an annual paper on MoF and BoJ *amakudari* positions on the boards of directors of the main private banks. However, this publication contains only limited information on *amakudari*. For example, it pays no attention to such issues as the former positions of the retirees at the MoF and BoJ and the specific function that they perform on the boards of private banks. Given that the goal of this study is to analyse the presence of former MoF and BoJ staff members on the boards of directors of the leading private banks over longer periods of time than the previously mentioned publications allow for, the main source used here is the publication *Nippon Kinyū Meikan* (Directory of Executives in the Japanese Finance Industry), published by Nippon Kinyū Tsūshinsha. This three-volume work, published since the early sixties, contains information on the composition of the boards of directors of all Japanese financial institutions, including since the early seventies the personal profiles of individual board members. By analysing these profiles it is possible to trace former MoF and BoJ staff members who accepted positions on the boards of private banks. The publication offers the following advantages. First, *Nippon Kinyū Meikan* shows the careers of the board members since graduation from high school or uni-versity until their present position. Thus, if the executive was employed previously by the MoF or BoJ, this will be shown. Consequently, the so-called 'hopping birds', who worked at other corporations and institutions during the period between retiring from the MoF or BoJ and entering the boards of the private banks, are covered as well. Second, the publication allows for the construction of a database covering post-retirement positions of former MoF and BoJ staff members in the private banking industry over a long time period, i.e. since the early seventies. Third, in particular for the highest functions in the boards, *Nippon Kinyū Meikan* provides information about the *amakudari kanryō*'s careers at the MoF and BoJ. This information can be used to analyse possible relationships between specific career patterns at the MoF and BoJ and the acceptance of post-retirement jobs at private banks.

7.3   Analysis of data

The focus of my analysis is the presence of MoF and BoJ *amakudari kanryō* on the board of directors, i.e. the highest executive functions that for most banks comprise the following positions: chairman (*torishimariyaku kaichō*), sometimes a deputy-chairman (*torishimariyaku fuku kaichō*), president (mostly called *torishimariyaku tōdori*, sometimes *torishimariyaku shachō*), deputy president (*fuku torishimariyaku*), executive directors (*senmu torishimariyaku*), managing directors (*jōmu torishimariyaku*), directors (*torishimariyaku*), one or more advisory directors (*torishimariyaku sōdanyaku*) and statutory auditors (*kansayaku*). The chairman's main functions are to advise the president, to take care of public relations and the selection of top executives (Schaede 1992, p.28). It is often argued that the chairman does not have real power as regards daily bank management and that therefore his importance and influence is not that significant. However, in the context of this study, the function of chairman is included, since even if a chairman does not have a lot of actual power, he is well informed about strategic decisions and consequently could serve as an important source of information for the supervisory authorities. The president operates as the chief executive officer: together with the deputy-president and the executive and managing directors, he constitutes the so-called *jōmukai* or executive committee of the board that takes the most important decisions. Directly under the *jōmukai* are a number of directors, who are often assisted by one or more advisory directors. The latter are mostly former chairmen or presidents and remain on the board in an advisory role. Finally, the statutory auditors are charged with overseeing the discharge of duties by the directors (Sheard 1994, p.90).

The definition of the board of directors that is used is somewhat strict and is followed in empirical studies on *amakudari* such as Calder (1989) and Schaede (1992), and in other studies involving the boards of Japanese companies such as Sheard (1994). A broader definition of the board, which is used in various annual reports of Japanese banks, includes the functions of advisor (*komon*) and counsellor (*sōdanyaku*). The latter are former chief executive officers; both operate in advisory roles. This study does not take these functions systematically into account for two reasons. First, I found many discrepancies in the number of advisors and counsellors reported in *Nippon Kinyū Meikan* and in the annual reports of various banks. Furthermore, for some banks the figures on their advisors and counsellors were not consistently reported. Second, according to various interviewees, the functions of advisor and counsellor are relatively low in the hierarchy of the board and are not that influential. Occasionally, former high-ranking retirees from the MoF and BoJ enter the board in the function of advisor, but most move shortly afterwards into higher executive functions. The remaining advisors who were former MoF or BoJ staff members are said to be not that influential.[4]

In the following analysis I shall concentrate on the positions of MoF and BoJ *amakudari kanryō* on the boards of city banks, long-term credit banks, trust banks and regional banks for the period 1975–1993, as reported in the relevant issues of *Nippon Kinyū Meikan*.[5] Furthermore, I shall analyse the figures for the Second Tier regional banks for the years 1979, 1984 and 1988–1993. Owing to time constraints, the analysis of these smallest regional banks is concentrated on the post-'bubble' years, during which numerous Second Tier regional banks got into severe difficulties and received assistance from public and private institutions (see the previous chapter). Former MoF and BoJ bureaucrats who accepted positions on the boards when they were still relatively young, i.e. younger than the standard retirement age of 50–55, have been taken into account as well. Furthermore, the figures include the MoF officials who worked at the local finance bureaus, the customs houses, the National Tax Administration Agency, the regional taxation bureaus and the tax offices, and in the case of the former BoJ employees at its branches and offices.[6] Owing to a lack of data, I have not included MoF and BoJ retirees who moved into research institutes affiliated with private banks: anecdotal evidence suggests that the number of these *amakudari kanryō* could be substantial, in

[4] For example, some advisors of the Industrial Bank of Japan (IBJ) who were formerly at the MoF or BoJ were famous for being well paid and chauffeur driven in company cars but operating in a very low-key and relaxed mode. A senior executive of a major bank reported that he was asked to employ a former MoF bureaucrat, but replied that he wanted to accept this person only on the condition that this *amakudari kanryō* would operate similar to the IBJ *amakudari* advisors (various interviews with a former high-ranking staff member of the BoJ and leading executives at various Japanese private banks, February–April 1995).
[5] A full overview of all *amakudari* positions at individual banks is presented in van Rixtel (1997).
[6] See Appendices 5.2 and 5.3 of chapter 5.

particular in more recent years. In total, I have analysed around 45,000 personal profiles of board members of Japanese private banks: around 35,000 for 13 city banks (later 11 due to two mergers involving city banks only), 3 long-term credit banks, 7 trust banks and 64 regional banks and approximately 10,000 for a maximum of 70 Second Tier regional banks. The interpretation of the data results in the following conclusions.

First, relatively few *amakudari kanryō* were employed on the boards of city, long-term credit and trust banks, and relatively many on the boards of regional and second Tier Regional banks. For example, the large and influential city banks that are related to the *keiretsu* or industrial groupings, i.e. Sumitomo Bank, Dai-Ichi Kangyo Bank, Mitsui Bank (name later changed to Sakura Bank), Fuji Bank and Mitsubishi Bank (present Bank of Tokyo-Mitsubishi), employed no retired MoF and BoJ staff members on their boards (following the strict definition) during the period 1975–1993 (see also Moerke 1997). To compare the relative presence of these retirees on the boards of individual banks in the various bank groups, the number of individual banks per percentage-category of MoF and BoJ retirees on the boards for the years 1979, 1988 and 1993 are shown in table 7.1. The categories show whether the percentage of MoF and BoJ *amakudari kanryō*, calculated as the number of former MoF/BoJ staff members on the boards divided by the total number of board members, was 0%, between 0% and 5%, between 5% and 10%, between 10% and 15% or above 15%. Comparison between the commercial banks, i.e. city, regional and Second Tier regional banks, show that particularly the latter two groups had MoF and BoJ retirees on their boards. In the years 1979, 1988 and 1993, only 24%, 23% and 27% of the regional banks had none of these former bureaucrats in top executive positions. The figures for the smaller Second Tier regional banks were even lower (respectively, 6%, 6% and 9%). These figures differ sharply from those of the city banks, of which 54%, 54% and 46% did not have former MoF and BoJ staff members on their boards. Furthermore, also in relative terms, the regional and Second Tier regional banks employed more MoF and BoJ retirees than the city banks. As shown in table 7.1, during 1979, 1988 and 1993, respectively, 46%, 46% and 34% of the regional banks were characterised by having boards with more than 10% of the board members being former MoF or BoJ staff members. For the Second Tier regional banks, these figures were even higher (49%, 53% and 53%, respectively). However, the relative presence of MoF and BoJ retirees on the boards of the city banks decreased sharply over the years: in 1979, at 31% of the city banks more than 10% of the board positions were occupied by former MoF or BoJ bureaucrats, but in 1988 and 1993 at not a single city bank were more than 10% of the board members former MoF/BoJ staff

Table 7.1. *Number of banks per percentage-category of MoF and BoJ retirees on the boards in 1979, 1988 and 1993*

Bank-groups	Total number of banks per bank-group	Percentage of former MoF and BoJ officials on boards of individual banks				
		0	0–5	5–10	10–15	15+
1979						
City banks	13	7 (54%)	1 (8%)	1 (8%)	3 (23%)	1 (8%)
LTCBs	3	–	1 (33%)	1 (33%)	1 (33%)	–
Trust banks	7	5 (71%)	–	1 (14%)	– (–)	1 (14%)
Regional	63	15 (24%)	1 (2%)	18 (29%)	19 (30%)	10 (16%)
Second Tier	69	4 (6%)	1 (1%)	30 (44%)	11 (16%)	23 (33%)
1988						
City banks	13	7 (54%)	2 (15%)	4 (31%)	–	–
LTCBs	3	–	1 (33%)	2 (67%)	–	–
Trust banks	7	5 (71%)	2 (29%)	–	–	–
Regional	64	15 (23%)	3 (5%)	17 (27%)	19 (30%)	10 (16%)
Second Tier	68	4 (6%)	2 (3%)	26 (38%)	16 (24%)	20 (29%)
1993						
City banks	11	5 (46%)	3 (27%)	3 (27%)	–	–
LTCBs	3	–	1 (33%)	2 (67%)	–	–
Trust banks	7	4 (57%)	2 (29%)	1 (14%)	–	–
Regional	64	17 (27%)	5 (8%)	20 (31%)	16 (25%)	6 (9%)
Second Tier	65	6 (9%)	2 (3%)	23 (35%)	16 (25%)	18 (28%)

Notes: Numbers in brackets show the number of banks in a specific bank-group as a percentage of the total number of banks per group. The strict definition of the board is followed (i.e. excluding advisors and counsellors). Due to rounding-off, sums of the percentages may not equal 100.

members. Regarding the long-term credit and trust banks, I have also found a decrease in the relative presence of these former bureaucrats, which in the case of the trust banks had already been quite limited. For example, during the years 1979 and 1988, five out of seven trust banks did not employ a single MoF or BoJ retiree in their board. Thus, it has to be concluded that in particular the smaller banks, i.e. the regional and Second Tier regional banks, employed retired MoF and BoJ staff members. This conclusion contrasts the remarks in Prestowitz (1988), van Wolferen (1989) and Schaede (1992) that in particular the large or leading banks had former bureaucrats on their boards. The presented data clearly show that the leading and most powerful private banks in Japan employed very few *amakudari kanryō* from the MoF and BoJ. Thus, this finding does not support the claim of the interventionist or government control school (see section 3.4 of chapter 3) that the system of *amakudari* is used to exercise strong control over private business. After all, if the Japanese government bureaucracy were as powerful and interventionist oriented as this school suggests, and if it were substantially and systematically to use *amakudari* as an instrument of monetary policy, one would expect to find large numbers of MoF and BoJ *amakudari kanryō* on the boards of the largest and most important private banks. However, as demonstrated, this was not the case during the period investigated. From various interviews with executives from leading city, long-term credit and trust banks, it became clear that these banks did not want former MoF or BoJ bureaucrats in their highest executive functions: for reasons such as bureaucratic interference and meddling with company policy, obstruction of internal promotion schemes and high salary costs, the pre-eminent banks preferred not to have MoF/BoJ *amakudari kanryō* on their boards. Furthermore, given the fact that the MoF and BoJ needed the co-operation of the leading banks to obtain necessary information and knowledge of new technological developments and other financial innovations, these banks could more easily refuse to accept retired bureaucrats than the smaller banks.

Second, among the city, long-term credit and trust banks, the smaller banks were more likely to employ former MoF and BoJ bureaucrats on their boards. For example, relatively large numbers of ex-MoF bureaucrats occupied positions on the boards of the relatively small Bank of Tokyo (present Bank of Tokyo-Mitsubishi) and Hokkaido Takushoku Bank. In the case of the former, between 6% and 9% of these positions were obtained by MoF and BoJ retirees; in the case of the latter, this figure was between 4% and 12%. Furthermore, the boards of several small city banks such as Taiyo Kobe Bank, Kyowa Bank and Saitama Bank, especially during the years before they merged, were dominated by

MoF and BoJ *amakudari kanryō*.[7] In terms of size of total assets, these banks were among the smallest city banks. The concentration of former MoF/BoJ officials was highest among the smaller long-term credit and trust banks, too. For example, Nippon Credit Bank, which was the smallest long-term credit bank, had the highest percentage of positions on the board filled by former bureaucrats (between 6% and 24% during the period 1975–1993). At the trust banks, retirees from the MoF and BoJ were concentrated at Chuo Trust & Banking Co. and Nippon Trust Bank, which were also the smallest banks.

Third, the previous conclusion, however, does not apply to the regional banks: among these banks, MoF and BoJ *amakudari kanryō* were not predominantly concentrated at the smallest banks. For example, among the 10 largest regional banks, nine banks – the exception being Shizuoka Bank – employed former MoF/BoJ staff members on their boards during 1975–1993, whereas among the 10 smallest regional banks seven banks accepted these former bureaucrats in high-ranking positions (exceptions being Tajima Bank, Bank of Okinawa and Shimizu Bank). Furthermore, a considerably high relative presence of MoF and BoJ retirees was observed at the largest regional banks: for example, of the board positions of the second largest regional bank (Chiba Bank), 17% were filled in 1993 by MoF and BoJ *amakudari kanryō*. This figure was close to the highest relative presence of MoF and BoJ retirees on the boards of the 10 smallest regional banks in 1993 (a figure of 20% for both Tohoku Bank and Kanto Bank). Thus, among the regional banks, I have not found the clear pattern of concentration of MoF and BoJ *amakudari kanryō*, in particular at the smallest banks, that was observed for the city, long-term credit and trust banks.

Fourth, the concentration of retired MoF and BoJ staff members on the boards of the smallest banks was more pronounced for the group of Second Tier regional banks than for the group of regional banks. Of the 10 smallest Second Tier regional banks, all banks employed MoF and BoJ retirees during at least some of the years 1979, 1984 and 1988–1993.[8] However, of the 10 largest Second Tier regional banks, one bank (Keiyo Bank, the former Chiba Sogo Bank) employed no retired MoF/BoJ staff members during these years. More importantly, among the six smallest

---

[7] Taiyo Kobe Bank merged with Mitsui Bank in 1990 into Mitsui Taiyo Kobe Bank (later renamed Sakura Bank). Kyowa Bank and Saitama Bank merged in 1991 into Kyowa Saitama Bank (later Asahi Bank). The number of positions on their boards filled by former MoF and BoJ officials were between 8 and 19%, 3 and 26%, and 4 and 15% of the total number of their board positions, respectively. These figures came down drastically after the mergers.

[8] I have not taken into account Toho Sogo Bank, Higo Family Bank, Heiwa Sogo Bank and Fuso Sogo Bank, which did not exist during some of these years.

Second Tier regional banks in 1993, at five banks more than 15% of all board positions were occupied by MoF/BoJ retirees.[9] This compared with only one bank (Aichi Bank) among the 10 largest Second Tier regional banks (percentage of 17%). Hence, the relative presence of MoF and BoJ *amakudari kanryō* at the smallest Second Tier regional banks was higher than at the largest banks.

Fifth, the presence of former MoF and BoJ staff members on the boards of private banks during the sample period showed a very consistent pattern at specific banks. The analysis leads to the conclusion that four different types of banks can be distinguished: one category of banks which employed only former MoF bureaucrats, one group of banks with only former BoJ staff members, one category with both MoF and BoJ *amakudari kanryō* and a number of banks that never employed former MoF or BoJ bureaucrats in the highest executive functions. It is important to note that this distribution was extremely persistent during the sample period: at the specific banks belonging to these four different categories of banks, the very fundamental characterisation of the presence of former MoF and BoJ bureaucrats never changed. An overview of these categories is presented in table 7.2. The first and second columns show for the city, long-term credit, trust and regional banks the banks which employed during at least 15 of the 19 years in the sample period only former MoF (BoJ) staff members in executive positions and during the other years not a single BoJ (MoF) retiree. In the case of the Second Tier regional banks the criterion is whether banks employed during the years 1979, 1984 and at least five of the 1988–1993 years only former MoF (BoJ) staff members and not a single BoJ (MoF) retiree during the other years. The third column shows the banks that during the period 1975–1993 employed no MoF or BoJ *amakudari kanryō* on their boards. The table shows that 27 banks employed consistently only former MoF bureaucrats, 11 banks had only former BoJ staff members on their boards and 23 banks never employed an ex-MoF or ex-BoJ official. It is observed that particularly among the Second Tier regional banks a relatively large number of banks employed consistently only MoF retirees: out of a total number of 65–69 Second Tier regional banks that existed during the years of the sample period, 16 (or around 25%) experienced a consistent presence of only former MoF officials. This figure contrasts sharply with the situation at the group of 'only BoJ' banks, in which only two Second Tier regional banks were represented. Furthermore, the table shows that 13 regional banks were among the banks that

---

[9] These banks were (with the percentage of MoF/BoJ retirees on the board between brackets): Nara Bank (25%), Saga Kyoei Bank (18%), Shimane Bank (20%), Fukuoka Chuo Bank (18%) and Tsukuba Bank (23%).

Table 7.2. Amakudari *characterisation of the boards of private banks*[1]

Only MoF retirees	Only BoJ retirees	No MoF/BoJ retirees
City banks:	*City banks:*	*City banks:*
Sakura Bank[2]	Tokai Bank	Sumitomo Bank
Long-term credit banks:	*Regional banks:*	Dai-Ichi Kangyo Bank
Industrial Bank of Japan	77 Bank	Mitsui Bank
Trust banks:	Higo Bank	Fuji Bank
Nippon Trust Bank	Toho Bank	Mitsubishi Bank
Regional banks:	Kagoshima Bank	*Trust banks:*
Hokuriku Bank	Fukui Bank	Mitsui Trust & Banking Co.
Hiroshima Bank	Oita Bank	Yasuda Trust & Banking Co.
Hokkaido Bank	Awa Bank	Toyo Trust & Banking Co.
Shikoku Bank	Miyazaki Bank	*Regional banks:*
Bank of Iwate	*Second Tier regional banks:*	Shizuoka Bank
Mie Bank	Hiroshima-Sogo Bank	Yamaguchi Bank
Tottori Bank	Kita-Nippon Bank	Nanto Bank
Chikuho Bank		Iyo Bank
Second Tier regional banks:		Hyakujushi Bank
Tochigi Bank		Daishi Bank
Bank of Kansai		Suruga Bank
Kyushu Bank		Akita Bank
Niigata Chuo Bank		Hokuetsu Bank
Kagawa Bank		Yamagata Bank
First Bank of Toyama		Shimizu Bank
Fukushima Bank		Bank of Okinawa
Sapporo Bank		Tajima Bank
Hanwa Bank		*Second Tier regional banks:*
Daito Bank		Keiyo Bank
Sendai Bank		Yamagata Shiawase
Bank of Naniwa		
Kyoto Kyoei Bank		
Shizuoka Chuo		
Taisho Bank		
Saga Kyoei Bank		

Notes: [1] Again, the strict definition of the board was followed, i.e. the positions of counsellor and advisor were not taken into account. The sample period for the city, long-term credit, trust and regional banks is the period 1975–1993. For the Second Tier regional banks, the sample period consists of the years 1979, 1984 and 1988–1993.
[2] For Sakura Bank the sample period includes the years 1990–1993 only.
Source: Nippon Kinyū Tsūshinsha.

never employed any MoF or BoJ retirees, which implies that one out of five regional banks never accepted any MoF or BoJ *amakudari kanryō* on their boards. Furthermore, the banks that were completely dominated by either MoF or BoJ retirees were characterised by high succession rates. That is, when a MoF or BoJ *amakudari kanryō* left a top-position at one of these banks, another former MoF/BoJ bureaucrat very often succeeded him. The situation at three banks is illustrative.[10] At the Industrial Bank of Japan (dominated by MoF retirees), Shokichi Funayama, a former Administrative Vice-Minister, was auditor during a period of 10 years. After his resignation from this position, he was succeeded in 1981 by Kaneo Ishihara, also a former Administrative Vice-Minister. When Kaneo left in 1984, another former Administrative Vice-Minister, Fumio Takagi, joined the board, again in the position of auditor. Another example was Tokai Bank (dominated by BoJ retirees), where Shigemitsu Miyake, a former Executive Director of the BoJ, occupied the position of chairman until 1986. When he resigned to become advisory director, Eikichi Arai, a former Director of the International Department of the BoJ, was promoted executive director and became deputy chairman in 1987. Arai left the board in 1992 and was again succeeded by a former high-ranking BoJ staff member, Kenichi Kajii, former Director of the BoJ's Bank Supervision Department, who was appointed auditor. Finally, at the MoF-monopolised Kyushu Bank (Second Tier regional bank), a former Director-General of MoF's Mint Bureau, Kunio Miyakawa, entered the board in 1973 to hold the function of president for 12 years and then became chairman. After his resignation in 1990, a former Director of a tax office, Yūsuke Watanabe, entered as advisor, soon becoming deputy president in 1991. In April 1993, Watanabe was appointed president.

The presence of former MoF and BoJ bureaucrats on the boards of the 'only MoF' and 'only BoJ' banks that are reported in table 7.2 was, for certain banks, extremely dominant. Especially at some regional and Second Tier regional banks, relatively large percentages of board positions were occupied by MoF or BoJ *amakudari kanryō*. For example, at Hokkaido Bank and Shikoku Bank (regional banks), which were dominated by former MoF officials, in certain years 14% and 20% of all board positions were filled by former MoF bureaucrats. In addition, the number one (chairman) and sometimes also the number two (president) position were occupied by ex-MoF bureaucrats. Kagoshima Bank and Oita Bank, which were continuously dominated by BoJ *amakudari kanryō*, had maximum occupation rates of 20% and 23%, respectively. Also among the 'only MoF' and 'only BoJ' Second Tier regional banks, I have found banks with high percentages of their board positions filled by MoF or BoJ retirees. The bank with the highest percentage was Tochigi Bank, at which at the end of the seventies more than half (54%) of all board positions were occupied by former MoF staff members. Among the banks that employed both MoF and BoJ retirees on their boards, certain banks had significantly

---

[10] The various functions in the MoF and BoJ that will be referred to have been discussed in appendices 5.2 and 5.3 of chapter 5, respectively.

Table 7.3. *Number of MoF(M)/BoJ(B) amakudari kanryō in specific positions on the boards of city banks*

	1975	1976	1977	1978	1979	1980	1981	1982	1983	1984	1985	1986	1987	1988	1989	1990	1991	1992	1993
Chairman	M2 B4	M2 B3	M1 B3	M2 B1	M2 B1	M2 B2	M2 B2	M3 B2	M2 B2	M2 B2	M2 B2	M2 B1	M2 B1	M2 B1	M2 B1	M2 B1	M2 –	M2 –	M2 –
Deputy Chairman	–	–	–	–	–	–	–	–	B1	–	–	–	–	–	–	B1	B1	B1	B1
President	M2 B1	M2 B1	M3 B1	M3 B1	M2 B1	M2 B1	M2 B1	M2 B1	B1	M1 B1	M1 B1	M1	M1	M1	M1	M1 B1	M1 B2	B1	M1 B1
Deputy President	M1	M3	M3	M3 B3	M1 B3	M1 B1	M1 B1	M4	M3	M2	M2 B1	M2 B1	M1	M2	M1	–	B1	M1 B1	B1
Executive Director	M4 B2	M2 B3	M2 B3	M1 B1	M2 B1	M3 B1	M3 B1	B2	B2	M1 B2	M1 B1	M1 B1	M1 B1	B1	M1	M1	M1	M1	B1
Managing Director	B4	B2	–	M2 B1	M1 B1	–	–	M1 B1	M1 B1	B1	M1 B2	B1	M1 B1	M1 B2	M2 B2	M3 B1	M3 B1	–	M1
Advisory Director	–	–	–	–	M1	M1	M1	M1	M3	M3	M3	M3 B1	M1 B1	M2 B1	M2 B1	M1 B2	B1	–	–
Director	–	–	–	B1	–	–	–	–	–	M1 B1	M1	M1 B2	–	–	–	–	–	–	–
(Standing) Auditor	–	–	–	–	B1	–	–	–	B1	B1	–	M1	M1	M1	M1	B1	B1	B2	B1
Advisor	B2	(M2) (B2)	–	–	B1	(M2) (B1)	(M2) (B1)	(M2) (B1)	(M3) (B1)	(M3) (B1)	(M3) (B1)	(M2) (B2)	(M3) (B2)	(M3) (B2)	(M2) (B2)	(M2) (B2)	(M2) (B3)	(M2) (B3)	(M2) (B3)
Total	M9 B13	M9 B11 (M11) (B13)	M9 B9	M11 B8	M9 B9	M9 B7 (M11) (B8)	M9 B7 (M11) (B8)	M11 B7 (M13) (B8)	M10 B8 (M13) (B9)	M10 B7 (M13) (B8)	M11 B7 (M14) (B8)	M12 B5 (M14) (B7)	M8 B4 (M11) (B6)	M8 B5 (M11) (B7)	M8 B5 (M10) (B7)	M9 B5 (M11) (B7)	M7 B5 (M9) (B8)	M5 B6 (M7) (B9)	M5 B4 (M7) (B7)

more retirees from either the MoF or BoJ. For example, looking at the group of city banks, the former Taiyo Kobe Bank and Bank of Tokyo were dominated by former MoF bureaucrats, whereas the former Kyowa Bank experienced a significant presence of ex-BoJ staff members on its board.[11] In the case of the former Bank of Tokyo, the acceptance of relatively large numbers of MoF retirees should at least be interpreted partly as returning a favour to the MoF for having been given the task of managing the government's foreign exchange reserves (Brown 1999, p.35).

Sixth and finally, on average the relative numbers of MoF and BoJ *amakudari kanryō* on the boards of city, long-term credit, trust and regional banks decreased during the 1975–1993 period. Notable exceptions were among the city banks Daiwa Bank, and in the group of regional banks Hiroshima Bank, Nishi Nippon Bank, Hokkaido Bank, Bank of Osaka, Bank of Iwate and Tohoku Bank. Also at the Second Tier regional banks, the relative presence of former MoF and BoJ staff members diminished for most banks. However, in particular in the early nineties, a number of Second Tier regional banks, more specifically Hyogo Bank, Fukutoku Bank, Kumamoto Family Bank, Setouchi Bank, Fukushima Bank, Akita Akebono Bank, Saga Kyoei Bank and Nara Bank experienced an increase in the percentage of board positions occupied by these former bureaucrats.

The specific functions performed by MoF and BoJ *amakudari kanryō* on the boards of city, long-term credit, trust, regional and Second Tier regional banks are shown in tables 7.3–7.7. Within brackets are the number of MoF and BoJ retirees who were employed as advisor or counsellor and the total number of ex-MoF and ex-BoJ officials including advisors and counsellors. Table 7.3 shows that at the city banks, in particular during the seventies and mid-eighties, MoF and BoJ *amakudari kanryō* were predominantly employed in the function of chairman and in *jōmukai* positions such as president, deputy president, executive director and managing director. However, this concentration diminished during the early nineties, in particular after a number of mergers involving some of the smallest city banks. Relatively few former MoF and BoJ staff members were employed at the city banks in the lower-ranking functions of director and auditor. However, the opposite situation was observed for the long-term credit banks such as presented in table 7.4. During most of the 1975–1993 period, these banks employed relatively large numbers

---

[11] This pattern was widely known in the financial community in Tokyo. According to Johnson (1974), p.957, 'in financial circles the new Taiyo Kobe Bank is commonly referred to as the "Finance Ministry Bank" (*Ōkura Ginkō*)'. The winter 1990 edition of the *Japan Company Handbook* refers to Kyowa Bank as 'close to Bank of Japan' (Toyo Keizai 1990, p.1024). Supported by various interviews, October 1992–June 1993.

Table 7.4. *Number of MoF(M)/BoJ(B) amakudari kanryō in specific positions on the boards of long-term credit banks*

	1975	1976	1977	1978	1979	1980	1981	1982	1983	1984	1985	1986	1987	1988	1989	1990	1991	1992	1993
Chairman	—	—	—	—	—	—	—	—	—	—	—	—	—	—	—	—	—	—	—
Deputy Chairman	—	—	—	—	—	—	—	—	—	—	—	—	—	—	—	—	—	—	—
President	—	—	—	—	M1	M1	M1	M1	—	—	—	—	—	—	—	—	—	—	M1
Deputy President	M1	M1	—	M1	—	—	—	—	M1	M1	—	—	—	—	—	—	M1	M1 B1	M1 B1
Executive Director	B1	B1	B2	B1	B1	—	—	—	—	—	—	M1 B1	M1 B1	M1 B1	M1 B1	M1 B1	B1	—	—
Managing Director	M2 B1	M1 B1	M1	M1 B1	M1 B1	M1 B1	M1	M1	—	—	M1 B1	—	—	—	—	—	—	—	—
Advisory Director	—	—	—	—	—	—	—	—	M1	M1	—	—	—	—	—	—	—	—	—
Director	M3	M2	M1	—	—	—	—	—	—	M1	—	—	—	—	—	—	—	—	—
(Standing) Auditor	M2	M2	M2	M2	—	M2 B1	M2 B2	M2 B2	M2 B2	M2 B2	M3 B1	M2 B1	M2 B1	M2 B1	M2 B1	M2 B1	M2 B1	M2 B1	M2 B1
Advisor	—	—	—	—	—	(M1) (B1)	(M1)	(M2)	(M2) (B1)	(M2) (B1)	(M3) (B1)	(M3) (B1)	(M3)	(M3)	(M2)	(M2)	(M2)	(M2)	(M2)
Total	M8 B2	M6 B2	M4 B2	M4 B2	M2 B2	M4 B2 (M5) (B3)	M4 B2 (M5)	M4 B2 (M6)	M4 B2 (M6) (B3)	M5 B2 (M7) (B3)	M4 B2 (M7) (B3)	M3 B2 (M6) (B3)	M3 B2 (M6)	M3 B2 (M6)	M3 B2 (M5)	M3 B2 (M5)	M3 B2 (M5)	M3 B2 (M5)	M4 B2 (M6)

of MoF and BoJ *amakudari kanryō* as auditor and relatively few in higher-ranking positions. This changed somewhat in the beginning of the nineties, when a renewed presence of former MoF and BoJ officials in the higher functions such as president and deputy-president occurred. A similar pattern is also shown for the trust banks in table 7.5. MoF and BoJ retirees were relatively concentrated in the lower-ranking positions of director and auditor throughout the period 1975–1993. An increase in the number of MoF/BoJ retirees on the boards of trust banks in higher-level functions such as deputy president, executive director and managing director was observed during the early nineties. At the group of regional banks, which are presented in table 7.6, MoF and BoJ *amakudari kanryō* were particularly well represented in the functions of chairman, president, executive director and managing director. Furthermore, since the mid-eighties, in particular the number of MoF retirees employed as chairman increased. Finally, at the Second Tier regional banks, which continuously employed almost twice as many MoF *amakudari kanryō* than BoJ retirees, the major developments were the following: an increase of MoF and BoJ *amakudari kanryō* employed as chairman, a decrease in ex-MoF and ex-BoJ staff members in the lower-ranking function of director, a sharp decrease of MoF retirees employed as managing director and an increase of former BoJ officials working as managing director (table 7.7). The continuous presence of almost double the number of retired MoF staff members on the boards of Second Tier regional banks compared with the number of BoJ retirees could be explained by the fact that, via the local finance bureaus, customs houses and regional taxation bureaus, the MoF was much better represented across the various prefectures than the BoJ and consequently had closer and more intimate contacts with at least some of these regional banks.[12]

The conclusions presented here have in my opinion serious implications for the credibility of the various theoretical interpretations of *amakudari*, which were discussed in section 3.4 of chapter 3. First, the fact that particularly the largest banks did not employ significant numbers of MoF and BoJ *amakudari kanryō* is fundamentally at odds with the basic argument of the interventionist or government control interpretation which claims that *amakudari* is used as an important means of government control over private business. Of course, this does not imply that *amakudari* is not used as an instrument of government control or intervention.

---

[12] Given the large number of officials employed by these local MoF offices (around 68,000 as of October 1996; see table 5.1 in chapter 5), it is not surprising that former MoF officials showed up in larger numbers in post-retirement positions on the boards of Second Tier regional banks than former BoJ staff members (the BoJ employed at its regional branches and offices only around 3,000 officials).

Table 7.5. *Number of MoF(M)/BoJ(B) amakudari kanryō in specific positions on the boards of trust banks*

	1975	1976	1977	1978	1979	1980	1981	1982	1983	1984	1985	1986	1987	1988	1989	1990	1991	1992	1993
Chairman	–	–	–	–	–	M1	M1	M1	M1	–	–	–	–	–	–	–	–	–	–
Deputy Chairman	–	–	–	–	–	–	–	–	–	–	–	–	–	–	–	–	–	–	–
President	M1	M1	M1	M1	M1	–	–	–	–	–	–	–	–	–	–	–	–	–	–
Deputy President	–	–	–	–	–	–	–	–	–	–	–	–	–	–	–	–	–	–	M1
Executive Director	B1	B1	B1	B1	–	–	–	–	–	–	M1	–	–	–	–	–	M1	M1	–
Managing Director	–	–	–	–	–	–	B1	M1 B1	M1 B1	M1 B1	B1	B1	B2	B1	–	M1	–	–	B1
Advisory Director	B1	–	–	–	–	–	–	–	–	M1	M1	M1	–	–	–	–	–	–	–
Director	–	–	–	–	B1	B1	B1	B2	B2	B1	–	–	–	–	B1	B1	B2	B2	B1
(Standing) Auditor	M1 B1	M1 B1	M1 B1	M1 B1	M1 B1	M1 B1	B1	M1 B1	M1 B1	M1 B1	M1 B1	M1 B1	M1	M1	M1	M1	M1	M1	M1
Advisor	–	–	–	–	–	(B1)	(B1)	(M1) (B1)	(M1) (B1)	(M1) (B1)	(M1) (B1)	(M1)	(M2)	(M2)	(M2)	(M3)	(M3)	(M1)	(M1)
Total	M2 B3	M2 B2	M2 B2	M2 B2	M2 B2	M2 B2 (B3)	M1 B3 (B4)	M3 B4 (M4) (B5)	M3 B4 (M4) (B5)	M3 B3 (M4) (B4)	M3 B2 (M4) (B3)	M2 B2 (M3)	M1 B2 (M3)	M1 B1 (M3)	M1 B1 (M3)	M2 B1 (M5)	M2 B2 (M5)	M2 B2 (M3)	M2 B2 (M3)

Table 7.6. *Number of MoF(M)/BoJ(B) amakudari kanryō in specific positions on the boards of regional banks*

	1975	1976	1977	1978	1979	1980	1981	1982	1983	1984	1985	1986	1987	1988	1989	1990	1991	1992	1993
Chairman	–	M1	–	–	M1	M2	M1	M1	M2	M4	M6	M8	M6	M6	M7	M7	M5	M7	M8
	B4	B5	B6	B4	B5	B5	B5	B6	B5	B5	B5	B5	B7	B6	B6	B7	B5	B5	B6
Deputy Chairman	–	–	–	–	–	–	–	–	–	–	–	–	–	–	–	–	–	–	B1
President	M7	M8	M9	M10	M7	M9	M9	M10	M10	M11	M11	M11	M10	M11	M9	M9	M9	M9	M8
	B11	B11	B11	B13	B14	B13	B13	B13	B12	B11	B11	B10	B9	B8	B8	B8	B8	B9	B9
Deputy President	M5	M3	M3	M4	M4	M2	M2	M4	M3	M2	M2	M1	M1	–	M1	M1	M3	M2	M2
	B9	B7	B5	B5	B4	B3	B4	B4	B2	B1	B1	B2	B5	B5	B5	B3	B5	B3	B3
Executive Director	M6	M11	M9	M8	M9	M12	M11	M7	M10	M8	M7	M7	M6	M6	M6	M8	M9	M8	M8
	B4	B5	B5	B4	B2	B4	B6	B7	B6	B8	B8	B7	B4	B5	B5	B5	B6	B7	B6
Managing Director	M8	M6	M9	M9	M9	M7	M7	M9	M9	M9	M6	M7	M8	M13	M12	M10	M7	M10	M8
	B10	B8	B7	B8	B8	B6	B8	B7	B7	B5	B6	B7	B9	B11	B9	B8	B6	B7	B5
Advisory Director	M1	M1	M1	M1	M2	M3	M3	M2	M1	M1	M1	M1	M2	M1	M2	M1	M2	M2	M1
	–	–	–	–	–	B1	–	–	B1	–	–	–	–	–	B1	B1	B2	B1	B1
Director	M4	M4	M5	M6	M4	M5	M6	M8	M5	M5	M4	M5	M6	M6	M6	M8	M6	M5	M7
	B5	B4	B2	B2	B4	B4	B1	B3	B2	B4	B5	B6	B4	B4	B5	B4	B3	B1	B5
(Standing) Auditor	M1	M3	M4	M4	M4	M3	M4	M6	M5	M7	M7	M6	M7	M8	M7	M6	M6	M4	M5
	B6	B6	B7	B7	B6	B7	B6	B6	B6	B5	B5	B5	B5	B5	B5	B6	B7	B6	B4
Advisor	–	–	–	–	–	–	–	–	–	–	–	–	M1	–	–	(M2)	(M1)	–	(M1)
	(B1)	(B1)	(B1)	(B1)	(B1)	(B2)	(B1)	(B2)	(B3)	(B3)	(B3)	(B4)	(B6)	(B5)	(B5)	(B6)	(B5)	(B4)	(B2)
Total	M32	M37	M40	M42	M40	M43	M43	M47	M45	M47	M44	M47	M47	M51	M50	M50	M47	M47	M47
	B49	B46	B43	B43	B43	B43	B43	B46	B41	B39	B41	B42	B43	B44	B44	B42	B42	B39	B40
																(M52)	(M48)		(M48)
	(B50)	(B47)	(B44)	(B44)	(B44)	(B45)	(B44)	(B48)	(B44)	(B42)	(B44)	(B46)	(B49)	(B49)	(B49)	(B48)	(B47)	(B43)	(B42)

Table 7.7. *Number of MoF(M)/BoJ (B)* amakudari kanryō *in specific positions on the boards of Second Tier regional banks*

	1979	1984	1988	1989	1990	1991	1992	1993
Chairman	–	M4	M4	M6	M8	M7	M5	M7
	–	–	–	–	B1	B2	B2	B1
Deputy Chairman	–	–	–	–	–	–	M1	M1
	–	–	B1	B1	B1	–	–	–
President	M12	M13	M14	M15	M13	M14	M14	M15
	B8	B6	B7	B7	B7	B7	B7	B6
Deputy President	M4	M3	M3	M3	M2	M5	M4	M4
	B1	B1	B4	B4	B4	B3	B4	B5
Executive Director	M10	M13	M8	M8	M8	M5	M9	M12
	B7	B7	B7	B5	B3	B3	B2	B2
Managing Director	M23	M20	M19	M17	M16	M15	M13	M11
	B11	B10	B6	B9	B14	B16	B17	B18
Advisory Director	–	M1	–	M1	M1	–	M1	M1
	B1	B3	–	B1	B2	B2	–	–
Director	M22	M25	M17	M16	M17	M12	M12	M12
	B4	B7	B12	B13	B9	B8	B6	B5
(Standing) Auditor	M13	M13	M14	M12	M14	M14	M15	M16
	B7	B7	B7	B2	B2	B1	B2	B2
Advisor	(M1)	(M1)	(M1)	(M2)	(M1)	(M1)	–	–
	–	(B2)	(B1)	(B1)	–	–	–	–
Total	M84	M92	M79	M78	M79	M72	M74	M79
	B39	B41	B44	B42	B43	B42	B40	B39
	(M85)	(M93)	(M80)	(M80)	(M80)	(M73)		
		(B43)	(B45)	(B43)				

However, it does cast serious doubts on the validity of the somewhat extreme claims of the interventionist school. Second, the finding that among the city, long-term credit and trust banks the smaller banks in particular employed former MoF and BoJ staff members seems to support the equalisation hypothesis ('buying influence'), as discussed in section 3.4 of chapter 3, which argues that the smaller and weaker banks especially want to hire ex-bureaucrats in order to establish better connections with the government bureaucracy. However, this finding could also be explained by interpreting the MoF and BoJ as paternalistic caretakers who want to strengthen the management of the smaller and weaker banks and keep a close watch ('monitoring') on their financial stability by strategically positioning their retired staff members in high-level executive positions: an interpretation that could also be considered as a softened version of the interventionist or government control school. Third, the conclusion that a significant number of the smaller regional banks employed very few or no MoF or BoJ *amakudari kanryō* is fundamentally at odds with the equalisation hypothesis. Of course, this finding also conflicts with the softened version of the interventionist school. Fourth, however, I have found a concentration of retired MoF and BoJ staff members on the boards of the smallest banks in particular among the Second Tier regional banks. In other words, the equalisation hypothesis seems to be more valid for the Second Tier regional banks than for the regional banks. Finally, the analysis does not support the consensual policy interpretation (see section 3.4 of chapter 3), which sees *amakudari* as a general mechanism for informal consultations and consensus building between the public and private sectors. According to this interpretation, MoF and BoJ *amakudari kanryō* should be employed by the banks that act as chairmen of the various banking associations in particular.[13] However, these banks are always the leading banks of the specific bank groups, and as I have demonstrated before, the leading banks among the city and long-term credit banks employed very few *amakudari kanryō*. Only in the group of regional banks, did the chair bank (Bank of Yokohama) of the group association (Zenkoku Chihō Ginkō Kyōkai or Regional Banks Association of Japan) have a large presence of retirees from the MoF.

7.4   Alternative explanation of *amakudari*

As is shown by the empirical findings in the previous section, the traditional interpretations of *amakudari* cannot convincingly explain by themselves the presence of MoF and BoJ *amakudari kanryō* on the boards of the major private banks. In my view, the pattern of employment of former MoF and BoJ staff members on the boards of specific banks during the period 1975–1993 involved elements of patterned equalisation, bureaucratic intervention and career management.

Patterned equalisation

Particularly among the regional banks, a pattern can be observed that I call 'patterned equalisation', a kind of 'buying influence' behaviour: MoF and BoJ *amakudari kanryō* were employed in executive positions at specific banks in a very consistent but random pattern, which can be explained only by assuming that the decision whether or not to employ former bureaucrats was taken at the individual bank level. I want to stress that the concept of patterned equalisation is related in particular to the

---

[13] These banking associations play an important role in the formulation of policy between the banking industry and monetary authorities; various interviews with MoF officials, February–March 1993.

decision of banks whether or not to accept MoF/BoJ *amakudari kanryō* on their boards. When banks decided to accept these former bureaucrats, the specific pattern of the presence of MoF and BoJ retirees at these banks, for example the existence of 'only MoF' and 'only BoJ' banks, can be explained by a possible mutual understanding between the MoF and BoJ: a kind of implicit agreement to respect each other's 'dropping zones' and not to interfere with the other's post-retirement employment policy.

Regarding the two key elements of patterned equalisation, consistency and randomness, I would like to put forward the following remarks. The consistency is shown by the fact that during the 1975–1993 period a fairly constant group of regional banks did employ former MoF or BoJ staff members in executive positions who were very often succeeded by other MoF or BoJ retirees, whereas another fairly constant group employed no MoF and BoJ *amakudari kanryō* at all. The randomness is shown by the presence of ex-bureaucrats at both large and small regional banks: it is hard to find clear general criteria to explain the distribution of former MoF and BoJ bureaucrats among the regional banks. Obviously, a number of regional banks believed that it was in their own interest to hire these former bureaucrats, whereas other regional banks simply did not want to employ them. Otherwise, it would be difficult to explain why 13 regional banks (around 20% of the total number of regional banks), which are in many ways very different and ranked at different positions, employed no MoF or BoJ retirees during the period 1975–1993.

The element of patterned equalisation also seems to have applied to the situation at Daiwa Bank, one of the smaller city banks. As a result of the Mitsui–Taiyo Kobe and Kyowa–Saitama mergers, Daiwa Bank lost considerable market share. It responded by hiring two former high-ranking bureaucrats in 1990 and 1991, respectively Shigeyoshi Genjida, the former Director-General of the Printing Bureau, MoF, and Takeshi Ohta, the former Deputy Governor for International Relations of the BoJ. The hiring of the latter could have been an indication of the desire of Daiwa Bank to strengthen its international activities, a strategy that also seemed to have been followed by the smallest city bank, Hokkaido Takushoku Bank.[14] Furthermore, the idea of patterned equalisation could also explain the continuing relatively strong presence of MoF and BoJ *amakudari kanryō* at the two smallest trust banks. Finally, the fact that during the years 1979, 1984 and 1988–1993 only two out of 65–69 Second Tier regional banks never employed MoF and BoJ retirees and that the others

---

[14] Around the same time, Hokkaido Takushoku Bank hired two former MoF and BoJ officials who also had great experience in international finance: Hirotake Fujino, ex-MoF and former Executive Director IMF (hired in 1989), and Yoshiyuki Ohkuma, former Director of the Foreign Exchange Division of the International Department of the BoJ (hired in 1990).

employed considerable numbers at the highest executive positions (particularly by the smallest banks among the Second Tier regional banks) supports the validity of equalisation in two ways. First, as a group, Second Tier regional banks 'bought' former MoF/BoJ officials as a means to strengthen their position vis-à-vis the regional banks (inter-group competition). Second, the smallest Second Tier regional banks hired former MoF/BoJ bureaucrats to compete with the larger Second Tier regional banks (intra-group competition). Inter-group competition could also explain the relatively large numbers of MoF and BoJ retirees on the boards of the largest regional banks. As I explained in section 5.3 of chapter 5, the MoF controlled the branch network of regional banks through its administrative guidance. Since the largest regional banks, such as the Bank of Yokohama and Chiba Bank, were natural competitors of the smallest city banks in particular, they could have tried to influence the MoF's guidance and thereby their competitive strength towards city banks by hiring in particular former MoF staff members.

All in all, patterned equalisation implies that specific banks accepted MoF and BoJ retirees in order to 'buy influence' from the monetary authorities. In the context of principal-agent theory, the banks were agents which were looking for certain 'favours' from the MoF/BoJ (the principals) in return for well-paid post-retirement positions. Of course, as principal-agent theory also suggests, the different incentives for both parties may have generated conflicts, leading to agency costs. This element will be investigated in more detail in chapter 8. As regards the aspect of 'buying influence', the analysis at the micro level could be extended to the macro level. It has been observed that the regulated industries in Japan such as the banking and construction sectors were particularly likely to hire former bureaucrats (see table 7.8; see also US Embassy Tokyo 1999).[15] Thus, it seems fair to conclude that the element of 'patterned equalisation' or 'buying influence' did exist, and that the mechanism of *amakudari* was used by the banking industry at least to some extent to mitigate or circumvent existing regulations.

Bureaucratic intervention

The presence of former MoF and BoJ staff members on the boards of private banks involved elements of what I call 'bureaucratic intervention'

---

[15] The element of equalisation or 'buying influence' in relation to *amakudari* is further supported by Moerke (1997). He finds that Japanese firms that are not related to a *keiretsu* have on average more *amakudari kanryō* from the MoF and BoJ on their boards than member-firms of a *keiretsu*, apparently to 'outbalance the better bank-firm relations of the *keiretsu*'. It is also found that *keiretsu* firms on average hire more retirees from government institutions related directly to their business.

Table 7.8. Amakudari *and regulated industries*

	Number of firms[1]	Number of *amakudari kanryō* on the board	Percentage of *amakudari* positions as of total number of board members
Regulated industries			
Construction	30	150	12.8
Second-Tier regional banks	30	60	11.4
Telecommunication	4	13	9.7
Air transport	5	11	8.2
Regional banks	30	36	5.7
Electricity and gas	20	20	3.9
Unregulated industries			
Steel	30	6	0.9
Automotive	30	6	0.9

Note: [1] The firms included in the survey are the listed companies with the largest sales in each industrial category.
Source: OECD (1999c), p.6.

or ex-post monitoring (see section 4.3 of chapter 4). First, the clearest case of intervention involved a concentration of relatively young MoF and BoJ *amakudari kanryō* moving into executive positions at private banks in a short period of time (one or two years). The involvement of young bureaucrats, i.e. bureaucrats who were much younger than the standard retirement age of 50–55, pointed at the dispatching of former staff members at the initiative of the MoF and BoJ: it would have been impossible for private banks to hire at their own initiative relatively large numbers of comparatively young elite bureaucrats in a short period of time. I have found numerous examples of this form of intervention. Among the city and long-term credit banks, this intervention was concentrated at some of the smallest banks in the years 1958–1961. For example, the Bank of Kobe, which merged with Taiyo Bank in October 1973 to become Taiyo Kobe Bank, in 1960 moved two former BoJ officials (Bunjirō Matsumura and Yoji Kobayashi) at age 40 and 39 into two branch offices. Both officials obtained positions on the board afterwards. At Kyowa Bank, four ex-BoJ bureaucrats, three of them in their early forties, moved into executive positions during 1958–1960. As a result, in 1975 26% of the board positions at Kyowa Bank were occupied by former BoJ staff members, a figure that dropped sharply to 14% in 1978. At the smallest long-term credit bank (Nippon Credit Bank), four ex-MoF bureaucrats in their late thirties and early forties entered into executive positions in 1961. In general, the intervention by relatively young bureaucrats was sometimes linked to clear structural changes at the bank involved. For example, in January 1951, Niwa Bank moved into Kyoto under the name of Bank of Kyoto, with Niwa Bank in Fukuchiyama continuing to be the parent body. This development was followed by the movement of three former MoF bureaucrats at the ages of 27, 37 and 39 into executive positions at the Bank of Kyoto in 1951 and 1952.

Second, I have observed the movement of 'older' MoF and BoJ bureaucrats at retirement age (i.e. real *amakudari kanryō*) into strategic executive positions at private banks, which seems to have been related to structural developments such as establishment, mergers, listing at stock exchange and changing of bank status. For example, the establishment of Chuo Trust & Banking Co. in May 1962 was accompanied by the appointment of two former high-ranking BoJ staff members and one former MoF official to its board.[16] Of course, these movements of MoF and BoJ *amakudari kanryō* could also be explained by patterned equalisation. From interviews with former MoF and BoJ staff members, however, I got the impression that the Japanese monetary authorities felt responsible for banks that experienced at a specific moment structural changes which were often initiated by the MoF/BoJ. In this respect, the MoF and BoJ could be seen more as paternalistic caretakers that assisted the banks involved at that specific moment. The merger between Saitama Bank and Kyowa Bank seems to have been another example of this strategic intervention policy: Takuya Mori, who was the representative of the MoF at the BoJ's Policy Board, entered Saitama Bank in 1985 and became the deputy chairman of Kyowa Saitama Bank (present Asahi Bank) after the merger. Against the background of the facts that the board of Kyowa Bank had always been dominated by former BoJ staff members, that mergers in the banking industry were characterised by strong MoF involvement and that Mori, as a result of his previous function, had established good relations with the BoJ, he was perfectly suited to assist in the difficult task of establishing a coherent organisation.

Third, I have found an increase in the number of MoF and BoJ *amakudari kanryō* on the boards of a number of well-known problem banks that were typified as such in chapter 6, as they either failed or were forced to restructure, often requiring support from other banks. Examples are Hokkaido Bank and the Bank of Osaka among the regional banks and various Second Tier regional banks such as Fukutoku Bank, Hyogo

---

[16] The BoJ officials were Kiyoka Shirane, former Executive Director (left the BoJ at age 54), and Takemi Iga, former Councillor (left the BoJ at age 45); the MoF official was Hisao Fukuda, former Director-General of the Foreign Exchange Bureau (present International Bureau).

Bank, Kumamoto Family Bank and Taiheiyo Bank. After the collapse of the 'bubble', these banks experienced inflows of MoF and BoJ retirees, which were often announced in the media as being part of large-scale rescue packages ('signalling effect').[17] Given the fact that *amakudari* is a structural phenomenon, the Japanese monetary authorities had during each year of the sample period 1975–1993 a group of well-educated bureaucrats at their disposal who needed to find post-retirement jobs (as explained in section 3.4 of chapter 3) and consequently could be sent as 'troubleshooters' to problem-banks. That is to say, the MoF and BoJ killed two birds with one stone: on the one hand, the retirees could start a private sector career and on the other hand, their movement into problem banks, as an element of prudential policy, restored public confidence to some extent at least.

Career management

Finally, the presence of MoF and BoJ *amakudari kanryō* in the highest executive positions during the period 1975–1993 was also clearly related to bureaucratic career management. In other words, *amakudari* was an important incentive mechanism within the Japanese government bureaucracy. This aspect is supported by the finding of the existence of 'only MoF' and 'only BoJ' groups of banks and high succession rates at the banks of these groups, the high succession rates at numerous banks that employed MoF and BoJ *amakudari kanryō* in general, the linking of specific functions in the organisational structure of both the MoF and BoJ with specific post-retirement positions on the boards of private banks, and the presence of former bureaucrats in specific functions at certain banks. That is to say, both the MoF and BoJ seemed to have 'secured' a number of post-retirement positions for their staff members at private banks as rewards for good performance (see section 3.4 of chapter 3).

To get a better insight into the career management aspects of *amakudari*, I present in tables 7.9–7.12 for former staff members of the MoF and BoJ on the boards of city, long-term credit, trust and regional banks the number of years that they worked at the MoF or BoJ (columns) and their age at leaving these organisations (rows).[18]

Table 7.9 shows that the retirees from the MoF and BoJ on the boards of city banks were relatively concentrated in the '25 < 30' (number of years

---

[17] Various articles in *Nihon Keizai Shimbun*, which were retrieved from the Nikkei Database System, covered these appointments of former MoF/BoJ officials.

[18] The former MoF and BoJ bureaucrats include both the 'real' *amakudari kanryō* who left at the standard retirement age of 50–55 and the others who left at sometimes much younger ages. Given the gaps in the time span of the investigation of the Second Tier regional banks presented in this chapter, I have not included them.

Table 7.9. *Profile of MoF/BoJ retirees on the boards of city banks, 1975–1993*[1]

Age at leaving the MoF/BoJ	Number of years at the MoF/BoJ				
	15 < 20	20 < 25	25 < 30	30 < 35	>35
35 < 40					
	B3 (12%)				
40 < 45					
	B2 (8%)	B1 (4%)			
45 < 50		M4 (20%)	M3 (15%)		
		B2 (8%)	B3 (12%)		
50 < 55			M8 (40%)	M2 (10%)	
			B7 (28%)	B1 (4%)	
55 < 60				M2 (10%)	M1 (5%)
			B1 (4%)	B3 (12%)	B1 (4%)
>60					
					B1 (4%)

Note: [1] M indicates former MoF official. B indicates former BoJ official. Numbers following M or B show the number of retirees. Percentages show the number of MoF(BoJ) retirees in a specific category as a proportion of the total number of MoF(BoJ) retirees. The total number of MoF retirees is 20, total number of BoJ retirees is 25. Owing to rounding, the percentages may not sum to 100.

at MoF/BoJ) and '50 < 55' (age at retiring from MoF/BoJ) intervals: 8 out of 20 ex-MoF officials (40%) and 7 out of 25 ex-BoJ officials (28%) worked between 25 and 30 years at the MoF and BoJ and left these institutions at ages between 50 and 55 years. Furthermore, the table shows that a relatively large number of young former BoJ staff members obtained positions on the boards of city banks: 20% of the ex-BoJ bureaucrats was under 45 years of age when they entered the city banks' boards, mainly the board of Kyowa Bank. In accordance with the aspect of bureaucratic intervention in my explanation of *amakudari*, this finding could explain some of the problems experienced at Kyowa Bank in the past. Table 7.9 also shows that the majority of both MoF and BoJ retirees on the boards of city banks were over 50 years of age when they left the bureaucracy (65% of the MoF retirees and 56% of the BoJ retirees).

As table 7.10 indicates, I also have found a concentration of MoF and BoJ retirees in the '25 < 30 years at the MoF/BoJ' and '50 < 55 years of retirement age' intervals (respectively, 45% and 60%) who accepted positions on the boards of long-term credit banks. These banks experienced a relatively significant presence of young former MoF bureaucrats: 32% of the MoF retirees on their boards were under 40 years of age when they

Table 7.10. *Profile of MoF/BoJ retirees on the boards of long-term credit banks, 1975–1993*[1]

Age at leaving	Number of years at the MoF/BoJ						
the MoF/BoJ	5 < 10	10 < 15	15 < 20	20 < 25	25 < 30	30 < 35	>35
30 < 35	M1 (8%)	M1 (8%)					
35 < 40	M1 (8%)	M1 (8%)					
40 < 45			M1 (8%)				
45 < 50				M1 (8%)	M2 (15%)		
50 < 55					M2 (15%)	M1 (8%)	
					B3 (60%)	B1 (20%)	
55 < 60					M1 (8%)	M1 (8%)	
							B1 (20%)

Note: [1] See table 7.9. The total number of MoF retirees is 13, total number of BoJ retirees is 5.

Table 7.11. *Profile of MoF/BoJ retirees on the boards of trust banks, 1975–1993*[1]

Age at leaving	Number of years at the MoF/BoJ			
the MoF/BoJ	15 < 20	20 < 25	25 < 30	30 < 35
40 < 45	M1 (20%)			
	B1 (11%)	B3 (33%)		
45 < 50		M1 (20%)	M1 (20%)	
		B1 (11%)	B1 (11%)	
50 < 55			M1 (20%)	M1 (20%)
			B3 (33%)	

Note: [1] See table 7.9. The total number of MoF retirees is 5, total number of BoJ retirees is 9.

began working at these banks. This could be explained by the movement of a relatively large number of young ex-MoF officials on to the board of Nippon Credit Bank in the early sixties, which seems to have been related to its establishment in 1957. In addition, all retirees from the BoJ on the boards of the long-term credit banks left the BoJ after age 50, which compares with a percentage of 69% in the case of former MoF officials.

The MoF and BoJ *amakudari kanryō* on the boards of trust banks, as shown in table 7.11, were mostly employed for between 20 and 30 years

Table 7.12. *Profile of MoF/BoJ retirees on the boards of regional banks, 1975–1993*[1]

Age at leaving the MoF/BoJ	Number of years at the MoF/BoJ							
	0 < 5	5 < 10	10 < 15	15 < 20	20 < 25	25 < 30	30 < 35	>35
≤ 25	M1 (1%)	M1 (1%)						
25 < 30		M3 (3%)						
30 < 35		B1 (1%) M1 (1%)	B1 (1%) M1 (1%)					
35 < 40								
40 < 45				M4 (4%) B2 (2%)	M3 (3%) B3 (3%)	B1 (1%)		
45 < 50		M1 (1%)		M2 (2%)	M17 (17%) B6 (6%)	M8 (8%) B12 (12%)	M1 (1%)	
50 < 55					M3 (3%)	M29 (29%) B40 (40%)	M18 (18%) B20 (20%)	M1 (1%) B2 (2%)
55 < 60					B1 (1%)	M1 (1%)	M4 (4%) B8 (8%)	M1 (1%) B1 (1%)
>60						M1 (1%)		B1 (1%)

Note: [1] See table 7.9. The total number of MoF retirees is 101, total number of BoJ retirees is 99.

by the MoF/BoJ and left predominantly at ages between 45 and 55 years (80% of the MoF retirees and 55% of the BoJ retirees), although the concentration in the '25 < 30'/'50 < 55' cell is less than at the city and long-term credit banks. Also in contrast with the situation at the city and long-term credit banks is the presence on the boards of trust banks of a minority of both MoF and BoJ ex-bureaucrats who left the MoF and BoJ at an age above 50 (40% of the MoF retirees and 33% of the BoJ retirees).

The background of former MoF and BoJ staff members on the boards of regional banks, as presented in table 7.12, shows a relative dominance of MoF and BoJ retirees in the '25 < 30 years at the MoF/BoJ' and the '50 < 55 years of retirement age' intervals. In fact, respectively 29% and 40% of the MoF and BoJ *amakudari kanryō* were employed between 25 and 30 years by the MoF/BoJ and left at an age between 50 and 55 years. Furthermore, also in accordance with the situation at the city and long-term credit banks, was a majority presence of former MoF and BoJ officials with a retirement age over 50 (58% of the MoF and 73% of the BoJ retirees).

In conclusion, with the exception of the trust banks, I have found a relative dominance of MoF and BoJ *amakudari kanryō* who retired at ages between 50 and 55 years and worked for between 25 and 30 years at the MoF/BoJ, and an absolute dominance of MoF and BoJ retirees on the boards of private banks who retired from these organisation at ages over 50 years. Clearly, the majority of former MoF and BoJ staff members on the boards of city, long-term credit and regional banks left at the end of a regular career at the MoF and BoJ and thus can be interpreted as 'real' retirees. I have also found examples of retirement at relatively early ages, of which at least some are, in my view, as discussed before, examples of bureaucratic intervention (or ex-post monitoring). It is also noteworthy that at the groups of the city and regional banks similar numbers of both MoF and BoJ retirees were employed in board positions: the city banks employed a total number of 20 MoF and 25 BoJ *amakudari kanryō*, the regional banks 101 against 99. However, I have found no evidence of implicit or explicit agreements between the MoF and BoJ regarding the allocation of post-retirement positions at these banks.

Regarding career management, the existence of 'only MoF' and 'only BoJ' groups of banks as reported in table 7.2 and the high succession rates at these groups have already been mentioned. To investigate the second element of career management in relation to *amakudari*, i.e. the succession of retired MoF and BoJ bureaucrats to the boards of city, long-term credit, trust and regional banks by other former bureaucrats, I have constructed table 7.13. This table presents the strictly and broadly defined succession rates for MoF/BoJ retirees who were employed by

Table 7.13. *Succession rates of MoF/BoJ retirees on the boards of major banks, 1975–1993*[1]

	MoF		BoJ	
	SSR	SBR	SSR	SBR
City banks				
Taiyo Kobe Bank	50%	50%	0%	0%
Sanwa Bank	0%	0%	0%	0%
Tokai Bank	—[2]	—[2]	50%	50%
Kyowa Bank	0%	0%	40%	40%
Saitama Bank	100%	100%	66.7%	66.7%
Bank of Tokyo	100%	100%	100%	100%
Hokkaido Takushoku Bank	0%	50%	—[2]	—[2]
Long-term credit banks				
Industrial Bank of Japan	100%	100%	—[2]	—[2]
Long-Term Credit Bank of Japan	66.7%	66.7%	100%	100%
Nippon Credit Bank	25%	25%	100%	100%
Trust banks				
Mitsubishi Trust Bank	—[2]	—[2]	0%	100%
Sumitomo Trust Bank	—[2]	—[2]	0%	0%
Chuo Trust Bank	0%	0%	66.7%	66.7%
Nippon Trust Bank	100%	100%	—[2]	—[2]
Regional banks				
Bank of Yokohama	66.7%	100%	100%	100%
Chiba Bank	100%	100%	0%	0%
Hokuriku Bank	50%	100%	—[2]	—[2]
Joyo Bank	0%	0%	100%	100%
Ashikaga Bank	50%	50%	—[2]	—[2]
Bank of Fukuoka	—[2]	—[2]	0%	50%
Hiroshima Bank	0%	0%	—[2]	—[2]
Hachijuni Bank	—[2]	—[2]	0%	0%
Gunma Bank	100%	100%	100%	100%
Chugoku Bank	0%	0%	—[2]	—[2]
Juroku Bank	0%	0%	100%	100%
Bank of Kyoto	0%	40%	100%	100%
Shiga Bank	0%	0%	0%	0%
Kiyo Bank	100%	100%	100%	100%
San-In Godo Bank	—[2]	—[2]	0%	0%
Hyakugo Bank	0%	0%	0%	0%
Higo Bank	—[2]	—[2]	100%	100%
Ogaki Kyoritsu Bank	100%	100%	0%	0%
Hokkoku Bank	0%	0%	—[2]	—[2]
Tokyo Tomin Bank	0%	100%	100%	100%
Toho Bank	—[2]	—[2]	0%	0%
Kagoshima Bank	—[2]	—[2]	66.7%	66.7%
Musashino Bank	50%	50%	66.7%	66.7%

Table 7.13. (*cont.*)

	MoF		BoJ	
	SSR	SBR	SSR	SBR
Bank of Osaka	100%	100%	100%	100%
Shikoku Bank	50%	50%	$-^2$	$-^2$
Chiba Kogyo Bank	0%	0%	0%	50%
Oita Bank	$-^2$	$-^2$	33.3%	33.3%
Yamanashi Chuo Bank	$-^2$	$-^2$	0%	0%
Eighteenth Bank	0%	0%	0%	0%
Awa Bank	$-^2$	$-^2$	50%	100%
Aomori Bank	0%	0%	100%	100%
Ikeda Bank	66.7%	66.7%	100%	100%
Senshu Bank	$-^2$	$-^2$	100%	100%
Shinwa Bank	40%	60%	50%	100%
Michinoku Bank	100%	100%	0%	0%
Bank of Saga	100%	100%	0%	0%
Miyazaki Bank	$-^2$	$-^2$	0%	0%
Bank of the Ryukyus	0%	0%	$-^2$	$-^2$
Mie Bank	50%	50%	$-^2$	$-^2$
Kanto Bank	$-^2$	$-^2$	0%	0%
Ugo Bank	$-^2$	$-^2$	0%	0%
Shonai Bank	$-^2$	$-^2$	0%	0%
Tottori Bank	100%	100%	$-^2$	$-^2$
Tohoku Bank	$-^2$	$-^2$	0%	0%
Chikuho Bank	0%	100%	$-^2$	$-^2$
Toyama Bank	50%	50%	$-^2$	$-^2$

Notes: [1] SSR is the strictly defined succession rate (succession within ± one year). SBR is the broadly defined succession rate (succession within ± two years). Banks where no MoF and BoJ *amakudari kanryō* left during the period 1975–1993 (for example Daiwa Bank, 77 Bank) are omitted, as are banks active for only for a small number of years during the period 1975–1993.
[2] A dash indicates that there were no MoF or BoJ *amakudari kanryō* on the board or that no MoF or BoJ *amakudari kanryō* left the board during the period 1975–1993.

these banks from 1975 until 1993.[19] The strictly defined succession rate (SSR) is calculated as the number of times when a new MoF or BoJ *amakudari kanryō* entered the board in the same, previous or following year (i.e. during a time-span of three years) that another former MoF/BoJ official left the board, divided by the number of MoF/BoJ retirees who left the board during the period 1975–1993. For example, if two former

[19] Owing to the large number of missing years in the coverage of the Second Tier regional banks in this chapter, these banks are not included in the analysis.

BoJ staff members left the board and only one new BoJ retiree joined it in the previous, same or following year, the SSR would be 50%. The broadly defined succession rate (SBR) is similar to the SSR with the difference that the new entries take place in the same, previous two or following two years (a time-span of five years). I have found for a large number of banks SSRs and SBRs of 100%, which means continuous succession of MoF and BoJ *amakudari kanryō* on the boards of private banks by other former MoF and BoJ staff members. For example, the former Bank of Tokyo was an obvious landing spot for former MoF/BoJ officials for career management purposes, with succession rates of 100% for both MoF and BoJ retirees. Major banks with SSRs and SBRs of 100% for MoF *amakudari kanryō* were the former Saitama Bank, the Industrial Bank of Japan and Nippon Trust Bank. In the case of retirees from the BoJ, banks with SSRs and SBRs of 100% included the smaller long-term credit banks, i.e. the Long-Term Credit Bank of Japan and Nippon Credit Bank. It must be emphasised that some banks which show a clear dominance of either MoF or BoJ *amakudari kanryō* experienced very low succession rates. For example, during the period 1975–1993 Chiba Bank consistently employed BoJ retirees. However, during this period only one former BoJ official left, and he was not succeeded by another BoJ retiree, so the succession rate was 0%. It is clear that a low succession rate is not necessarily an indication of a lack of dominance by either MoF or BoJ *amakudari kanryō* on the board of the respective bank.

Third, I have found an explicit linking of functions in the organisation of the MoF and BoJ and at private banks that provides further support for the hypothesis that *amakudari* was used for career management purposes during the period 1975–1993. MoF and BoJ staff members who retired from specific high-ranking functions (such as Administrative Vice-Minister at the MoF) were frequently employed in specific functions on the boards of certain private banks. In numerous cases there seems to have been an explicit link between the specific executive position of the *amakudari kanryō* at the bank and his last function at the MoF or BoJ. I have found many examples of this matching of functions during the sample period that runs from 1975 until 1993. A former Vice-Minister of Finance for International Affairs consistently occupied one of the functions of deputy-president, president or chairman at the former Bank of Tokyo. At the same bank, former BoJ staff members, all of whom initially occupied the position of managing director and then became executive director, retired from an executive position at the Personnel Department of the BoJ. The former Taiyo Kobe Bank employed a significant number of former Administrative Vice-Ministers as chairman and/or president. During the whole sample period, a former Administrative Vice-Minister of

Table 7.14. *Last position at the MoF of MoF* amakudari kanryō *on the boards of private banks, 1975–1993*

	City banks	Long-term credit banks	Trust banks	Regional banks
Administrative vice-minister, etc.[1]	8 (40%)	4 (31%)	0	3 (3%)
Director-general[2]	6 (30%)	4 (31%)	1 (20%)	15 (15%)
Deputy director-general	1 (5%)	0	0	2 (2%)
Director division or director department	2 (10%)	2 (15%)	0	11 (11%)
Councillor	2 (10%)	1 (8%)	1 (20%)	9 (9%)
Counsellor	0	0	1 (20%)	0
Director of customs office	0	0	0	3 (3%)
Bank examiner or bank inspector (prudential supervision tasks)	0	0	1 (20%)	13 (13%)
Director tax office, director regional taxation bureau	1 (5%)	0	0	7 (7%)
Director of local finance bureau or other regional office	0	0	1 (20%)	9 (9%)
Rest[3]	0	0	0	24 (24%)
?[4]	0	2 (15%)	0	5 (5%)
Total	20	13	5	101
	(100%)	(100%)	(100%)	(100%)

Notes: [1] Administrative Vice-Minister, Vice-Minister of Finance for International Affairs, Deputy Vice-Minister, Deputy Vice-Minister for Policy Co-ordination, MoF's Representative at the Policy Board of the BoJ and the Special Advisor to the Minister of Finance.
[2] Includes the Director-General (DG) of Tokyo Customs, DG Mint Bureau, DG Printing Bureau and the Commissioner of the National Tax Administration Agency.
[3] Includes positions such as: secondment to Economic Planning Agency, officer for research on banking, director tax business tax office, deputy-director division, manager division, function at local finance bureau, function at regional taxation office, deputy-director department, function at Banking Bureau, chief clerk at local finance bureau, function in finance division, director of Tokyo Office-Mint Bureau.
[4] Last function not known.

the MoF continuously occupied the position of auditor at the Industrial Bank of Japan. This linking of functions also existed at numerous regional banks. From 1977 onwards, former Administrative Vice-Ministers filled the highest executive position at the Bank of Yokohama. At Chiba Bank, former Directors of departments and Executive Directors of the BoJ continuously occupied the top positions on the board. In general, with very few exceptions, former BoJ staff members who obtained the number one or number two executive positions on the board of a regional bank retired from the BoJ as Director of a department (*kyokuchō*).

A more structural analysis of the linkage of specific functions is presented in tables 7.14 and 7.15. The tables show an overview of the last function of MoF and BoJ *amakudari kanryō* at the MoF/BoJ for the retirees who moved on to the boards of city, long-term credit, trust and

Table 7.15. *Last position at the BoJ of BoJ* amakudari kanryō *on the boards of private banks, 1975-1993*

	City banks	Long-term credit banks	Trust banks	Regional banks
Governor etc.[1]	0	0	0	0
Executive director etc.[2]	4 (16%)	1 (20%)	1 (11%)	6 (6%)
Director department etc.[3]	10 (40%)	2 (40%)	0	25 (25%)
General manager branches and offices	4 (16%)	0	3 (33%)	8 (8%)
Deputy-director department, deputy general manager of branches and local offices	1 (4%)	0	0	8 (8%)
Director division (chief manager)	1 (4%)	1 (20%)	0	8 (8%)
Bank supervisor, manager of bank supervision department	1 (4%)	0	0	22 (22%)
Rest[4]	2 (8%)	0	1 (11%)	14 (14%)
?[5]	2 (8%)	1 (20%)	4 (44%)	8 (8%)
Total	25 (100%)	5 (100%)	9 (100%)	99 (100%)

Notes: [1] Governor, Senior Deputy-Governor and Deputy-Governor for International Relations.
[2] Executive Director, Executive Auditor and Director of the Governor's Office.
[3] Including Director of the Institute for Monetary and Economic Studies.
[4] Examples are: deputy auditors, advisors, other managers, deputy auditor or manager of a department.
[5] Last function not known.

regional banks during the 1975–1993 period.[20] I have found that relatively large numbers of MoF retirees on the boards of city banks retired from the highest positions at the MoF: 40% were former Administrative Vice-Ministers or occupied a similar function, and 30% retired as Director-General. In total, 85% of the former MoF staff members on the boards of city banks were employed at or above the level of Director of a division or department in their last position at the MoF. A similar situation existed at the long-term credit banks: 77% of the MoF *amakudari kanryō* on the boards of these banks retired from the highest positions at the MoF. Thus, bureaucrats who reached the top at the MoF had a very good chance of landing a top job on the boards of city and long-term credit banks, which are the most important private banks in Japan.

However, the reverse applies to the trust and regional banks: the last functions at the MoF of MoF retirees who entered the boards of these banks were in general at the lower levels in the MoF's organisation. At the trust banks, only 20% of the MoF *amakudari kanryō*'s last functions were at or above the level of Director of a division or department. In the

[20] The specific functions at the MoF and BoJ were explained in appendices 5.2 and 5.3 of chapter 5, respectively.

case of the regional banks, this percentage was 31%. A relatively large number of ex-MoF bureaucrats on the boards of regional banks retired from functions at regional and local MoF institutions such as tax offices, regional taxation bureaus and local finance bureaus. For example, of the 24% shown in the 'Rest' category in table 7.14, most of the MoF *amakudari kanryō* (18%) moved from one of these functions into the boards of regional banks.

As regards the BoJ *amakudari kanryō*, table 7.15 shows that the situation was comparable to the situation of the MoF retirees. That is, relatively more ex-BoJ bureaucrats who retired from the highest functions at the BoJ (at or above the level of Director of a department) occupied positions on the boards of city and long-term credit banks than on the boards of trust and regional banks. The regional banks employed relatively large numbers of former bank supervisors or managers from the BoJ's Bank Supervision Department. In particular this latter finding could have led to agency costs or conflicts of interest ('collusive practices'), which will be discussed in the next chapter.

To conclude, in general most of the MoF and BoJ officials who retired from the highest positions in the bureaucratic 'heaven' 'descended' into new jobs on the boards of the most important Japanese banks, i.e. the city and long-term credit banks. Of course, generally speaking these banks also offered the best conditions in terms of salary, prestige and prospective career development. Thus, the empirical findings indicate the existence of a reward mechanism in both the MoF and BoJ during the period 1975–1993 that was related to the system of *amakudari*.

Fourth and finally, the aspect of bureaucratic career management that involved the hiring of MoF and BoJ retirees for specific functions on the board was evident for a number of banks. For example, since 1980 the Long-Term Credit Bank of Japan consistently employed one former MoF official and one former BoJ official in the low-ranking board function of auditor. During the sample, the MoF-coloured Bank of Yokohama continuously accepted one former BoJ bureaucrat as auditor. At the same time, the BoJ-dominated Chiba Bank always employed one former MoF official who started in the position of managing director and then became executive director. Another example was the smaller Ashikaga Bank, which consistently hired one MoF *amakudari kanryō* as auditor.

All in all, the presented evidence clearly leads to the conclusion that the mechanism of *amakudari* was used by both the MoF and BoJ for career management purposes during the period 1975–1993. That the acceptance of *amakudari* positions was not simply just an individual decision of retiring staff members but a structural element of personnel management at the (semi-)public sector was shown by the 'carrot-and-stick' policy of the BoJ. On the one hand, banks that provided *amakudari* landing spots were rewarded, as the BoJ provided them with relatively more direct credit – the cheapest form of funds – that it could extend solely at its own discretion (various interviews with private bankers and former BoJ staff members, February–May 1995 and October 1998, Tokyo; this is also suggested as a possible incentive mechanism by Horiuchi and Shimizu 1998, p.20). According to various interviewees, this reward mechanism was used in particular during the period when the BoJ enforced direct credit restrictions (window guidance or *madoguchi shidō*), such as described in section 5.5 of chapter 5.[21] On the other hand, the BoJ applied sanctions to banks that did not comply with its *amakudari* policy or treated BoJ retirees on their boards 'disrespectfully'. Various interviewees, from both the private banking sector and the BoJ, described the rather astonishing incident involving Tokai Bank, one of the city banks. When Tokai Bank reprimanded a BoJ *amakudari kanryō* who was employed on its board, allegedly the BoJ reacted furiously by reducing its direct lending to Tokai Bank to zero for the course of one reserve maintenance period (around one month) (interviews with high-ranking Japanese staff of Western commercial banks, June 1993, and with various (former) BoJ staff members, May 1995 and October 1998, Tokyo; the incident is also reported in M.A Suzuki 1992, p.118).

7.5   Comparison of empirical findings with more recent data

This section will compare the empirical findings of the previous section (period 1975–1993) with some of the latest data available on *amakudari* (for 1999). Owing to logistical problems, I have not been able to use the publication *Kinyū Meikan* again. Instead, I have chosen for the yearly overview on *amakudari* positions in the private banking industry the data published by Teikoku Databank. Possible differences in coverage and definitions mean that comparison of the data from both sources should be pursued with caution. For example, it is not clear whether the figures published by Teikoku Databank include advisors and counsellors, the 'hopping birds' (*watari-dori*) who move from one institution to another and, in the case of MoF retirees, former officials who retired from various government tax institutions such as the National Tax Administration Agency, the regional taxation bureaus and tax offices to the boards of private banks. Nevertheless, despite these caveats, comparison of the figures gives some indication, though nothing more, of the trends in the acceptance of positions on the boards of private banks by former MoF and BoJ staff members from 1993 until 1999. In table 7.16 the *amakudari*

---

[21] Horiuchi and Shimizu (1998, p.20), raise the possibility that these restrictions in themselves could have been 'an important reason why banks accepted *amakudari* from the BoJ'.

Table 7.16. *MoF and BoJ* amakudari kanryō *on the boards of private banks, end-March 1999 compared with 1993*

Bank	1999[1] MoF	BoJ	1993[2] MoF	BoJ	Change in total number of amakudari kanryō[3]
Bank of Tokyo–Mitsubishi	–	–	2[4]	1[4]	−2M, −1B
Dai-Ichi Kangyo Bank	–	–	–	–	=
Asahi Bank	–	–	–	1	−1B
Fuji Bank	–	–	–	–	=
Sumitomo Bank	–	–	–	–	=
Daiwa Bank	–	–	1	1	−1M, −1B
Sakura Bank	–	–	1	–	−1M
Sanwa Bank	–	–	–	–	=
Tokai Bank	–	–	–	1	−1B
Industrial Bank of Japan	1	–	1	–	=
Mitsubishi Trust	–	1	–	1	=
Sumitomo Trust	–	–	–	–	=
Mitsui Trust	–	–	–	–	=
Yasuda Trust	–	–	–	–	=
Toyo Trust	–	–	–	–	=
Chuo Trust	–	1	1	1	−1M
Nippon Trust	–	–	1	–	−1M
Bank of Yokohama	1	1	1	1	=
Chiba Bank	1	1	1	3	−2B
Shizuoka Bank	–	–	–	–	=
Hokuriku Bank	1	–	1		=
Joyo Bank	1	–	2	1	−1M, −1B
Ashikaga Bank	–	–	1	–	−1M
Bank of Fukuoka	1	2	1	1	+1B
Hiroshima Bank	1	–	2	–	−1M
Hachijuni Bank	–	1	1	–	−1M, +1B
Gunma Bank	1	1	1	1	=
Chugoku Bank	1	–	1	–	=
Yamaguchi Bank	–	–	–	–	=
Nishi-Nippon Bank	2	1	2	1	=
77 Bank	–	1	–	1	=
Nanto Bank	–	–	–	–	=
Juroku Bank	–	–	1	1	−1M, −1B
Bank of Kyoto	–	1	1	1	−1M
Iyo Bank	–	–	–	–	=
Hokkaido Bank	1	–	3	–	−2M
Hyakujushi Bank	–	–	–	–	=
Daishi Bank	–	–	–	–	=
Shiga Bank	–	2	–	1	+1B
Kiyo Bank	1	1	1	1	=
San-in Godo Bank	–	1	1	2	−1M, −1B
Hyakugo Bank	–	–	1	–	−1M
Suruga Bank	–	–	–	–	=

Table 7.16. (*cont.*)

Bank	1999[1] MoF	BoJ	1993[2] MoF	BoJ	Change in total number of *amakudari kanryō*[3]
Higo Bank	−	1	−	1	=
Ogaki Kyoritsu Bank	−	1	1	1	−1M
Hokkoku Bank	−	−	−	1	−1B
Tokyo Tomin Bank	−	1	1	1	−1M
Toho Bank	−	1	−	2	−1B
Kagoshima Bank	−	1	−	1	=
Musashino Bank	1	−	1	1	−1B
Bank of Osaka	2	−	2	1	−1B
Shikoku Bank	−	−	1	−	−1M
Chiba Kogyo Bank	1	−	1	−	=
Fukui Bank	−	−	−	1	−1B
Oita Bank	−	1	−	1	=
Akita Bank	−	−	−	−	=
Yamanashi Chuo Bank	−	−	−	−	=
Eighteenth Bank	1	1	1	−	−1B
Hokuetsu Bank	−	1	−	−	+1B
Awa Bank	−	1	−	2	−1B
Bank of Iwate	1	−	3	−	−2M
Aomori Bank	1	−	−	1	+1M, −1B
Bank of Ikeda	−	1	1	1	−1M
Senshu Bank	1	1	2	1	−1M
Shinwa Bank	1	1	1	1	=
Michinoku Bank	1	1	1	1	=
Bank of Saga	3	−	2	−	+1M
Miyazaki Bank	−	1	−	1	=
Yamagata Bank	−	−	−	−	=
Bank of the Ryukyus	−	−	−	−	=
Mie Bank	1	−	−	−	+1M
Shimizu Bank	−	−	−	−	=
Bank of Okinawa	1	−	−	−	+1M
Kanto Bank	−	1	1	2	−1M, −1B
Hokuto Bank	1	1	1	2	−1B
Shonai Bank	−	−	−	−	=
Tajima Bank	−	−	−	−	=
Tottori Bank	−	−	1	−	−1M
Tohoku Bank	1	−	3	−	−2M
Chikuho Bank	1	−	1	−	=
Toyama Bank	−	1	1	1	−1M

Notes: [1] Teikoku Databank (1999).
[2] *Nippon Kinyū Meikan* (1993).
[3] Change in number of MoF (M) and BoJ (B) *amakudari kanryō* (1999 compared with 1993). The character = indicates no change.
[4] Bank of Tokyo only.

positions of MoF and BoJ retirees on the boards of city, long-term credit, trust and regional banks – in total 81 banks – are shown for 1993 and 1999 based on respectively *Nippon Kinyū Meikan* and Teikoku Databank. The figures for the failed Hokkaido Takushoku Bank, Nippon Credit Bank and Long-Term Credit Bank of Japan, which employed relatively large numbers of *amakudari kanryō*, are not included. All in all, the general trend seems to indicate a significant drop in the presence of former MoF and BoJ staff members on the boards of the major private banks. Among the city banks, the number of both MoF and BoJ retirees decreased by four, leaving apparently no former MoF and BoJ officials on the boards of city banks. It has to be said that this development was influenced significantly by the merger between the Bank of Tokyo and Mitsubishi Bank: being one of the more independent and powerful banks related to a *keiretsu* or industrial grouping, Mitsubishi Bank reportedly resisted very strongly the continuing presence of MoF and BoJ *amakudari kanryō* on the board of the new bank, and insisted that incumbent MoF and BoJ retirees on the board of the Bank of Tokyo moved into advisor positions at the Bank of Tokyo-Mitsubishi (see also Brown 1999). The situation at the Industrial Bank of Japan, which is the only long-term credit bank reported, remained unchanged. Among the trust banks, retired MoF officials disappeared completely from the boards; only two former BoJ staff members maintained a position. The situation at the regional banks also points at a considerable decrease in the number of MoF and BoJ *amakudari kanryō*: the total numbers of MoF and BoJ retirees on their boards dropped by, respectively, 22 and 15 in 1999 compared with 1993. On the other hand, certain regional banks experienced an increase of these officials, by a total of four for both the MoF and BoJ. Taking all banks into account, the comparison between 1999 and 1993 also leads to the conclusion that the mechanism of *amakudari* in the private banking industry was characterised by a strong pattern of continuity: at almost half (39) of the 81 banks that are reported in table 7.16, nothing changed in a time-span of six years.

7.6   Conclusions

As was discussed in chapter 3 and shown in chapter 6, the phenomenon of *amakudari* is one of the most delicate topics in the ongoing debate about the specific nature of the Japanese political-economic system and the functioning of the Japanese government bureaucracy. The acceptance of highly paid jobs after retirement by former government bureaucrats raises suspicious feelings among the general public and media of possible conflicts of interest and collusive practices. Of course, the delicate nature

Table 7.17. *Movement of MoF* amakudari kanryō *into private financial institutions, 1968–1993*

	Shinkin banks	*Sogo* banks/Second Tier regional banks	Regional banks	City, long-term credit and trust banks	Securities firms
1968–1969	22	10	5	3	2
1970–1974	82	24	8	2	9
1975–1979	103	18	7	3	11
1980–1984	107	18	5	8	19
1985–1989	106	13	10	7	27
1990–1993	95	16	8	3	19
Totals	515	99	43	26	87

Source: Yamori and Fujiwara (1995), p.6.

of *amakudari* also obstructs independent and objective research. However, as is shown by a relatively small number of empirical studies such as reported in this chapter, this research is certainly not impossible. The data on *amakudari* positions can be found, and the analysis presented in this chapter provides a number of sources that can be used to conduct in-depth empirical research.

The analysis in this chapter has also shown that despite the enormous changes in the Japanese financial system during the years 1975–1993, the presence of MoF and BoJ *amakudari kanryō* on the boards of private banks during this period was characterised by a pattern of continuity. Furthermore, it was also demonstrated that the traditional general interpretations of *amakudari* cannot explain convincingly the presence of MoF and BoJ retirees in the highest executive functions of private banks. The movement of former MoF and BoJ staff members into these functions can only be explained at the firm level, and involves elements of patterned equalisation, bureaucratic intervention and career management.[22] In my view, the general explanations of *amakudari* at the macro level by the various schools that were presented in chapter 3 need to be supplemented or even replaced by studies at the micro level. Only then will it be possible to solve the fundamental differences of opinion regarding the basic role and functioning of the Japanese government bureaucracy and its post-retirement employment system.

Finally, comparison of the figures on *amakudari* positions in the private banking industry between 1999 and 1993, despite being possibly

---

[22] Another explanation has been presented in Katayama (2000), p.283, where it is asserted that 'the government has also sent *amakudari* bureaucrats to private banks as a form of government sanction imposed on those who do not obey government regulations'.

flawed by inconsistencies in definitions and coverage owing to the use of
different sources, leads to the conclusion that the presence of MoF and
BoJ on the boards of private banks has decreased significantly in recent
years. Thus, the increasing criticism of *amakudari* in Japanese society
and the measures adopted in the second half of the nineties by both the
MoF and BoJ to limit the acceptance of post-retirement jobs in the private banking sector by their staff members (see chapters 5 and 6) seem
to have worked to some extent at least. Again, it has to be emphasised
that this conclusion is only tentative and that further research is needed.
For example, I have not investigated the possible existence of substitution
effects, such as an increase of *amakudari* positions at research institutes
affiliated with banks, at other private financial institutions such as securities firms, pension funds and foreign financial institutions located
in Japan, and at the smallest private sector financial institutions such
as *shinkin* banks and credit co-operatives. Yamori and Fujiwara (1995)
report that large numbers of MoF officials descended into *shinkin* banks
compared with other private financial institutions (see table 7.17). More
specifically, over a 25-year period, out of a total of 770 MoF officials who
accepted post-retirement positions at private financial institutions, 515
or 67% moved into *shinkin* banks. Furthermore, the reported decline in
the number of MoF and BoJ *amakudari kanryō* on the boards of private
banks should not be misinterpreted as signalling the end of the system of
post-retirement employment at the Japanese government bureaucracy in
general or *amakudari* in particular. This will be discussed in chapter 9.
In the meantime, chapter 8 will be devoted to a quantitative investigation
of the determinants of the inflow of MoF and BoJ retirees in the private
banking sector. This analysis will shed light on the relevance of the explanation of *amakudari* in terms of patterned equalisation, bureaucratic
intervention and career management that was presented in the previous
paragraphs. It will also reveal some of the negative aspects of *amakudari*,
in particular the possible existence of collusive practices that undermined
the effectiveness of Japanese prudential policy during the period 1975–
1993 and promoted the Japanese banking crisis.

8   *Amakudari* and the performance of Japanese banks

> To understand everything must mean to know nothing.
>
> Old Buddhist saying

8.1   Introduction

The objective of this chapter is to investigate further quantitatively the three aspects of the explanation of the presence of MoF and BoJ *amakudari kanryō* on the boards of private banks for the period 1975–1999 as described in chapter 7: patterned equalisation (or 'buying influence'), bureaucratic intervention or ex-post monitoring in the context of prudential policy, and career management.[1] These three elements will be formulated as hypotheses that will be tested using econometric techniques. Furthermore, I shall pay attention to certain possible negative effects of *amakudari* on the performance of Japanese private banks. In this respect, the element of patterned equalisation will be reformulated into a more negative version that departs from the notion that equalisation attempts could possibly lead to collusive practices involving former MoF and BoJ officials and private banks. Thus, the first hypothesis will concentrate on the behaviour of banks in terms of agency costs. This hypothesis is in line with Horiuchi and Shimizu (1998), Hanazaki and Horiuchi (1998) and Yamori (1998), where it is concluded that the mechanism of *amakudari* has led to 'cosy' relationships between supervisors and banks that most likely have undermined the effectiveness of Japanese prudential policy. The hypothesis can be explained as follows. Banks in trouble bid for the services of well-connected officials from the MoF/BoJ in order to receive support or regulatory forbearance. These retired senior officials have the respect of their former subordinates at the MoF/BoJ and still wield much influence over their actions. Troubled banks are willing to

---

[1] This chapter draws heavily on joint work with Wolter H.J. Hassink. An abridged version of the chapter is forthcoming in the *Journal of the Japanese and International Economies*. Helpful comments by two anonymous referees are highly appreciated.

pay the highest 'rewards' to the former MoF/BoJ officials – that is to offer them *amakudari* positions – because regulatory forbearance is much more valuable to them than to healthy banks. Hence, this first hypothesis predicts that poorly performing banks are the most successful in persuading these retirees to join their boards. In addition, troubled banks are generally willing to take more risks, but usually prudential supervisors would stop them. The retirees could try to persuade the supervisory authorities to bend the rules and to allow them to take risks such as extending more loans to relatively risky industries in order to try to restore profitability. Hence, the hypothesis predicts that there the inflow of *amakudari kanryō* has a negative impact on the bank's financial performance.

The second hypothesis departs from the element of bureaucratic intervention. In this view, the system of *amakudari* is used for monitoring purposes, since the MoF and the BoJ are supervisory agencies involved in the implementation of prudential policy. The inflow of former MoF or BoJ staff members is a signal to deposit-holders and other stakeholders of the bank that the supervisory authorities are actively supporting the troubled bank. Hence, *amakudari* is used to restore confidence in the bank's financial continuity ('ex-post monitoring'). This second hypothesis predicts a negative correlation between a bank's financial situation and the inflow of *amakudari kanryō*. A second implication of this monitoring hypothesis is that there should be a lagged improvement in the performance of the bank following the inflow of the MoF/BoJ retirees.

Finally, the third hypothesis reflects the aspect of career management in my explanation of *amakudari* as presented in the previous chapter. According to this hypothesis, the system of *amakudari* is used solely as an instrument for career development and retirement purposes at the MoF and BoJ. It implies that there the inflow of *amakudari* officials on to the boards of private banks has no effect on the financial situation of these banks.

All in all, this chapter will provide an in-depth analysis of the three hypotheses. Section 8.2 describes the relationship between *amakudari*, prudential policy and corporate governance, which is relevant for the second hypothesis covering the element of bureaucratic intervention in particular, and the various hypotheses are discussed in more detail. In section 8.3, I explain the data and the dependent and independent variables. Section 8.4 presents the estimates of the determinants of *amakudari* appointments and analyses the results. Section 8.5 investigates whether the performance of banks improved after the inflow of MoF and BoJ retirees. In section 8.6, I discuss certain detrimental effects of the system of *amakudari*, and present evidence that it has been responsible at least to some extent for the Japanese banking crisis of the nineties. Section 8.7 concludes.

8.2   *Amakudari,* prudential policy and corporate governance

My second hypothesis, which suggests that *amakudari* is used as a form of bureaucratic intervention, relates to the monitoring of private banks by the Japanese monetary authorities; in other words the implementation of prudential policy. In this respect the MoF and BoJ could use *amakudari* in the following ways. First, the presence of retired MoF and BoJ officials on the boards of private banks could be helpful in exercising the ex-ante and interim monitoring functions discussed in section 4.3 of chapter 4. In this so-called 'stock' approach, MoF and BoJ *amakudari kanryō* operate as 'watchdogs', who monitor the banks' management and financial development from the inside. Second, in the ex-post monitoring sense, officials of the MoF and BoJ could be sent as 'troubleshooters' to the threatened bank in cases of acute financial crisis or threat of insolvency. This dispatching of monetary bureaucrats could be made public as a signalling effect, in order to restore confidence. As I have discussed in the previous chapters, this is the case regarding the *amakudari* appointments, which are made public in the media and published in reference books. The use of *amakudari* for ex-post monitoring purposes – in other words, a form of intervention by the supervisory authorities – could be interpreted as a 'flow' approach.

Both the ex-ante and interim monitoring ('stock' approach) and ex-post monitoring ('flow' approach) by outsiders appointed to the boards of Japanese firms have been investigated in depth in various studies. Following a stock approach to examine the monitoring of private firms by their main banks, Sheard (1994) found that main banks' executives who are on the boards of their client firms perform ex-ante and interim monitoring functions. Morck and Nakamura (1992), Kaplan and Minton (1994), and Kang and Shivdasani (1995) have investigated the ex-post monitoring by main banks in the form of new appointments of their executives on the boards of client firms.

The possibility of monitoring functions being exercised by former MoF and BoJ officials on the boards of private banks has been investigated as well, particularly during the second half of the nineties (Okazaki 1995; Yamori and Fujiwara 1995; van Rixtel and Hassink 1996a, 1996b; Fujiwara and Yamori 1997; Horiuchi and Shimizu 1998). Most of these studies found evidence of a relationship in one form or another between *amakudari* positions on the boards of private banks and the implementation of prudential policy. Therefore, in this chapter I shall concentrate in more detail on the ex-post monitoring by MoF and BoJ *amakudari kanryō* on the boards of private banks. This element of prudential policy has been formulated as the second hypothesis. Ex-post monitoring involves the sending of new retirees to these banks, and covers both new appointments and the replacement of incumbent retirees leaving the boards of private banks.

I have discussed in section 4.3 of chapter 4 a number of specific characteristics of the corporate governance system in Japan, such as the *keiretsu* or industrial groupings and the main bank system, which could have implications for the implementation of prudential policy by the supervisory authorities and thus also for the formulation of the second hypothesis of bureaucratic intervention. This discussion resulted in the development of a model of 'hierarchical delegated monitoring', which sees the public monitors (monetary authorities) and private monitors (*keiretsu* and main banks) as complementary institutions regarding the ex-post monitoring of private banks ('the monitoring of the monitors'). Following this model, I argue that besides the (ex-post) monitoring or prudential policy implemented by the public monitors, monitoring of Japanese private banks could be exercised by the *keiretsu* and main banks as well.

The ex-post monitoring or 'flow' approach that I follow in this chapter can be interpreted in two ways: one way could be to measure the actual inflow of retirees, another could be a 'binary' approach, i.e. whether or not these retirees enter the boards of private banks. I use the latter approach, which is also used by Kaplan and Minton (1994) and Kang and Shivdasani (1995).

The form of the equation that will be estimated is as follows. The number of new MoF and BoJ retirees appointed at some individual bank (A) may be influenced by:

$$A_{it} = \alpha_0 + \alpha_1 x_{1i,t} + \alpha_2 x_{2i,t} + \alpha_3 x_{3i,t} \tag{8.1}$$

Index i refers to bank i and index t refers to period t. α_0 is a constant. α_n, n = 1,2,3, are vectors of coefficients on the independent variables x_k, k = 1,2,3. I classify the independents as belonging to one of the following groups: the performance variables (x_1), the relationship variables (x_2) and the governance variables (x_3).

Equation (8.1) will be used to test the three hypotheses. If the appointment of MoF/BoJ retirees is initiated by the banks because they experience financial distress then a negative impact of the performance variables on the appointment of new retirees should be found (hypothesis 1: 'buying influence').[2] If the inflow of *amakudari kanryō* is because of any financial distress at the individual bank, then this negative

---

[2] With the exception of bank lending, where a positive relationship should be expected.

impact should be observed as well (hypothesis 2: ex-post monitoring). If the system of *amakudari* is used as a system of retirement then the coefficients on x_1 will be zero (hypothesis 3: *amakudari* as a reward system from the perspective of career management).

Equation (8.1) will be controlled for so-called relationship effects (x_2) and governance effects (x_3). As regards the former, certain individual banks may have a better relationship with the monetary authorities than others. Thus, retirees from the MoF and BoJ may be appointed more easily to the boards of these banks. The relationship variables consist of variables representing common university backgrounds between top MoF and BoJ officials on the one hand and private banks' executives on the other, whether a bank's headquarters is located close to Tokyo and whether a bank was previously owned or controlled by the government ('public' bank). The governance variables represent the main bank and *keiretsu* systems. I include five dummy variables, i.e. one for banks that operate as a main bank, one for those banks which have a main bank, two for banks which maintain links with a *keiretsu* and one for banks that are the leading bank of a *keiretsu*.

The first and second hypotheses will be further investigated by considering what happens to the financial results of banks after the appointment of a new MoF/BoJ retiree. This will be measured by:

$$x_{1,i,t} = \sum_{j=1}^{K} \beta_j A_{i,t-j} \qquad (8.2)$$

The performance of the bank is measured by information on developments in profits, solvency, liquidity, deposits and lending. A positive impact of the inflow of *amakudari kanryō* on these performance variables in (8.2) confirms the hypothesis about 'buying influence'. Furthermore, it implies that the second hypothesis covering ex-post monitoring cannot be rejected.

The bank's attitude towards risk may be measured by loans to risky industries such as the construction and real estate sectors. A positive impact of the inflow of MoF/BoJ retirees on lending to risky industries in (8.2) has different implications for the hypotheses. According to the first hypothesis, the troubled bank may persuade the supervisory authorities to allow it to increase its risky lending as a desperate attempt to improve profitability ('go-for-broke' behaviour'; see Herring 1998, pp.21ff.). So, a positive impact of the inflow of *amakudari kanryō* on risky loans implies that the first hypothesis cannot be rejected. A positive impact means that the second hypothesis is rejected, since a growth of risky lending is at odds with the prudential policy goals of the monetary authorities.

8.3   Data, dependent and independent variables

In this section, I shall discuss the data, the dependent variables and the independent variables. The latter consist of a number of governance, performance and relationship variables. (See appendix 8.1 for definitions.)

Data and dependent variables

The analysis uses three different samples. The first sample includes the four largest groups of private banks, i.e. the city, long-term credit, trust and regional banks. The banks are observed for the period 1977–1993. Basically, the second sample follows the same set of banks as the previous one. The data set contains additional information on loans to three risky industries (real estate, construction and non-bank financial companies). However, observations on the long-term credit banks are not available. This data set covers the period 1981–1993. The third set of data consists of observations for the five largest groups of banks in Japan: city, long-term credit, trust, regional and Second Tier regional banks.[3] It covers the period 1989–1993, when the 'bubble' economy collapsed. As discussed in chapter 6, this development had a huge impact on the Second Tier regional banks in particular. Furthermore, the analysis will be based on balanced panels. Thus, the number of banks in each year is constant for each panel; hence, banks that merged in a specific year are excluded. In addition, the samples do not include non-listed banks, about which only limited information is available. As a result, the number of banks used in the analysis is 77 in the first sample, 74 in the second one and 115 in the third. The data on the MoF and BoJ retirees on the boards of private banks are obtained from the same source as in chapter 7, i.e. the publication *Nippon Kinyū Meikan*. Again, a strict definition of the board of directors is followed, which does not include the functions of advisors and counsellors.

The inflow of MoF/BoJ retirees on to the boards during a certain period may have various definitions. As discussed in the previous section, I use the 'binary' approach used in Kaplan and Minton (1994), for which the following two definitions will be applied. First, the variable A in equation (8.1) has the value 0 but becomes 1 if one or more former MoF or BoJ staff member(s) is/are appointed to one or more of the functions of chairman, deputy-chairman, president, deputy-president, executive director, managing director, director, advisory director and auditor in a specific year. This variable is denoted by NEWALL. Because in the majority of appointment years only one former MoF or BoJ official is

---

[3] Because of lack of data regarding lending to risky industries, the Industrial Bank of Japan is not included.

Table 8.1. *Number of former MoF and BoJ staff members on the boards of private banks in the years t − 1 and t, 1977–1993*[1]

t − 1	t					
	0	1	2	3	4	5
0	402	15	1			
1	15	272	32	1		
2		27	329	24		
3		2	23	124	9	
4		1	2	6	17	1
5				2	1	3

Note: [1] Total number of cases = 1,309 (77 banks, 17 years).

appointed, the dependent variable NEWALL takes the value 1 for both single and multiple appointments. Thus, NEWALL takes the value 1 for all appointments of MoF and BoJ retirees, including those in which a new MoF or BoJ retiree replaces an incumbent MoF/BoJ-retiree board member. Second, I use another variable, NEW, to measure the inflow of *amakudari kanryō* A in equation (8.1). The variable NEW is equal to NEWALL, except for the cases in which a new MoF or BoJ retiree replaces an incumbent or old MoF/BoJ retiree. That is, the difference between NEWALL and NEW is that NEW takes the value 0 for outside appointments in which one former MoF or BoJ staff member replaces or succeeds another MoF or BoJ staff member already present on the board. The dependent variable NEW is used because replacements of one or more MoF/BoJ staff members could take place for other than intervention or prudential policy reasons. For example, as shown in chapter 7, the MoF and BoJ seem to have 'secured' a number of positions for their retirees on the boards of several banks. Basically, NEWALL registers gross flows of MoF and BoJ retirees, whereas NEW measures net flows. In the following analysis, both NEWALL and NEW are used as measures of A in equation (8.1).

Table 8.1 presents information on the presence of BoJ and MoF retirees on the boards of private banks during the period 1977–1993. Since during this period no bank ever employed more than five former MoF and/or BoJ staff members, the number of retired MoF and BoJ officials employed by a specific bank in a particular year ranges between 0 and 5. The area to the right of the diagonal reflects the cases in which new MoF/BoJ retirees enter the boards, i.e. are the cases in which the dependent variable NEW takes the value 1. I find the following cases (t − 1, t) in which one or more

Table 8.2. *Dependent variables NEWALL$_{i,t}$ and NEW$_{i,t}$*

NEWALL$_{i,t}$ = 1 if:		NEW$_{i,t}$ = 1 if:	
year t − 1	year t	year t − 1	year t
$y_i^1 = 0$	$y_i > 0$	$y_i = 0$	$y_i > 0$
$y_i = n$	$y_i > n$	$y_i = n$	$y_i > n$
$y_i = n$	$y_i = n$ but outside succession		

Note: [1] y_i is the number of MoF and BoJ retirees on the board of bank i.

MoF/BoJ retirees enter the boards: $(0, 1) = 15$, $(0, 2) = 1$, $(1, 2) = 32$, $(1, 3) = 1$, $(2, 3) = 24$, $(3, 4) = 9$ and $(4, 5) = 1$, resulting in a total of 83 cases in which NEW is 1. Thus, only in two cases two MoF/BoJ retirees were appointed simultaneously to the board of a specific bank in a particular year.

Table 8.2 presents an overview of the specification of the variables NEWALL and NEW. Furthermore, investigation of the data shows that for the first data set (1977–1993), out of 1,309 observations (77 banks per year), there are 133 cases where NEWALL is equal to 1, and 83 with NEW equal to 1. So, during this period, a recently retired MoF or BoJ staff member replaced on 50 occasions an incumbent MoF or BoJ retiree already present on the board. For the second data set (1981–1993), with 74 banks per year generating a total of 962 observations, NEWALL = 1 in 100 cases and NEW = 1 in 62 cases, leaving 38 cases of outside replacement. Finally, the third data set (1989–1993), with 115 banks per year (total of 575 observations), yields for NEWALL and NEW, respectively, 71 and 44 cases with the value 1.

Independent variables

The independent variables in equation (8.1) may be classified towards a group of performance variables, a group of relationship variables and a group of governance variables. I first shall discuss all independent variables in more detail. Appendix 8.1 gives the exact definitions and sources of all variables. Tables 8.3, 8.4 and 8.5 contain the descriptive statistics of the variables.

Performance variables The performance of individual banks in equation (8.1) will be represented by eight variables: PROFIT, SOLVENCY, LIQUIDITY, DEPOSITS, LOANS, LR, LC and LF.[4]

---

[4] The first data set 1977–1993 contains the variable LOANS. The two other data sets contain the variables LR, LC and LF.

First, a variable PROFIT for profitability is used, which is measured as net return on equity, i.e. net unappropriated profits divided by total stockholders' equity. I expect a negative sign of profit in equation (8.1) for both the first and second hypotheses. Second, an indicator SOLVENCY for bank solvency is used, calculated as the ratio of total stockholders' equity to total assets. The definition of capital includes only core or Tier I capital. The reason for this is that I have not found reliable data on Tier II capital for individual Japanese banks, which includes 45% of their latent gains on securities holdings. Furthermore, the solvency ratios are not weighted for various assets. Again, I expect a negative impact of SOLVENCY in (8.1) for the first two hypotheses. Third, the ratio of banks' liquid assets to total assets is used as an indicator for bank liquidity (LIQUIDITY). Liquid assets are represented by the most liquid assets, i.e. cash and assets due from banks. The liquidity position has a negative impact on the inflow of retirees from the MoF/BoJ, that is a deterioration of a bank's liquidity position would lead to the inflow of *amakudari kanryō* from the MoF/BoJ. Fourth, I take into account deposits as ratio of total assets (DEPOSITS). For both the first and second hypotheses, MoF and BoJ retirees enter banks that show a relatively worse performance in terms of deposits, which could indicate a deterioration of depositors' confidence in the banks' health. Fifth, a variable LOANS is included, i.e. loans as the ratio of total assets, as a general measure of the risky behaviour of each bank. It should be expected that as a form of prudential policy former MoF or BoJ staff members enter banks that show relatively high levels of lending in terms of assets. Finally, to take into account loan exposure to so-called risky sectors, I add for the sample periods 1981–1993 and 1989–1993 the variables LR, LC and LF, which represent lending by individual banks to the real estate, construction and non-bank financial sectors as ratios of their total lending. These variables are included to capture the possible reaction of the monetary authorities to the rise and collapse of the 'bubble' economy, as described in chapter 6. Given that objective and independent estimates of non-performing loans of individual banks hardly exist, the variables LR, LC and LF are taken as proxies for this variable.

In the estimations the performance variables x_1 are specified in first differences, for which the main reason is to capture the dynamics of the relationship that is going to be estimated. That is, the goal is to estimate in which way the inflow of *amakudari kanryō* (i.e. the change in the number of MoF/BoJ retirees on the boards of private banks) is related to the change in the performance variables:[5]

$$\Delta x_{1,t} = x_{1,t} - x_{1,t-1} \qquad\qquad (8.3)$$

[5] Alternative specifications are used in van Rixtel and Hassink (1996a).

Relationship variables Three so-called relationship variables are incorporated in equation (8.1), which represent the existence of specific relations between the MoF and BoJ and the private banking industry: GAKUBATSU, DUMHQ and DUMFGOVTB. The variable GAKUBATSU represents the link between the MoF/BoJ and private banks based on the mechanism of *gakubatsu* – common university backgrounds of government officials and the banks' board members – that was discussed in section 3.4 of chapter 3. It is to be expected that banks employing significant numbers of graduates from the elite universities in their highest executive positions have easier access to and better-established relationships with the monetary authorities. That means that the MoF and BoJ should also be better informed about the actual situation of these banks and consequently should be able to advise their former classmates about required changes in management policy. Thus, I expect that banks which have relatively large numbers of elite universities' graduates on their boards are less likely to experience the entry of MoF and BoJ retirees. To take this relationship into account, the variable GAKUBATSU is constructed, which is the ratio of the number of graduates from the 'Big Five' universities (Tokyo, Hitotsubashi, Kyoto, Keio and Waseda) to the total number of executives in the highest board positions (*jōmukai*, see the previous chapter). The expected sign of GAKUBATSU is negative. The alternative variables TODAI and TODAILAW have been used as well, which are the ratios of the number of graduates from the University of Tokyo and its Law Faculty to the total number of highest executives in the *jōmukai*. As was demonstrated in sections 5.4 and 5.5 of chapter 5 and section 6.4 of chapter 6, the highest functions at both the MoF and BoJ are to a large extent filled by graduates from the University of Tokyo in general and its Law Faculty in particular. Since the estimations using GAKUBATSU, TODAI or TODAILAW did not yield significantly different results only the results for GAKUBATSU will be presented. Second, the dummy variable DUMHQ is used, which is 1 when the headquarters of a bank is located in Tokyo or one of the adjacent prefectures. The expected sign of DUMHQ is negative: the MoF and BoJ should be relatively better informed about banks that are located in the Tokyo region, given the concentration of their supervisory responsibilities in Japan's capital and the availability of information resulting from their informal contacts with the financial services industry, central government and news media, all of which are concentrated in Tokyo. Finally, the dummy variable DUMFGOVTB is included, which takes the value 1 when a bank was formerly owned or directly controlled by the government. Examples are the Bank of Tokyo and Hokkaido Takushoku Bank. Because of these historical ties, these banks possibly still enjoy a 'special' relationship with the MoF and BoJ. That is, to some extent the MoF and BoJ will still feel responsible for the actual development of these banks and consequently will feel more inclined to send their retirees when things have turned for worse (positive sign).

Governance variables Finally, five time-invariant dummy variables that represent governance relationships are used: DUMHMAINB, DUMINFORMAL, DUM8KEI, DUMIMAINB and DUMALKEI. First, to test possible monitoring by main banks (i.e. mainly city and long-term credit banks) of their smaller client banks such as Second Tier regional banks the dummy variable DUMHMAINB (DUM Has MAIN Bank) is constructed, which takes the value 1 for a regional or Second Tier regional bank if this bank has a bank as its main shareholder. Where the main shareholder is represented by stock ownership of employees, DUMHMAINB is 1 if a regional or Second Tier regional bank has a bank as its second largest shareholder. The expected sign of DUMHMAINB is positive: since the focus in the analysis is on ex-post monitoring, the expectation is to find complementary, that is positive, relationships between this variable and the inflow of retirees from the MoF and BoJ. The Japanese system of corporate governance also suggests that the *keiretsu* or industrial groupings could perform monitoring functions of banks. This is investigated by including two dummy variables DUMINFORMAL and DUM8KEI. The dummy variable DUMINFORMAL takes the value 1 if a regional or Second Tier regional bank maintains an informal link with a *keiretsu* such as reported by a main Japanese data-source (*Kigyō Keiretsu Sōran*). The expected sign of DUMINFORMAL is positive: when things at a particular regional or Second Tier regional bank have gone wrong, which implies that the MoF and BoJ have to intervene, the monitoring conducted by the *keiretsu* is supplemented by intervention of the MoF and BoJ. The dummy variable DUM8KEI is 1 if the largest shareholder of a small city, small long-term credit, small trust, regional or Second Tier regional bank is a leading financial firm of one of the seven *keiretsu* (Dai-Ichi Kangyō, Fuyō, Mitsubishi, Mitsui, Sanwa, Sumitomo and Tokai), as explained in section 4.3 of chapter 4, or is the Industrial Bank of Japan. The importance of IBJ in this respect is extensively discussed in Calder (1993). A small bank means (again) a bank that is not the main bank of other banks. The variable DUM8KEI is added to take into account the smaller city, long-term credit and trust banks, whose possible relationship with a *keiretsu* is not fully incorporated in the variable DUMINFORMAL. The expected sign of DUM8KEI is also positive. Furthermore, I assume that the monetary authorities concentrate their supervisory policies on the main banks, given their important monitoring roles. Consequently, it is expected that MoF and BoJ retirees move in particular into banks that operate as main bank. This relationship is investigated by including the following dummy variables. First, the dummy variable DUMIMAINB (DUM Is MAIN Bank) is used, which takes the value 1 for a bank which is the largest shareholder of one or more regional or Second Tier regional banks. Thus, for a bank that is the main bank of a regional or Second Tier regional bank the variable DUMIMAINB takes the value 1, whereas for a regional or Second Tier regional bank that has a main bank the variable DUMHMAINB takes the value 1. The expected sign of DUMIMAINB is positive. Second, I include the dummy variable DUMALKEI that is unity for banks that are a leading bank of one of the seven *keiretsu* and for the Industrial Bank of Japan. The expected sign of DUMALKEI is positive.

Summary statistics are presented in tables 8.3–8.5.

8.4   Empirical results

This section presents the estimation results of equation (8.1) using the two dependent variables NEWALL and NEW for the three sample periods. The empirical equation is formulated as a Probit model. The marginal effects are reported, which are the change in probability for a change in the independent variable.[6] Table 8.6 shows the results for the sample period 1977–1993, which includes the city, long-term credit, trust and regional banks, in total 77 banks for each year. The results for the dependent variable NEWALL (the first column) can be summarised as follows. With respect to the five performance variables, the marginal effects related to profitability and solvency are significant at respectively the 1% and 10% level, both with the negative sign that is in accordance with the first and second hypotheses, i.e. the 'buying influence' and 'ex-post monitoring' hypotheses. To get some feeling for the size of the effect, the change in the probability that corresponds to the range of the independent variable is calculated. The marginal effect of PROFIT of -1.387 implies that the range of observed values (in first differences) of this variable is in accordance with a change of NEWALL of 30 percentage points.[7] For

---

[6] The marginal effect is calculated as the mean of the independent variable using the estimated coefficients of the regressions. To be precise, the marginal effect of the jth independent variable is $\partial \Phi / \partial x_j = \phi(\bar{x} a)x_j$, where a is the vector of the estimated coefficients (the Probit estimates of (8.1)) on the independent variables and $\bar{x}$ is a vector of the averages of all independents.

[7] For continuous independent variables, the increase in Φ is calculated as follows. I change the independent variable by its range and calculate the impact on the change in Φ. The range of PROFIT is equal to 0.2184 units (the difference between the maximum value (0.0783) and the minimum value (-0.1401), as reported in table 8.3). The marginal

Table 8.3. *Summary statistics of the sample 1977–1993*

	Mean	St. dev.	Minimum	Maximum
NEWALL	0.102	0.302	0	1
NEW	0.063	0.244	0	1
Performance variables				
PROFIT	0.0889	0.0310	0.0156	0.2529
SOLVENCY	0.0339	0.0089	0.0132	0.0674
LIQUIDITY	0.0800	0.0570	0.0159	0.3610
DEPOSITS	0.7653	0.1700	0.0231	0.9180
LOANS	0.5997	0.0845	0.2712	0.7679
ΔPROFIT	−0.0043	0.0175	−0.1401	0.0783
ΔSOLVENCY	−0.0001	0.0033	−0.0510	0.0137
ΔLIQUIDITY	−0.0003	0.0218	−0.1162	0.1669
ΔDEPOSITS	−0.00004	0.0261	−0.2919	0.1828
ΔLOANS	−0.0005	0.0287	−0.3335	0.3799
Relationship variables				
GAKUBATSU	0.389	0.245	0	1
DUMHQ	0.299	0.458	0	1
DUMFGOVTB	0.091	0.288	0	1
Governance variables				
DUMHMAINB	0.273	0.446	0	1
DUMINFORMAL	0.260	0.439	0	1
DUM8KEI	0.545	0.498	0	1
DUMIMAINB	0.104	0.305	0	1
DUMALKEI	0.169	0.375	0	1

Keys: NEWALL: 1 if one or more former MoF/BoJ staff members are appointed in the highest positions on the board of a private bank, NEW: see NEWALL but replacements of incumbent ex-MoF/BoJ retirees are not taken into account. PROFIT: net return on equity, SOLVENCY: stockholders' equity/total assets, LIQUIDITY: liquid assets/total assets, DEPOSITS: total deposits/total assets, LOANS: total loans and bills discounted/total assets, GAKUBATSU: number of graduates from elite universities/total executives, DUMHQ: headquarters are close to Tokyo, DUMFGOVTB: bank was formerly owned or controlled by government, DUMHMAINB: bank is main (or second-largest) shareholder, DUMINFORMAL: informal relationship with a *keiretsu*, DUM8KEI: largest shareholder is a leading firm of *keiretsu* or the Industrial Bank of Japan, DUMIMAINB: bank is largest shareholder of regional banks, DUMALKEI: main bank of *keiretsu* or Industrial Bank of Japan.
Total number of observations is 1,309, number of banks is 77, number of years is 17.

SOLVENCY, which has a marginal effect of −4.615, the range in its observed values (in first differences) corresponds to a change in NEWALL of 32 percentage points. The results show no significant results for liquidity,

effect (−1.387) gives the change in Φ for a change in PROFIT. The range of PROFIT corresponds to a change in Φ of 0.2184 × 1.387 × 100% = 30%. For dummy variables, the variation of the probability is equal to the estimated coefficient on the dummy variable.

Table 8.4. *Summary statistics of the sample 1981–1993*

	Mean	St. dev.	Minimum	Maximum
NEWALL	0.104	0.305	0	1
NEW	0.064	0.246	0	1
Performance variables				
PROFIT	0.0816	0.0284	0.0156	0.2529
SOLVENCY	0.0331	0.0080	0.0132	0.0587
LIQUIDITY	0.0826	0.0637	0.0159	0.3610
DEPOSITS	0.7852	0.1341	0.1541	0.9180
LR	0.0722	0.0370	0.0046	0.2725
LC	0.0673	0.0259	0.0079	0.1478
LF	0.0557	0.0436	0.0046	0.2440
ΔPROFIT	−0.0040	0.0175	−0.0975	0.0783
ΔSOLVENCY	0.0004	0.0030	−0.0275	0.0137
ΔLIQUIDITY	−0.0001	0.0232	−0.1162	0.1669
ΔDEPOSITS	−0.00001	0.0268	−0.2919	0.3293
ΔLR	0.0023	0.0068	−0.0318	0.0392
ΔLC	0.0009	0.0050	−0.0138	0.0268
ΔLF	0.0041	0.0118	−0.0621	0.0602
Relationship variables				
GAKUBATSU	0.366	0.234	0	0.976
DUMHQ	0.270	0.444	0	1
DUMFGOVTB	0.054	0.226	0	1
Governance variables				
DUMHMAINB	0.284	0.451	0	1
DUMINFORMAL	0.270	0.444	0	1
DUM8KEI	0.541	0.499	0	1
DUMIMAINB	0.095	0.293	0	1
DUMALKEI	0.162	0.369	0	1

Keys: NEWALL: 1 if one or more former MoF/BoJ staff members are appointed in the highest positions on the board of a private bank, NEW: see NEWALL but replacements of incumbent ex-MoF/BoJ retirees are not taken into account. PROFIT: net return on equity, SOLVENCY: stockholders' equity/total assets, LIQUIDITY: liquid assets/total assets, DEPOSITS: total deposits/total assets, LR: loans to real estate/total loans, LC: loans to construction sector/total loans, LF: loans to non-bank financial sector/total loans, GAKUBATSU: number of graduates from elite universities/total executives, DUMHQ: headquarters are close to Tokyo, DUMFGOVTB: bank was formerly owned or controlled by government, DUMHMAINB: bank is main (or second-largest) shareholder, DUMINFORMAL: informal relationship with a *keiretsu*, DUM8KEI: largest shareholder is a leading firm of *keiretsu* or the Industrial Bank of Japan, DUMIMAINB: bank is largest shareholder of regional banks, DUMALKEI: main bank of *keiretsu* or Industrial Bank of Japan.

Total number of observations is 962, number of banks is 74, number of years is 13.

Table 8.5. *Summary statistics of the sample 1989–1993*

	Mean	St. dev.	Minimum	Maximum
NEWALL	0.123	0.329	0	1
NEW	0.077	0.266	0	1
Performance variables				
PROFIT	0.0683	0.0355	−0.2176	0.3993
SOLVENCY	0.0355	0.0074	0.0111	0.0724
LIQUIDITY	0.0697	0.0543	0.0140	0.3028
DEPOSITS	0.7869	0.1453	0.1541	0.9186
LR	0.0922	0.0485	0.0216	0.3067
LC	0.0761	0.0301	0.0082	0.1623
LF	0.0677	0.0482	0.0067	0.2440
ΔPROFIT	−0.0109	0.0363	−0.2379	0.6953
ΔSOLVENCY	0.0019	0.0039	−0.0275	0.0222
ΔLIQUIDITY	−0.0031	0.0238	−0.1162	0.1073
ΔDEPOSITS	0.0032	0.0334	−0.2919	0.3293
ΔLR	0.0011	0.0082	−0.0371	0.0392
ΔLC	0.0020	0.0064	−0.0228	0.0268
ΔLF	0.0024	0.0141	−0.0621	0.0656
Relationship variables				
GAKUBATSU	0.277	0.228	0	0.935
DUMHQ	0.243	0.430	0	1
DUMFGOVTB	0.052	0.223	0	1
Governance variables				
DUMHMAINB	0.417	0.494	0	1
DUMINFORMAL	0.296	0.457	0	1
DUM8KEI	0.583	0.494	0	1
DUMIMAINB	0.061	0.239	0	1
DUMALKEI	0.070	0.255	0	1

Keys: NEWALL: 1 if one or more former MoF/BoJ staff members are appointed in the highest positions on the board of a private bank, NEW: see NEWALL but replacements of incumbent ex-MoF/BoJ retirees are not taken into account. PROFIT: net return on equity, SOLVENCY: stockholders' equity/total assets, LIQUIDITY: liquid assets/total assets, DEPOSITS: total deposits/total assets, LR: loans to real estate/total loans, LC: loans to construction sector/total loans, LF: loans to non-bank financial sector/total loans, GAKUBATSU: number of graduates from elite universities/total executives, DUMHQ: headquarters are close to Tokyo, DUMFGOVTB: bank was formerly owned or controlled by government, DUMHMAINB: bank is main (or second-largest) shareholder, DUMINFORMAL: informal relationship with a *keiretsu*, DUM8KEI: largest shareholder is a leading firm of *keiretsu* or the Industrial Bank of Japan, DUMIMAINB: bank is largest shareholder of regional banks, DUMALKEI: main bank of *keiretsu* or Industrial Bank of Japan.

Total number of observations is 575, number of banks is 115, number of years is 5.

Table 8.6. *Probit estimates for NEWALL and NEW, sample 1977–1993*

	NEWALL		NEW	
	Marginal effect	t-statistic	Marginal effect	t-statistic
Performance variables				
Δ PROFIT	−1.387	(−3.05)***	−1.225	(−3.60)***
Δ SOLVENCY	−4.615	(−2.05)**	−4.877	(−2.88)***
ΔLIQUIDITY	0.026	(0.06)	−0.363	(−1.07)
ΔDEPOSITS	0.150	(0.46)	0.285	(1.11)
Δ LOANS	0.081	(0.28)	−0.068	(−0.31)
Relationship variables				
GAKUBATSU	−0.117	(−2.34)**	−0.091	(−2.33)**
DUMHQ	0.065	(2.94)***	0.015	(0.89)
DUMFGOVTB	0.110	(2.86)***	0.060	(1.91)*
Governance variables				
DUMHMAINB	0.062	(2.99)**	0.035	(2.18)**
DUMINFORMAL	−0.021	(−1.14)	−0.025	(−1.81)*
DUM8KEI	−0.004	(−0.20)	−0.004	(−0.26)
DUMIMAINB	−0.010	(−0.24)	−0.019	(−0.61)
DUMALKEI	−0.045	(−1.31)	−0.011	(−0.38)

Keys: NEWALL: 1 if one or more former MoF/BoJ staff members are appointed in the highest positions on the board of a private bank, NEW: see NEWALL but replacements of incumbent ex-MoF/BoJ retirees are not taken into account. PROFIT: net return on equity, SOLVENCY: stockholders' equity/total assets, LIQUIDITY: liquid assets/total assets, DE-POSITS: total deposits/total assets, LOANS: total loans and bills discounted/total assets, GAKUBATSU: number of graduates from elite universities/total executives, DUMHQ: headquarters are close to Tokyo, DUMFGOVTB: bank was formerly owned or controlled by government, DUMHMAINB: bank is main (or second-largest) shareholder, DUMIN-FORMAL: informal relationship with a *keiretsu*, DUM8KEI: largest shareholder is a leading firm of *keiretsu* or the Industrial Bank of Japan, DUMIMAINB: bank is largest shareholder of regional banks, DUMALKEI: main bank of *keiretsu* or Industrial Bank of Japan.
Total number of observations is 1,309, number of banks is 77, number of years is 17.
Estimate of constant is not reported
* Statistically significant from zero at the 10% level.
** Statistically significant from zero at the 5% level.
*** Statistically significant from zero at the 1% level.

deposits and lending. Thus, retirees from the MoF and BoJ enter the boards of private banks when profitability and solvency are deteriorating, and not in reaction to changes in liquidity, deposits and lending. This finding implies that the third hypothesis that *amakudari* is 'just' a reward mechanism in bureaucratic career management is not supported. Second, the results of the NEWALL estimates for the relationship variables are as follows. For the variable GAKUBATSU, I find a marginal effect of −0.117. In other words, banks that have only graduates from the elite universities on their boards have an 11.7% lower probability of receiving retirees from the MoF and/or BoJ. The marginal effect of DUMHQ (0.065) indicates that banks that have their headquarters close to Tokyo have a 6.5% higher probability of receiving MoF/BoJ retirees on to their boards. The marginal effect of DUMFGOVTB of 0.110 implies that banks that were previously controlled by the government have an 11% higher probability of employing former MoF/BoJ officials. Third, with respect to the governance variables, the marginal effect of the variable DUMHMAINB is 0.062. Thus, banks that have a main bank have a 6.2% higher probability of enrolling MoF/BoJ retirees. Obviously, monetary authorities and main banks act as complements in the ex-post monitoring sense. Regarding the monitoring by the *keiretsu*, the results show that this aspect of corporate governance is not present. The results indicate that the coefficients on the variables DUMINFORMAL and DUM8KEI are not significant at all. Furthermore, the estimates of the coefficients on the variables DUMIMAINB and DUMALKEI, i.e. the variables that represent banks that operate as main banks, are not significant.

The second column of table 8.6 gives the results for the dependent variable NEW (that is without outside succession of incumbent MoF and BoJ retirees on the boards of private banks by other retired MoF and BoJ staff members). Similar to the results of the NEWALL estimate, the estimate with the variable NEW yields significant and negative co-efficients on the performance variables PROFIT and SOLVENCY. The range of the first differences of the actual values observed for PROFIT in table 8.3 corresponds to a change in NEW of 27 percentage points, given the marginal effect of PROFIT of −1.225. For SOLVENCY, which has a marginal effect of −4.877, the range of values observed in first differences relates to a change in the variable NEW by 32 percentage points. The marginal effect (−0.091) for the relationship variable GAKUBATSU is slightly lower for NEW than for NEWALL. It means that banks that have solely graduates from the top five universities on their boards have a 9.1% lower probability of hiring MoF and/or BoJ retirees than banks that have no graduates from these universities on their boards. Furthermore, I find that banks which were previously controlled by the government have a 6% higher probability of employing former MoF/BoJ officials. However, the coefficient on DUMHQ is not significant: when succession is not included, obviously MoF and BoJ retirees are less likely to move on to the boards of banks which have their headquarters located close to Tokyo. This could mean that because of closer links or geographical advantages, the MoF and BoJ have 'secured' certain retirement positions for their staff members at banks with their main office located close to Tokyo. Thus, when a former MoF/BoJ staff member leaves his position on the board of a private bank, another MoF/BoJ retiree succeeds him. This finding is in line with the results presented in chapter 7, such as the high succession rates of former MoF and BoJ officials on the boards of private banks by other ex-MoF/BoJ officials and the links between specific positions in the MoF/BoJ and on the boards of private banks. With respect to the governance variables, the marginal effect of DUMHMAINB slightly decreases from 6.2% (NEWALL) to 3.5% (NEW). Furthermore, the marginal effect of −0.025 for the variable DUMINFORMAL is significant at the 10% level. Thus, banks that maintain an informal relationship with a *keiretsu* have a 2.5% lower probability of enrolling new ('first time') or additional MoF and/or BoJ retirees.

Table 8.7 presents the results for the sample period 1981–1993, which includes three additional performance variables representing loans to risky industries. It shows that the results for both dependent variables are largely the same. The estimates for both NEWALL and NEW yield significant and negative results for the performance variable PROFIT (marginal effects of, respectively, −2.049 and −1.700). The range of this variable is in accordance with a change of NEWALL and NEW of 36 and 30 percentage points, respectively. An interesting finding now is the negative marginal effect for lending to the construction sector (LC), which is not in accordance with the second hypothesis that the mechanism of *amakudari* is used as an instrument of prudential policy. Namely, in that case it should be expected that MoF/BoJ retirees move particularly on to the boards of banks that expand their lending to risky industries. Instead, the negative result confirms the first hypothesis of 'buying influence': banks that experience a decrease in profitable lending to the construction industry hire retired MoF/BoJ officials, hoping that they can be instrumental in restoring profitability in one way or another. The marginal effects for NEWALL and NEW of, respectively, −5.747 and −4.872 imply that the ranges of LC correspond to changes in both dependent variables of 22% and 20% respectively. As regards the other variables, DUMHQ (0.043) is significant for NEWALL, and DUMHMAINB for both NEWALL and NEW (0.069 and 0.040, respectively).

Finally, I investigate whether the collapse of the 'bubble' economy had consequences for the movement of MoF and BoJ retirees on to the boards of banks. As mentioned before, this collapse affected in particular the Second Tier regional banks. Table 8.8 presents the results for the sample period 1989–1993 that includes the Second Tier regional banks. The results show that for both estimates the marginal effect of the variable PROFIT is significant and has the expected negative sign. The range of PROFIT, which has a marginal effect of −1.057, corresponds to a change

Table 8.7. *Probit estimates for NEWALL and NEW, sample 1981–1993*

	NEWALL		NEW	
	Marginal effect	t-statistic	Marginal effect	t-statistic
Performance variables				
ΔPROFIT	−2.049	(−3.65)*****	−1.700	(−4.10)***
ΔSOLVENCY	−2.471	(−0.77)	−2.546	(−1.06)
ΔLIQUIDITY	−0.060	(−0.14)	−0.321	(−0.93)
ΔDEPOSITS	0.229	(0.59)	0.291	(1.00)
ΔLR	−0.548	(−0.38)	0.677	(0.60)
ΔLC	−5.747	(−2.84)***	−4.872	(−3.11)***
Δ LF	−1.104	(−1.32)	−0.215	(−0.35)
Relationship variables				
GAKUBATSU	−0.049	(−0.86)	−0.044	(−1.01)
DUMHQ	0.043	(1.71)*	−0.001	(−0.05)
DUMFGOVTB	0.070	(1.45)	0.052	(1.33)
Governance variables				
DUMHMAINB	0.069	(2.94)***	0.040	(2.19)**
DUMINFORMAL	−0.018	(−0.86)	−0.021	(−1.34)
DUM8KEI	0.010	(0.44)	−0.004	(−0.25)
DUMIMAINB	−0.012	(−0.24)	−0.019	(−0.62)
DUMALKEI	−0.057	(−1.54)	−0.013	(−0.43)

Keys: NEWALL: 1 if one or more former MoF/BoJ staff members are appointed in the highest positions on the board of a private bank, NEW: see NEWALL but replacements of incumbent ex-MoF/BoJ retirees are not taken into account. PROFIT: net return on equity, SOLVENCY: stockholders' equity/total assets, LIQUIDITY: liquid assets/total assets, DEPOSITS: total deposits/total assets, LR: loans to real estate/total loans, LC: loans to construction sector/total loans, LF: loans to non-bank financial sector/total loans, GAKUBATSU: number of graduates from elite universities/total executives, DUMHQ: headquarters are close to Tokyo, DUMFGOVTB: bank was formerly owned or controlled by government, DUMHMAINB: bank is main (or second-largest) shareholder, DUMIN-FORMAL: informal relationship with a *keiretsu*, DUM8KEI: largest shareholder is a leading firm of *keiretsu* or the Industrial Bank of Japan, DUMIMAINB: bank is largest shareholder of regional banks, DUMALKEI: main bank of *keiretsu* or Industrial Bank of Japan.
Total number of observations is 962, number of banks is 74, number of years is 13.
Estimate of constant is not reported.
* Statistically significant from zero at the 10% level.
** Statistically significant from zero at the 5% level.
*** Statistically significant from zero at the 1% level.

of NEWALL of 23 percentage points (NEW: 26 percentage points). Furthermore, for NEW, the marginal effect for the variable LC is significant (with a negative sign) at the 10% level. Again, this finding implies a rejection of the second hypothesis about *amakudari* being used as an

Table 8.8. *Probit estimates for NEWALL and NEW, sample 1989–1993*

| | NEWALL | | NEW | |
	Marginal effect	t-statistic	Marginal effect	t-statistic
Performance variables				
ΔPROFIT	−1.057	(−1.83)*	−1.181	(−2.83)***
ΔSOLVENCY	1.096	(0.29)	2.029	(0.73)
ΔLIQUIDITY	0.483	(0.80)	−0.174	(−0.36)
ΔDEPOSITS	0.334	(0.79)	0.287	(0.92)
ΔLR	−0.999	(−0.65)	0.608	(0.52)
ΔLC	−2.918	(−1.33)	−2.912	(−1.74)*
ΔLF	−1.394	(−1.38)	−0.349	(−0.47)
Relationship variables				
GAKUBATSU	−0.042	(−0.45)	−0.083	(−1.16)
DUMHQ	0.065	(1.70)*	0.001	(0.03)
DUMFGOVTB	0.214	(2.52)**	0.146	(2.00)**
Governance variables				
DUMHMAINB	0.068	(2.24)**	0.031	(1.33)
DUMINFORMAL	−0.023	(−0.84)	−0.029	(−1.38)
DUM8KEI	−0.028	(−0.92)	−0.034	(−1.45)
DUMIMAINB	0.060	(0.68)	0.017	(0.28)
DUMALKEI	−0.110	(−2.33)**	−0.048	(−1.13)

Keys: NEWALL: 1 if one or more former MoF/BoJ staff members are appointed in the highest positions on the board of a private bank, NEW: see NEWALL but replacements of incumbent ex-MoF/BoJ retirees are not taken into account. PROFIT: net return on equity, SOLVENCY: stockholders' equity/total assets, LIQUIDITY: liquid assets/total assets, DEPOSITS: total deposits/total assets, LR: loans to real estate/total loans, LC: loans to construction sector/total loans, LF: loans to non-bank financial sector/total loans, DUMH-MAINB: bank is main (or second-largest) shareholder, GAKUBATSU: number of graduates from elite universities/total executives, DUMHQ: headquarters are close to Tokyo, DUMFGOVTB: bank was formerly owned or controlled by government, DUMINFORMAL: informal relationship with a *keiretsu*, DUM8KEI: largest shareholder is a leading firm of *keiretsu* or the Industrial Bank of Japan, DUMIMAINB: bank is largest shareholder of regional banks, DUMALKEI: main bank of *keiretsu* or Industrial Bank of Japan.
  Total number of observations is 575, number of banks is 115, number of years is 5.
  Estimate of constant is not reported.
* Statistically significant from zero at the 10% level.
** Statistically significant from zero at the 5% level.
*** Statistically significant from zero at the 1% level.

ex-post monitoring device. At the same time, the first hypothesis cannot be rejected. For the relationship variables, in the case of NEWALL the marginal effect for DUMHQ is significant (0.065). Furthermore, for both NEWALL and NEW the variable DUMFGOVTB is significant at the 5%

level. Finally, as regards the governance variables, both DUMHMAINB
(6.8%) and DUMALKEI (−11%) have a significant impact on NEWALL.

8.5   The effect of *amakudari* on bank performance

This section investigates whether the performance of banks improved
after the inflow of retired MoF/BoJ staff members. More specifically,
for the periods 1977–1993 and 1981–1993 the following relationship is
estimated:

$$\Delta x_{1,j,t} = c_{1,j} + \sum_{i=2}^{6} \beta_i \, NEW_{t-i} + \sum_{t=7}^{T} \gamma_t \, YEAR_t \qquad (8.4)$$

with $x_{1,j,t}$ is performance variable j, $\Delta x_{1,j,t} = x_{1,j,t} - x_{1,j,t-1}$, $j = 1, \ldots, K$,
$c_{1,j}$ is a constant and NEW_t is the dependent variable without succession.[8]
YEAR is a year dummy for year t, and $t = 7, \ldots, T$. For the period
1977–1993 the number of performance variables K and years T are respectively 5 and 17; for the period 1981–1993 K and N are respectively 7
and 13. I have included five lags to measure the impact of the appointment of new or additional MoF/BoJ retirees on the performance variables.

The OLS estimates of the impact of the *amakudari* appointments on
the performance variables for the periods 1977–1993 and 1981–1993 are
presented in tables 8.9 and 8.10, respectively.[9] The appointments of new
or additional MoF/BoJ retirees have in particular a significant positive
impact on the development of profitability. For example, for the period
1977–1993 the results show that the profitability of a bank in a particular
year improves after MoF/BoJ retirees have been appointed to the board
of this bank two, four, five and six years earlier. This positive impact of
amakudari appointments on the development of future bank profitability
is also found for the period 1981–1993. Furthermore, I find for both
sample periods a negative impact on the development of deposits of the
appointment of MoF/BoJ retirees that took place four years earlier, and a
positive impact on deposits of these appointments five years earlier. The
estimates also show that the *amakudari* appointments have no influence
on the development of solvency and liquidity.

However, the estimates for the 1981–1993 period show that the growth
of lending to the real estate, construction and non-bank financial

---

[8] The same specification was estimated for the performance variables using the variable
NEWALL. The results of these estimations are similar to those with the variable NEW.
[9] Given the small number of five years in the sample period 1989–1993, the equation was
not estimated for this period. Furthermore, the estimates of the year dummies are not
reported as well, although it might be interesting to note that the coefficients for the years
of the 'bubble' period were significant.

Table 8.9. *Impact of the appointments of MoF/BoJ retirees on the performance of private banks, 1977–1993*

	CONSTANT	NEW_{t-2}	NEW_{t-3}	NEW_{t-4}	NEW_{t-5}	NEW_{t-6}	SE
$\Delta PROFIT_t$	−0.027	0.003	−0.001	0.004	0.004	0.003	0.014
	(−16.6)***	(1.73)*	(−0.568)	(2.23)**	(2.27)**	(1.79*)	
$\Delta SOLVENCY_t$	−0.002	−0.0004	−0.0001	0.0001	0.0005	−0.000	0.003
	(−6.69)***	(−1.01)	(−0.31)	(0.41)	(1.31)	(−0.001)	
$\Delta LIQUIDITY_t$	0.002	−0.001	−0.002	−0.0004	−0.004	−0.001	0.023
	(0.94)	(−0.35)	(−0.75)	(−0.12)	(−1.26)	(−0.44)	
$\Delta DEPOSITS_t$	0.010	−0.007	−0.0001	−0.009	0.010	0.003	0.025
	(3.24)***	(−0.22)	(−0.034)	(−2.65)***	(3.00)***	(0.89)	
$\Delta LOANS_t$	−0.001	0.002	0.003	−0.001	0.003	0.005	0.028
	(−0.43)	(0.44)	(0.70)	(−0.34)	(0.81)	(1.25)	

Notes: Reported values are the coefficient estimates (OLS), with t-ratios in parentheses. The estimates of the lagged performance variables are reported. The values of year dummies are not reported. SE is the standard error of regression.

A specification with a dummy variable that takes the value 1 for the years 1990–1993 was used, i.e. the period during which the 'bubble' collapsed. This specification yielded similar results. (Specifications with different lag-structures generated similar results.)

The specification was re-estimated for the various performance variables using the variable $NEWALL_t$. The results of these estimations were similar to those with the variable NEW_t.

Table 8.10. *Impact of the appointments of MoF/BoJ retirees on the performance of private banks, 1981-1993*

	CONSTANT	NEW_{t-2}	NEW_{t-3}	NEW_{t-4}	NEW_{t-5}	NEW_{t-6}	SE
$\Delta PROFIT_t$	−0.002	0.005	−0.003	0.005	0.006	0.005	0.015
	(−1.00)	(1.79)*	(−1.12)	(1.81)*	(2.32)**	(1.78)*	
$\Delta SOLVENCY_t$	−0.0002	−0.0006	−0.0001	0.0002	0.0002	0.00003	0.023
	(−0.49)	(−1.12)	(−0.15)	(0.34)	(0.41)	0.06)	
$\Delta LIQUIDITY_t$	−0.007	−0.002	−0.003	0.004	−0.003	0.0003	0.023
	(−2.66)***	(−0.45)	(−0.65)	(1.09)	(−0.74)	(0.08)	
$\Delta DEPOSITS_t$	−0.015	0.0005	0.002	−0.014	0.014	0.005	0.029
	(−4.32)***	(0.10)	(0.34)	(−2.89)***	(2.90)***	(0.93)	
ΔLR_t	0.006	0.001	−0.0001	0.004	0.004	−0.0005	0.008
	(6.17)***	(0.84)	(−0.08)	(3.12)***	(3.41)***	(−0.38)	
ΔLC_t	0.0006	−0.001	−0.001	0.0003	0.001	−0.0005	0.004
	(1.22)	(−0.99)	(−0.97)	(0.42)	(1.93)*	(−0.68)	
ΔLF_t	0.005	0.002	0.007	−0.003	0.002	−0.002	0.013
	(3.10)***	(0.81)	(2.98)***	(−1.42)	(0.99)	(−0.81)	

Notes: See table 8.9.

industries is positively influenced by the appointment in previous years of retired MoF and/or BoJ staff members. This clearly contradicts the idea that the mechanism of *amakudari* is being used as an instrument of prudential policy. Namely, in that case appointments of retired MoF/BoJ staff members on the boards of private banks should result in a decrease in lending to risky industries in future years. Thus, the second hypothesis of ex-post monitoring is rejected. On the contrary, the finding of a positive impact on the growth in lending to risky industries is in line with the 'buying influence' hypothesis (first hypothesis): troubled banks persuade prudential supervisors to allow an increase in risky lending in return for retirement positions on the banks' boards in the future. Thus, the system of *amakudari* undermined the effectiveness of prudential supervision during the years in the sample periods, which could have been responsible at least to some extent for the problems in the Japanese banking sector during the past decade.

8.6   The detrimental effects of *amakudari*

The empirical results from the investigation in this chapter strongly suggest that the mechanism of *amakudari* involving retirees from the MoF and BoJ moving on to the boards of private banks had a detrimental effect on Japanese prudential policy during the period from the mid-seventies until the mid-nineties (see also van Rixtel 1996, 1997, 1998a and 1998c; van Rixtel and Hassink 1996b). This conclusion is in line with other recent research, in particular Horiuchi and Shimizu (1998), and has been supported in the 1998 edition of the OECD *Economic Survey – Japan* and the *Wall Street Journal* (see also Jarrett 1998).[10] Of course, the question arises whether this finding can be linked directly to the problems in the Japanese banking industry that became so evident during the second half of the nineties. To investigate this hypothesis, I have constructed table 8.11, which shows the characterisation of the boards of well-known problem banks in terms of the presence of MoF and BoJ *amakudari kanryō* (AK). This characterisation is classified 'weak' (†), 'significant' (††) or 'strong' (†††). The identification of the problem banks is based on the discussion of the policy reaction to the banking crisis in section 6.4 of chapter 6. In total, I have found a total of 20 problem banks for which I also could find information on their *amakudari* positions. These banks either failed or were kept alive with DIC and/or BoJ support and/or financial assistance from their main banks and/or other private financial institutions, including takeovers by healthier banks. The period investigated is from 1975 until 1993, i.e. way ahead of the collapse of the 'bubble' economy at the end of the eighties and the years when the problems

---

[10] The OECD asserted that the 'discretionary nature of prudential policy could have been sustained by the mechanism of *amakudari*' (OECD 1998, p.184). See also the *Wall Street Journal*, 'Revolving Door: Many Japanese Banks Ran Amok While Led By Former Regulators', 16 January 1996.

Table 8.11. Amakudari kanryō *(AK) on the boards of problem banks, 1975–1993*[1]

	Bank type	No AK on the board	Only MoF AK	Only BoJ AK	Both MoF/BoJ AK
Hokkaido Takushoku Bank	City bank				†††
Long-Term Credit Bank of Japan	Long-term credit bank				††
Nippon Credit Bank	Long-term credit bank				†††
Ashikaga Bank	Regional bank				††
Bank of the Ryukyus	Regional bank		†		
Chiba Kogyo Bank	Regional bank				††
Hokkaido Bank	Regional bank		†††		
Hokuriku Bank	Regional bank		††		
Kanto Bank	Regional bank				†††
Fukutoku Bank	Second Tier regional				††
Hanwa Bank	Second Tier regional		††		
Hiroshima-Sogo Bank	Second Tier regional			†††	
Hyogo Bank	Second Tier regional				††
Kofuku Bank	Second Tier regional				††
Kokumin Bank	Second Tier regional				†††
Kumamoto Family Bank	Second Tier regional				†††
Niigata Chuo Bank	Second Tier regional		††		
Taiheiyo Bank	Second Tier regional				†††
Tokuyo City Bank	Second Tier regional				†††
Tokyo Sowa Bank	Second Tier regional				†††

Note: [1] Years investigated 1975–1993.
Weak presence †: presence of some *amakudari kanryō* for several years only (less than 10% of the total number of board members are former MoF/BoJ officials for several years).

Significant presence ††: presence of some *amakudari kanryō* during most years or the full period (less than 10% of the total number of board members are former MoF/BoJ officials for most years or full period).

Strong presence †††: presence of large numbers of *amakudari kanryō* during the full period (more than 10% of the total number of board members are former MoF/BoJ officials for most years or full period).

Source: Nippon Kinyū Meikan.

in the banking sector started to erupt. Thus, the choice of this period should correct to a large extent for the possible sending of MoF/BoJ retirees to banks as part of prudential policy. In other words, the presence of MoF and BoJ *amakudari kanryō* on the boards of these banks should be seen as a structural characteristic of these banks and should be separated from the possible dispatching of former MoF/BoJ officials to the banking sector from the perspective of bureaucratic intervention. Without exaggeration, the results are striking. First, all problem banks employed MoF/BoJ *amakudari kanryō* during the period 1975–1993. Second, only one problem bank (Bank of the Ryukyus) experienced a 'weak' (that is for some years only) presence of retired monetary bureaucrats. Third, only one problem bank employed retired BoJ staff members only (Hiroshima-Sogo Bank). In other words, all problem banks except for one employed retired MoF officials during many years before the problems in the banking industry surfaced. Thus, the presence of former MoF officials on the board of private banks turned out to be a particularly good leading indicator for future problems. The relatively harmless role of BoJ retirees in this respect is supported by Horiuchi and Shimizu (1998). Fourth, 14 of the 20 problems banks employed significant numbers of both MoF and BoJ *amakudari kanryō* during many years.[11]

Furthermore, against the background of the reported perverse – i.e. positive – effects of *amakudari* on lending to risky industries, I present in table 8.12 the specific *amakudari* positions on the boards of the city bank (Hokkaido Takushoku Bank) and three Second Tier regional banks (Hyogo Bank, Taiheiyo Bank and Hanwa Bank) that failed around the mid-nineties. The table shows that these banks continuously employed former high-ranking MoF and/or BoJ staff members in the highest board positions including functions such as president, deputy-president and executive director. Investigation of two other major banks that failed in the second half of the nineties, i.e. the long-term credit banks Long-Term Credit Bank of Japan and Nippon Credit Bank, also yielded the result that these banks continuously employed former MoF and BoJ officials (between one and two ex-MoF and one ex-BoJ official at LTCB, and between one and five ex-MoF and one ex-BoJ official at NCB). It has to be emphasised that the last functions of some of the retirees at these banks were the highest in the MoF and BoJ, such as Director-General of a bureau (MoF) and Director of a department (BoJ). Investigations of newspapers and annual reports, analysis of financial statements and several interviews did not lead to the conclusion that these institutions

[11] In the context of these findings it is interesting to note that Suruga Bank, which has been typified as the best-run bank in Japan (Fiorillo 2000b), employed no retirees from the MoF and BoJ during the period 1975–1993.

Table 8.12. *Specific* amakudari *positions on the boards of failed banks*[1]

Name retiree	MoF/BoJ	Last function at MoF/BoJ	Highest function at bank (ranking)	Period at bank
Hokkaido Takushoku Bank				
T. Tojo	MoF	Director-General, Banking Bureau	President (no. 2)	1959–1991
K. Kawaguchi	MoF	Councillor, Minister's Secretariat	Executive director (no. 5)	1976–1987
K. Hirose	MoF	Director, Kobe Customs Office	Deputy-president (no. 3)	1980–1987
K. Agawa	MoF	Director, Commercial Banks Division, Banking Bureau	Managing director (no. 6)	1984–1991
H. Fujino	MoF	Secondment in high position at IMF	Deputy-president (no. 4)	1989–
Y. Okuma	BoJ	Director, Foreign Exchange Division, International Department	Director	Not clear
Hyogo Bank				
T. Ito	BoJ	Director, Bank Supervision Dept.	Executive director (no. 3)	November 1977–1985/1988
N. Taniguchi	MoF	Deputy Director-General, National Tax Administration Agency	President (no. 2)	August 1980–1990/1991
M. Yamada	MoF	Councillor, Minister's Secretariat	President (no. 2)	May 1989–1992/1993
M. Yoshida	MoF	Director-General, Banking Bureau	President (no. 1)	April 1993–
K. Ōra	BoJ	Adviser to the Governor	Deputy-president (no. 2)	November 1992–
K. Otsubo	MoF	Banking Inspector, Banking Bureau	Executive director (no. 3)	December 1992–

Hanwa Bank				
M. Matsuhiro	MoF	Banking Inspector, Banking Inspection Department, Banking Bureau	Managing director (no. 3)	May 1975–1990/1991
T. Okada	MoF	Director, Department of Local Finance Bureau	Executive director (no. 2)	May 1992–
Taiheiyo Bank				
Y. Aoyama	MoF	Director-General, Printing Bureau	President (no. 2)	1974–1985/1988
M. Nakagawa	BoJ	Deputy-General Manager, Branch	Auditor (no. 16)	June 1976–1980/1984
S. Nagai	MoF	Director, Department of Tokyo Taxation Bureau	Executive director (no. 4)	June 1984–1987/1988
Y. Sakaue	BoJ	Director, Issue Department	Auditor (no. 17)	June 1982–1987/1988
H. Suzuki	BoJ	Director, Budget and Management Department	Auditor (no. 16)	June 1987–1988/1989
N. Sekiguchi	MoF	Director, Regional Taxation Office	Chairman (no. 1)	December 1988–
H. Tsujishita	BoJ	Banking Supervisor	Advisory director (no. 7)	December 1988–1991/1992
K. Imada	BoJ	Banking Supervisor	Deputy President (no. 3)	June 1992–

Note: [1] Hokkaido Takushoku Bank: 1975–1993. Second Tier regional banks: the years 1979, 1984 and 1988–1993. In the case of the Second Tier regional banks, the exact year of leaving the board is not known.

experienced financial problems before allowing MoF or BoJ *amakudari kanryō* on to their boards.

The indications of possible collusive practices and 'buying influence' behaviour related to *amakudari* in the banking industry during the period 1975–1993 are further supported by the relatively strong presence of former MoF and BoJ banking supervisors on the boards of private banks. I have already presented evidence of this pattern in chapter 7 for both the MoF and BoJ. Further evidence is presented in Yamori and Fujiwara (1995) and Fujiwara and Yamori (1997). As regards the latter study, it is shown that 27% (25 out of 94) of the MoF and 54% (41 out of 76) of the BoJ retirees on the boards of Second Tier regional banks, of whom it could be determined what their last function was in the MoF and BoJ, were employed in functions related to the implementation of prudential policy during the period 1975–1995.

8.7   Conclusions

In this chapter I have investigated the relationship between the movement of retirees from the MoF and BoJ on to the boards of private banks and a number of performance, relationship and governance variables, by testing the significance of three hypotheses that are based on the elements of patterned equalisation, bureaucratic intervention and career management which were introduced in chapter 7. The first hypothesis focuses on the behaviour of troubled banks from the perspective of agency problems related to 'equalisation' attempts ('buying influence'). These banks bid for the inflow of banking supervisors, i.e. retirees from the MoF and BoJ (*amakudari kanryō*). This is confirmed by the result of a negative impact of profitability upon the inflow of these retirees. The troubled banks then try to bend the rules by persuading the MoF and BoJ to allow them to increase their risky but profitable lending. The estimates in this chapter support this hypothesis of 'buying influence'. That is, I find a clear positive impact from the appointments of former MoF/BoJ officials on the lending to risky industries. In general, in addition to the existence of (patterned) equalisation or 'buying influence' behaviour through *amakudari* that I have evidenced in this chapter for the banking industry, empirical research also supports the existence of this behaviour for the Japanese corporate sector as a whole. Moerke (1997) suggests that firms that are not a member of a *keiretsu* hire on average more MoF and BoJ *amakudari kanryō* than *keiretsu* member-firms. OECD (1999c) finds that in particular regulated industries, which most likely could benefit more from close relationships with the government bureaucracy than unregulated industries, hire former government officials.

The second hypothesis refers to the use of *amakudari* as an instrument of bureaucratic intervention or prudential policy ('ex-post monitoring'). Indeed, for all samples a negative impact from changes in profitability on the inflow of retirees from the MoF/BoJ is registered. Furthermore, I find a clear impact of the inflow of former MoF/BoJ officials on the development of profitability in subsequent periods. However, I also find an increase in lending to risky industries after the inflow of MoF/BoJ retirees. This is at odds with the implementation of prudential policy by the monetary authorities. Therefore, the second hypothesis of *amakudari* being used as an effective ex-post monitoring mechanism is rejected.

The third hypothesis that was tested implies that the movement of MoF/BoJ retirees on to the boards of private banks is used as an instrument for retirement purposes only. However, the estimates of the three sample periods show an impact of the performance of individual banks on the appointment of former MoF/BoJ staff members. Hence, this finding casts doubts on the interpretation by some authors that *amakudari* is predominantly used as a reward system.[12] For example, Kaplan and Minton (1994), p.233, remark that *amakudari* appointments 'are generally considered rewards' and therefore do not consider other possible uses of *amakudari*. As I have discussed in chapter 7, the element of career management is important as an explanation of *amakudari*, but certainly not the only or most important explanation, as is shown by the empirical results in both chapters 7 and 8.

Another interesting finding is that the estimates show a negative relationship between MoF/BoJ *amakudari* appointments and common university backgrounds (*gakubatsu*) between MoF and BoJ officials on the one hand and board members of private banks on the other. They also show that former government-controlled banks are more likely to accept MoF/BoJ retirees. Finally, regarding several governance variables, support is found for the complementary relationship between intervention by the MoF/BoJ and monitoring by main banks. Banks that have a main bank are more likely to experience an inflow of MoF/BoJ retirees than banks that do not have main bank relationships. Finally, I have found no strong evidence for monitoring by industrial groupings or *keiretsu*.

All in all, there is mounting evidence of detrimental effects of the presence of MoF and BoJ *amakudari kanryō* on the boards of private banks on their performance during the period 1975–1993. In earlier research, I have demonstrated that Second Tier regional banks that did not employ former MoF/BoJ on their boards were 4.6% more profitable than those employing ex-BoJ staff members and 7.4% more so than those with

---

[12] This point is stressed in particular by Ramseyer and Rosenbluth (1993).

former MoF officials (*The Economist*, 6 May 1995, p.32). Based on the empirical findings in this chapter, Japanese banks should be careful in hiring *amakudari kanryō*, in particular those from the MoF.

As such, the negative side-effects of *amakudari* are nothing new: in addition to the scandals involving financial institutions, many non-financial Japanese firms have been involved in scandals that were linked in one way or another to the post-retirement employment system of the Japanese government bureaucracy. For example, Kyocera, which refused to accept *amakudari kanryō*, was allegedly punished by government agencies in the form of confidential information leaks to its competitors. In the mid-nineties, the HIV-contaminated blood scandal was linked directly to Ministry of Health and Welfare officials turning a blind eye to warnings about this situation, possibly because of the large number of landing spots in the pharmaceutical industry (Miyamoto 1996; *The New York Times* 1996; Gibney 1998b, p.8; Nakano 1998, p.95). Various scandals rocked the Japanese defence industry, implicating significant numbers of *amakudari kanryō* from the Self-Defence Forces and the Defence Agency.[13] In the construction industry, a significant number of problem firms, such as Kumagai Gumi (see section 6.4 of chapter 6), employed many retirees from the Ministry of Construction.[14] In 1998, the government-owned Japan National Oil Corporation was hit by a huge bad-loan scandal that implicated former high-ranking officials from the Ministry of International Trade and Industry on its board (*Daily Yomiuri*, 2 March 1999). The airline company All Nippon Airways (ANA) experienced a power struggle between its president and two *amakudari kanryō* from the Ministry of Transport on its board (*Japan Times*, 22 May 1997). Even more interesting, it has been reported that former high-ranking police officers have accepted positions in firms related to the Japanese pinball gambling (*pachinko*) industry (*Asia Times* Online, 30 March 2000). All these examples suggest that the practice of *amakudari* should be investigated carefully but thoroughly on its merits and demerits. A start will be made in chapter 9, where lessons will be drawn from the Japanese experience with informality and banking problems.

---

[13] According to a government report, a total of 756 former senior officials of the Self-Defence Forces and the Defence Agency accepted jobs after retirement at 50 defence contractors during the nineties (*Kyodo News*, 22 February 2000).

[14] According to the *Weekly Post*, a high number of bureaucrats from the Ministry of Construction descended into troubled construction companies. For example, Kumagai Gumi employed six retired Construction Ministry officials in positions such as vice-president, managing director and heads of branch offices. Also other problem firms such as Aoki Construction Co., Sato Industrial Co., Hazama Construction Co. and Tokai Kogyo employed these *amakudari kanryō* (*Weekly Post*, 25 September–1 October 2000; http://www.weeklypost.com/000925/000925a.html).

Appendix 8.1 *Definitions*

Sample periods

Data set 1 1977–1993 period: 77 banks for each year. Included are the city, long-term credit, trust and regional banks for which data are being published by the Federation of Bankers Associations of Japan (Zenginkyō) in *Zenkoku Ginkō Zaimu Shō Hyō Bunseki* (Analysis of Financial Statements of All Banks). Not included are the banks that merged with each other or are the result of a merger (i.e. Mitsui Bank, Taiyo Kobe Bank, Mitsui Taiyo Kobe Bank, Sakura Bank, Kyowa Bank, Saitama Bank, Kyowa Saitama Bank, Asahi Bank and Nishi Nippon Bank) and five non-listed regional banks (Ugo Bank, Shonai Bank, Tohoku Bank, Tajima Bank and Tottori Bank), for which only limited information is available.

Data set 2 1980–1993 period: 74 banks for each year. Included are the city, trust and regional banks. Excluded are the three long-term credit banks and the banks that were also excluded from the 1976–1993 sample.

Data set 3 1989–1993 period: 115 banks for each year. Included are the city, long-term credit, trust, listed regional and listed Second Tier regional banks. Excluded are the banks which merged with each other or were taken over by other larger banks, banks which are the result of a merger, all non-listed regional and non-listed Second Tier regional banks and the Industrial Bank of Japan (IBJ). IBJ is excluded because the database on loans to the three risky industries does not contain the data for 1988, which are needed to calculate the first differences for 1989.

Dependent variables

- NEWALL$_{i,t}$: 1 for bank i in year t if one or more former MoF or BoJ staff members is/are appointed in one or more of the functions of chairman, deputy-chairman, president, deputy-president, executive director, managing director, director, advisory director or auditor in that year. Because in the majority of appointment years only one former MoF or BoJ official is appointed, the dependent variable NEWALL$_{i,t}$ takes the value 1 for both single and multiple appointments. This variable includes both new entries and succession. Source: *Nippon Kinyū Meikan*.

- NEW$_{i,t}$: equal to NEWALL$_{i,t}$, except that the cases in which a new MoF or BoJ retiree replaces an incumbent or old MoF/BoJ retiree are now not taken into account. Source: *Nippon Kinyū Meikan*.

Independent variables in all data sets

- PROFIT: profitability, measured as net return on equity, is calculated as net unappropriated profits (*tōki mishobun riekikin*, reference code (RC) as used in Zenginkyō (a) and (b) is *q*), total figure for fiscal year, divided by total stockholders' equity (*shihon no bu gōkei*, RC is *bx*), end of fiscal year.[15] Source: Zenginkyō (a) and (b). Until Zenginkyō (1981a), the data on net profits reported in Zenginkyō (a) and (b) are half-year figures. Therefore, the figures on yearly net profits for the 1976–1981 period are combinations of the figures reported in Zenginkyō (a) and (b): for example, the figure on net profits for Fiscal Year 1975 (as of 31 March 1976) is the sum of the figures reported in Zenginkyō (1975b) and Zenginkyō (1976a). From Zenginkyō (1982a), the figures on net profits reported in Zenginkyō (a) are yearly figures.
- SOLVENCY: calculated as the ratio of total stockholders' equity (*shihon no bu gōkei*, RC is *bx*), end of fiscal year, to total assets (*shisan no bu gōkei*, RC is *dx*), end of fiscal year. Source: Zenginkyō (a).
- LIQUIDITY: calculated as the ratio of most liquid assets, i.e. cash and due from banks (*genkin azuke kin*, RC is *da*), end of fiscal year, to total assets (*shisan no bu gōkei*, RC is *dx*), end of fiscal year. Source: Zenginkyō (a).
- DEPOSITS: calculated as the ratio of total deposits (*yokin*, RC is *aa*), end of fiscal year, to total assets (*shisan no bu gōkei*, RC is *dx*), end of fiscal year. Source: Zenginkyō (a).
- LOANS: calculated as the ratio of loans and bills discounted (*kashidashikin*, RC is *dh*), end of fiscal year, to total assets (*shisan no bu gōkei*, RC is *dx*), end of fiscal year. Source: Zenginkyō (a).
- DUMHMAINB: 1 if a regional or Second Tier regional bank has a bank as its main shareholder (main bank), 0 otherwise; where the main shareholder is the banks' employees, DUMHMAINB is 1 when a regional or Second Tier regional bank has a bank as its second largest shareholder. Banks which operate as main bank are mainly city, long-term credit and trust banks. Source: *Nippon Kinyū Meikan*.
- DUMINFORMAL: 1 if a regional or Second Tier regional bank maintains an informal relationship with a *keiretsu* as reported in *Kigyō Keiretsu Sōran*, 0 otherwise. *Kigyō Keiretsu Sōran* reports in particular for regional

---

[15] In Japan, the fiscal year runs from 1 April, to 31 March.

and Second Tier regional banks if these banks are 'close, intimate' (*missetsu*) or have a 'close friendship' (*shimmitsu*) with a *keiretsu*. In these cases DUMINFORMAL is 1. Source:*Kigyō Keiretsu Sōran*.

- DUM8KEI: 1 if the largest shareholder of a small city, small long-term credit, small trust, regional or Second Tier regional bank is a leading financial firm of one of the seven *keiretsu* (i.e. the five *keiretsu* that are the successors to the pre-war *zaibatsu* (Mitsui, Mitsubishi, Sumitomo, Fuyō and Dai-Ichi Kangyō) and the two groups informally organised around Sanwa Bank and Tokai Bank) or the Industrial Bank of Japan, 0 otherwise. Source: *Nippon Kinyū Meikan*.
- DUMIMAINB: 1 for a bank that is the largest shareholder of one or more regional or Second Tier regional banks. In other words, the bank that takes the value 1 is its/their main bank. Source: *Nippon Kinyū Meikan*.
- DUMALKEI: 1 if a city or trust bank is the main bank of one of the five *keiretsu* that are the successors to the pre-war *zaibatsu* (Mitsui, Mitsubishi, Sumitomo, Fuyō and Dai-Ichi Kangyō), the two groups informally organised around Sanwa Bank and Tokai Bank or the Industrial bank of Japan, 0 otherwise. The specific banks which take the value 1 are Mitsui Trust & Banking Co., Mitsubishi Bank, Mitsubishi Trust & Banking Co., Sumitomo Bank, Sumitomo Trust & Banking Co., Fuji Bank, Yasuda Trust & Banking Co., Dai-Ichi Kangyo Bank, Sanwa Bank, Toyo Trust & Banking Co., Tokai Bank, Chuo Trust & Banking Co. and the Industrial Bank of Japan. Since balanced data are used, the leading bank of the Mitsui *keiretsu*, i.e. Mitsui Bank, which merged with Taiyo Kobe Bank in April 1990 into Mitsui Taiyo-Kobe Bank (name changed into Sakura Bank as from April 1, 1992), is not included. Source: *Kigyō Keiretsu Sōran*.
- GAKUBATSU: calculated as the ratio of the number of graduates from the elite universities (Tokyo, Hitotsubashi, Kyoto, Keio and Waseda) to the total number of executives in the highest board positions (*jōmukai*), both as of August–September. Source: *Nippon Kinyū Meikan*.
- DUMHQ: 1 if the headquarters of a bank is located close to Tokyo, i.e. located in Tokyo or one of the adjacent prefectures, 0 otherwise. The criteria for being located close to Tokyo is whether the headquarters is located in the Kanto District, i.e. in one of the following prefectures adjacent to Tokyo: Ibaraki, Tochigi, Gunma, Saitama, Chiba, Tokyo, and Kanagawa. Source: *Nippon Kinyū Meikan*.
- DUMFGOVTB: 1 if a bank was formerly owned or directly controlled by the government, 0 otherwise. Source: Bank of Japan and *Nippon Kinyū Meikan*.

Additional independent variables in data sets 2 and 3

• LR: calculated as the ratio of loans to the real estate sector, end of fiscal year, to total lending (*kashidashikin*, RC is *dh*), end of fiscal year. Source: loans to the real estate sector are from the Nikkei Needs Database, total lending is from Zenginkyō (a). Data are available from 1980; however, for the long-term credit banks data are available from 1989 only.

• LC: calculated as the ratio of loans to the construction sector, end of fiscal year, to total lending (*kashidashikin*, RC is *dh*), end of fiscal year. Source: loans to the construction industry are from the Nikkei Needs Database, total lending is from Zenginkyō (a). Data are available from 1980; however, for the long-term credit banks data are available for a shorter period only.

• LF: calculated as the ratio of loans to the non-bank financial sector, end of fiscal year, to total lending (*kashidashikin*, RC is *dh*), end of fiscal year. Source: loans to the non-bank financial sector are from the Nikkei Needs Database, total lending is from Zenginkyō (a). Data are available from 1980; however, for the long-term credit banks data are available for a shorter period only

9 Conclusion: Informality, monetary policy and bank performance – lessons from the Japanese experience

> In terms of maintaining order, we feel we have an indisputable, remarkable record.
>
> M. Tsuchida, former Director-General, Banking Bureau, MoF, 1991[1]

9.1 Introduction

The second half of the 1990s certainly will not go unnoticed by Japanese historians. As described in this study, in 1997 and 1998 some of the largest banks and securities houses collapsed, followed in 2000 by bankruptcies of several insurance companies. A large number of scandals shook the foundations of Japan's monetary establishment, and ultimately caused the fall of some of its most respected and powerful representatives. These events severely increased doubts about the health of Japanese financial institutions and the stability of the Japanese financial system as a whole. The developments also resulted in a large number of studies that tried to explain the causes and consequences of the Japanese banking problems. Although some of these publications incorporated analyses of the fundamental characteristics of the Japanese monetary authorities and financial system, to a large extent the research remained limited to investigations of the banking crisis as such, taking little account of broader concepts such as the structure of the government bureaucracy, economic policy and political economy. This study has taken the opposite approach, first developing a qualitative framework which formed the basis for institutional and empirical analysis of several structural informal aspects that may have been partly responsible for the banking problems. I leave it to the reader to judge to what extent this attempt has been successful. I have concentrated particularly on informality for two reasons. Firstly, informality seems to lie at the heart of the discussions on the specific nature of the Japanese political economy and economic system, and thus, secondly, could have major implications for the organisation of Japanese

---

[1] Cited in Vogel (1996), p.170.

macro and micro monetary policy. As was mentioned in chapters 3 and 4, informality in general and its importance in the operation of monetary policy in particular are certainly not unique Japanese phenomena. For example, several central banks have publicly acknowledged the use of informal instruments – often referred to as moral suasion – in the implementation of their policies. However, what is unique is the passionate debate on the relevance and importance of informality in Japanese economic policy that has been going on for some time in the field of Japanese economic and political studies. For no other major economic power does opinion on this matter differ so greatly as for Japan. In chapters 2 and 3, it was argued that, fundamentally, this debate touches the issue of market versus government control (see also van Rixtel 1997 and Katz 1998). The adherents of the market view, who have gained influence after the Asian crisis and the economic and financial problems in Japan,[2] do not believe in effective government control of the Japanese economy and regard the importance of informal factors as public control mechanisms as negligible. At the other extreme are those of the interventionist or government control school – sometimes also typified as the 'revisionists' – who see the Japanese economy as subject to strong control by the government bureaucracy. In this view, such control is exercised particularly through the use of informal instruments. Because of their sometimes extreme views and harsh criticism of mainstream Japanese (economic) studies, the 'revisionists' have been on the defensive for some time now (see, for example, Lindsey and Lukas 1998). However, they certainly deserve credit for drawing attention to certain institutional aspects such as informality that could have played (or may even still play) an important role in the Japanese economic system and economic policy. Several other and more recent schools, which have been collectively identified in this study as network schools and which are less radical than the interventionist school in their views, also stress the importance of informal aspects in Japanese economic policy. In general, the findings of this study support the main assertion of the interventionist and network schools that informality has been of relevance and importance for the implementation of economic policy in Japan, and possibly to some extent still is. However, contrary to the revisionists' general view, I have also found evidence that the use of certain informal instruments often had detrimental effects and occasionally was even counterproductive. In other words, evidence suggests that certain informal institutional characteristics of the mode of Japanese monetary policy implementation may turn out to have been structural weaknesses instead. In the following sections, this general

---

[2] See, for example, Wolf (1998).

conclusion will be discussed in more detail. First, section 9.2 looks at the Japanese banking crisis and summarises what went wrong in line with the assessment made in chapter 6. Second, I shall discuss the limitations of informal instruments in section 9.3, departing from the qualitative framework developed in chapters 2, 3 and 4, which has been investigated institutionally as such in chapter 5. I shall also pay attention to the effectiveness of informal instruments in the context of the on-going process of financial and administrative reform. Third, in section 9.4, the findings of chapters 7 and 8 on *amakudari* will be related to the apparent shortcomings of Japanese prudential policy during the nineties. Finally, in section 9.5 I shall draw some lessons from the Japanese experience and present some forward-looking observations.

9.2   The Japanese banking crisis: what went wrong

In chapter 6, I discussed the policy response to the banking problems. In that context, the worsening of the situation in the banking sector in terms of the evolution of bad loans and growing number of troubled institutions was also described. Indeed, many observers share the view that Japan experienced a banking crisis. Some, in particular in the revisionist camp, however, believe that the rise and collapse of the 'bubble' and the subsequent economic recession and banking crisis were deliberate policies that aimed to achieve structural reforms in both the financial and non-financial industries. In other words, the story of the Phoenix arising from its ashes. For example, Chalmers Johnson asserted that there 'was not a bubble, this is governmental policy' (Katz 1998, p.22). In the view of Hollerman (1998), 'the regulatory strategy of the economic bubble and the recession that followed it induced great structural changes in the Japanese economy'; the 'bubble' 'was a calculated demonstration by MoF of Japan's industrial policy on the international plane'.[3] It seems that, according to these observers, the brilliant exponents of the Japanese government bureaucracy simply cannot make mistakes, and that every development in the Japanese economic system is the intended outcome of a carefully orchestrated policy move. I do not subscribe to this view. During the nineties, Japan experienced a severe banking crisis that to a large extent was the result of policy inaction and even policy mistakes, and which contributed significantly to the protracted sluggish economic development of recent years.

In my view, the Japanese banking crisis was due to a number of general and Japan-specific causes. From a general perspective, the following

[3] See also van Wolferen (2001), p.73.

factors can be distinguished, which also played a major role in the development of banking crises in numerous other developed countries, such as the United States and several Scandinavian countries (see, for example, Sheng 1996; FDIC 1997; Caprio et al. 1998; Herring 1998; Demetriades 1999; Herring and Wachter 1999; Hoshi and Kashyap 1999; Hutchison et al. 1999; Moody's Investors Service 1999a; Hoshi 2000; Ueda 2000, pp.6ff.). First, the process of financial reform increased the competition between various groups of banks and between banks and other financial institutions, and increased the exposure of the banks in terms of their lending to relatively risky industries such as real estate and non-bank financial companies. Second, Japan experienced a classical 'boom and burst' scenario of asset prices, as described in chapter 6. As in many other countries, this consisted of a credit-induced spiral of booming asset prices and increasing lending beyond prudent risk-return considerations on the side of banks, which, when it turned out not to be sustainable, resulted in the burst of the 'bubble' leading to a severe economic downturn and a fast accumulation of bad loans that would exceed the self-absorbing capacity of the banking sector. Third, this was partly due to the existence of an inadequate system of prudential supervision. In other words, regulation was 'too little' (Ito 2000, p.8). Fourth, as has been discussed extensively in chapter 6, the policy response of the monetary policy authorities was dominated by regulatory forbearance, which most likely, as in other countries, exacerbated the problems. The other element in the policymakers' reaction, i.e. financial reform, came often too late. Thus, in addition to 'too little', regulation was at the same time 'too much' (Ito 2000, p.8). Finally, just as in other countries, the existence of a financial safety net could have provoked moral hazard in the banking sector.

However, in addition to these general factors, in my view first and foremost a number of Japan-specific factors were responsible for the seriousness and protracted length of the problems in the Japanese banking sector. In this respect, the government bureaucracy, the banking sector and the political system all can be held accountable, each of them at least to some extent. With the benefit of hindsight, the policymakers share some blame for several unfortunate macro-economic policy decisions, which have been typified by some as 'mistakes' (van Rixtel 1996, 1997; Cargill 1998, 2000; Patrick 1998; Posen 1998; Curtis 1999; Hoshi and Patrick 2000b; Ito 2000; see also various publications of international organisations, particularly the OECD). In all fairness, it has to be said that economic policymaking is never easy and is surrounded by great uncertainties. Nevertheless, Japanese policymakers should have taken more lessons from the experiences of their counterparts in other countries, where banking crises had accurred, such as the costs of regulatory forbearance and 'buying time' policies which so dominantly characterised the Japanese policy response (see chapter 6; see also Kane 1993; Ueda 2000). Furthermore, in the course of the developing banking crisis, major scandals often erupted that implicated the monetary authorities, seriously undermined their credibility and delayed prompt and effective intervention (see chapter 6; see also Duck 1996, p.1724; van Rixtel 1996, 1997; Katz 1998; Lincoln 1998a; pp.58ff., 1998b, p.359; US Embassy Tokyo 1999). In addition, many share the view that the specific (informal) safety net that characterised the post-World War II Japanese financial structure – i.e. the 'convoy system' which was promoted and supported as such by the monetary authorities – exacerbated the possible moral hazard that has been often related to the existence of safety nets for the financial services industry in other countries and which caused additional problems (Horiuchi 1996, p.1; Schaede 1996; Cargill 1998, 2000; Kuroda 1998, pp.219–220; Beason and James 1999; Spiegel 1999, p.26; Ito 2000, p.11; Ueda 2000, pp.6ff.). According to Milhaupt (1999), pp.40ff., an implicit or informal financial safety net such as adopted in Japan turned out to be inferior to a well-designed explicit system: 'The lack of a formal institutional structure for failed bank resolutions compounded the country's financial problems. . . . The informal safety net may also have contributed to the poor profitability of the Japanese banking sector.' Finally, several structural deficiencies of Japanese prudential policy hampered the effective implementation of financial supervision and contributed significantly to the perseverance of the problems (Schaede 1996; van Rixtel 1996; Kuroda 1998, pp.219–220). For example, for many years a large number of authorities were involved in the operation of prudential policy. To say the least, the co-ordination between them was often less than satisfactory. Besides the MoF – later replaced by the Financial Supervisory Authority (FSA) and Financial Services Authority (FSEA) – and the BoJ, the Ministry of Trade and Industry was responsible for the supervision of the non-bank industry, the Ministry of Agriculture, Forestry and Fisheries for the financial agricultural co-operatives, the Ministry of Labour for the labour credit associations, and the prefectural governors (i.e. politicians) for the credit co-operatives. As of today, several of these government organisations are still entrusted with certain tasks in the field of prudential policy. The nineties saw numerous conflicts between these various supervisory authorities regarding their actual authority and responsibilities towards the financial institutions under their jurisdiction. A clear example in this respect is the problems with the housing loan companies (*jūsen*) (see chapter 6). Furthermore, the number of overall staff engaged in prudential policy activities was very small, in both relative and absolute terms, especially against the background of the large number of financial institutions under their jurisdiction and the problems in the Japanese financial services sector. Increases in staff active in prudential policy activities were often blocked by budgetary constraints and strict regulations on the total number of civil servants, which were imposed by the political system. In addition, the expertise of Japanese prudential supervisors, in particular those from the MoF, was often doubted, which was made worse by the rotation schemes that characterise the Japanese government bureaucracy (various interviews with private bankers, 1995 and 1998, Tokyo). Over the years, this custom of rotating staff every two to three years made it almost impossible for them to acquire the specialised knowledge necessary to understand banking business and prudential supervision matters. Another problem regarding a fast and effective resolution of the banking problems has been for many years the lack of well-developed bankruptcy proceedings and accounting standards (Craig 1998b, p.3; Fukao 1998, pp.401ff.; Kuroda 1998, pp.219–220). Finally, and in my view most importantly, independent and prudent supervision in Japan has been frustrated by the existence of too cosy relations between banks' executives, politicians and monetary authorities, in other words by the vast informal networks connecting the public with the private (see also: van Rixtel 1996, 1998c; Schaede 1996; Cargill 1998; Lincoln 1998b). The absence of arm's-length relationships between banks and prudential supervisors promoted supervisory ineffectiveness in general and regulatory forbearance in particular, and provoked in various instances sheer corruption and other collusive practices. In chapter 6, I explained the importance in this respect of mechanisms such as the MoF-*tan* system, and the somewhat similar BoJ-*tan* system, *ama-agari* ('ascending into heaven') and *amakudari* ('descending from heaven'). The detrimental effects of the latter have been discussed extensively in chapter 8, and will be assessed in more detail in section 9.4. The existence of these informal networks promoting close and intimate relationships between supervisors and financial institutions has been largely responsible for the occurrence of various scandals such as the stock-loss compensation scandal in 1991, the credit co-operatives scandal of early 1995, the trading-losses scandal of Daiwa Bank in the United States in 1995 and the corruption scandals at the MoF and the BoJ during the first quarter of 1998 (see: chapters 5 and 6; see also van Rixtel 1996 and 1998c; Lincoln 1998b; Brown 1999). Closely related to the existence of informal networks has been the use of informal instruments such as administrative guidance in the implementation of prudential policy, including in the policy response to the banking problems (chapters 5 and 6).[4] This guidance has been often non-transparent and consequently arbitrary and ambiguous in nature. The ambiguity inherent to administrative guidance has been blamed for causing several scandals and contributing to the apparent lack of effectiveness that has characterised Japanese prudential policy during the nineties, and will be discussed further in section 9.3 (Van Rixtel 1996, 1998c; Schaede 1996; Cargill et al. 1998).

To a large extent, the role of the policymakers in the Japanese banking crisis has been overshadowed by that of the banks themselves. Bank behaviour has been characterised by imprudent lending policies, inadequate provisioning, resistance against effective measures to dispose of bad loans in the hope that collateral values would recover ('wait and see' attitude), limited disclosure and transparency. For example, the banking sector successively blocked on several occasions government initiatives for the introduction of regulations that would have stimulated disclosure and transparency, for example in the case of the design of the new Banking Law at the end of the seventies (McCall Rosenbluth 1989).[5] Furthermore, the banking sector managed to thwart rare attempts to enhance the effectiveness of prudential policy by safeguarding political support via substantial financial injections (Rosenbluth and Thies 1999). The banks also managed to 'buy influence' or protection from the supervisory authorities, for example by offering post-retirement positions to former staff members from the MoF and BoJ, as has been shown in chapter 8. Finally, more and more evidence, in particular of an empirical nature, has become available to support the view that the Japanese banking sector has been lacking an effective corporate governance system with respect to the banks' management (Fukao 1998; Hanazaki and Horiuchi 1998; Anderson and Campbell 2000; Morck and Nakamura 1999a, 1999b; Kanaya and Woo 2000).

Finally, to complete the picture, the Japanese political system often proved to be too rigid and entrenched to take swift action in response to the increasing banking problems. Despite the clear progress made during

---

[4] For example, the OECD has mentioned administrative guidance explicitly as one of the causes of the banking problems: 'the implicit guarantees against institutional bankruptcy inherent in the convoy system and administrative guidance, encouraged problem institutions to continue with imprudent lending policies and for healthy institutions to lend to unhealthy institutions, increasing the risk of systemic collapse' (OECD 1999b, p.33).

[5] The importance of accurate disclosure and transparency was demonstrated by, for example, the experience with the collapse of Hokkaido Takushoku Bank in 1997. The official statements of the bank for fiscal year 1996 reported total capital in order of 297.6 billion yen, whereas official inspections later revealed a negative capital position of 1,172.5 billion yen as of 31 March 1998 (Fukao 1998, p.402).

the nineties in terms of political differentiation, the lack of an effective opposition – that could be seen by the Japanese electorate as a credible alternative to the ruling Liberal Democratic Party (LDP) – hindered for many years the process of financial reform in general and the adoption of measures that could have solved the problems in the banking sector much faster in particular.[6] In this respect, the experiences with the formulation and adoption of the financial revitalisation legislation in the summer and autumn of 1998 were telling (see chapter 6). As regards the importance of the existence of a credible political opposition, I would cite Nobel prizewinner Merton H. Miller, who made the following statement at a 1993-conference in Tokyo with reference to the political environment in the Unites States:

> Until that kind of political competition comes to Japan, I am sorry, as an academic, to have to conclude that all talk of financial deregulation and reform in Japan is likely to be just that – academic. (Miller 1993, p.25)

Furthermore, politicians defended on numerous occasions the interests of (specific segments) of the banking sector, which reportedly rewarded them generously,[7] and of specific constituencies with specific interests in the banking industry, such as the agricultural co-operatives which were heavily exposed to the troubled housing loan companies (*jūsen*). Finally, politicians often engaged in 'bureaucrat bashing', blaming the monetary authorities for all the problems and policy 'mistakes', and arguing that their own hands were clean.[8] This occasionally resulted in political demands for the introduction of administrative and financial reforms which unfortunately later turned out to be merely cosmetic.

9.3   Policy effectiveness: the limitations of informal instruments

The investigation of the importance and relevance of informality in the implementation of Japanese monetary policy in general and micro monetary policy (prudential policy) in particular has been the main thread of

---

[6] In this regard, it is interesting to note that according to Carlile (1998), p.109, 'none of the non-LDP parties played a significant role in formulating administrative reform proposals'.

[7] Based on various interviews, in particular in October 1998, with several private bankers, Tokyo. The financial relationship between the banking industry and several political parties (the LDP in particular) and the question whether this benefited the banks effectively is beyond the scope of this study. See in this respect, for example: McCall Rosenbluth 1989, 1993; Calder 1993; Rosenbluth and Thies 1999.

[8] According to Hiwatari (2000), the breaking-up of the MoF was a strategy of 'blame avoidance' by non-LDP parties in particular.

this study. As has been discussed in chapter 3, according to the majority of the schools on the Japanese political economy and economic system, informal aspects are relevant for Japanese economic policy, at least as a fundamental institutional characteristic. Based on the related literature, I have distinguished two main elements of informality: administrative guidance and informal networks based on personal relations. The common denominators of these informal policy instruments are the dimensions of non-legal enforceability – compliance cannot be coerced by legal means – and, generally, also non-transparency. I have separated administrative guidance into published and unpublished administrative guidance. The former consists of the *tsūtatsu* or circulars published by the MoF, which were virtually abolished in the summer of 1998 (see section 6.4 of chapter 6). I have demonstrated in chapter 5 that these circulars were predominantly issued for micro monetary policy purposes, and that the effectiveness of the few *tsūtatsu* that aimed at achieving certain macro policy goals must be seriously doubted – in my view they were mainly used as publicity instruments on behalf of the ruling LDP. The informal networks that have been identified in the context of economic policy are constituted by former government bureaucrats descending from bureaucratic 'heaven' into private business (*amakudari*), the reverse process of private sector staff ascending into 'heaven' (*ama-agari* or *shukkō*), and common university backgrounds (*gakubatsu*). The mechanism of *amakudari* involving former staff from the MoF and BoJ has been discussed theoretically in chapters 3 and 4, institutionally in chapters 5 and 6 and empirically in chapters 7 and 8; an overall review will be presented in the next section. The movement of staff members from private financial institutions into the MoF and BoJ (*ama-agari*) has reportedly reduced substantially since the 1998 scandals, certainly when compared with the entrenched and institutionalised pattern of the earlier years (see, for example, table 5.5 on page 108 for the MoF, and section 5.5 for the BoJ). However, as described in section 6.5 of chapter 6, private financial institutions' staff continued to dominate the overall *ama-agari* process related to the Japanese government: as of 15 August 1999, according to official government figures almost half of all *ama-agari* movements into the central government bureaucracy originated from the financial services industry. In my view, this shows how important this mechanism is for private financial institutions, given their deplorable financial situation and the drain on their human resources that it entails. Furthermore, I proved that the importance of graduating from specific universities (*gakubatsu*) – in particular from the University of Tokyo – for reaching the top at the MoF actually increased during the nineties, despite official promises to reverse this pattern (see table 6.7 on page 220).

As reported in chapter 6, the monetary authorities, in particular the MoF, made quite extensive use of various forms of published and unpublished administrative guidance in their response to the growing banking problems. The MoF actively promoted non-disclosure and non-transparency in the banking industry via its administrative guidance aimed at masking the magnitude of the problems, for example by discretionary changing accounting standards. It used administrative guidance to arrange rescue mergers between healthy and troubled banks, to adjust the operational procedures of commercial banks and to 'convince' various private financial institutions to provide financial support to problem banks, as, for example, in the case of Nippon Credit Bank (see chapter 6). Furthermore, the MoF used various forms of administrative guidance in its 'price keeping operations' (PKOs) related to the stock market. Closely linked to its use of administrative guidance, MoF's officials actively maintained and treasured various informal networks with the banking sector such as the MoF-*tan* and *amakudari* systems. From the limited information available, the overall record of the BoJ regarding the use of informal instruments seems to have been much less 'unfavourable' than the MoF's. In general, the BoJ has always been much more in favour of market-oriented policy instruments than the MoF, partly because this was seen as the most effective strategy in enhancing its independence from the government (various interviews, former MoF and BoJ staff members and private bankers, April–June 1993, April–May 1995 and October 1998, Tokyo). On the other hand, however, BoJ officials also participated systematically and extensively in informal networks with private banks as well, leading to accusations of collusive practices and one of the most serious crises in the BoJ's existence in 1998 when both the Governor and Deputy-Governor were forced to resign. Furthermore, to keep things in perspective, I must mention the drastic sanctions that the BoJ imposed on Tokai Bank when the latter 'punished' a former high-ranking BoJ staff member employed on its board (see chapter 7).

Looking back at the heavy, deliberately chosen dependence on informal instruments in the conduct of Japanese prudential policy in general (see chapter 5) and in the policy response to the banking crisis during the nineties in particular (see chapter 6), it is clear by any objective standard that this strategy has not been very effective in ex-post terms, given the deplorable situation of the Japanese banking sector and economy at the start of the new millennium.[9] Moreover, some even assert that the use of administrative guidance was partly responsible for the creation of the

[9] That is, I relegate to the realm of fantasy the revisionists' conspiracy stories of a deliberate government attempt to create order out of chaos by creating and destroying the 'bubble'.

banking problems and the deterioration of the situation in the first place (van Rixtel 1996, 1998c; Schaede 1996; OECD 1999b; Cargill 2000; Kanaya and Woo 2000). The question arises why the use of informal instruments, firstly, did not prevent the banking crisis from happening and, secondly, failed to achieve in a much faster and less costly way the official policy goals of solving this crisis and maintaining overall financial stability. In essence, this question relates to the issue of the policy effectiveness of administrative guidance and the required preconditions to ensure this. Most of these conditions have been listed by Okimoto (1989), p.94, and Murakami and Rohlen (1992), pp.91–95, as follows (see also chapter 2). First, the guidance should be aimed at a relatively small number of companies in a given industry, which have a clear market-leader among them. Second, the industry should be characterised by a fairly high degree of market concentration and a mature stage in the industry's life cycle, which makes it difficult for newcomers to enter this market. This specific market structure should also facilitate compliance with the guidance, as it is in the companies' own interests to maintain the status quo. Furthermore, the industry should have a strong association or another mechanism for consensus building. Third, the industry should be highly dependent on the government body that imposes the administrative guidance, which involves elements of both 'carrot' (i.e. lifting of regulations) and 'stick' (i.e. imposing sanctions) considerations. This relates to the permissive authorisation such as licensing (*kyoninka*) of the public body that in the end has to ensure that the 'voluntary' compliance to the government's guidance is effectuated (see chapter 3). Fourth, there should be common problems of sufficient severity to guarantee co-operation between the companies, i.e. a certain degree of group solidarity needs to exist. I would like to add two additional factors. Fifth, in my view, it is also of great importance that informal policy networks between the public and private spheres exist which allow for the co-ordination and consensus-building necessary to ensure compliance with administrative guidance. Namely, as discussed in chapter 3, compliance with ministerial guidance depends significantly on the involvement of the regulated parties in its formulation ('interactive' dimension). Sixth and finally, a certain concentration of regulatory power (*kyoninka*) in a specific regulatory body is required. This is why numerous observers of the Japanese situation and certain Japanese opposition parties have been demanding for many years that the MoF should be broken up into several sections.

Applying these six preconditions for effective administrative guidance in the policy response to the banking crisis in the nineties shows a differentiated picture. Although the number of banks in specific bank groups

remained relatively small – i.e. the degree of concentration remained
relatively high – the process of financial reform and the resulting functional desegmentation of the banking sector and blurring of demarcation
lines in the financial services industry promoted competition between
various bank groups, and increasingly individual banks' interests diverged
(see chapters 5 and 6). In other words, the element of group solidarity
became less important. This frustrated a coherent overall adoption of administrative guidance by policymakers, because certain individual banks
considered it to be in their own interest to shirk this government control
and so took advantage of certain loopholes in this guidance – for example
circumventing guidance by conducting specific activities through affiliated non-bank companies (Schaede 1996; Hartcher 1998). This process was further strengthened by the progressing internationalisation of
the Japanese financial system, which was, for example, one of the main
reasons for the BoJ to abolish its administrative guidance towards bank
lending (so-called 'window guidance' or *madoguchi shidō*, see section 5.5
of chapter 5). All in all, these developments should tend to limit the
effectiveness of administrative guidance. On the other hand, the banking
industry has always had a clear leader, at least in institutional terms (the
chair-bank of the Federation of Bankers Associations of Japan), a factor
that should have been beneficial to the use of administrative guidance.
Furthermore, the degree of concentration in the Japanese banking industry increased significantly during the nineties, as was shown in chapter 6
(see table 6.11 on page 250), which should also promote its effectiveness.
The situation regarding the third condition – substantial dependence
of the banks on the MoF and BoJ – is more difficult to assess. True,
without doubt the great dependence of banks on funds provided by the
monetary authorities during the post-war 'high growth period', which
was characterised by overloan, overborrowing and underdeveloped capital markets (see section 5.2 of chapter 5), decreased significantly with
the change in the flow of funds and financial structure towards a greater
role for direct finance in the financing of private business (Calder 1997,
p.21; Norville 1998, p.113; Pempel 1998, pp.75–76; Hoshi and Kashyap
1999). Furthermore, the lifting over the years of various regulations such
as interest rate controls, limitations to establish new branches, regulations that maintained the functional segmentation in the financial services
industry and restrictions on international transactions, eroded the monetary authorities' ability to implement administrative guidance effectively.
Thus, these developments as such certainly curtailed the use of administrative guidance by the monetary authorities. In more general terms
and at first sight, the on-going process of financial reform should have
undermined the effectiveness of administrative guidance, as instinctively

it should be accompanied by a decrease in the number of both formal and informal regulations and consequently the number of sanctions at the monetary authorities' disposal to 'force' compliance with their guidance. For example, as has been discussed in chapter 6, the published informal regulations or circulars (*tsūtatsu*) have been virtually abolished. On the other hand, however, it has been asserted in several studies that the process of (financial) reform in Japan is characterised by a substantial degree of re-regulation: replacement of one form of formal regulation by another, and informal re-regulation that compensates for formal deregulation (see in particular Vogel 1996, supported by Dattel 1996; Calder 1997, p.26–27; Carlile 1998; Carlile and Tilton 1998b; Norville 1998, pp.127–128; Pempel 1998, p.137; Tilton 1998; Wood 1998, p.222).[10] In this regard, it should be recalled that a significant part of the abolished *tsūtatsu* were continued in another regulatory format (see section 6.4 of chapter 6). Examples of formal deregulation accompanied by formal re-regulation are the imposition of new reporting requirements for liberalised foreign exchange transactions in order to avoid tax evasion (Lincoln and Litan 1998), or the lifting of regulations on the establishment by banks of new branches, which had lost most of their usefulness anyway (see chapter 6), on the one hand, but introducing licensing approval for the establishment of financial subsidiaries to conduct new activities, such as the establishment of securities subsidiaries by banks under the Financial System Reform Act of 1993, on the other (Vogel 1996; see also section 6.4 of chapter 6). The alleged pattern of re-regulation that accompanies the official (financial) reform programme has been most ardently defended in Vogel (1996, pp.257 and 210):

In Japan, where government officials have traditionally relied on administrative guidance as a critical tool of policy, and administrative guidance has in turn relied on discretionary authority over industry, officials have been particularly keen to create new sources of this authority. This explains the most distinctive feature of Japanese reform: the ministries' effort to turn liberalisation into a protracted process in which their ability to determine the timing and conditions of new market entry generates a powerful new source of leverage over industry... The ministries have written the reform laws in a way that maximizes their own discretion in interpreting and implementing them. This discretion generates power because its expands their freedom to interpret the laws to their own liking, and it makes companies more reliant on the ministries to implement them in a manner

---

[10] In various personal interviews, this pattern was acknowledged by active and former MoF staff members, who asserted on the one hand that bureaucrats do not want to lose control (sometimes motivated by paternalistic concerns such as 'otherwise the private sector would be at a loss'), and on the other hand that weak companies want to remain protected and thus ask for guidance.

that suits the industry. Furthermore, it gives the ministries the ability to discriminate between market players, and this ability is critical to their power to enforce compliance with administrative guidance.

Thus, the pattern of re-regulation described above would have contributed to maintain, at least to some extent, the effectiveness of administrative guidance. Furthermore, it can be asserted that the process of formal financial liberalisation, the development of which may be measured by the number of formal statutes that have been eliminated by the monetary authorities, has not progressed convincingly. For example, according to official figures published by the Management and Co-ordination Agency, despite the on-going process of financial reform, the number of licences used by the MoF for policy purposes increased from 1,116 in 1985 to 1,469 in 1997, an increase of 32% in just 12 years; the combined number of these regulations under the jurisdiction of the MoF and FSA in 1998 was 1,623, an increase of 45% compared with 1985.[11] In relative terms, as a percentage of the total number of licences issued by Japanese ministries and agencies, the share of MoF's licences grew from 11% in 1985 to 13% in 1997 and to 15% in 1998 (including the FSA). Thus, the process of financial and administrative reform did not prevent, in either absolute or relative terms, an increase in MoF's formal regulation during the eighties and nineties, leaving it with considerable regulatory power (*kyoninka*). All in all, it should be concluded that the MoF still possesses significant numbers of 'carrots' and 'sticks' which it can use to a considerable extent and at its own discretion in relation to the implementation of administrative guidance. As regards the fourth condition, it is clear that the aspect of group solidarity, despite the magnitude of the problems in the banking sector, has been severely eroded owing to increasing interest differentiation between groups of banks and individual banks – a development that should have undermined the effectiveness of administrative guidance. Furthermore, the existence of informal networks between the monetary authorities and banks has come under pressure, although it is very difficult to assess to what extent their relevance and importance has actually declined. Finally, the situation regarding the sixth condition – i.e. sufficient concentration of regulatory power in one body – is relatively unclear as well. On the one hand, as shown above, the number of licences under the direct control of the MoF decreased significantly with the establishment of the FSA in 1998. On the other hand, it is not clear – at least not to me – whether the MoF and the current Financial Services Authority (FSEA) can be regarded as policy bodies each of which operates

---

[11] This analysis follows Carlile and Tilton (1998b, p.8). Updated figures are used from *Sōmuchō* (1999).

in a fashion completely independent of the other.[12] That is, it is not clear whether or not their combined regulatory power should be the yardstick against which to measure the actual ability and potential of these regulatory authorities to implement administrative guidance effectively.

Thus, the analysis of the conditions that determine the effectiveness of administrative guidance does not point clearly in a certain direction. It looks like there is a slight bias towards a less favourable environment for the use of informal instruments, but it is much too early to judge whether they can no longer be regarded as effective policy instruments. This is also reflected in the OECD's assessment of the use of administrative guidance by the Japanese government, which states that 'there is considerable disagreement about whether it continues to be an important regulatory tool', and that 'the degree of progress in eliminating guidance as a regulatory tool is not clear' (OECD 1999b, p.56). In any case, the deregulation programme that was approved by the Japanese government in March 1999 explicitly admitted that administrative guidance was still being used as a policy instrument. Despite these uncertainties, however, I believe that it is clear that three important lessons can be drawn from the Japanese experience with informal instruments. First, the policy response to the banking crisis in Japan has shown the limitations of these instruments as tools for crisis management. As has been discussed extensively in chapter 3, the effective implementation of administrative guidance requires consensus building and a certain degree of group solidarity between the various parties involved. However, in a crisis situation, the interests of individual banks are likely to begin to diverge sharply. To put it more aptly, with the development of the banking crisis, fewer banks were willing to pay the bill to clean-up the mess caused by other banks. This became clear when the monetary authorities' most favoured policy instruments in times of crisis – rescue mergers and 'voluntary' financial assistance – became more and more difficult to organise. Sometimes the MoF was able to force compliance, as, for example, in the case of Nippon Credit Bank (see chapter 6). However, it has also become clear that this practice was tolerated less and less, as public testimonies from angry executives of financial institutions which had to provide the funds have shown. Second, as has been remarked in Cargill (2000), administrative guidance is not the most appropriate instrument to monitor risk, which should be the central element in any prudent implementation of prudential policy. This is in my view mainly because the effectiveness of governmental guidance depends to

---

[12] One should also not forget the substantial powers of the MoF regarding tax matters, given its control of the National Tax Administration Agency and the Regional Taxation Bureaus. See *Jihyō Sha* (1998).

a considerable extent on the specific nature of the 'give-and-take' relationship between regulator and regulated party, which relates to the element of 'social exchange' (see chapters 2 and 3).[13] That is, to maintain the effectiveness of administrative guidance, occasionally supervisory authorities have to turn a blind eye to situations that require swift action. This brings me to the third lesson, which is related to the dimension of informality and the close and intimate relations between supervisors and banks that are part and parcel of the infrastructure necessary for administrative guidance to be effective. The policy response to the banking crisis has shown that, on the one hand, policymakers held on to their old habit of using informal instruments, perhaps for want of something better, perhaps because they could not or did not want to act differently. On the other hand, the large number of scandals implicating both supervisory authorities and banks and the general demand for more transparency and disclosure exposed the existence of the vast and deeply entrenched informal networks between them.

In the end, I believe that it was the inextricable link between the use of informal instruments and the necessary 'give-and-take' relationships ('carrot-and-stick' policy) between policymakers and financial institutions, which were firmly embedded into elaborate informal networks and ensured the effectiveness of the guidance, that was eventually the reason for the apparent increasing ineffectiveness of administrative guidance. That is, when the latter part of the relationship turned out to be increasingly unsustainable – see the large and increasing number of scandals and consequent public outrage and demands for restrictions on informal networks such as *amakudari* and the MoF-*tan* system – the continuation of the former part also became more and more problematic. In general, the element of 'social exchange' ('give-and-take' – see chapters 2 and 3) has declined in importance in parallel with changes in Japanese society, and this has undermined the effectiveness of administrative guidance, as asserted by the pluralistic network school and to a lesser extent by the consensual policy school (see chapters 2 and 3; Murakami and Rohlen 1992; Pempel 1998). Furthermore, the general tendency towards more legal transparency and the announced intention of the Japanese government to move towards ex-post monitoring of compliance with general rules instead of ex-ante approvals (see Cabinet Decision 1999) should make it more difficult to use informal instruments, although various observers differ sharply on this matter.[14] In addition, evidence has mounted

[13] In chapter 2, social exchange was defined as implicit give-and-take operating in a long-term framework in which both government and private firms get what they want.
[14] Pempel (1998), p.160, asserts that 'administrative guidance was reduced by requirements for the publicized transparency of all government directives'. Also Schwartz (1998),

that the 'give and take' element embedded in administrative guidance can have the rather unwelcome side-effect that 'over time, the regulator gets entangled in a web of obligations and favours that render rule enforcement difficult' (Schaede 1996, p.6). Finally, the ambiguity inherent in the informal nature of administrative guidance has been blamed on numerous occasions for causing confusion and scandals, embarrassing both regulators and financial institutions (various interviews, November–December 1992 and April–May 1995, Tokyo; Shindo 1992; Duck 1996, p.1723; van Rixtel 1998c). Even the published part of the guidance – i.e. the circulars or *tsūtatsu* – was often extremely difficult to understand, and not only for non-native speakers.

All in all, the Japanese experience with informal instruments has revealed serious shortcomings in their use. Whether or not they will continue to play a role in the implementation of Japanese monetary policy in general and prudential policy in particular will depend to a large extent on the progress made with further administrative (including legal) and financial reform.[15] Many observers remain sceptical about financial reform in Japan, including the 'Big Bang' programme, and doubt that the regulatory authorities are really serious about fundamentally changing the basic structure of the Japanese financial system (among many others: Dattel 1996; Murphy 1997; Keehn 1998, p.204; Nakatani 1998, p.37; Norville 1998). They accuse adherents of the market school of being naïve, and assert that deregulation in Japan is more 'a relaxation or loosening rather than a removal of regulation' (Carlile and Tilton 1998b, p.3). Some believe that because of electoral reasons, the ruling parties will be satisfied with just the appearance of reform (see for example: Carlile 1998; Lincoln 1998c; Pempel 1998). The pessimists among these sceptics promote the view, mentioned before, that the official process of financial reform is accompanied by a process of re-regulation, often of an informal nature, leaving the monetary authorities in control as strongly as before.

p.27, believes that, given certain legal developments, 'the utility of administrative guidance has diminished'. On the other hand, several observers have concluded that despite the introduction of the Administrative Procedures Law (see chapter 3), the ability of the government to use administrative guidance has not been effectively hampered (Lake 1998, p.135; see also Grier 1997). In this respect, various interviewees argued that the use of administrative guidance could be curtailed only by fundamental changes in the legal system, which still provides government bureaucrats with substantial powers to interpret existing regulations at their own discretion. The OECD has explicitly supported the importance of legal reform: 'The move from a regulatory system characterised by administrative guidance to one based on universal rules requires a strengthening of the legal profession' (OECD 2000).

[15] For more elaborate discussions of administrative and regulatory reform see Ozawa (1994), Carlile and Tilton (1998a), Gibney (1998a), Pempel (1998), Schwartz (1998), Curtis (1999), La Croix and Mak (1999), OECD (1999b) and Stockwin (1999).

Others subscribe to the importance of the reform measures adopted and the progress that has been made so far, but point at several improvements that still have to be implemented in several areas such as corporate governance in order to achieve more liberalised and efficient financial markets (see, for example, Cargill 2000; Hoshi and Patrick 2000a).[16] The Chairman of the Federal Reserve Board, Allan Greenspan, regarding the financial measures implemented by the Japanese government, emphasised that 'it has yet to make significant progress in diversifying the financial system' (Greenspan 1999).[17] The OECD concluded that the process of structural reform in Japan, with the possible exception of financial reform, appears to have been largely ineffective (IMF 1999b, p.98; OECD 1999b). Many international organisations and foreign governments stress the need for promoting administrative transparency and disclosure, and moving from discretionary guidance to rule-based governance (see, for example, US Embassy Tokyo 1999; United States 2000; OECD 1999, 2000). The apparent lack of success in structural reform has been reflected in official figures that showed that the government has completed only 58% of the deregulation measures announced (only 55% for the banking, brokerage and insurance sectors) (*Nikkei Weekly*, 18 December 2000). As regards the relationship between administrative and financial reform on the one hand and the use of informal instruments on the other, I would like to end with the following observations of two of the most renowned researchers on Japanese regulatory reform:

The pervasiveness of informal regulatory mechanisms has a number of implications for analyzing the Japanese regulatory reform process. It means that meaningful treatment of regulatory reform in Japan requires that the scope of analysis moves beyond looking simply at the formal regulatory mechanisms and scrutinize the often hidden world of informal administration and private sector regulation. Without this expanded purview, it is impossible to fully grasp the sources of reform initiatives and the roots of resistance to them. Furthermore, it implies that removing statutory and codified rules alone will frequently be insufficient to ensure that the private sector will be given free rein or to guarantee that a competitive market will necessarily follow. (Carlile and Tilton 1998b, p.9)

[16] One of the most positive assessments of the process of financial reform in Japan has been put forward by Beason and James (1999), p.201, where it is asserted that the Japanese financial system 'will certainly be more liberal than that in the US and many other industrialised nations. Japan will certainly enter the club of countries with essentially free financial markets.'

[17] In this respect, empirical evidence has become available that points at the costs of the heavy dependence on bank borrowing as a source of corporate finance in Japan. Weinstein and Yafeh (1998) show that the dominance of indirect finance in Japan in combination with underdeveloped capital markets may have inhibited economic growth. Kang and Stulz (2000) find that firms which relied more on bank credit reduced investment more than other firms in the early 1990s in Japan. See also Bayoumi (2001).

9.4   *Amakudari* and prudential policy: too close for comfort

The practice of *amakudari* – the descending from bureaucratic heaven of retired civil servants into private business – involving former staff members from the MoF and BoJ has been investigated extensively in this study. The main findings of the relevant chapters, in particular chapters 7 and 8, have already been discussed in their concluding sections. Therefore, I shall concentrate here on the general overview and present an assessment of the experiences with the post-retirement employment system of the Japanese government.

In chapter 7 it was demonstrated that the traditional interpretations of *amakudari* cannot convincingly explain the presence of MoF and BoJ retirees on the boards of Japanese private banks. Therefore, I proposed an alternative explanation that involves the elements of patterned equalisation, bureaucratic intervention and career management. In Chapter 8, this explanation was reformulated in three hypotheses, linking the various elements to, respectively,' 'buying influence', prudential policy or 'ex-post monitoring' and reward mechanisms. The empirical results strongly point at the importance and relevance of the first hypothesis, i.e. troubled Japanese private banks employed former MoF and BoJ officials in order to buy regulatory protection that would allow them to engage in desperate final attempts to survive ('go-for-broke' behaviour). Furthermore, I have shown that banks that did not employ these former bureaucrats performed on average significantly better (in terms of profitability) than banks which consistently hired them (see *The Economist*, 6 May 1995, p.32). I have also presented substantial qualitative evidence that provides further support for the detrimental effects of *amakudari* on bank performance. For example, out of 20 well-known problem banks, all but one employed retired MoF staff members long before any problem surfaced; in fact, all employed MoF and/or BoJ retirees for many years. The adverse impact on performance seems also to have occurred at the *jūsen* or housing loan companies, which were established with active support from the MoF and employed significant numbers of former high-ranking MoF staff members. There has been no sector in the Japanese financial system where former MoF officials were so heavily involved as the housing lenders; neither has there been any sector where the percentage of bankruptcies has been so high. It seems more than just a coincidence that more or less every bank that failed or got into serious problems experienced an inflow of MoF and/or BoJ retirees at some stage, which was not related to prudential supervisory concerns (because no problems were then apparent) but to other reasons such as 'buying influence' behaviour, and the persistent presence of these retirees in high-ranking positions thereafter. In this respect, it should be remembered (as discussed in chapters 7 and 8) that many MoF and BoJ retirees on the boards of private banks were previously employed in functions related to prudential policy. Thus, bank supervisors often had to inspect their previous superiors, which was probably not beneficial to the quality of banking inspections, for example because of the importance attached to seniority in Japanese society. The presence of former high-ranking staff members from the MoF and BoJ on the boards of private banks could also in numerous cases have delayed intervention by the supervisory authorities, given reasons of loss of reputation and prestige. It does nothing for the reputation of the MoF or BoJ if they have to admit – by intervening – that a bank under the guidance of one of their former top officials is close to bankruptcy. Through *amakudari*, the supervisory authorities became too entangled with the private banking sector, and often turned a blind eye to the deplorable situation of many Japanese banks. All in all, in my view, there is ample evidence to suggest that the practice of *amakudari* instigated collusive practices between supervisors and banks that have seriously undermined the implementation of an effective and independent prudential policy in Japan, and thereby contributed to the prolonged length and seriousness of the Japanese banking crisis (see also van Rixtel 1996, 1998c). That is, *amakudari* has been 'too close for comfort'. It has obstructed the development of arm's-length relations between supervisors and banks which are one of the guiding principles, accepted in many countries and based on broadly shared academic insights, for the establishment of a really prudent operation of prudential policy.[18]

As has been shown in chapter 8, it is clear that the detrimental effects of *amakudari* have not been restricted to the financial services industry. Indeed, many sectors in Japanese society and its economic system have experienced scandals and problems related in one way or another to the post-retirement system of the Japanese government bureaucracy. This system has also led to the establishment of many public sector related organisations whose main function seems to be to provide landing spots for retiring government bureaucrats.[19] Further, it discriminates between

---

[18] Some observers, such as Richardson (1997) and Brown (1999), do not subscribe to this view. However, they do not present any empirical analyses or show figures to support their claims. The empirical findings presented in this book and in other empirical studies available strongly point at a different conclusion.

[19] For example, 309 of the 726 executive positions (i.e. more than 40%) at 72 special legal entities were occupied by retired government bureaucrats (*Mainichi Daily News*, 10 August 2000). Furthermore, certain private companies seem to be functioning primarily as landing spots for retired civil servants. A clear example is the private company in charge of the operation of the Kansai International Airport: 8 of its 10 board members were former government officials (as of April 2000; see *Nihon Keizai Shimbun*, 24 April 2000).

'insiders' – firms that have established close connections with the government bureaucracy through *amakudari* relationships – and 'outsiders' (US Embassy Tokyo 1999). From the perspective of private business, the costs of hiring former civil servants can be high, particularly when firms have to be 'persuaded' to do so.[20] These hirings frustrate internal promotion schemes and easily can result in less efficient business operations. They are also costly, in particular at times of economic crisis and dwindling revenues. Not surprisingly, private corporations seem to be increasingly reluctant to provide *amakudari* landing spots (Duck 1996, pp.1698–1699; Brown 1999, p.38). Thus, in my view, there are convincing arguments in favour of the proposition that the practice of *amakudari* should be severely restricted. It is clear that this can only be achieved through structural reforms of the basic characteristics of the Japanese government bureaucracy. First, the financial incentives that are the raison d'être behind the existence of the post-retirement system of the government should be removed. That is, public pension schemes should be brought to the same or similar levels as private pension schemes. Second, the strict principle of seniority in the government bureaucracy should be abolished, so ending the custom that every year a certain number of civil servants have to retire at relatively early ages, and consequently need to find employment elsewhere. However, it does not seem likely that these conditions will be met soon (see also Komiya 1999).

As regards the current situation of *amakudari*, I have shown in chapter 7 that, at first sight and based on different sources, the numbers of retired MoF and BoJ staff members on the boards of Japanese private banks have come down considerably between 1993 and 1999. However, this does not necessary imply that the practice of *amakudari* in the financial services industry has decreased in importance. I have not investigated possible substitution effects, for example a compensation for the decrease in landing spots at the large and medium-sized private banks by an increase in post-retirement positions at smaller banks such as *shinkin* banks and credit co-operatives, research institutions affiliated with the large banks, other financial institutions or associations of financial institutions.[21] Furthermore, the MoF in particular has numerous possibilities to send its retirees to post-retirement positions in organisations affiliated with the public sector, such as public corporations

---

[20] In this respect, a very critical assessment of *amakudari* is presented by Komiya (1999), p.85: 'The practice of *amakudari* has given rise to the emergence and growth of a large number of what might be called "government–industry complexes". They have multiplied and proliferated over the 50 years since the end of the Second World War and have become a heavy burden on both tax-payers and the private sector.'
[21] For the importance of the latter in providing post-retirement positions for MoF and BoJ officials see Komiya (1999).

(*kodan*), special corporations (*tokushu gaisha*) and other so-called 'special legal entities' (*tokushu hōjin*), and public non-profit associations, foundations and research institutes (see also: Johnson 1974; Stockwin 1999, p.107).[22] Very often these positions serve as landing spots to wait out the two-year period stipulated by the National Public Service Law for retiring bureaucrats who want to accept positions in private business areas related to their previous position in the government bureaucracy (see chapter 3). These bureaucrats often become the *watari-dori*, or 'hopping birds', who jump from one post-retirement position to another.[23] The possibility exists that numerous MoF and BoJ retirees have descended into private companies unrelated to the financial services industry, various public entities and other organisations such as universities, simply waiting for things to turn better, such as a recovery of the economy or calming down of the public outrage over the many scandals related to *amakudari*. Thus, the decline of the direct movement into *amakudari* positions could be partly compensated by an increase in the number of *watari-dori* positions, leading to a renewed importance of *amakudari* in the near future. In this respect, it should be noted that the practice of *watari-dori* is of considerable importance for the MoF as a post-retirement employment system. Based on figures presented in Colignon and Usui (1999, p.55), it can be concluded that almost 40% of all *amakudari* movements from the MoF can be typified as *watari-dori*, predominantly consisting of an initial movement to the semi-public sector and then to the private sector (see table 9.1). In any case, official figures published by the Management and Coordination Agency in December 2000 showed that the post-retirement system of the Japanese government bureaucracy is still 'alive and kicking': of 538 bureaucrats who occupied positions of division chief or higher at the central government and retired between August 1999 and August 2000, 485 were re-employed within three months of retirement, of which more than half at quasi-government bodies (*Japan Times*, 21 December 2000; *Nihon Keizai Shimbun*, 21 December 2000). Hence, at the start of the new millennium, around 90% of all retiring high-ranking civil servants found new employment within a very short period of time. It is interesting to note that these figures are considerably

[22] The MoF is particularly known for its control of high-ranking positions at public corporations. According to media reports, MoF retirees filled the highest executive positions at almost 40% of these corporations (*Mainichi Daily News*, 16 August 2000).

[23] Figures published by the Management and Coordination Agency in May 2000 showed that 'hopping' around can be financially extremely rewarding: 200 retired bureaucrats who descended into public non-profit associations and corporations received onetime payouts of more than 30 million yen each for employment periods of less than 10 years, whereas in the private sector the average retirement bonus amounted to 32 million yen for no less than 35 years of service (*Mainichi Shimbun*, 5 May 2000).

Table 9.1. Amakudari *and* watari-dori *movements to the boards of private firms (based on Seikai-Kancho Jinjiroku 1995)*

Originating ministry/ agency	Total number of amakudari	Watari-dori paths 1[1]	2[2]	3[3]	4[4]	5[5]	Total number of wataridori	Number of watari-dori/ number of amakudari	Number of watari-dori/ total number of watari-dori
Police Agency	43	1	3	0	0	1	5	0.12	0.018
Defence Agency	22	2	2	1	0	0	5	0.227	0.018
Ministry of Finance	213	58	3	20	0	0	81	0.38	0.289
National Tax Agency	84	0	0	2	0	0	2	0.023	0.007
Ministry of Education	1	0	0	0	0	0	0	0	0
Ministry of Health & Welfare	6	0	0	0	0	0	0	0	0
Ministry of Agriculture	58	17	0	5	0	0	22	0.379	0.079
Ministry of Justice	7	0	0	0	0	0	0	0	0
Ministry of Foreign Affairs	1	0	0	0	0	0	0	0	0
MITI	115	34	1	16	2	0	53	0.46	0.189
Ministry of Posts & Telecom.	28	5	1	4	0	0	10	0.357	0.036
Ministry of Labour	3	0	0	0	0	0	0	0	0
Ministry of Construction	180	42	3	13	0	0	58	0.322	0.207
Ministry of Home Affairs	1	NA	NA	NA	NA	NA	NA	NA	NA

Notes: [1] Movement from a ministry to a *tokushu hōjin* (special legal entity such as a public corporation) and then to the private sector.
[2] Movement from a ministry to *zaidan-shadan* (public foundation) and then to the private sector.
[3] Movement from a ministry to a quasi-governmental entity and then to the private sector.
[4] Movement from a ministry to a private firm and then to another private firm.
[5] Movement from a ministry to an educational institution and then to the private sector.
Source: Colignon and Usui (1999), p.55.

higher than comparable figures for 1998, when only 375 retired government officials of the level of division chief or above found re-employment positions, of which 242 in public corporations (Kyodo World Service, 5 March 2000). This development does not look like a real regime-shift or the effective result of a profound administrative reform process. Furthermore, based on March 2000 figures, 126 executives (including 28 presidents), out of a total of 1,763 board members, at 115 regional and Second Tier regional banks originated from central or local government. Thus, as of March 2000, one in 14 board members and almost one in four presidents of regional and Second Tier regional banks was a former government official. In other words, despite the apparent decline in the inflow of government retirees into the boards of regional and Second Tier regional banks (flows), the number of incumbent former government bureaucrats on the boards of these banks (stocks) still remained high. Apparently, old habits die slowly. As regards the monetary authorities' perception of administrative reform, the real question is whether the 'voluntarily' restraints imposed by both the MoF and BoJ on the post-retirement employment practices of their staff will be maintained after the criticism of *amakudari* has faded away.[24] All in all, I remain rather sceptical about the effective reform of the post-retirement employment system of the Japanese government bureaucracy in general and of the practice of *amakudari* in particular. In this regard, I would like to hold with the assessment of the OECD: 'Recent scandals have thrown the habit into question, but if the fundamental incentives to hire former officials are not changed, *amakudari* is unlikely to disappear' (OECD 1999c, p.7).

9.5   Lessons from the Japanese experience

This study has focused explicitly on the relevance and importance of informal instruments in the implementation of Japanese monetary policy in general and of prudential policy in particular. I have adopted the qualitative theoretical framework, which has been developed in chapters 2, 3 and 4, for an institutional empirical investigation of the organisation and functioning of both the MoF and BoJ and their reaction to the banking crisis of the nineties in chapters 5 and 6 as well as a quantitative empirical investigation of the informal network constituted by *amakudari* in chapters 7 and 8. In my view, the results of the analysis are clear. Opaque regulation and discretion have serious drawbacks compared with rule-based prudential supervision. That is, transparency and disclosure cannot easily be replaced effectively by informal practices, a conclusion supported by economic theories departing from such universal concepts as agency costs (moral hazard) and corporate governance (see for example

[24] The experience with the Ministry of Construction makes one fear the worst. After severe criticism of its *amakudari* practices, which were related to several bribery scandals, the Ministry announced in 1993 that it would exercise restraint in this respect. However, in 1996 it was accused of reviving *amakudari* appointments for its retiring staff (*Daily Yomiuri* 2000). That old habits die slowly was also reflected in, for example, the appointment of another former high-ranking MoF official as president of the Tokyo Stock Exchange in May 2000. This time the only difference was that the new president did not retire from the MoF as administrative vice-minister but as Commissioner of the National Tax Administration Agency (*Nihon Keizai Shimbun*, 31 March 2000). Finally, a good example of the 'reform-minded' attitude towards the post-retirement employment practices at the central government bureaucracy was reflected in the revelation in April 2000 of a secret deal between the Ministry of International Trade and Industry (MITI) and a semi-public organisation to provide attractive management positions for retired MITI officials (*Nihon Keizai Shimbun*, 24 April 2000).

Llewellyn 2000; see also Milhaupt 1999). This may not be to the liking of some in the revisionist camp, who believe that general economic rules contribute little to achieving a better understanding of the 'unique' developments in Japan (see, for example, van Wolferen 1997). However, often their conclusions and analyses are steeped in generalist assertions, which almost without exception lack convincing empirical arguments and econometric analysis to support them. Furthermore, they seem virtually unaware of recent developments in economic theory and econometrics. Economics is much more than just old-fashioned neo-classical analysis and has much to offer, for example in the field of comparative institutional analysis, as has been demonstrated by the excellent studies of Aoki (2000) and Dore (2000). Economic theoretical investigations have also led to the conclusions that the Japanese monetary authorities should proceed cautiously with repeated capital injections and that the banks should be made aware of the threat of unavoidable closure in the event of non-compliance with prudential policy, in order to mitigate the risk of moral hazard (Diamond 2000). One can only hope that Japanese policy-makers have learned these lessons, but in any case, conventional economic 'wisdom' offers more than enough starting points to reach comprehensive solutions.

Furthermore, the Japanese experience has shown that the existence of too close connections between supervisory authorities and banks, instead of 'arm's-length' relations, can lead to collusive practices, in particular in an environment characterised by a weak and non-credible political opposition.[25] The vast informal networks blurring the separation between the public and the private undermined prudential policy, as interests of supervisors and banks frequently coincided, which delayed and frustrated necessary supervisory action. Thus, the dimension of informality contributed to the adoption of the policy of regulatory forbearance instead of a direct and adequate resolution of the banking problems. Similar to other international experiences with policy reactions to banking crises, this policy of delay turned out to be very costly in terms of the total amount of public money injected into the banking system and the repercussions for economic growth and financial stability (see also Eisenbeis and Horvitz 1993; Kane 1993; FDIC 1997; Herring 1998). The Japanese experience also shows that the 'magic' policy toolkit does not exist: informal instruments can have major drawbacks and limitations compared with clear and transparent rules, even when taking into account important

[25] In this respect, as has been observed in Milhaupt (1999), it should be noted that in a political economy characterised by a weak opposition and one dominant political party, with close relations between supervisory authorities and private banks, an informal safety net could easily be used to protect special interests.

historical and cultural differences between countries. Although informal
instruments may have been of relevance and importance at certain times
during the post-war 'high growth period' – opinions differ sharply on this
(see chapter 3) – their effects seem to have been increasingly counterproductive during the nineties.[26] If, for whatever reason, policymakers
wish to continue to employ administrative guidance, the major chal-
lenge will be for them to maintain the 'give-and-take' relationship with
the regulated companies that is necessary for compliance without this
leading to more scandals, in an environment demanding greater transparency and accountability and influenced by the rapidly proceeding
international integration of financial markets and the establishment of
international financial alliances. Given the experiences of recent years in
particular, it is clear to me that this will be a tall order. The increasing
concentration in the Japanese banking industry and the move towards
a small number of financial conglomerates in Japan could be helpful in
maintaining to some extent the effectiveness of various forms of 'moral
suasion'. However, these developments are also part of an international
trend towards greater consolidation and efficiency in the financial services industry, implying more emphasis on return on investment and
profitability, which is fundamentally at odds with managerial decision-
making processes being thwarted by informal government interference.
Furthermore, the Japanese financial structure is moving irrevocably towards greater diversification in the sources of corporate finance from
indirect to more direct finance, in parallel to similar developments cur-
rently taking place in the euro area (Santillán, van Rixtel and Marques
2000). This development will decrease the importance of the banking sector in the financing of the corporate sector and undermine the relevance
and importance of administrative guidance that departs from regulation
of the banking industry, as financial markets – given their close interdependence with international financial developments – are significantly less
under the control of monetary authorities than domestic banks. Finally,
the Japanese experience has demonstrated the importance of political
differentiation, in other words the existence of an effective and credible
political opposition. Unfortunately, during the nineties the banking crisis
in Japan was accompanied not only by an economic recession and a de-
moralised government bureaucracy, but also by a political crisis (see, for
example, Stockwin 1999, pp.8–9). These crises mutually reinforced each

---

[26] Some empirical evidence is also starting to emerge that leads to the conclusion that the
effects of administrative guidance in the Japanese financial services industry on productivity growth and technological progress have been negative (Katayama 1998, 2000). For
other research in this field see, for example, Weinstein (1992), and Beason and Weinstein
(1993).

other and promoted the policy of regulatory forbearance and inaction. For example, the paralysis in the political system that became so evident to international policymakers and investors during the summer of 1998, when government parties and opposition failed to agree on urgently needed financial support measures, seriously undermined national and international confidence in the stability of the Japanese financial system.

Of course, at the end of this study, one wonders what the future may bring. As has been remarked by Pempel (1998), p.138, 'change in Japan has typically been a matter of two steps forward and one step back'. The experiences with financial reform have indeed shown that changes come slowly and are often of such an ambivalent nature that they give rise to accusations of re-regulation instead of praise for deregulation. Progress is also slow with respect to the convergence of assessments of the developments in the Japanese political economy and financial system by various schools of thought and individual observers, which continue to differ fundamentally in opinion (see chapters 2 and 3). Some tend to be optimistic, believing in the impetus for change towards more structural reform, transparency and disclosure, and the strength of the Japanese people and policymakers to overcome the economic and financial difficulties of the nineties, which are, in the context of Japan's history, nothing more than a hiccup (see, for example, Posen 1998; Patrick 1999; Helweg 2000). In this respect, several observers argue that Japan has shown, in the past, a capacity to move fast where necessary, and that it will do so again, this time to 'embrace a new economic strategy' for the twenty-first century (Porter et al. 2000, pp.189–190). Others are much more pessimistic, sometimes slipping into 'gloom and doom' scenarios in which Japan is portrayed as being on the verge of disaster, and that only very fundamental reforms and drastic measures can prevent the total collapse (see in particular Morishima 1999; see also Katz 1998 and Mulgan 2000). A sense of growing impatience about developments in Japan, in particular regarding the financial services industry, has gripped international policymakers, as was demonstrated for example by the declaration of the February 2001 G7 meeting at Palermo (see also Köhler 2001).

Thus, at the start of the new millennium, concerns about the health of the Japanese financial system persist. When observing developments in Japan, one cannot avoid the impression of a continuous feeling of déjà vu. Some lessons have been learned, as demonstrated by the careful move towards greater transparency and disclosure in the form of the announced introduction of mark-to-market accounting in Fiscal Year 2001 and the breaking-up of the MoF, which has largely been the result of greater political differentiation. However, the need for further reforms is clear, as a continuous stream of bad news continues to dominate the economic headlines on Japan. As discussed in chapter 6, the credibility of prudential supervisors deteriorated again in the course of 2000. A new estimate of the total amount of bad loans of Japanese private banks was revealed by the FSEA at the request of the opposition in April 2001, which totalled around 150 trillion yen (22% of all outstanding loans) and overshadowed any figure published previously by the supervisory authorities. The deplorable situation of the Japanese insurance sector and public financial institutions added to the concerns of international policymakers and private bankers.

It is to be hoped that the Japanese supervisory authorities will finally take the necessary next steps, in particular the introduction of elements of debt forgiveness and loan workout programmes to solve the bad-loan problems and the further improvement of transparency and disclosure in the financial industry, including much more stringent measures to eliminate collusive practices emanating from the existence of informal networks between the public and the private sectors. Combined with the on-going 'Big Bang' financial deregulation programme, these steps could result in a restructured, revitalised and stronger Japanese financial system in the twenty-first century. However, any delay in further necessary regulatory reforms will make it more difficult to achieve this situation. Or, as Yukio Mishima wrote, citing the Master Jōchō: 'Now is the time, and the time is now' (Sparling 1992, p.149).

Bibliography

Abegglen, J.C. (1995). *Sea Change: Pacific Asia as the New World Industrial Center* (New York: The Free Press)

Abrahams, P. (1998). 'Gripped by Policy Paralysis', *Financial Times*, 28 September

The Accountant (1998). 'Japan – Fears over Effectiveness of Loan Reporting Rules', September

Ackley, G. and Ishi, H. (1976). 'Fiscal, Monetary, and Related Policies', in Patrick, H. and Rosovsky, H. (eds.), *Asia's New Giant: How the Japanese Economy Works* (Washington, DC: The Brookings Institution), 153–247

Administrative Reform Council (1997). 'Final Report of the Administrative Reform Council (Executive Summary)', 3 December, http://www.kantei.go.jp/

Alletzhauser, A. (1990). *The House of Nomura – The Rise to Supremacy of the World's Most Powerful Company: The Inside Story of the Legendary Japanese Dynasty* (London: Bloomsbury)

Allinson, G.D. and Sone, Y. (1993). *Political Dynamics in Contemporary Japan* (Ithaca: Cornell University Press)

Amyx, J.A. (1998). 'Banking Policy Breakdown and the Declining Institutional Effectiveness of Japan's Ministry of Finance: Unintended Consequences of Network Relations', dissertation submitted to the Department of Political Science and the Committee on Graduate Studies of Stanford University, July

(1999). 'Political Impediments to Far-Reaching Banking Reforms in Japan: Implications for Asia', in Noble, G. and Ravenhill, J. (eds.), *The East Asian Financial Crisis and the Architecture of Global Finance* (Cambridge: Cambridge University Press), 132–151

Anderson, C.W. and Campbell II, T.L. (2000). 'Corporate Governance of Japanese Banks', mimeo

Angel, R.C. (1991). *Explaining Economic Policy Failure: Japan in the 1969 and 1971 International Monetary Crisis* (New York: Columbia University Press)

Aoki, M. (1988a). 'The Japanese Bureaucracy in Economic Administration: A Rational Regulator or Pluralist Agent?', in Shoven, J.B. (ed.), *Government Policy Towards Industry in the United States and Japan* (Cambridge: Cambridge University Press), 265–300

——— (1988b). *Information, Incentives, and Bargaining in the Japanese Economy* (Cambridge: Cambridge University Press)

——— (2000). *Information, Corporate Governance, and Institutional Diversity: Competitiveness in Japan, the USA, and the Transitional Economies* (Oxford: Oxford University Press)

Aoki, M., Kim, H.-K. and Okuno-Fujiwara, M. (eds.) (1996). *The Role of Government in East Asian Economic Development: Comparative Institutional Analysis* (Oxford: Clarendon Press)

Aoki, M. and Patrick, H. (eds.) (1994). *The Japanese Main Bank System: Its Relevance for Developing and Transforming Economies* (Oxford: Oxford University Press)

Aoki, M., Patrick, H. and Sheard, P. (1994). 'The Japanese Main Bank System: An Introductory Overview', in Aoki and Patrick, 3–50

Aoki, M. and Saxonhouse, G.R. (eds.) (2000). *Finance, Governance, and Competitiveness in Japan* (Oxford: Oxford University Press)

Asahi Shimbun. Various issues.

Asiaweek (1998). 'Big Stink at the MoF – A New Scandal Unveils Lurid Tales of Corruption', 13 February, http://cnn.com/ASIANOW/asiaweek/98/0213/nat5.html

Balassa, B. and Noland, M. (1988). *Japan in the World Economy* (Washington, DC: Institute for International Economics)

Balling, M., Henry, E. and O'Brien, R. (eds.) (1998). *Corporate Governance, Financial Markets and Global Convergence* (Boston: Kluwer Academic Publishers)

Ballon, R.J. (1990). 'Decision Making in Japanese Industry', Sophia University, Institute of Comparative Culture, Business Series Bulletin no. 132

Ballon, R.J. and Tomita, I. (1988). *The Financial Behavior of Japanese Corporations* (Tokyo: Kodansha International)

Bank for International Settlements (BIS) (1986). *Changes in Money-Market Instruments and Procedures: Objectives and Implications* (Basle, BIS)

——— (1994). *Exploring Aggregate Asset Price Fluctuations across Countries: Measurement, Determinants and Monetary Policy Implications* (Basle, BIS)

Bank of Japan (1973). *Money and Banking in Japan* (Basingstoke: Macmillan)

——— (1988). 'Functions and Organization of the Bank of Japan', mimeo

——— (1990). 'Reorganization of the Bank of Japan', International Department, mimeo

——— (1992). 'Recent Developments in Monetary Aggregates', Bank of Japan Special Paper no. 221 (Tokyo)

——— (1993). 'Treasury Business of the Bank of Japan', Bank of Japan Special Paper no. 226 (Tokyo)

(1997). 'Revision of the Organisation and Operations of the Bank of Japan', http://www.boj.or.jp/en/about/bojlaw2.htm

(1998a). 'Utilization of Financial Institutions' Self-Assessment in Enhancing Credit Risk Management', *Bank of Japan Quarterly Bulletin*, February, 19–32

(1998b). 'Revisions to the Organisation and Operations of the Bank of Japan', International Department, mimeo

(1999). 'Principles for On-site Examination and Off-site Monitoring for Fiscal 1999', 30 March

(2000). *Annual Review 2000* (Tokyo: Bank of Japan)

(2001). *Monthly Report of Recent Economic and Financial Developments* (February) (Tokyo: Bank of Japan)

Annual Review, various issues (Tokyo: Bank of Japan)

Economic Statistics Monthly, various issues (Tokyo: Bank of Japan)

Quarterly Bulletin, various issues (Tokyo: Bank of Japan)

The Banker (1998). 'Bridge Plan to Nowhere', August, 26–29

(2001a). 'Bad Debts Haunt Japan', (January), 88–89

(2001b). 'Foreign Interest Stirs Trouble', January, 89–90

Banno, J. (ed.) (1997). *The Political Economy of Japanese Society*, Volume I: *The State or the Market?* (Oxford: Oxford University Press)

(1998). *The Political Economy of Japanese Society*, Volume II: *Internationalisation and Domestic Issues* (Oxford: Oxford University Press)

Barron's (2000). *Dictionary of Banking Terms* (Hauppauge, NY: Barron's Educational)

Batten, D., Blackwell, M., Kim, I., Nocera, S. and Ozeki, Y. (1989). 'The Instruments and Operating Procedures for Conducting Monetary Policy in the Group of Five Countries', IMF Working Paper WP/89/57

Bayoumi, T. (2001). 'The Morning After: Explaining the Slowdown in Japanese Growth in the 1990s', *Journal of International Economics*, 53, 241–259

Beason, D. and James, J. (1999). *The Political Economy of Japanese Financial Markets: Myths versus Reality* (Basingstoke: Macmillan)

Beason, R. and Weinstein, D.E. (1993). 'MITI and the Japanese Myth: Growth, Economics of Scale, and Targeting in Japan (1955–1990)', mimeo.

Benston, G.J. (1998). 'Regulating Financial Markets: A Critique and Some Proposals', The Institute of Economic Affairs, Hobart Paper no. 135

Berglöf, E. (1994). 'Corporate Governance in Transition Economies: The Theory and its Policy Implications', paper presented at CEPR/ECARE Workshop 'Competing Models of Capitalism', Brussels, 28–29 October

Berglöf, E. and Perotti, E. (1994). 'The Governance Structure of the Japanese Financial Keiretsu', *Journal of Financial Economics*, 36, 259–284

Bernanke, B. (2000). 'Japanese Monetary Policy: A Case of Self-Induced Paralysis?', mimeo, January

Bingham, C.F. (1989). *Japanese Government Leadership and Management* (Basingstoke: Macmillan)

Blumenthal, T. (1985). 'The Practice of *Amakudari* within the Japanese Employment System', *Asian Survey*, 25 (3), 310–321

Borio, C., Kennedy, N. and Prowse, S. (1994). 'Exploring Aggregate Asset Price Fluctuations across Countries: Measurement, Determinants and Monetary Policy Implications', BIS Economic Papers no. 40

Boyd, R. (1987). 'Government–Industry Relations in Japan: Access, Communication, and Competitive Collaboration', in Wilks, S. and Wright, M. (eds.), *Comparative Government–Industry Relations: Western Europe, the United States and Japan* (Oxford: Clarendon Press), 61–90

Brainard, W. (1967). 'Uncertainty and the Effectiveness of Policy', *American Economic Review, Papers and Proceedings*, 57(2), 411–425

Brouwer, G. de (1992). 'An Analysis of Recent Developments in the Japanese Money Market', Australian National University, Australia–Japan Research Centre, Pacific Economic Paper no. 211

Brown Jr., J.R. (1999). *The Ministry of Finance: Bureaucratic Practices and the Transformation of the Japanese Economy* (Westport: Quorum Books)

Burger, A.E. (1971). *The Money Supply Process* (Belmont: Wadsworth)

Burstein, D. (1988). *Yen! Japan's New Financial Empire and Its Threat to America* (New York: Simon and Schuster)

Buruma, I. (1989). *God's Dust: A Modern Asian Journey* (New York: Farrar, Straus and Giroux)

Cabinet Decision (1999). 'The Three-Year Programme for Promoting Deregulation as Revised, Cabinet Decision', 30 March

Calder, K.E. (1988). *Crisis and Compensation: Public Policy and Political Stability in Japan* (Princeton: Princeton University Press)

(1989). 'Elites in an Equalizing Role: Ex-Bureaucrats as Coordinators and Intermediaries in the Japanese Government–Business Relationship', *Comparative Politics*, July, 379–403

(1993). *Strategic Capitalism: Private Business and Public Purpose in Japanese Industrial Finance* (Princeton: Princeton University Press)

(1997). 'Assault on the Bankers' Kingdom: Politics, Markets, and the Liberalization of Japanese Industrial Finance', in Loriaux et al., 17–56

Capital Markets Research Institute (Japan). *Review*, various issues (Tokyo: Capital Markets Research Institute)

Caprio, Jr., G., Hunter, W.C., Kaufman, G.G. and Leipziger, D.M. (eds.) (1998). *Preventing Bank Crises: Lessons from Recent Global Bank Failures*, World Bank, EDI Development Studies (Washington, DC: World Bank)

Cargill, T.F. (1989). 'Central Bank Independence and Regulatory Responsibilities: The Bank of Japan and The Federal Reserve', Salomon Brothers Center for the Study of Financial Institutions, Monograph Series in Finance and Economics, 1989–2 (New York: Salomon Brothers Center for the Study of Financial Institutions at the Leonard N. Stern School of Business of New York University)

(1995). 'The Statistical Association between Central Bank Independence and Inflation', *Banca Nazionale del Lavoro Quarterly Review*, 159–172

(1998).'What Caused Japan's Banking Crisis?', mimeo, 31 May

(2000). 'What Caused Japan's Banking Crisis?', in Patrick and Hoshi, 37–58

Cargill, T.F., Hutchison, M.M. and Ito, T. (1997). *The Political Economy of Japanese Monetary Policy* (Cambridge, MA: MIT Press)
(1998). 'The Banking Crisis in Japan', in Caprio et al., 173–193
(2000). *Financial Policy and Central Banking in Japan* (Cambridge, MA: MIT Press)
Cargill, T.F. and Royama, S. (1988). *The Transition of Finance in Japan and the United States: A Comparative Perspective* (Stanford: Hoover Institution Press)
Carlile, L.E. (1998). 'The Politics of Administrative Reform', in Carlile and Tilton, 76–110
Carlile, L.E. and Tilton, M.C. (eds.) (1998a). *Is Japan Really Changing Its Ways? Regulatory Reform and the Japanese Economy* (Washington, DC: Brookings Institution)
(1998b). 'Regulatory Reform and the Developmental State', in Carlile and Tilton, 1–15
(1998c). 'Is Japan Really Changing?', in Carlile and Tilton, 197–218
Castells, M. (1996). *The Rise of the Network Society* (Oxford: Blackwell)
Cecchetti, S.G., Genberg, H., Lipsky, J. and Wadhwani, S. (2000). 'Asset Prices and Central Bank Policy', International Center for Monetary and Banking Studies/CEPR, Geneva Reports on the World Economy no. 2
Centre for Economic Policy Research (1998). *Financial Crises and Asia*, CEPR Conference Report no. 6 (London: CEPR)
Chant, J.F. and Acheson, K. (1986). 'The Choice of Monetary Instruments and the Theory of Bureaucracy', in Toma, E.F. and Toma, M. (eds.), *Central Bankers, Bureaucratic Incentives, and Monetary Policy* (Boston: Kluwer Academic Publishers), 107–128
Chew, D.H. (ed.) (1997). *Studies in International Corporate Finance and Governance Systems* (New York: Oxford University Press)
Choate, P. (1990). *Agents of Influence: How Japan Manipulates America's Political and Economic System* (New York: Touchstone)
Chow, G.C. (1975). *Analysis and Control of Dynamic Economic Systems* (New York: John Wiley & Sons)
Chowdhury, A. and Islam, I. (1993). *The Newly Industrialising Economies of East Asia* (London: Routledge)
Claessens, S., Djankov, S. and Klingebiel, D. (1999). 'Financial Restructuring in East Asia: Halfway There?', World Bank, Financial Sector Discussion Paper no. 3, (September)
Colignon, R.A. and Usui, C. (1999). 'Serial Retirements of Administrative Elites: *Wataridori*', in Meek, C.B. and Schvaneveldt, S.J. (eds.), *Best Papers Proceedings 1999 Association of Japanese Business Studies Conference*, Salt Lake City, 4–6 June, 43–60
Corbett, J. (1998). 'Changing Corporate Governance in Japan', in Balling et al., 113–136
(1999). 'Crisis? What Crisis? The Policy Response to Japan's Banking Crisis', in Freedman, 191–224
(2000). 'Japan's Banking Crisis in International Perspective', in Aoki and Saxonhouse, 139–175

Craig, V.V. (1998a). 'Japanese Banking: A Time of Crisis', Federal Deposit Insurance Corporation, *Banking Review*, 11(2), 9–17
(1998b). 'Financial Deregulation in Japan', Federal Deposit Insurance Corporation, *Banking Review*, 11(3), 1–12
Curtis, G.L. (1999). *The Logic of Japanese Politics: Leaders, Institutions, and the Limits of Change* (New York: Columbia University Press)
Daily Yomiuri. Various issues
Dattel, E.R. (1994). *The Sun that Never Rose* (Chicago: Probus)
(1996). 'Cultural Captivity – Japan's Crippled Financial System', *World Policy Journal*, Spring, 27–35
Davis, P.A. (1972). 'Administrative Guidance in Japan: Legal Considerations', Sophia University, Socio-Economic Institute, Bulletin no. 41
De Nederlandsche Bank (1995). *Jaarverslag 1994* (Annual Report 1994) (Amsterdam: De Nederlandsche Bank)
Demetriades, P.O. (1999). 'Financial Liberalisation and Credit-Asset Booms and Bust in East Asia', mimeo
Dennis, G.E.J. (1981). *Monetary Economics* (Harlow: Longman)
Deutsche Bank (2000). 'Frankfurt Voice – Japanese Life Insurers: The Second Movement of the Bad-asset Concerto?', *Deutsche Bank Research*, 11 February, 2–5
(2001). 'Japanese Banking System: Overview', Deutsche Bank, *Financial Institutions Worldwide*, 12 January, 147–152
Dewatripont, M. and Tirole, J. (1994). *The Prudential Regulation of Banks* (Cambridge, MA: MIT Press)
Diamond, D.W. (1984). 'Financial Intermediation and Delegated Monitoring', *Review of Economic Studies*, 51, 393–414
(2000). 'Should Japanese Banks Be Recapitalised?', mimeo, August
Dore, R. (2000). *Stock Market Capitalism: Welfare Capitalism – Japan and Germany versus the Anglo-Saxons* (Oxford: Oxford University Press)
Dotsey, M. (1986). 'Japanese Monetary Policy: A Comparative Analysis', *Federal Reserve Bank of Richmond Economic Review*, November/December, 12–24
Drucker, P.E. (1998). 'In Defense of Japanese Bureaucracy', *Foreign Affairs*, 77(5), 68–80
Duck, K. (1996). 'Now that the Fog Has Lifted: The Impact of Japan's Administrative Procedures Law on the Regulation of Industry and Market Governance – Comments', *Fordham International Law Journal*, 19, 1686–1763
Düser, T. (1990). *International Strategies of Japanese Banks: The European Perspective* (Basingstoke: Macmillan)
Eads, G.C. and Yamamura, K. (1987). 'The Future of Industrial Policy', in Yamamura and Yasuba, 423–468
Economic Strategy Council of Japan (1999). 'Strategies for Reviving the Japanese Economy – Report to Prime Minister Obuchi', 26 February (Tokyo: Ministry of Finance)
The Economist. Various issues, including
(1995). 'Japan's Unheavenly Insiders', 6 May, 32
(1998). 'Bruised, Battered and Broke', 15 August, 59–60

(2000). 'Japanese Financial Regulation: A Loss of Appetite', 16 September, 106

(2001a). 'Financial Regulation in Japan: In with the Old . . .', 6 January, 67–68

(2001b). 'Japanese Banks: Fiddling while Marunouchi Burns', 27 January, 73–79

EHS Law Bulletin Series (1991). *Japanese Laws Relating to Banks* (Tokyo: Eibun-Horeisha)

Eijffinger, S.C.W. (1986). *Over de Beheersbaarheid van de Geldhoeveelheid* (On the Controllability of the Money Supply) (Amsterdam: VU Uitgeverij)

Eijffinger, S.C.W. and de Haan, J. (1996). 'The Political Economy of Central-Bank Independence', Princeton University, Department of Economics, International Finance Section, Special Papers in International Economics no. 19

Eijffinger, S.C.W. and van Rixtel, A.A.R.J.M. (1992). 'The Japanese Financial System and Monetary Policy: A Descriptive Review', *Japan and the World Economy*, 4, 291–309

Eijffinger, S.C.W., van Rooij, M. and Schaling, E. (1996), 'Central Bank Independence: A Paneldata Approach', *Public Choice*, 89, 163–182

Eisenbeis, R.A. and Horvitz, P.M. (1993). 'The Role of Forbearance and Its Costs in Handling Troubled and Failed Depository Institutions', in Kaufman, G. (ed.), *Reforming Financial Institutions and Markets in the United States: Towards Rebuilding a Safe and More Efficient System* (Boston: Kluwer Academic Publishers), 49–68

Ernst & Young (1989). *A Guide for Foreign Securities Dealers Doing Business in Japan* (Tokyo: Ernst & Young)

Euromoney (1999a). 'A Little Help from My Friends', June, 30

(1999b). 'Cruel and Unusual Punishment', September, 48–51

(2000). 'Playing a Whole New Ball Game', August, 32–35

(2001). 'Bureaucrats give up a great treasure', February, 103–107

Evans Jr., R. (1990). 'Japan's Economy: An Economist's View', *The Japan Foundation Newsletter*, 17(3) 14–18

Federal Deposit Insurance Corporation (FDIC) (1995). 'Press Release – Regulators Terminate the US Operations of Daiwa Bank, Ltd. Japan', PR-67-95, 2 November

(1997). 'History of the Eighties – Lessons for the Future', Symposium Proceedings, 16 January

Federal Reserve Bank of Kansas City (1999). *New Challenges for Monetary Policy*, proceedings symposium, Jackson Hole, 26–28 August

Federation of Bankers Associations of Japan (1984). *Banking System in Japan* (Tokyo: Federation of Bankers Associations of Japan)

(1988). *Report on Specialized Financial Institution System in Japan* (Tokyo: Federation of Bankers Associations of Japan)

(1990a). *On a New Japanese Financial System* (Tokyo: Federation of Bankers Associations of Japan)

(1990b). *Japanese Banks '90* (Tokyo: Federation of Bankers Associations of Japan)

(1994). *The Banking System in Japan* (Tokyo: Federation of Bankers Associations of Japan)

(1996). *Japanese Banks '96* (Tokyo: Federation of Bankers Associations of Japan)

Japanese Banks, various issues (Tokyo: Federation of Bankers Associations of Japan)

Feldman, R.A. (1986). *Japanese Financial Markets: Deficits, Dilemmas, and Deregulation* (Cambridge, MA: MIT Press)

Financial Services Agency (1999). 'Publication of the Program Year 2000 Basic Guidelines and Basic Plan for Inspections', 28 July (Tokyo: Financial Services Agency)

(2000). 'Statement by the Commissioner on the Establishment of the Financial Services Agency', 3 July (Tokyo: Financial Services Agency)

Financial Supervisory Agency (1999). 'Publication of the 1999 Program Year Basic Guidelines and Basic Plan for Inspections', 3 August (Tokyo: Financial Supervisory Agency)

Financial System Council (1999a). 'Summary of the Interim Report of the First Committee of the Financial System Council', 6 July (Tokyo: Ministry of Finance)

(1999b). 'Report on the Framework of the Deposit Insurance System and Resolution of Failed Financial Institutions after the Termination of Special Measures', 21 December (Tokyo: Ministry of Finance)

Financial System Research Council (1997a). 'Report on the Revision of the Bank of Japan Law', 6 February (Tokyo: Ministry of Finance)

(1997b). 'Regarding the Reform of the Japanese Financial System', 13 June (Tokyo: Ministry of Finance)

Financial Times (1998). 'Western Banks Reduce Yen Deposit Rates to below Zero', 6 November

(2001). 'Reformist Minister Walks Financial Sector Tightrope', 21 December

Fingleton, E. (1995). 'Japan's Invisible Leviathan', *Foreign Affairs*, 74(2), 69–85

Fiorillo, J. (1999a). 'The FSA – Full Speed Ahead', ING Barings, *Japanese Financial News*, 15 February

(1999b). 'Creation of a New Banking Universe', ING Barings, *Japan Research*, 14 December

(2000a). 'Banking Reform Postmortem – FRC's Ochi and the LDP are Backtracking on System Rehabilitation', ING Barings, *Japan Research*, 12 January

(2000b). 'Suruga Bank – Against Which all Others Should Be Judged', ING Barings, *Financial News*, 26 June

(2000c). 'The New FSA – What to Expect', ING Barings, *Financial News*, 26 July

(2000d). 'Sogo Causes Dramatic Upturn in Bankruptcies', ING Barings, *Financial News*, 14 August

(2000e). 'Good Old Boy Mori at the Finance Agency – A Second Round of Reform?', ING Barings, *Industry News*, 14 December

(2000f). 'The NPL Problem – Which Banks to Avoid!', ING Barings, *Industry News*, 20 December

Flannery, M.J. (1995). 'Prudential Regulation for Banks', in Sawamoto, Nakajima and Taguchi, 281–318

Flynn, N. (1999). *Miracle to Meltdown in Asia* (Oxford: Oxford University Press)

Foundation for Advanced Information and Research (1991). *FAIR Fact Series II: Japan's Financial Markets* (Tokyo: Foundation for Advanced Information and Research)

Frankel, A.B. and Morgan, P.B. (1992). 'Deregulation and Competition in Japanese Banking', *Federal Reserve Bulletin*, August, 579–593

Freedman, C. (ed.) (1998). *Japanese Economic Policy Reconsidered* (Cheltenham: Edward Elgar)

—— (1999). *Why Did Japan Stumble? Causes and Cures* (Cheltenham: Edward Elgar)

Friedman, B.M. (1975). 'Targets, Instruments, and Indicators of Monetary Policy', *Journal of Monetary Economics*, 1(4), 443–473

—— (1990). 'Targets and Instruments of Monetary Policy', in Friedman, B.M. and Hahn, F.H. (eds.), *Handbook of Monetary Economics*, Volume II (Amsterdam: North-Holland), 1185–1230

Friedman, D. (1988). *The Misunderstood Miracle: Industrial Development and Political Change in Japan* (Ithaca: Cornell University Press)

Friedman, M. (1969). *The Optimum Quantity of Money and Other Essays* (Chicago: Aldine)

Friesen, C.M. (1986). *International Bank Supervision* (London: Euromoney Publications)

Fruin, W.M. (ed.) (1998). *Networks, Markets, and the Pacific Rim: Studies in Strategy* (Oxford: Oxford University Press)

Fujiwara, K. and Yamori, N. (1997). 'Kinyū Kikan e no Yakuin Haken ni tsuite – Dai-ni Chihō Ginkō no Ba-ai' (The Dispatching of Officials to Financial Institutions – The Case of the Second Tier Regional Banks), *Kinyū Keizai Kenkyū*, 13(14), 70–85

Fukao, M. (1998). 'Japanese Financial Instability and Weaknesses in the Corporate Governance Structure', *Seoul Journal of Economics*, 11(4), 381–422

—— (1999). 'Recapitalising Japan's Banks: The Functions and Problems of the Financial Revitalisation Act and Bank Recapitalisation Act', mimeo, 30 June

Fukui, T. (1986). 'The Recent Development of the Short-term Money Market in Japan and Changes in the Techniques and Procedures of Monetary Control used by the Bank of Japan', in Bank for International Settlements (ed.), *Changes in Money-Market Instruments and Procedures: Objectives and Implications* (Basle: BIS), 94–126

Funabashi, Y. (1989). *Managing the Dollar: From the Plaza to the Louvre* (Washington, DC: Institute for International Economics)

Gerlach, M.L. (1992). *Alliance Capitalism: The Social Organization of Japanese Business* (Berkeley: University of California Press)

Gerlach, M.L. and Lincoln, J.R. (1998). 'Structural Analysis of Japanese Economic Organization – A Conceptual Framework', in Fruin, 293–321

Gertler, M., Goodfriend, M., Issing, O. and Spaventa, L. (1998). *Asset Prices and Monetary Policy: Four Views*, (Basle: BIS/CEPR)

Gibney, F. (ed.) (1998a). *Unlocking the Bureaucrat's Kingdom: Deregulation and the Japanese Economy* (Washington, DC: Brookings Institution Press)

—— (1998b). 'Introduction', in Gibney, 1–15

Gibson, M.S. (1998). 'Big Bang Deregulation and Japanese Corporate Govern-ance: A Survey of the Issues', Board of Governors of the Federal Reserve System, International Finance Discussion Paper no. 624.

Goldman Sachs (1998). 'Financial Services – Major Banks: Bridge Bank – Great Propaganda?', *Goldman Sachs Investment Research*, 29 July

(2000). 'Banks – City Banks: How Many Loan Losses Still to Go? An Alternative Methodology to Looking at Category 2s', *Goldman Sachs Investment Research*, 26 April

Goodhart, C.A.E. (1988). *The Evolution of Central Banks* (Cambridge, MA: MIT Press)

(1989). *Money, Information and Uncertainty* (2nd edn) (Basingstoke: Mac-millan)

(1995). 'The Objectives for, and Conduct of, Monetary Policy in the 1990s', in Goodhart, C.A.E. (ed.), *The Central Bank and the Financial System* (Basingstoke: Macmillan), 216–235

Goodhart, C.A.E. and Sutija, G. (eds.) (1990). *Japanese Financial Growth* (Basingstoke: Macmillan)

Goodman, G.K. (1986). *Japan: The Dutch Experience* (London/Dover: Athlone Press)

Gool, P. van (1987). *Monetaire Transmissie: Een Geschiedenis* (A History of Monetary Transmission) (Amsterdam: VU Uitgeverij)

Gordon, R.H. (1976). 'An Interpretation of the Costs on the Instruments in Deterministic Linear-Quadratic Control', *International Economic Review*, 17(3), 779–781

Government Ruling Party Conference (1998a). 'Comprehensive Plan for Financial Revitalisation (1st Version) – Government-Ruling Party Con-ference to Promote the Comprehensive Plan for Financial Revitalisation', 23 June

(1998b). 'Comprehensive Plan for Financial Revitalisation (Second Report) – Government-Ruling Party Conference to Promote the Comprehensive Plan for Financial Revitalisation', 2 July

Greenspan, A. (1999). 'Do Efficient Financial Markets Mitigate Financial Crises?', deposition to the 1999 Financial Markets Conference of the Federal Reserve Bank of Atlanta, 19 October, http://www.federalreserve.gov/boarddocs/speeches/1999/

Grier, J.H. (1997). 'Information Disclosure and Deregulation', speech delivered at the Tokyo American Center, 27 June, http://www.jipr.org

Groenewegen, J. (1994). 'A Changing Japanese Market for Corporate Control', mimeo

Group of Ten (2001). 'Report on Consolidation in the Financial Sector'

Haitani, K. (1976). *The Japanese Economic System: An Institutional Overview* (Lexington, MA: Lexington Books)

Haley, J.O. (1986). 'Administrative Guidance versus Formal Regulation: Resolv-ing the Paradox of Industrial Policy', in Saxonhouse, G.R. and Yamamura, K. (eds.), *Law and Trade Issues of the Japanese Economy: American and Japanese Perspectives* (Seattle and London: University of Washington Press), 107–128

(1989). 'The Context and Content of Regulatory Change in Japan', in Button, K. and Swann, D. (eds.), *The Age of Regulatory Reform* (Oxford: Clarendon Press), 124–138

(1991). *Authority Without Power* (New York: Oxford University Press)

(1992). 'Consensual Governance: A Study of Law, Culture, and the Political Economy of Postwar Japan', in Kumon and Rosovsky, 32–62

Hall, M.J.B. (1993). *Banking Regulation and Supervision: A Comparative Study of the UK, USA and Japan* (Aldershot: Edward Elgar)

(1998a). *Financial Reform in Japan – Causes and Consequences* (Cheltenham: Edward Elgar)

(1998b). 'Financial Reform in Japan: Redefining the Role of the Ministry of Finance', *Journal of International Banking Law*, 5, 171–177

Hamada, K. (1995). 'Bubbles, Bursts and Bailouts: A Comparison of Three Episodes of Financial Crises in Japan', in Okabe, M. (ed.), *The Structure of the Japanese Economy: Changes on the Domestic and International Fronts* (Basingstoke: Macmillan), 263–286

(1998). 'The Japanese Big Bang as a Unilateral Action', mimeo

Hamada, K. and Hayashi, F. (1985). 'Monetary Policy in Postwar Japan', in Ando, A., Eguchi, H., Farmer, R. and Suzuki, Y. (eds.), *Monetary Policy in Our Times* (Cambridge, MA: MIT Press), 83–121

Hamada, K. and Horiuchi, A. (1987). 'The Political Economy of the Financial Market', in Yamamura and Yasuba, 223–260

Hanazaki, M. and Horiuchi, A. (1998). 'A Vacuum of Governance in the Japanese Bank Management', Center for International Research on the Japanese Economy, Discussion Paper CIRJE-F-29, December

Handelsblatt (1998). 'IWF besorgt um Tokios Finanzsystem', 17 August

Harner, S.M. (2000). *Japan's Financial Revolution – And How American Firms Are Profiting* (Armonk, NY: M.E. Sharpe)

Hartcher, P. (1998). *The Ministry – The Inside Story of Japan's Ministry of Finance* (London: HarperCollinsBusiness)

Hayashi, R. (1999). 'Changes in Bureaucracy', in Asia/Pacific Research Center Stanford University (ed.), *Crisis and Aftermath: The Prospects for Institutional Change in Japan*, Report of a Conference at Stanford University, 3 May, 19–25

Hellmann, D.C. (1988). 'Japanese Politics and Foreign Policy: Elitist Democracy Within an American Greenhouse', in Inoguchi and Okimoto, 345–378

Helweg, M.D. (2000). 'Japan: A Rising Sun?', *Foreign Affairs*, 79(4), 26–39

Henderson, D.F. (1973). *Foreign Enterprise in Japan: Laws and Policies* (Chapel Hill: University of North Carolina Press)

Henderson, D.W. and Turnovsky, S.J. (1972). 'Optimal Macroeconomic Policy Adjustment under Conditions of Risk', *Journal of Economic Theory*, 4, 58–71

Herring, R.J. (1998). 'Banking Disasters: Causes and Preventative Measures – Some Extrapolations from Recent U.S. Experience', paper presented at seminar 'Global Lessons in Banking Crisis Resolution for East Asia', The Economic Development Institute of the World Bank, Singapore, May

Herring, R.J. and Wachter, S. (1999). 'Real Estate Booms and Banking Busts: An International Perspective', University of Pennsylvania, The Wharton School, Financial Institutions Center, Discussion Paper 99–27

Hirsh, M. and Henry, E.K. (1997). 'The Unraveling of Japan Inc.: Multinationals as Agents of Change', *Foreign Affairs*, 76(2), 11–16

Hiwatari, N. (1998). 'Explaining the End of the Post-War Party System', in Banno, 285–319

(2000). 'The Reorganization of Japan's Financial Bureaucracy: The Politics of Bureaucratic Structure and Blame Avoidance', in Hoshi and Patrick, 109–136

Hodgman, D.R. (ed.) (1983). *The Political Economy of Monetary Policy: National and International Aspects'*, Federal Reserve Bank of Boston, Conference Series, 26

Hollerman, L. (1988). *Japan, Disincorporated: The Economic Liberalization Process* (Stanford: Hoover Institution Press, Stanford University)

(1998). 'Whither Deregulation? An Epilogue to Japan's Industrial Policy', in Gibney, 243–270

Horiuchi, A. (1984). 'The "Low Interest Rate Policy" and Economic Growth in Postwar Japan', *The Developing Economies*, 4, 349–369

(1996). 'Financial Fragility and Recent Developments in the Japanese Safety Net', revised version of paper prepared for the 71st Annual Western Economic Association International Conference, San Francisco, June

Horiuchi, A. and Shimizu, K. (1998). 'Did *Amakudari* Undermine the Effectiveness of Regulator Monitoring in Japan?', University of Tokyo, Faculty of Economics, Discussion Paper no. 98-F-10, April

Horne, J. (1985). *Japan's Financial Markets: Conflict and Consensus in Policymaking* (Sydney: George Allen & Unwin)

(1988). 'The Economy and the Political System', in Stockwin, J.A.A. (ed.), *Dynamic and Immobilist Politics in Japan* (Basingstoke: Macmillan), 141–170

Hoshi, T. (2000). 'What Happened to Japanese Banks', Bank of Japan, Institute for Monetary and Economic Studies, Discussion Paper no. 2000-E-7

Hoshi, T. and Kashyap, A. (1999). 'The Japanese Banking Crisis: Where Did it Come From and How will it End?', NBER Working Paper no. 7250

(2000). 'Japan Backtracks on Final Liberalisation', *Asian Wall Street Journal*, 21 February

Hoshi, T. and Patrick, H. (eds.) (2000a). *Crisis and Change in the Japanese Financial System* (Boston/Dordrecht, Kluwer Academic Publishers)

(2000b). 'Introduction', in Hoshi and Patrick, 1–33

Hoshi, T., Scharfstein, D. and Singleton, K.J. (1991). 'Japanese Corporate Investment and Bank of Japan Guidance of Commercial Bank Lending', paper presented at NBER Conference on Japanese Monetary Policy, Tokyo, April

Hsu, R.C. (1994). *The MIT Encyclopedia of the Japanese Economy* (Cambridge, MA: MIT Press)

Hutchison, M.M. (1988). 'Monetary Control with an Exchange Rate Objective: The Bank of Japan, 1973–1986', *Journal of International Money and Finance*, 7, 261–271

Hutchison, M., McDill, K. and Madrassy, R. (1999). 'Empirical Determinants of Banking Crises: Japan's Experience in International Perspective', in Freedman, 157–183

Imai, K.I. (1992). 'Japan's Corporate Networks', in Kumon and Rosovsky, 198–230

Inoguchi, T. and Okimoto, D.I. (1988). *The Political Economy of Japan*, Volume II: *The Changing International Context* (Stanford: Stanford University Press)

Inoki, T. (1993). 'Japanese Bureaucrats at Retirement: The Mobility of Human Resources from Central Government to Public Corporations', World Bank, Economic Development Institute, Working Paper no. 93–32

International Currency Review (1995). 'The Japanese Banking Crisis – The Daiwa Bank Catastrophe', *International Currency Review*, 23(2), 23–32

International Monetary Fund (IMF) (1992), *International Capital Markets: Developments, Prospects, and Policy Issues*, 1992 issue (Washington, DC: IMF)

(1993). *International Capital Markets: Developments, Prospects, and Policy Issues*, 1993 issue (Washington, DC: IMF)

(1997). *International Capital Markets: Developments, Prospects, and Policy Issues*, 1997 issue (Washington, DC: IMF)

(1998). *International Capital Markets: Developments, Prospects, and Policy Issues*, 1998 issue (Washington, DC: IMF)

(1999a). *International Capital Markets: Developments, Prospects, and Policy Issues*, 1999 issue (Washington, DC: IMF)

(1999b). 'Japan: Economic and Policy Developments', Staff Country Report no. 99/114 (Washington, DC: International Monetary Fund)

(2000a). 'International Capital Markets: Developments, Prospects, and Policy Issues – Annex I: Progress in Financial and Corporate Restructuring in Japan' (Washington, DC: International Monetary Fund)

(2000b). 'Japan: Staff Report for the 2000 Article IV Consultation', Staff Country Report no. 00/98, August (Washington, DC: International Monetary Fund).

(2000c). 'Japan: Economic and Policy Developments', Staff Country Report no. 00/143, November (Washington, DC: International Monetary Fund)

Ishizaka, M. (1992). 'The Course of Action Planned by the Securities and Exchange Surveillance Commission', *Capital Markets Research Institute Review*, 28, 13–23

Ito, T. (1992). 'Losing Face?', *The International Economy*, May/June, 46–49

(1999). 'Comments on Corbett', in Freedman, 225–229

(2000). 'The Stagnant Japanese Economy in the 1990s: The Need for Financial Supervision to Restore Sustained Growth', in Hoshi and Patrick, 85–107

Ito, T. and Harada, K. (2000). 'Japan Premium and Stock Prices: Two Mirrors of Japanese Banking Crises', NBER Working Paper no. 7997

Ito, T. and Melvin, M. (1999). 'Japan's Big Bang and the Transformation of Financial Markets', NBER Working Paper no. 7247

Itoh, M. (1990). *The World Economic Crisis and Japanese Capitalism* (Basingstoke: Macmillan)

Japan Economic Institute (1994). 'Uncertain Impact of Administrative Reform Law', Report B, 21 October

(1998). 'Japan's Banks and the Bad-Loan Problem: The Nightmare Continues', *Japan Economic Institute Report*, 25A, 3 July

Japan Economic Institute Report, various issues

Japan Economic Journal. Various issues

Japan Press Network (2000). 'Ruling Parties' Administrative Reform Panel Agrees on Proposal to Ban *Amakudari* Practices by 2005', 13 July, http://www.jpn.co.jp/

Japan Times. Various issues

Japanese Bankers Association (1998). *Banking Law (Japan)* (Tokyo: Japanese Bankers Association)

Jarrett, P. (1998). 'The Japanese Recession: What Caused It and What to Do about It', paper presented at the NBER/TCER Japan Project Conference, Tokyo, 29–30 October

Jihyō Sha. *Ōkurashō Meikan* (Personnel Directory of the MoF), various issues (Tokyo: Jihyō Sha)

Jinji In. *Eiri Kigyō e no Shūshoku no Shōnin ni kansuru Nenji Hōkokusho* (National Personnel Authority, Annual Report Concerning Approvals of Employment in Profit-making Enterprises), various issues (Tokyo: National Personnel Authority)

Johansen, L. (1973). 'Targets and Instruments under Uncertainty', in Bos, H.C., Linneman, H. and De Wolff, P. (eds.), *Economic Structure and Development: Essays in Honour of Jan Tinbergen* (Amsterdam: North-Holland), 3–20

Johnson, C.J. (1974). 'The Reemployment of Retired Government Bureaucrats in Japanese Big Business', *Asian Survey*, 14, 953–965

(1978). *Japan's Public Policy Companies* (Washington, DC: American Enterprise Institute for Public Policy Research)

(1982). *MITI and the Japanese Miracle: The Growth of Industrial Policy, 1925–1975* (Tokyo: Charles E. Tuttle)

(1988). 'Studies of Japanese Political Economy: A Crisis in Theory', *The Japan Foundation Newsletter*, 16(3), 1–11

(1993). 'Comparative Capitalism: The Japanese Difference', *California Management Review*, 35(4), 51–67

(1995a). 'Japan: Who Governs? An Essay on Official Bureaucracy', in Johnson, 115–140

(1995b). 'Puppets and Puppeteers: Japanese Political Reform', in Johnson, 212–231

(1995c). *Japan: Who Governs? The Rise of the Developmental State* (New York: W.W. Norton)

Johnson, C.J. and Keehn, E.B. (1994). 'A Disaster in the Making: Rational Choice and Asian Studies', *The National Interest*, Summer, 14–22

JP Morgan (2000a). 'New Deposit Insurance System and Treatment of Failed Banks', JP Morgan Securities Asia Pte Ltd, *Japan Credit Research*, 6 April

(2000b). 'The Bank Straight Bond Market in Japan', JP Morgan Securities Asia Pte Ltd, *Japan Credit Market Strategy*, 6 October

(2000c). 'Japan Credit Monthly', JP Morgan Securities Asia Pte Ltd, *Japan Credit Research*, 6 December

Juristo (1991). 'Gyōsei Shidō Tetsuzuki Hō Yōkō An' (Administrative Procedures Law, Outline of Bill), *Juristo*, 985, 73–78

Kanaya, A. and Woo, D. (2000). 'The Japanese Banking Crisis of the 1990s: Sources and Lessons', IMF Working Paper WP/00/7

Kanda, H. (1990). 'Legal Aspects of Securitization in Japan', paper presented at SOAS Conference 'Which Path for the Japanese Financial System?', London, March

Kane, E.J. (1993). 'What Lessons Should Japan Learn from the U.S. Deposit-Insurance Mess?', *Journal of the Japanese and International Economies*, 7, 329–355

Kang, J.-K. and Shivdasani, A. (1995). 'Firm Performance, Corporate Governance, and Top Executive Turnover in Japan', *Journal of Financial Economics*, 38, 29–58

Kang, J.-K. and Stulz, R.M. (2000). 'Do Banking Shocks Affect Borrowing Firm Performance? An Analysis of the Japanese Experience', *Journal of Business*, 73(1), 1–23

Kaplan, S.N. and Minton, B.A. (1994). 'Appointments of Outsiders to Japanese Boards: Determinants and Implications for Managers', *Journal of Financial Economics*, 36, 225–258

Kasa, K. and Popper, H. (1997). 'Monetary Policy in Japan: A Structural VAR Analysis', *Journal of the Japanese and International Economies*, 11, 275–295

Katayama, S. (1998). 'Administrative Guidance, and Productivity and Innovation: Japanese Financial Sector', APEA 1998 Spring Conference, *Papers and Proceedings*, 13–25

(2000). 'Japanese Political Culture and Government Regulation', *European Journal of Political Economy*, 16, 273–286

Katayama, T. and Makov, R. (1998). 'Deregulation of Financial Markets in Japan', *Journal of International Banking Law*, 128–133

Katz, R. (1998). *Japan: The System that Soured – The Rise and Fall of the Japanese Economic Miracle* (Armonk, NY: M.E. Sharpe)

Kawakita, T. (1991). 'The Ministry of Finance', *Japanese Economic Studies*, Summer, 3–29

Keehn, E.B. (1990). 'Managing Interests in the Japanese Bureaucracy: Informality and Discretion', *Asian Survey*, 30(11), 1021–1037

(1998). 'The Myth of Regulatory Independence in Japan', in Gibney, 204–219

Keidanren (1998). 'For the Promotion of Deregulation Aimed at Economic Revival and the Establishment of a Transparent System of Governmental Management', 20 October, http://www.keidanren.or.jp/

Kenrick, D.M. (1988). *The Success of Competitive-Communism in Japan* (Basingstoke: Macmillan)

Kinyū Kantoku Chō (1999). *Kinyū Kantoku Chō no 1 Toshi* (The First Year of the Financial Supervisory Agency) (Tokyo: Kinyū Kantoku Chō)

Kinyū Shōken Research (1992). *Kinyū Shihon Shijōni Kan suru Ōkurashō Kankei Shiryō Shu 1992 Nenban* (Financial and Securities Research, 1992 Overview of Capital Markets Based on the Ministry of Finance Data Collection) (Tokyo: Kinyū Shōken Research)

Kinyū Zaisei Jijō Kenkyū Kai, *Ginkō Kyoku Kinyū Nenpō* (Monetary and Financial Research Association, Banking Bureau, Ministry of Finance: Annual Review), various issues (Tokyo: Monetary and Financial Research Association) (1993). *Ginkō Kyoku Kinyū Nenpō Bessatsu, Ginkō Kyoku Genkō Tsūtatsu 1993 Nenban* (Monetary and Financial Research Association, Banking Bureau, Ministry of Finance, Supplement Annual Review 1993 Edition, Current *Tsūtatsu* Banking Bureau Ministry of Finance) (Tokyo: Monetary and Financial Research Association)

Kitagawa, Z. (1989). *Doing Business in Japan* (New York: Matthew Bender)

Kitami, R. (1998). 'Resolution and Collection Methods in Japanese Financial Markets', paper presented at World Bank seminar 'Global Lessons in Banking Crisis Resolution for East Asia', Singapore, 12–13 May

Kneeshaw, J.T. and van den Bergh, P. (1989). 'Changes in Central Bank Money Market Operating Procedures in the 1980s', BIS Economic Papers, no. 23.

Köhler, H. (2001). 'Home Free? Turning Crisis into Opportunity', *Asian Wall Street Journal*, 8 January

Kokusai Kyoku Shōgai Gurūpu (1990). *Shokui, Kyoku Shitsu Kenkyūjo Tō no Eibun Koshō* (Liaison Group, International Department, Bank of Japan: English Translations of Functions in Departments, Offices, Institute, etc.) (Tokyo: Kokusai Kyoku Shōgai Gurūpu)

Komiya, R.M. (1990). *The Japanese Economy: Trade, Industry and Government* (Tokyo: University of Tokyo Press)

(1999). 'Declining Population, the Size of the Government and the Burden of Public Debt: Some Economic Policy Issues in Japan', in Freedman, 74–109

Komiya, R.M., Okuno, M. and Suzumura, K. (eds.) (1988). *Industrial Policy of Japan* (Tokyo: Academic Press)

Komiya, R. and Suda, M. (1991). *Japan's Foreign Exchange Policy 1971–82* (North Sydney: Allen & Unwin)

Kosai, Y. (1987). 'The Politics of Economic Management', in Yamamura and Yasuba, 423–468

Kosai, Y. and Ogino, Y. (1984). *The Contemporary Japanese Economy – Studies in the Modern Japanese Economy* (Basingstoke: Macmillan)

Krasa, S. and Villamil, A.P. (1992). 'Monitoring the Monitor: An Incentive Structure for a Financial Intermediary', *Journal of Economic Theory*, 57, 197–221

Krugman, P. (1994). 'The Myth of Asia's Miracle', *Foreign Affairs*, November/December, 62–78

Kumon, S. (1992). 'Japan as a Network Society', in Kumon and Rosovsky, 109–141

Kumon, S., and Rosovsky, H. (eds.) (1992). *The Political Economy of Japan*, Volume III: *Cultural and Social Dynamics* (Stanford: Stanford University Press)

Kunze, S. (1994). 'Price-Keeping Measures on the Stock Market by the Japanese Ministry of Finance in 1987 and 1990', University of Tokyo, Institute of Social Science, Discussion Paper V2

Kuribayashi, Y. (1992). *Ōkurashō – Fushin no Kōzu* (The Ministry of Finance – The Plot of Unfaithfulness) (Tokyo: Kōdansha)

Kuroda, A. (1989). 'Financial Globalization and Monetary Policy in Japan: An Overview', paper presented at the Chulalongkorn University Conference on 'International Dimensions of Japanese Financial Development: Implications on ASEAN and Thailand', Bangkok, March
    (1998). 'Prudential Policy in Japan', in Freedman, 219–245
La Croix, S.J. and Mak, J. (1999). 'Regulatory Reform in Japan: The Road Ahead', Stockholm School of Economics, The European Institute of Japanese Studies, Working Paper, no. 63, April
Lake, C.D. II (1998). 'Liberalizing Japan's Insurance Market', in Gibney, 116–141
Langdon, F.C. (1963). 'Big Business Lobbying in Japan: The Case of Central Bank Reform', *American Political Science Review*, 527–538
Lapavistas, C. (1998). 'The Financial System and the State in Economic Development: Some Analytical Propositions', paper presented at the CEPR/ISESAO European Network on the Japanese Economy Conference, 16–17 January
Levy, J. (1999). 'Reform of Corporate Insolvency Laws in Japan', in IMF (1999b), 129–151
Lifson, T.B. (1992). 'The Managerial Integration of Japanese Business in America', in Kumon and Rosovsky, 231–266
Lincoln, E.J (1998a). 'Deregulation in Japan and the United States: A Study in Contrasts', in Gibney, 53–68
    (1998b). 'Japan's Financial Problems', *Brookings Papers on Economic Activity*, 2, 347–385
    (1998c). 'Japan's Financial Mess', *Foreign Affairs*, 77(3), 57–66
Lincoln, E.J. and Litan, R.E. (1998). 'The "Big Bang"? An Ambivalent Japan Deregulates Its Financial Markets', *The Brookings Review*, 16(1), 37–40
Lindblom, C.E. (1959). 'The Science of "Muddling Through"', *Public Administration Review*, 19, 79–88
Lindsey, B. and Lukas, A. (1998). 'Revisiting the "Revisionists": The Rise and Fall of the Japanese Economic Model', *Trade Policy Analysis*, 3 (31 July)
Llewellyn, D.T. (2000). 'Some Lessons for Regulation from Recent Bank Crises', *Open Economies Review*, 11, 69–109
Loriaux, M., Woo-Cumings, M., Calder, K.E., Maxfield, S. and Pérez, S.A. (eds.) (1997). *Capital Ungoverned: Liberalizing Finance in Interventonist States* (Ithaca and London: Cornell University Press)
Mabuchi, M. (1993). 'Financing Japanese Industry: The Interplay between the Financial and Industrial Bureaucracies', World Bank, Economic Development Institute, Working Paper no. 93–35
Macfarlane, I.J. (1989). 'Policy Targets and Operating Procedures: The Australian Case', in Federal Reserve Bank of Kansas City (ed.), *Monetary Policy Issues in the 1990s* (Kansas City: Federal Reserve Bank of Kansas City), 143–159
Management and Coordination Agency (1996). 'Summary of the 1996 Annual Report of Management and Coordination Agency'
Martin, T. and Truedsson, F. (1998). 'The Future of the Bank of Japan: An Analysis of the 1998 Bank of Japan Law Revision', Stockholm School of

Economics, The European Institute of Japanese Studies, Working Paper, no. 45, May

Matsuoka, M. and Rose, B. (1994). *The DIR Guide to Japanese Economic Statistics* (Oxford: Oxford University Press)

Matsushita, M. and Schoenbaum, T.J. (1989). *Japanese International Trade and Investment Law* (Tokyo: University of Tokyo Press)

Matsushita, Y. (1997a). 'Recent Monetary and Economic Conditions in Japan and the Reform of the Financial Markets', speech delivered to the Kisaragi-kai meeting, 14 April

——— (1997b). 'A New Framework of Monetary Policy under the New Bank of Japan Law', speech delivered to the meeting of the Yomiuri International Economic Society, 27 June

McCall Rosenbluth, F. (1989). *Financial Politics in Contemporary Japan* (Ithaca: Cornell University Press)

——— (1993). 'Financial Deregulation and Interest Intermediation', in Allinson and Sone, 107–129

Mera, K. (1998). 'The Making of Japan's Failed Land Policy', in Gibney, 178–203

Mikuni, A. (1997). 'Japan's Big Bang: Illusions and Reality', Japan Policy Research Institute, Working Paper no. 39, October

Milhaupt, C.J. (1996). 'A Relational Theory of Japanese Corporate Governance: Contract, Culture, and the Rule of Law', *Harvard International Law Journal*, 37, 3–64

——— (1999). 'Japan's Experience with Deposit Insurance and Failing Banks: Implications for Financial Regulatory Design?', Bank of Japan, *Monetary and Economic Studies*, August, 21–46

Milhaupt, C.J. and Miller, G.P. (1997). 'Cooperation, Conflict, and Convergence in Japanese Finance: Evidence from the "Jusen" Problem', *Law and Policy in International Business*, 29(1), 1–78

Miller, M.H. (1993). 'The Regulation of Financial Markets', keynote address to the Hitotsubashi University International Symposium 'Financial Markets in the Changing World', Tokyo, 23–24 March

Minami, H. (1990). *Gyōsei Hō* (Administrative Law) (Tokyo: Yuhikaku Press)

Ministry of Finance (1991). 'Organization and Functions Ministry of Finance', mimeo (Tokyo: Ministry of Finance)

——— (1992a). 'The Schedule of the Liberalization of Interest Rate on Deposits', mimeo, Banking Bureau (Tokyo: Ministry of Finance)

——— (1992b). 'Interest Rate Liberalization of Time Deposits and Postal Savings Deposits', mimeo, Banking Bureau (Tokyo: Ministry of Finance)

——— (1992c). 'MoF's Stance on Financial Policy: Securing the Stability of the Financial System and Promoting its Efficiency', mimeo, Banking Bureau (Tokyo: Ministry of Finance)

——— (1992d). 'Structures and Functions of the Ministry of Finance 1992', booklet, 'Seminar on Fiscal and Monetary Policy', Institute of Fiscal and Monetary Policy (Tokyo: Ministry of Finance)

——— (1993a). *The Mechanism and Economic Effects of Asset Price Fluctuations: A Report of the Research Committee* (Tokyo: The Institute of Fiscal and Monetary Policy, Ministry of Finance)

(1993b). 'Main Functions of Government Debt Division', mimeo, Financial Bureau (Tokyo: Ministry of Finance)

(1994). 'Policy Guidelines on the Problem of Non-performing Loans Held by Financial Institutions' (Tokyo: Ministry of Finance)

(1996). 'On the Reform of Financial Administrative Organisation' (Tokyo: Ministry of Finance)

(1997a). 'Financial System Reform: Toward the Early Achievement of Reform', 13 June (Tokyo: Ministry of Finance)

(1997b). 'Implementation of Prompt Corrective Action and Measures to Enhance Financial Facilities', 24 December (Tokyo: Ministry of Finance)

(1998a). 'Outline of Emergency Measures to Stabilise the Financial System, February (Tokyo: Ministry of Finance)

(1998b). 'Outline of the New Approach of Financial Institution Inspection' 31 March, http://www.mof.go.jp/english/gyousei/e1b040a.htm

(1998c). 'Reforms to the Financial Regulatory System', June (Tokyo: Ministry of Finance)

(1998d). 'Outline of the Report by the Council on the Ministry of Finance's Administration', 17 July, http://www.mof.go.jp/english/tosin/e1a201.htm

(1998e). 'Statement by the Minister of Finance – Outline of the Bridge Banks Scheme', http://www.mof.go.jp/english/daijin/ebbs.htm

(1998f). 'Financial Revitalisation Measures' (Tokyo: Ministry of Finance).

(1998g). 'Early Strengthening Measures for the Financial System' (Tokyo: Ministry of Finance)

(2000a). 'Japanese Big Bang', January (Tokyo: Ministry of Finance), http://www.mof.go.jp/

(2000b). 'Schedule for Financial System Reform', April (Tokyo: Ministry of Finance), http://www.mof.go.jp/

(2000c). 'Outline of the Amendment Bill of the Deposit Insurance Law', March (Tokyo: Ministry of Finance)

(2000d). 'Fiscal Measures on the Deposit Insurance Corporation (FY2000)' (Tokyo: Ministry of Finance) http://www.mof.go.jp/

Mishkin, F.S. and Eakins, S.G. (2000). *Financial Markets and Institutions* (Reading, MA: Addison-Wesley)

Miyajima, H. (1998). 'The Impact of Deregulation on Corporate Governance and Finance', in Carlile and Tilton, 33–75

Miyamoto, M. (1995). *Straitjacket Society: An Insider's Irreverent View of Bureaucratic Japan* (Tokyo: Kodansha International)

(1996). 'Mental Castration, the HIV Scandal, and the Japanese Bureaucracy', Japan Policy Research Institute, Working Paper no. 23, August

Miyashita, K. and. Russell, D. (1996). *Keiretsu: Inside the Hidden Japanese Conglomerates* (New York: McGraw-Hill)

Moerke, A. (1997). 'Does Governance Matter? Performance and Corporate Governance Structures of Japanese Keiretsu Groups', Wissenschaftszentrum Berlin, Discussion Paper FS IV, 97–43

Moody's Investors Service. *Banking System Outlook – Japan*, various issues, including Moody's Investors Service (1999a)

Moody's Investors Service (1999b). 'Regulatory Re-Engineering of Japan's Regional Banking System: Resolving, Recapitalising, Restructuring and Liquidating', August
Morck, R. and Nakamura M. (1992). 'Bank and Corporate Control in Japan', mimeo
(1999a). 'Banks and Corporate Control in Japan', *Journal of Finance*, 54(1), 319–339
(1999b). 'Japanese Corporate Governance and Macroeconomic Problems', Harvard Institute of Economic Research, Discussion Paper no. 1893
Mori, N., Shiratsuka, S. and Taguchi, H. (2000). 'Policy Responses to the Post-bubble Adjustments in Japan: A Tentative Review', Bank of Japan, Institute for Monetary and Economic Studies, Discussion Paper no. 2000-E-13
Morishima, M. (1982). *Why Has Japan 'Succeeded'? Western Technology and the Japanese Ethos* (Cambridge: Cambridge University Press)
(1999). 'Why Do I Expect Japan to Collapse?', in Freedman, 25–55
Morris-Suzuki, T. (1989). *A History of Japanese Economic Thought* (London: Routledge)
Morsink, J. and Bayoumi, T. (1999). 'A Peek Inside the Black Box: The Monetary Transmission Mechanism in Japan', IMF Working Paper WP/99/137, October
Mouer, R. and Sugimoto, Y. (1986). *Images of Japanese Society: A Study in the Structure of Social Reality* (London: KPI)
Mulgan, A.G. (2000). 'Japan: A Setting Sun?', *Foreign Affairs*, 79(4), 40–52
Murakami, Y. (1982). 'Toward a Socioinstitutional Explanation of Japan's Economic Performance', in Yamamura, K. (ed.), *Policy and Trade Issues of the Japanese Economy* (Seattle: University of Washington Press), 3–46
(1987). 'The Japanese Model of Political Economy', in Yamamura and Yasuba, 33–90
Murakami, Y. and Rohlen, T.P. (1992). 'Social-Exchange Aspects of the Japanese Political Economy: Culture, Efficiency, and Change', in Kumon and Rosovsky, 63–105
Muramatsu, M. and Krauss, E.S. (1987). 'The Conservative Policy Line and the Development of Patterned Pluralism', in Yamamura and Yasuba, 516–554
Murphy, R.T. (1996). *The Real Price of Japanese Money* (London: Weidenfeld & Nicolson)
(1997). 'Don't Be Fooled by Japan's Big Bang', *Fortune*, 29 December, 82–88
Muto, E. and Shirakawa, M. (eds.) (1993). *Nihon Ginkō* (The Bank of Japan) (Tokyo: Zaikei Shōhōha)
Nagashima, A. (1997). 'Role of the Central Bank During Problems of Bank Soundness: Japan's Experience', in Enoch, C. and Green, J.H. (eds.), *Banking Soundness and Monetary Policy – Issues and Experiences in the Global Economy* (Washington, DC: International Monetary Fund), 191–222
Nakajima, Z. and Taguchi, H. (1995). 'Toward a More Stable Financial Framework: Long-term Alternatives – An Overview of Recent Bank Disruption Worldwide', in Sawamoto, Nakajima and Taguchi, 41–98
Nakane, C. (1970). *Japanese Society* (1991 edn) (Tokyo: Charles E. Tuttle)

Nakano, K. (1998). 'Becoming a "Policy" Ministry: The Organization and *Amakudari* of the Ministry of Posts and Telecommunications', *Journal of Japanese Studies*, 24(1), 95–117

Nakao, M. and Horii, A. (1991). 'The Process of Decision-Making and Implementation of Monetary Policy in Japan', Bank of Japan, Special Paper no. 198

Nakaso, H. (1999). 'Recent Banking Sector Reforms in Japan', Federal Reserve Bank of New York, *Economic Policy Review*, July, 1–7

Nakatani, I. (1991). 'Network shihon-shugi no kōzai' (Merits and Demerits of Network Capitalism), *Shūkan Toyo Keizai*, 13, December, 4–8

(1998). 'Reforming the Catch-up Economy', in Gibney, 30–40

Namiki, M. (1996). 'A Comparison of the Japanese and American Financial Regulatory Systems', Harvard University, Program on US–Japan Relations, Occasional Paper no. 96–08

Narita, Y. (1968). 'Administrative Guidance: Law in Japan', reprinted in Tanaka, H. (ed.), *The Japanese Legal System: Introductory Cases and Materials* (Tokyo: University of Tokyo Press, 1976), 353–388

National Personnel Authority (1999a). *Annual Report 1997* (Tokyo: National Personnel Authority)

(1999b). *Jinji-in Geppō* (Monthly Review), May (Tokyo: National Personnel Authority)

Nester, W.R. (1990). *The Foundation of Japanese Power: Continuities, Changes, Challenges* (Basingstoke: Macmillan)

Neuffer, J.F. (1998). 'Behind the Screen: Roundup of Japanese Politics', 21 August

New York Times (1996). 'Japan's Vaunted Bureaucrats, the Real Power Behind the Throne, Are Under Siege', 5 May, 8

(2001). 'Official Japan Does Musical Chairs, and Desks', 4 January, 3

Nihon Ginkō Kinyū Kenkyūjo (Institute for Monetary and Economic Studies, Bank of Japan) (1993). *Nihon Ginkō no Kinō to Gyōmu* (The Functions and Business of the Bank of Japan) (Tokyo: Nihon Ginkō Kinyū Kenkyūjo)

Nihon Kinyū Nenpyō (Chronology of Japanese Finance), various issues (Tokyo: Institute for Monetary and Economic Studies, Bank of Japan)

Nihon Keizai Shimbun. Various issues

Nihon Keizai Shimbunsha (1992). *Ōkurashō no Yūutsu* (The Melancholy of the Ministry of Finance) (Tokyo: Nihon Keizai Shimbunsha)

Nikkei Net (2000). 'Govt To Allot 15 Trln Yen For Finance System Crisis In FY01', 30 August

Nikkei Weekly. Various issues

Nippon Kinyū Tsūshinsha (Japan Finance News Agency). *Nippon Kinyū Meikan* (Directory of Executives in Japanese Financial Industry), various issues (Tokyo: Nippon Kinyū Tsūshinsha)

Nippon Finance (1986). Technical Note no. 18, 30 September

Noble, G.W. (1989). 'The Japanese Industrial Policy Debate', in Haggard, S. and Moon, C. (eds.), *Pacific Dynamics: The International Politics of Industrial Change* (Boulder: Westview Press), 53–95

Norville, E. (1998). 'The Illiberal Roots of Japanese Financial Regulatory Reform', in Carlile and Tilton, 111–141

Odagiri, H. (1992). *Growth through Competition, Competition through Growth* (New York: Oxford University Press)

OECD. *Economic Surveys – Japan*, various issues (Paris: OECD) (1999a). *OECD Economic Surveys – Japan 1999* (Paris: OECD) (1999b). *The OECD Review of Regulatory Reform in Japan* (Paris: OECD) (1999c). 'Unblocking Japanese Reform', *OECD Observer*, 216, 5–7

Ohara, Y. (1995). *Japanese Financial Sector Overview: Financial System in Japan* (Tokyo: UBS Securities) (1998). 'Japan Banks – Problems With the Japanese Banking System', Morgan Stanley Dean Witter, 13 August

Okabe, M. (1990). 'The Conduct and the Transmission Mechanism of Japanese Monetary Policy 1975–1989: A Literature Survey', mimeo, Bank of Japan, Institute for Monetary and Economic Studies, March (1995). 'The Conduct and the Transmission Mechanism of Japanese Monetary Policy 1975–1989', in Okabe, M. (ed.), *The Structure of the Japanese Economy: Changes on the Domestic and International Fronts* (Basingstoke: Macmillan), 323–357

Okazaki, T. (1995). 'Sengo Nihon no Kinyū Shisutemu' (The Postwar Japanese Financial System), in Morikawa, H. and Yonekura, S. (eds.), *Kōdo Seichō o Koete, Nihonkeieishi* (Beyond High-level Growth: The History of the Japanese Economy and Business), Volume V (Tokyo: Iwanami-shoten), 137–204

Okimoto, D.I. (1988). 'Political Inclusivity: The Domestic Structure of Trade', in Inoguchi and Okimoto, 305–344 (1989). *Between MITI and the Market: Japanese Industrial Policy for High Technology* (Stanford: Stanford University Press) (1998). 'Theoretical Approaches to the Japan–America Security Alliance', in Freedman, 46–81

Okimoto, D.I. and Rohlen, T.P. (eds.) (1988). *Inside the Japanese System: Readings on Contemporary Society and Political Economy* (Stanford: Stanford University Press)

Okina, K. (1993). 'Market Operations in Japan: Theory and Practice', in Singleton, 31–62 (1999). 'Monetary Policy under Zero Inflation: A Response to Criticisms and Questions Regarding Monetary Policy', Bank of Japan, *Monetary and Economic Studies*, December, 157–197

Okina, K. and Oda, N. (2000). 'Further Monetary Easing Policies under Non-negativity Constraints of Nominal Interest Rates: Summary of Discussion Based on Japan's Experience', paper prepared for the ninth international conference sponsored by the Institute for Monetary and Economic Studies, Bank of Japan, Tokyo, 3–4 July

Okina, K., Shirakawa, M. and Shiratsuka, S. (2000). 'The Asset Price Bubble and Monetary Policy: Japan's Experience in the Late 1980s and the Lessons', Bank of Japan, Institute for Monetary and Economic Studies, Discussion Paper no. 2000-E-12

Okuno-Fujiwara, M. (1991). 'Industrial Policy in Japan: A Political Economy View', in Krugman, P. (ed.), *Trade with Japan: Has the Door Opened Wider?* (Chicago: University of Chicago Press), 271–301

Ōkura Zaimu Kyōkai (Ministry of Finance's Finance Association). *Ōkurashō no Kikō* (The Organisation of the Ministry of Finance), various editions (Tokyo: Ministry of Finance's Finance Association)

Ōkurashō Ginkō Kyoku (Banking Bureau, Ministry of Finance) (1998). *Tsūtatsu Tō no Seiri* (The Reorganisation of *Tsūtatsu* and Related Matters), 8 June (Tokyo: Ministry of Finance)

Olson, M. (1982). *The Rise and Decline of Nations: Economic Growth, Stagflation, and Social Rigidities* (New Haven: Yale University Press)

Osano, H. (1996). 'Intercorporate Shareholdings and Corporate Control in the Japanese Firm', *Journal of Banking and Finance*, 20, 1047–1068

Osugi, K. (1990). 'Japan's Experience of Financial Deregulation Since 1984 in an International Perspective', BIS Economic Papers no. 26

Ozawa, I. (1994). *Blueprint for a New Japan: The Rethinking of a Nation* (Tokyo: Kodansha International)

Packer, F. (1994). 'The Disposal of Bad Loans in Japan: A Review of Recent Policy Initiatives', Columbia University, Center for Japanese Economy and Business, Working Paper no. 88

Park, Y.H. (1986). *Bureaucrats and Ministers in Contemporary Japanese Government* (Berkeley: Institute of East Asian Studies)

Patrick, H. (1998). 'The Causes of Japan's Financial Crisis', Columbia University, Center for Japanese Economy and Business, Working Paper no. 146

(1999). 'Rumination on Morishima', in Freedman, 56–71

Pauly, L.W. (1988). *Opening Financial Markets – Banking Politics on the Pacific Rim* (Ithaca and London: Cornell University Press)

Peek, J. and Rosengren, E.S. (1997). 'The International Transmission of Financial Shocks: The Case of Japan', *American Economic Review*, 87(4), 495–505

(1998). 'Determinants of the Japan Premium: Actions Speak Louder Than Words', paper presented at NBER/TCER Japan Project Conference, Tokyo, 29–30 October

Pempel, T.J. (1982). *Policy and Politics in Japan: Creative Conservatism* (Philadelphia: Temple University Press)

(1998). *Regime Shift: Comparative Dynamics of the Japanese Political Economy* (Ithaca: Cornell University Press)

Pempel, T.J. and Muramatsu, M. (1993). 'The Japanese Bureaucracy and Economic Development: Structuring a Proactive Civil Service', World Bank, Economic Development Institute, Working Paper no. 93–26

Petit, M.L. (1990). *Control Theory and Dynamic Games in Economic Policy Analysis* (Cambridge: Cambridge University Press)

Porter, M.E, Takeuchi, H. and Sakakibara, M. (2000). *Can Japan Compete?* (Basingstoke: Macmillan)

Posen, A.S. (1998). *Restoring Japan's Economic Growth* (Washington, DC: Institute for International Economics)

Prestowitz, C.V. (1988). *Trading Places: How America Allowed Japan to Take the Lead* (Tokyo: Charles E. Tuttle)

Prowse, S.D. (1992). 'The Structure of Corporate Ownership in Japan', *Journal of Finance*, 47(3), 1121–1140

(1994). 'Corporate Governance in an International Perspective: A Survey of Corporate Control Mechanisms among Large Firms in the United States, the United Kingdom, Japan and Germany', BIS Economic Papers no. 41

Pye, L.W. (1985). *Asian Power and Politics: The Cultural Dimensions of Authority* (Cambridge, MA: The Belknap Press of Harvard University Press)

Ramseyer, J.M. (1985). 'The Costs of the Consensual Myth: Antitrust Enforcement and Institutional Barriers to Litigation in Japan', *Yale Law Journal*, 94, 604–645

(2000). 'Rethinking Administrative Guidance', in Aoki and Saxonhouse, 199–211

Ramseyer, J.M. and McCall Rosenbluth, F. (1993). *Japan's Political Marketplace* (Cambridge, MA: Harvard University Press)

Ramseyer, J.M. and Nakazato, M. (1999). *Japanese Law: An Economic Approach* (Chicago: University of Chicago Press)

Ramseyer, J.M. and Rosenbluth, F. (1998). *The Politics of Oligarchy: Institutional Choice in Imperial Japan* (Cambridge: Cambridge University Press)

Rebick, M.E. (2000). 'The Importance of Networks in the Market for University Graduates in Japan: A Longitudinal Analysis of Hiring Patterns', *Oxford Economic Papers*, 52, 471–496

Research Project Team for Japanese Systems (1992). *Japanese Systems: An Alternative Civilization?* (Yokohama: Sekotac)

Richardson, B.M. (1997). *Japanese Democracy: Power, Coordination, and Performance* (New Haven: Yale University Press)

Rixtel, A.A.R.J.M. van (1988). 'Financiële Liberalisatie, Financiële Innovaties en Monetaire Politiek in Japan' (Financial Liberalisation, Financial Innovations and Monetary Policy in Japan), unpublished MA thesis, Tilburg University

(1991). 'Monetary Control: In Search of an Operational Terminology', Free University of Amsterdam, Economics Department, Research Memorandum 1991-52

(1994a). '*Amakudari* in the Private Banking Industry: Empirical Verification of the Equalisation Hypothesis', in Fruin, M., Gerlach, M. and Ries, J. (eds.), *Best Papers Proceedings*, Association of Japanese Business Studies Meeting, Vancouver, 7–9 January, 657–686

(1994b). 'The Political Economy and Economic System of Japan: A Survey of Literature, Conflict and Confusion', Free University of Amsterdam, Economics Department, Research Memorandum 1994-14

(1994c). 'Informal Aspects of Japanese Economic Policy', Free University of Amsterdam, Economics Department, Research Memorandum 1994-15

(1994d). 'Monetary Policy, Optimal Control, Informality and Uncertainty: Is Japan Really Different?', mimeo, Free University of Amsterdam

(1995). 'The Change and Continuity of *Amakudari* in the Private Banking Industry', in Metzger-Court, S. and Pascha, W. (eds.), *Japan's Socio-Economic Evolution: Continuity and Change* (Folkestone: Japan Library, Curzon Press), 244–261

(1996). 'The Evolution of the Japanese Financial System and Monetary Policy: The Rise and Collapse of the New Financial Superpower Myth', De Nederlandsche Bank, Monetary and Economic Policy Department, MEB Series no.1996-16. Reprinted in Boonstra, W.W. and Eijffinger, S.C.W.

(eds.), *Banks, Financial Markets and Monetary Policy* (Amsterdam: NIBE), 57–98

(1997). *Informality, Bureaucratic Control and Monetary Policy: The Case of Japan*, Ph.D. thesis, Tinbergen Institute, Research Series no. 161 (Amsterdam: Thesis Publishers)

(1998a). 'Het Japanse financiële systeem: Wat ging er mis?' (The Japanese Financial System: What Went Wrong?), *Bank en Effectenbedrijf*, 47 (January/February), 20–25

(1998b). 'De Japanse "Big Bang": De start van een nieuw financieel systeem?' (The Japanese 'Big Bang': The Start of a New Financial System?), *Bank en Effectenbedrijf*, 47 (April), 4–9

(1998c). 'Het Financiële Hervormingsproces in Japan: Van Strikte Regulering tot de "Big Bang" (Financial Reform in Japan: From Strict Regulation to the 'Big Bang'), *Financiële & Monetaire Studies*, 16(3) (Groningen: Wolters-Noordhoff)

Rixtel, A.A.R.J.M. van and Hassink, W.H.J. (1996a). 'Monitoring the Monitors: Retired MoF and BoJ Officials and the Ex-Post Monitoring of Japanese Banks', paper presented at NBER Working Group on Japan Conference, Cambridge, MA 4 May, published as De Nederlandsche Bank, Monetary and Economic Policy Department, MEB Series, no. 1996-15

(1996b). '*Amakudari* and the Monitoring of Private Banks: Which Determinants and Has Performance Improved?', paper presented at CEPR/CEP/STICERD Japan Network Workshop, London School of Economics, 13–14 December. Published as CEPR Discussion Paper no. 1785, January 1998

Rixtel, A.A.R.J.M. van, van der Wal, D. and Swank, O.H. (1995). 'Are Central Banks Inflation-Averse? Evidence from Seven OECD-Countries', mimeo, Free University of Amsterdam

Rohlen, T.P. (1988). 'Education in Japanese Society', in Okimoto and Rohlen, 25–31

(1992). 'Learning: The Mobilization of Knowledge in the Japanese Political Economy', in Kumon and Rosovsky, 321–363

Romer, C.D. and Romer, D.H. (1993). 'Credit Channel or Credit Actions? An Interpretation of the Postwar Transmission Mechanism', in Federal Reserve Bank of Kansas City (ed.), *Changing Capital Markets: Implications for Monetary Policy* (Kansas City: Federal Reserve Bank of Kansas City), 71–116

Rosenbluth, F. and Thies, M.F. (1999). 'The Electoral Foundations of Japan's Financial Politics: The Case of *Jusen*', mimeo (June)

Royama, S. (1983). 'The Japanese Financial System: Past, Present, and Future', *Japanese Economic Studies*, 12 (Winter), 3–32

(1988). 'The Financial System of Japan: A New View', *Japanese Economic Studies*, 16 (Spring), 76–97

(1989). 'Monetary Policy under the Evolution of Open Money Markets in Japan', mimeo

Saito, M. and Shiratsuka, S. (2000). 'Financial Crises as the Failure of Arbitrage and Monetary Policy: Evidence from the "Japan Premium" Phenomenon', paper prepared for the ninth international conference sponsored by the Institute for Monetary and Economic Studies, Bank of Japan, Tokyo, 3–4 July

384   Bibliography

Sakakibara, E. and Feldman, R.A. (1983). 'The Japanese Financial System in Comparative Perspective', *Journal of Comparative Economics*, 7, 1–24

Samuels, R.J. (1987). *The Business of the Japanese State: Energy Markets in Comparative and Historical Perspective* (Ithaca: Cornell University Press)

Santillán, J., Rixtel, A.A.R.J.M. van, and Marques, D. (2000). 'Main Changes in the Financial Structure of the Euro-Zone since the Introduction of the Euro', *OECD Financial Market Trends*, July

Sawamoto, K., Nakajima, Z. and Taguchi, H. (eds.) (1995). *Financial Stability in a Changing Environment* (Basingstoke: Macmillan)

Saxonhouse, G.R. (1983). 'What is All this About "Industrial Targeting" in Japan?', *World Economy*, September, 253–274

(1998). 'Japan and the 1994 *Economic Report of the President*', in Freedman, 85–113

Schaede, U. (1992). 'Corporate Governance in Japan: Institutional Investors, Management Monitoring and Corporate Stakeholders', University of California at Berkeley, Walter A. Haas School of Business, CCC Working Paper no. 92-12

(1993). 'The "Old Boy" Network and Government–Business Relationships in Japan: A Case Study of "Consultative Capitalism"', paper presented at the 1994 Association of Japanese Business Studies meeting, Vancouver, 7–9 January

(1995). 'The "Old Boy" Network and Government–Business Relationships in Japan', *Journal of Japanese Studies*, 21(2), 293–317

(1996). 'The 1995 Financial Crisis in Japan', mimeo, University of California, San Diego Graduate School of International Relations and Pacific Studies, http://www.nmjc.org/jiap/dereg/papers/bbankfa.html

Schmiegelow, M. (ed.) (1986a). *Japan's Response to Crisis and Change in the World Economy* (Armonk, NY, and London: M.E. Sharpe)

(1986b). 'Introduction', in Schmiegelow, vii–xiii

Schwartz, F.J. (1998). *Advice and Consent: The Politics of Consultation in Japan* (Cambridge: Cambridge University Press)

Scott, J. (1988). 'Social Network Analysis and Intercorporate Relations', *Hitotsubashi Journal of Commerce and Management*, 23, 53–68

Securities and Exchange Council (1997). *Shōken Shijō no Sōgōteki Kaikaku* (Comprehensive Reform of the Securities Market), 13 June (Tokyo: Ministry of Finance)

Seirōkyō (Labour Union of Government-Related Institutes). *Amakudari Hakusho* (*Amakudari* White Paper), various issues (Tokyo: Seirōkyō)

Seisaku Jihō Sha (Policy Review Company) (1992). *Okurashō 1993, Nippon no Kanchō* (The Government Authorities of Japan: The Ministry of Finance) (Tokyo: Seisaku Jihō Sha)

Seisaku Jihō Shuppansha (Policy Review Publisher) (1991). *Nihon Ginkō, Nihon Kaihatsu Ginkō, Nihon Yushutsunyū Ginkō, Seifu Kei Kinyū Kikan: Soshiki to Shuyō Kambu, 1992 Nenban* (The Organisation and Main Executives of the Bank of Japan, the Japan Development Bank, the Export–Import Bank of Japan and Financial Institutions of the Government System) (Tokyo: Seisaku Jihō Shuppansha)

Semkow, B.W. (1993). 'Japan's Financial System Reform Act', *Butterworths Journal of International Banking and Financial Law*, October, 435–446

Sheard, P. (1994). 'Bank Executives on Japanese Corporate Boards', Bank of Japan, *Monetary and Economic Studies*, 12(2), 85–121

Sheng, A. (1996). 'Banking Fragility in the 1980s: An Overview', in Sheng, A. (ed.), *Bank Restructuring: Lessons from the 1980s* (Washington, DC: World Bank), 5–23

Shimamoto, R. (1982). 'Monetary Control in Japan', in Meek, P. (ed.), *Central Bank Views on Monetary Targeting* (New York: Federal Reserve Bank of New York), 80–85

Shimizu, Y. (1994). 'Accounting as a Flexible Instrument of Governmental Banking Policy', in Stein, H. von (ed.), *Banken in Japan heute* (Frankfurt-am-Main: Fritz Knapp), 323–330

Shindo, M. (1992). *Gyōsei Shidō – Kanchō to Gyōkai no Aida* (Administrative Guidance: Between the Government and Business) (Tokyo: Iwanami Shinsho)

Shinjo, H. (1962). *History of the Yen: 100 Years of Japanese Money Economy* (Kobe: The Research Institute for Economics and Business Administration, Kobe University)

Shleifer, A. and Vishny, R.W. (1997). 'A Survey of Corporate Governance', *Journal of Finance*, 52(2), 737–783

Shrieves, R.E. and Dahl, D. (1998). 'Staying Afloat in Japan: Discretionary Accounting and the Behavior of Banks Under Financial Duress', mimeo, December

Singleton, K.J. (ed.) (1993). *Japanese Monetary Policy* (Chicago: University of Chicago Press)

Smits, R. (1997). *The European Central Bank – Institutional Aspects*, International Banking and Finance Law Series (The Hague/London/Boston: Kluwer Law International)

Snider, H.K. and Bird, A. (1994). 'CEO Pay and Firm Performance in Japan', *Best Papers Proceedings*, Association of Japanese Business Studies meeting, Vancouver, 7–9 January, 497–535

Sohn, Y. (1998). 'The Rise and Development of the Japanese Licensing System', in Carlile and Tilton, 16–32

Sōmuchō (Management and Coordination Agency) (1999). *Kisei Kanwa no Genkyō* (The Present Situation on the Softening of [Government] Regulation) (Tokyo: Management and Coordination Agency)

Song, B.-N. (1990). *The Rise of the Korean Economy* (Hong Kong: Oxford University Press)

Sparling, K. (1992). *The Samurai Ethic and Modern Japan: Yukio Mishima on Hagakure* (Tokyo: Charles E. Tuttle)

Spiegel, M.M. (1999). 'Moral Hazard under the Japanese "Convoy" Banking System', *Federal Reserve Bank of San Francisco Economic Review*, 3, 3–13

Standard & Poor's Ratings Services (2000). 'Bank Industry Risk Analysis: Japan'

Steenbeek, O.W. (1996). *Financial Regulation in Japan: Systemic Risks and the Nikkei Futures Market*, Tinbergen Institute, Research Series no. 119 (Amsterdam: Thesis Publishers)

Stockwin, J.A.A. (1999). *Governing Japan: Divided Politics in a Major Economy*, 3rd edn (Oxford: Blackwell Publishers)

Sunday Mainichi (1992). 'Shūshoku Kurosu Rankingu 1992' (Cross Ranking of New Employment 1992), 19 July, 147–160

Suzuki, M. (1992). *Dare ga Nichigin wo Koroshita ka? Kinyū no Seitaikaku* (Who Killed the Bank of Japan? The Ecology of Finance) (Tokyo: Kodansha)

Suzuki, Y. (1980). *Money and Banking in Contemporary Japan: The Theoretical Setting and Its Application* (New Haven: Yale University Press)

—— (1984). 'Financial Innovations and Monetary Policy in Japan', in Bank for International Settlements (ed.), *Financial Innovation and Monetary Policy* (Basle: BIS), 133–170

—— (1985). 'Japan's Monetary Policy Over the Past 10 Years', Bank of Japan, *Monetary and Economic Studies*, 3(2), 1–9

—— (1986). *Money, Finance, and Macroeconomic Performance in Japan* (New Haven: Yale University Press)

—— (1987a). *The Japanese Financial System* (Oxford: Clarendon Press)

—— (1987b). 'Implications for Monetary Policy: Monetary Policy in Japan under Financial Liberalization and Internationalization', in Foundation for Advanced Information and Research (ed.), *Japan's Financial Markets*, FAIR Fact Series (Tokyo: Look Japan), 40

—— (1989a). *Japan's Economic Performance and International Role* (Tokyo: University of Tokyo Press)

—— (1989b). 'Policy Targets and Operating Procedures in the 1990s: The Case of Japan', in Federal Reserve Bank of Kansas City (ed.), *Monetary Policy Issues in the 1990s* (Kansas: Federal Reserve Bank of Kansas City), 161–173

—— (1994). 'Monetary Policy of Japan', *Japanese Economic Studies*, 21(6), 55–89

—— (2000). 'Strategies for Overcoming Japan's Economic Crisis', in Aoki and Saxonhouse, 9–15

Suzuki, Y., Kuroda, A. and Shirakawa, H. (1988). 'Monetary Control Mechanism in Japan', Bank of Japan, *Monetary and Economic Studies*, 6(2), 1–27

Suzuki, Y. and Yomo, H. (1986). *Financial Innovation and Monetary Policy: Asia and the West* (Tokyo: University of Tokyo Press)

Suzumura, K. and Okuno-Fujiwara, M. (1987). 'Industrial Policy in Japan: Overview and Evaluation', in Sato, R. and Wachtel, P. (eds.), *Trade Friction and Economic Policy: Problems and Prospects for Japan and the United States* (New York: Cambridge University Press), 50–79

Swank, O.H. (1990). *Policy Makers, Voters and Optimal Control: Estimation of the Preferences behind Monetary and Fiscal Policy in the United States*, Tinbergen Institute, Research Series no. 1 (Amsterdam: Thesis Publishers)

Taira, K. and Wada, T. (1987). 'Business–Government Relations in Modern Japan: A *Todai-Yakkai-Zaikai* Connection?', in Mizruchi, M. and Schwartz, M. (eds.), *Intercorporate Relations: The Structural Analysis of Business* (Cambridge: Cambridge University Press), 264–297

Takarajima Sha (1995). *Ōkura Kanryō no Shōtai* (The True Character of the Ministry of Finance) (Tokyo: Takarajima Sha)

Takeda, M. and Turner, P. (1992). 'The Liberalization of Japan's Financial Markets: Some Major Themes', BIS Economic Papers no. 34

Tamura, T. (1991). 'The Bank of Japan Mechanism', paper presented at BRI Conference 'Understanding the Bank of Japan & Its Effects on the Japanese Capital Markets', London, 5 March

Teikoku Databank (1999). 'Ōkurashō, Nichigin no Ginkō Amakudari', 14 September (Retirees from the MoF and BoJ on boards of private banks, press release)

——— (2001). 'Annual Report on Corporate Bankruptcy in Japan 2000', http://www.teikoku.com/news/acbjoo.html

Teranishi, J. (1986a). 'The "Catch-up" Process, Financial System, and Japan's Rise as a Capital Exporter', *Hitotsubashi Journal of Economics*, 27 (Special Issue), 133–146

——— (1986b). 'Economic Growth and Regulation of Financial Markets: Japanese Experience During Postwar High Growth Period', *Hitotsubashi Journal of Economics*, 27, 149–165

——— (1990). 'Finance and Economic Development in Postwar Japan', paper presented at the Conference on Financial Development in Japan, Korea and Taiwan, Institute of Academia Sinica, Taipei, August

——— (1993). 'Financial Sector Reform after the War', in Teranishi and Kosai, 153–177

——— (1997). 'Bank Governance in the Japanese Economic System', *Banca Nazionale del Lavoro Quarterly Review*, 41–65

Teranishi, J. and Kosai, Y. (eds.) (1993). *The Japanese Experience of Economic Reforms* (Basingstoke: Macmillan)

Theil, H. (1964). *Optimal Decision Rules for Government and Industry* (Chicago: Rand-McNally)

Tilton, M.C. (1998). 'Regulatory Reform and Market Opening in Japan', in Carlile and Tilton, 163–196

Tinbergen, J. (1952). *On the Theory of Economic Policy: Contributions to Economic Analysis I* (Amsterdam: North-Holland)

Tokyo Business Today (1991). 'Chalmers Johnson: What Is Wrong with Japan, and What Is Worth Emulating?', December, 20–23

Toshikawa, T. (1995). *Ōkurashō – Kenryoku no Himitsu* (The Ministry of Finance – The Mystery of Power) (Tokyo: Shōgaku Kan)

Toyo Keizai. *Japan Company Handbook*, various issues (Tokyo: Toyo Keizai)

Toyo Keizai Shinposha (1992). *Yakuin Shiki Hō 1993 Nenban* (Board of Directors Information, 1993) (Tokyo: Toyo Keizai Shinposha)

——— *Kigyō Keiretsu Sōran* (Directory of Corporate Affiliations), various issues (Tokyo: Toyo Keizai Shinposha)

Tresize, P.H. (1983). 'Industrial Policy Is Not the Major Reason for Japan's Success', *Brookings Review*, Spring, 13–18

Trezise, P.H. and Suzuki, Y. (1976). 'Politics, Government, and Economic Growth in Japan', in Patrick, H. and Rosovsky, H. (eds.), *Asia's New Giant: How the Japanese Economy Works* (Washington, DC: The Brookings Institution), 753–811

Tsutsui, W.M. (1988). *Banking Policy in Japan: American Efforts at Reform During the Occupation* (London: Routledge)

Tsutsumi, K. (1996). *Kanryō Amakudari Hakusho* (Bureaucracy *Amakudari* White Book), Iwanami Booklet, no. 425 (Tokyo: Iwanami)

Tyson, L.D. (1993). *Who's Bashing Whom? Trade Conflict in High-Technology Industries* (Washington, DC: Institute for International Economics)

Ueda, K. (1992). 'Institutional and Regulatory Frameworks for the Main Bank System', mimeo

(1993a). 'A Comparative Perspective on Japanese Monetary Policy: Short-run Monetary Control and the Transmission Mechanism', in Singleton, 7–29

(1993b). 'Japanese Monetary Policy from 1970 to 1990: Rules or Discretion?', in Shigehara, K. (ed.), *Price Stabilization in the 1990s: Domestic and International Policy Requirements* (Basingstoke: Macmillan), 191–212

(1994). 'Institutional and Regulatory Frameworks for the Main Bank System', in Aoki and Patrick, 89–108

(1996). 'Japanese Monetary Policy: Rules or Discretion? Part II', Bank of Japan, IMES Discussion Paper no. 96-E-16

(2000). 'Causes of Japan's Banking Problems in the 1990s', in Hoshi and Patrick, 59–81

Uekusa, M. (1987). 'Industrial Organization: The 1970s to the Present', in Yamamura and Yasuba, 469–515

(1990). 'Government Regulations in Japan – Towards Their International Harmonization and Integration', University of Tokyo, Faculty of Economics, Research Institute for the Japanese Economy, Discussion Paper no. 90-F-4

United States (2000). 'Annual Submission by the Government of the United States to the Government of Japan under the US–Japan Enhanced Initiative on Deregulation and Competition Policy', 12 October

United States General Accounting Office (1996). 'Bank Regulatory Structure – Japan: Report to the Honorable Charles E. Schumer, House of Representatives' (Washington, DC: General Accounting Office)

Upham, F.K. (1986). 'Legal and Institutional Dynamics in Japan's Cartel Policy', in Schmiegelow, 278–303

(1987). *Law and Social Change in Postwar Japan* (Cambridge, MA: Harvard University Press)

(1991). 'The Man Who Would Import: A Cautionary Tale about Bucking the System in Japan', *Journal of Japanese Studies*, 17(2), 323–343

Ursacki, T. (1994). 'CEO Succession in Japan: Who Gets to the Top and Why?', *Best Papers Proceedings*, Association of Japanese Business Studies Meeting, Vancouver, 7–9 January, 625–655

US Embassy Tokyo (1999). *Country Commercial Guide Japan, FY 2000*, July 15

US News & World Report (1990). 'The "Gang of Four" Defends the Revisionist Line', 7 May, 54–55

Viner, A. (1987). *Inside Japan's Financial Markets* (London: Economist Publications)

Visser, H. (1987). 'Macro-Economische Aspecten van Bedrijfseconomisch Toezicht' (Macroeconomic Aspects of Prudential Policy), in Bosman, H.W.J. and Brezet, J.C. (eds.), *Sparen en Investeren, Geld en Banken* (Leiden/Antwerp: Stenfert Kroese), 83–93

Vogel, S.K. (1996). *Freer Markets, More Rules: Regulatory Reform in Advanced Industrial Countries* (Ithaca: Cornell University Press)

Wade, R. (1990). *Governing the Market* (Princeton: Princeton University Press) (1998). 'The Asian Debt-and-Development Crisis of 1997-?: Causes and Consequences', mimeo, August

Wakiyama, T. (1987). 'The Implementation and Effectiveness of MITI's Administrative Guidance', in Wilks, S. and Wright, M. (eds.), *Comparative Government-Industry Relations: Western Europe, the United States and Japan* (Oxford: Clarendon Press), 211-232

Wall Street Journal, various issues, including (1996). 'Revolving Door: Many Japanese Banks Ran Amok While Led by Former Regulators – Far from Imposing Caution, Some Ex-Bureaucrats Fed the Binge of Risky Loans', January

Walsh, C.E. (1997). 'Inflation and Central Bank Independence: Is Japan Really an Outlier?', Bank of Japan, *Monetary and Economic Studies*, 15 (May), 89-117

Watanabe, K. and Sudo, H. (1998). *The Japanese Big Bang* (Tokyo: Japan Center for International Finance)

Watanabe, O. (1997). 'The Weakness of the Contemporary Japanese State', in Banno, 109-161

Weinstein, D.E. (1992). 'Micro-Managing Macro Cycles? Evaluating Administrative Guidance and Cartels in Japan', Harvard University, Department of Economics, mimeo

Weinstein, D.E. and Yafeh, Y. (1998). 'On the Costs of a Bank-Centered Financial System: Evidence from the Changing Main Bank Relations in Japan', *Journal of Finance*, 53(2), 635-672

Weiss, L. (1998). *The Myth of the Powerless State* (Ithaca: Cornell University Press)

Weiss, L. and Hobson, J.M. (1995). *States and Economic Development: A Comparative Historical Analysis* (Cambridge: Polity Press)

Wellink, A. (1994). 'Experience Gained with Monetary Policy Instruments in the Netherlands', in *Monetary Policy Instruments: National Experiences and European Perspectives*, Bankhistorisches Archiv, Beihefte no. 27 (Frankfurt-am-Main: Fritz Knapp), 22-41

Werner, R.A. (1992). 'A Quantity Theory of Disaggregated Credit and International Capital Flows with Evidence from Japan', mimeo

Wessels, R.E. (1987). 'Prudential Regulation of Banks', in Bosman, H.W.J. and Brezet, J.C. (eds.), *Sparen en Investeren, Geld en Banken* (Leiden/Antwerpn: Stenfert Kroese), 94-107

Wiersema, M. and Bird, A. (1993). 'Organizational Demography in Japanese Firms: Group Heterogeneity, Individual Dissimilarity and Top Management Team Turnover', *Academy of Management Journal*, 36, 996-1025

Willett, T.D. and Keen, E. (1990). 'Studying the Fed: Toward a Broader Public-Choice Perspective', in Mayer, Y. (ed.), *The Political Economy of American Monetary Policy* (Cambridge: Cambridge University Press)

Wilson, D. (1988). *The Sun at Noon: An Anatomy of Modern Japan* (London: Coronet Books)

Wolf, C. (1998). 'What Caused Asia's Crash?', *Wall Street Journal*, 4 February

Wolferen, K.G. van (1989). *The Enigma of Japanese Power* (London: Macmillan) (1991). *Japan: De Onzichtbare Drijfveren van een Wereldmacht (Dutch edition of van Wolferen* (1989)) (Amsterdam: Rainbow Pocketboeken)

(1997). 'Is Economic Science Worth Anything? The Conceptual Mismatch Between Economic Theory and Japanese Reality', mimeo

(2001). 'De Japan-crisis is een westers verzinsel' (The Japan Crisis Is Made Up by the West), *SAFE*, 20(2), 68–75 (Amsterdam: Multi Magazines)

Wood, C. (1993). *The Bubble Economy: The Japanese Economic Collapse* (Tokyo: Charles E. Tuttle)

(1998). 'Japan's Financial System', in Gibney, 220–230

World Bank (1993). *The East Asian Miracle: Economic Growth and Public Policy* (New York: Oxford University Press)

(1998). *East Asia: The Road to Recovery* (Washington, DC: World Bank)

Wright, R.W. and Pauli, G.A. (1987). *The Second Wave: Japan's Global Assault on Financial Services* (London: Waterlow Publishers)

Wytzes, H.C. (1978). *Financiële Instellingen en Markten* (Financial Institutions and Markets) (Leiden/Antwerp: Stenfert Kroese)

Yamamoto, S. (1992). *The Spirit of Japanese Capitalism: And Selected Essays* (Lanham, MD: Madison Books)

Yamamura, K. (1990). 'Will Japan's Economic Structure Change? Confessions of a Former Optimist', in Yamamura, K. (ed.), *Japan's Economic Structure: Should It Change?* (Seattle: Society for Japanese Studies), 13–64

Yamamura, K. and Yasuba, Y. (eds.) (1987). *The Political Economy of Japan, Volume I: The Domestic Transformation* (Stanford: Stanford University Press)

Yamawaki, T. (1996). 'The Forbearance Policy: What Went Wrong with Japanese Financial Regulation?', Loughborough University Banking Centre, Research Paper no. 106/96

Yamori, N. (1994). 'Kantoku Tōkyoku kara no Yakuin Haken to Shinyō Chitsujo – Hyogo Ginkō no keusu' (The Dispatching of Officials from Supervisory Authorities and the Credit System – The Case of Hyogo Bank), *Kinyū Journal*, (December), 79–86

(1997). 'Kantoku Tōkyoku kara no Shūshoku to Ginkō no Keiei Senryaku no Sentaku' (Re-employment of supervisory authorities and the selection of management strategies by banks), *Keizai Kagaku*, 45(3), 15–25

(1998). 'Bureaucrat Managers and Corporate Governance: Expense Preference Behaviors in Japanese Financial Institutions', *Economics Letters*, 61, 385–389

Yamori, N. and Fujiwara, K. (1995). 'Kantoku Tōkyoku kara no Shūshoku to Kinyū Kikan Keiei – Shinyō Kinko to Ōkurashō no "case" o Chūshin ni shite' (Re-employment of Supervisory Authorities and Financial Institutions Management – The Case of the Shinkin Banks and the Ministry of Finance), *Keizai Kagaku*, 43(3), 1–15

Yoshikawa, H. (1995). *Macroeconomics and the Japanese Economy* (Oxford: Oxford University Press)

Yoshikawa, H. and Okazaki, T. (1993). 'Postwar Hyper-Inflation and the Dodge Plan, 1945–50: An Overview', in Teranishi and Kosai, 86–104

Young, M.K. (1984). 'Judicial Review of Administrative Guidance: Governmentally Encouraged Consensual Dispute Resolution in Japan', *Columbia Law Review*, 84, 923–983

Zenginkyō (a). *Zenkoku Ginkō Zaimu Shō Hyō Bunseki* (Federation of Bankers Associations of Japan, Analysis of Financial Statements of All Banks, 1 April–31 March), issues 1976–1993 (Tokyo: Zenginkyō)

(b). *Zenkoku Ginkō Chūkan Zaimu Shō Hyō Bunseki* (Federation of Bankers Associations of Japan, Analysis of Interim Financial Statements of All Banks, 1 April–30 September), issues 1975–1980 (Tokyo: Zenginkyō)

(1993). *Zenkoku Ginkō Zaimu Shō Hyō Bunseki* (Analysis of Financial Statements of All Banks) (Tokyo: Zenginkyō), 31 March

Zenginkyo Financial Review. Various issues (Tokyo: Federation of Bankers Associations of Japan)

Zysman, J. (1983). *Governments, Markets, and Growth: Financial Systems and the Politics of Industrial Change* (Oxford: Martin Robertson)

Index

Acheson, K. 79
Ackley, G. 41
Administrative Reform Council 197
administrative guidance 4–5, 23, 28, 34,
    69, 336–337
  ambiguous 347
  classified 43
  compliance 45–47
  consensual policy school 51
  criticism of 48–50
  definition 35, 40–43
  effectiveness 122–123
  efficiency-oriented 121–122
  informal 29
  interventionist school 50
  market school 50–51
  non-transparent 36, 48
  policymakers' attachment to 356
  revised 218, 233, 248
  to support stock market 189
  unpublished 91, 116–117, 119, 131,
    134, 218
  see also tsūtatsu
Administrative Procedures Law 49, 233
administrative reform 194–199, 212–222
Administrative Reform Bill 219, 243
Administrative Reform Council (ARC)
    203–204
agency costs 297–298
agriculture 194
Aizawa, Hideyuki 234–235
Alletzhauser, A. 48
amakudari 6–7, 53, 54–65, 69, 71, 92,
    133, 134, 174, 248, 339, 340
  adverse impact 349
  age 278–279, 284
  and banks: performance 191, 317–324;
    size 263–264; bank type 261–265

BoJ 56–57, 129
  career management 280–291
  claims for 257
  classification 57–58
  and consensual policy school 63–64
  criticism of 208–209
  data analysis 259–275
  data sources 256–259
  declining numbers 196, 294, 296,
    351
  definitions 54–57
  a delicate subject 256–257
  detrimental effects 297, 319–324,
    325–326
  empirical: investigation 255–296; results
    308–317
  equalising: information 62–63;
    patterned 275–277
  functions of 269–274, 287–291
  incentive 280
  interpretations of 60–65
  and interventionism 263, 277–280
  MoF 104–106
  private corporations' reluctance 351
  reward system 59, 60–61, 301, 312,
    325
  succession of 284–287, 313–314
  'too close for comfort' 349–354
  trends 291–294
Anti-Monopoly Law 93, 175
Anzen Credit Co-operative 189
Aoki, M. 17, 25, 55, 60, 62, 84, 355
Arai, Eikichi 267
Arai, Shokei 205
asset prices
  bubbles 172–173
  inflation 171
Austria 60

For EU product safety concerns, contact us at Calle de José Abascal, 56–1°, 28003 Madrid, Spain or eugpsr@cambridge.org.

www.ingramcontent.com/pod-product-compliance
Ingram Content Group UK Ltd.
Pitfield, Milton Keynes, MK11 3LW, UK
UKHW042211180425
457623UK00011B/145